Praise for *The River and the Horsemen: A Novel of the Little Bighorn*

"Robert Skimin's *The River and the Horsemen* is a slashing good yarn that grabs attention and never lets go. A great storyteller, Skimin is also a skilled researcher whose deft blending of fact and fiction works a special kind of magic. All the great actors on the Little Bighorn stage are here—Custer, his beloved wife Libbie, Reno, Benteen, Sitting Bull, Crazy Horse, and some added attractions. Custer's Last Stand has never been better told. This book will jump to the top of the historical novel lists and likely stay there."

—Frank E. Vandiver

"Being a purest like most Custer buffs, I had a hard job getting into *The River and the Horsemen*. But once I got into it I could not put it down. It is good reading, and Skimin sticks to the historical facts of the Custer story more often than not. He skillfully and inclusively takes you from June 1875 to the Last Stand. . . . Skimin is a master storyteller. He weaves a very engrossing story around the main characters that we are all familiar with: The Custers, Reno, Benteen, John Burkman, Vincent Charley, and all the officers of the 7th and their women. . . . Skimin also brings the Indian side of the story into play. He tells of the Indian way of life, the emotions that they felt and the plans that they made as the inevitable battle with the Blue Coats nears. He writes of the Indian chiefs: Gall, Sitting Bull, and Crazy Horse. . . . I highly recommend it."

—W. Donald Horn

"Intensely researched and entirely credible fiction."

—*Rocky Mountain News*

"Robert Skimin brings the Battle of the Little Bighorn into sharp focus through his adept research and perceptive analysis. Although his treatise is in fiction format, his conclusions are based upon his knowledge of battle from a professional army officer's view and his use of information from such highly respected sources as famed historian Robert Utley, noted Little Bighorn historian Brian Pohanka, the writings of Dr. John S. Gray, as well as recent articles from the Army's Command and General Staff College. He also had the advantage of picking Jay Smith's fertile mind before that Little Bighorn authority died. His presentation of the Native American side is a rich look into Sioux life. No one will ever truly know what really happened on that famous/infamous June day in

Montana in 1876, and forever the conjecture will be argued, but Skimin may have come as close as anyone. For anyone interested in American history, *The River and the Horsemen* is a valuable and fascinating look at one of our most intriguing events.

—**William Moody**

"The author knows what he's doing."   —*Texas Monthly*

"By bold invention and skillful adaptation of the diverse threads of legend, lore, and history, Skimin has woven a surprisingly unified account of events leading up to the climactic battle. . . . Skimin spends the bulk of the book developing individual characters—Custer, his wife, Libbie; Sitting Bull; and Crazy Horse—adding flesh and blood, frailties and foibles to familiar names and making three-dimensional historical figures most of us only know from school textbooks. . . . This portrait shows Custer, warts and all. [It] relates the great love affair between Custer and his lovely and loyal wife, Libbie. . . . The author excels at detail as the tale opens with a scene of the post-massacre inquest in a sweaty Chicago hotel, then switches seamlessly from the American West to President Grant's White House. Native American life is artfully captured; Custer's foe, the spiritual and political leader Sitting Bull, is insightfully portrayed as the two men prepare for the great denouement at the Little Bighorn. . . . Truly distinguished historical fiction."   —*Library Journal*

"Perhaps no other event recorded in the annals of American military history has inspired greater controversy than that which has come to be know as Custer's Last Stand. During the past 120 years, volumes, both fact and fiction, have been written about the events that occurred on June 25, 1876, yet the saga of the little Bighorn continues. . . . In this mesmerizing book, Robert Skimin has penned an epic novel that clearly details the battle and the events that led up to Custer's ill-fated encounter with the Sioux at the Little Bighorn. Even more important, he exercises his masterful ability as a storyteller and has blended together a fascinating array of historical and fictional characters that provides his readers with indelible insights into the human elements that held such sway in shaping the history that would be written that day. . . . Skimin has created a spellbinding novel which readers are certain to applaud as his finest work yet."

—*El Paso Times*

THE RIVER
AND THE
HORSEMEN

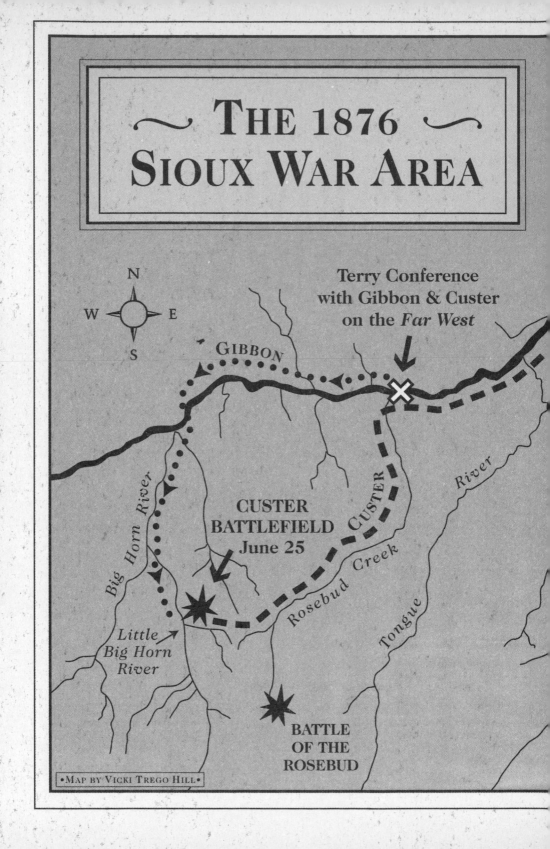

THE 1876 SIOUX WAR AREA

N W E S

GIBBON

Terry Conference
with Gibbon & Custer
on the *Far West*

Big Horn River

CUSTER
BATTLEFIELD
June 25

CUSTER

Rosebud Creek

River

Little
Big Horn
River

Tongue

BATTLE
OF THE
ROSEBUD

•MAP BY VICKI TREGO HILL•

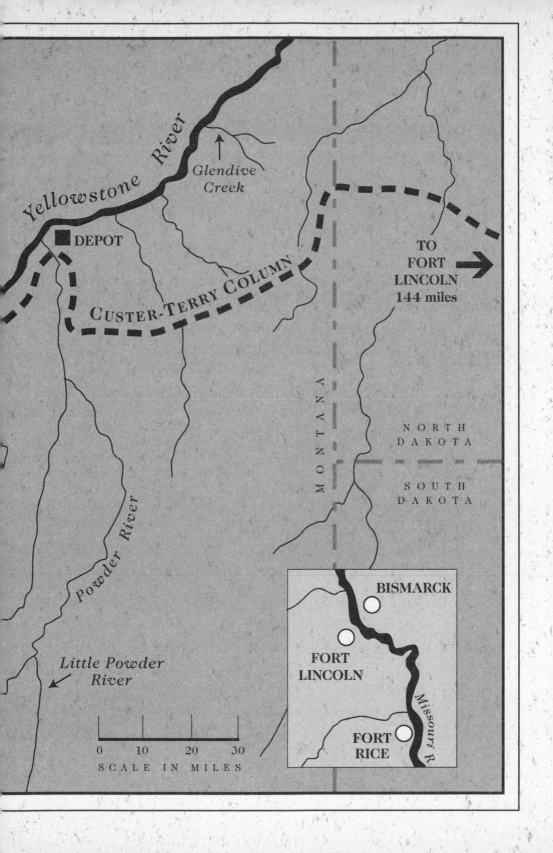

Yellowstone River

Glendive Creek

■ DEPOT

CUSTER-TERRY COLUMN

TO
FORT
LINCOLN
144 miles

MONTANA

NORTH
DAKOTA

SOUTH
DAKOTA

Powder River

Little Powder
River

0   10   20   30
SCALE IN MILES

BISMARCK

FORT
LINCOLN

FORT
RICE

Missouri R.

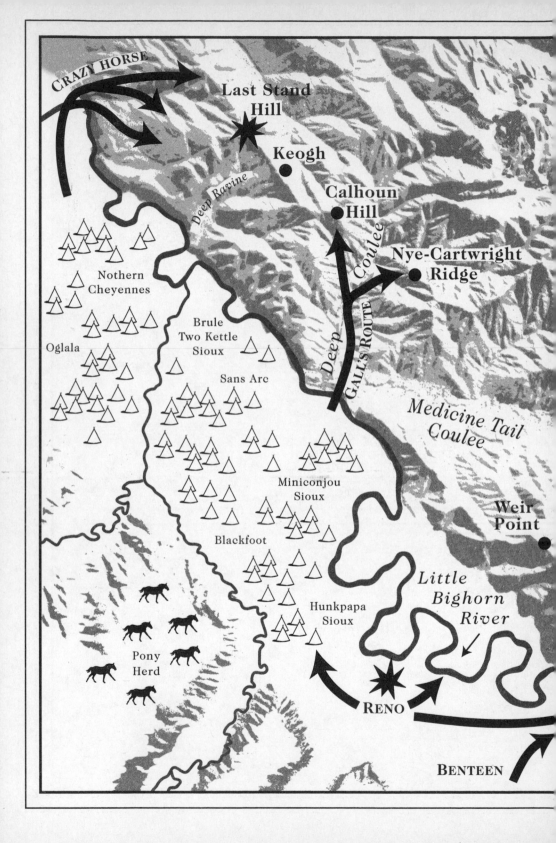

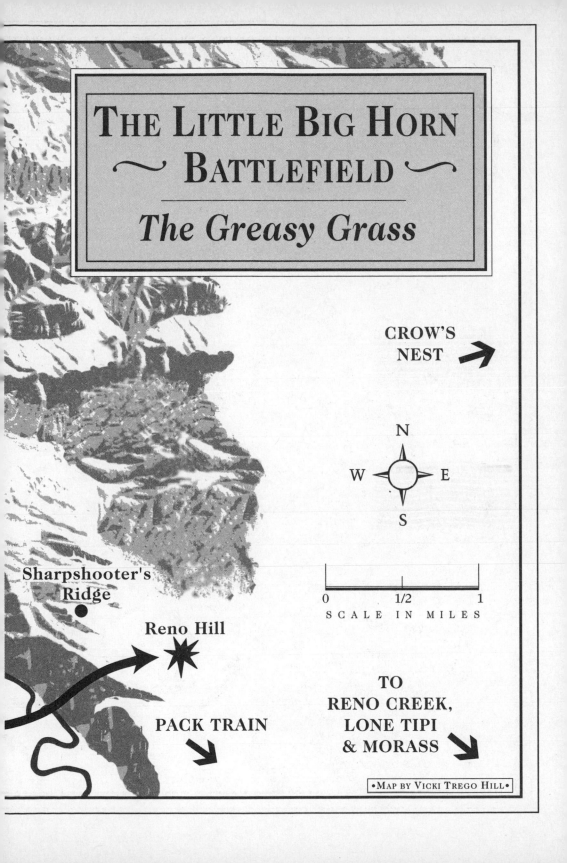

THE LITTLE BIG HORN
∼ BATTLEFIELD ∼
The Greasy Grass

CROW'S NEST →

N
W ⊕ E
S

0   1/2   1

SCALE IN MILES

Sharpshooter's Ridge

Reno Hill

TO
RENO CREEK,
LONE TIPI
& MORASS ↘

PACK TRAIN ↘

• MAP BY VICKI TREGO HILL •

THE RIVER AND THE HORSEMEN

★ A Novel *of the* Little Bighorn ★

Robert Skimin

B&B
BUNIM & BANNIGAN
New York Charlottetown

Published simultaneously in the United States and Canada by

Bunim & Bannigan, Ltd., PMB 157 111 East 14th Street
New York, NY 10003-4103
Bunim & Bannigan, Ltd., Box 636
Charlottetown, PEI C1A 7L3 Canada

www.bunimandbannigan.com

Manufactured in the United States of America
Design by Jean Carbain
Maps by Vicki Trego Hill

Cover photographs courtesy of the U.S. Army Military
History Institute, Carlisle, PA.
Custer: Vol. 69, p. 3407A
Sitting Bull: RG 31S, D of USA, 464
Little Bighorn battlefield: RG48S, E.S. Godfrey Coll. 2.16

Library of Congress Cataloging-in-Publication Data

Skimin, Robert.
The River and the horsemen : a novel of the Little Bighorn /
by Robert Skimin. — 1st B&B ed.
p. cm.
ISBN-13: 978-1-933480-13-8 (trade pbk. : alk. paper)
ISBN-10: 1-933480-13-0 (trade pbk. : alk. paper) 1. Custer, George
Armstrong, 1839-1876—Fiction. 2. Sitting Bull, 1834?-1890—Fiction.
3. Little Bighorn, Battle of the, Mont., 1876—Fiction. 4. Indians of
North America—Wars—1866-1895—Fiction. I. Title.

PS3569.K49R58 2007
813'.54—dc22

2007002044

ISBN: 978-1-933480-13-8
ISBN-10: 1-933480-13-0

135798642

First B&B edition 2007

To all of those who died at the Little Bighorn

In appreciation to the late Jay Smith, Jim Court, Brian Pohanka, Robert Utley, and all of the other authors whose books aided me, and the many librarians who helped with my research (particularly those of the U.S. Army Sergeant's Major Academy at Fort Bliss), the Horn buffs who gave me input, the U.S. Army Command and Staff College, and finally to the insightful editing of Paul Williams

Prologue

Ira Vandiver doodled in his notebook as the court stenographer neared the end of his reading of the preceding days' testimony. He covered a yawn. To break his drowsiness, he pulled out his copy of the order constituting the court and reread it.

Special Orders, No. 255. By direction of the president, and on application of Major Marcus A. Reno, Seventh Cavalry, a court of inquiry is hereby appointed to assemble at Chicago, Ill., on Monday, the 13th of January 1879, or as soon thereafter as practicable, for the purpose of inquiring into Major Reno's conduct at the Little Big Horn River on the 25th and 26th of June 1876. The court will report the facts, and its opinion as to whether, from all the circumstances in the case, any further proceedings are necessary. The detail of the court is as follows:

Colonel John H. King, 9th Infantry
Colonel Wesley Merritt, 5th Cavalry
Lieut. Colonel W. B. Royal, 3rd Cavalry
1st Lieut. Jesse M. Lee, Adjutant, 9th Infantry, is appointed
recorder of the court.
By Order of the Secretary of War

It seemed to Vandiver that Merritt was still a lieutenant colonel, but surely the order would be correct. He'd check on it later.

He glanced over at the T-shaped table where the members of the court sat. The courtroom itself was actually made up of two large rooms, Nos. 14 and 16 on the *entresol,* or mezzanine, of the Palmer House. The hotel was also serving as the temporary headquarters of General Philip Sheridan, in whose jurisdiction the court had been convened. The spectator area in the adjoining room was jammed and spilling over with onlookers. Bright colors flooded the benches, from blue army uniforms to civilian suits and gaudy neckties, to the more subtle hues of the ladies' dresses and fancy hats. Women hadn't attended at first, but when word got out that they could get in, more and more showed up each day. Anything about the dashing Custer and his terrible tragedy was enough to bring them out. One woman, whose identity was carefully hidden under a veil, was widely believed to be Libbie Custer, the wife of the deceased general. But sources in her hometown of Monroe, Michigan, insisted that she was cloistered in the family house there, where she and others closest to her were hanging on every newspaper account of the court's progress.

Vandiver had tried to catch the mystery lady twice, but she was always up and out before he could reach her as the court adjourned. He liked the idea that it might be Libbie Custer. It gave a sad and romantic twist to the story of the court. After all, the lady had been doing her utmost to clear her beloved husband's name ever since the battle, so why *shouldn't* she be here?

Anything could happen in this court, he thought. This damned thing had the whole country watching for the morning paper with bated breath—it was the most fascinating event since Lincoln's assassination, and was nearly as divisive as the Civil War itself. It seemed as if almost everyone had lined up on one side or the other, pro-Custer or anti-Custer. Half the country thought the yellow-haired boy general was an arrogant, glory-seeking killer of innocent soldiers; the other half thought he was a great hero who had been unjustly vilified for his greatest act of heroism.

At the outset of the battle, Custer had split his command, ordering Major Reno, with three companies of troopers, to attack the huge Sioux village that was his objective. He subsequently took five companies several miles ahead of Reno's command, to a place where they were annihilated. No one had ever determined what truly happened in what became known as "Custer's Last Stand."

Not just in America were people captivated by what happened by that obscure river in the western United States; most of the civilized world was enthralled as well. Custer's Last Stand had superseded the Charge of the Light Brigade as a tragic and heroic battle.

This court of inquiry was supposed to provide the answers.

It was warm in the crowded rooms, with body heat adding to the stick-iness of an unseasonably warm rain blowing in from Lake Michigan. Handkerchiefs mopped and dabbed at brows and sweaty necks. A low murmur of sporadic conversation, mostly whispering, provided a soft buzz that the president of the court silenced now and then with a tap of his gavel.

Vandiver, a reporter from the New York *Times* was one of over two dozen newspapermen sitting in the front two rows of the gallery. At thirty-seven, he was an experienced newspaperman who had been a young cavalry officer during the Civil War. Since he had served under Custer in the Wolverine Brigade late in the war, he had a special interest in this case; he also had interviewed the general several months before the battle. In attendance since the court opened, reporters had been banned from taking notes in the courtroom—a restriction that was removed when it had in no way inhibited the country's newspapers from full reports of the proceed-ings. Notebooks stuffed in the reporters' hats were to blame.

Vandiver sketched a drawing of the "T." Seated at the end of it was Lieutenant Jesse Lee, the recorder. Lee was a big man, courteous and inclined to fiddle with his thick black hair. He had served in the war, and was now the adjutant of the Ninth Infantry. His role was roughly equiva-lent to that of a prosecuting attorney in a civilian court, although in the truest sense, a court of inquiry was simply supposed to make a finding of fact. Mr. Hollister, the official stenographer, sat to his right.

At the top of the "T" in the center sat Colonel John Haskell King, the president of the court. A portly man with gray hair, a full and flowing mustache and muttonchop whiskers, King was sixty years old and the colonel of the 9th Infantry. He had fought in the Mexican War, had led a battalion at Shiloh, a brigade at Chickamauga, and a division in the Atlanta campaign. He had been in the army for forty-one years, and had been brevetted major general during the war. A brevet is a commission promoting an officer to a higher rank with no increase in pay, usually awarded for heroism or exceptional performance. The colonel's joviality seemed to lurk just below the solemnity he outwardly wore to maintain order in the court.

To his right sat Colonel Wesley Merritt the commander of the Fifth United States Cavalry. Six feet tall and slender, with a scraggly blond

Jeff Davis beard, the forty-one-year-old Merritt had graduated from West Point in 1860. In June of 1863, he was promoted directly to brigadier general from captain and had commanded the reserve cavalry brigade at Gettysburg. He finished the war as one of its brightest young major generals, and became the lieutenant colonel of the Ninth Cavalry—the Buffalo Soldiers—in 1866. Although his demeanor on the court was severe, he was noted for his affability nearly as much as his competence.

The third member of the court, seated on Colonel King's left, was the fifty-four-year-old Lieutenant Colonel William Bedford Royal, who had been in the army since 1846. He had a brilliant Civil War record as well, having been brevetted brigadier general. He had also been brevetted for his actions under Crook at the Rosebud, just prior to the battle of the Little Bighorn in 1876. He seemed the most reserved and formal of the three senior officers. He was currently in field command of the Brave Rifles, the Third Cavalry.

All of the officers, including the much younger Lieutenant Lee, were attired in their dark-blue dress uniforms.

Seated at a table off to the side, and also wearing his dress uniform, including the white gloves, but minus the sword, was Major Marcus Albert Reno. A graduate of West Point, class of 1857, he was five-feet-eight-inches in height and of stocky build. His face was rather round, with a sparse mustache and a touch of goatee peeking out from under his lower lip. His eyes and straight hair were dark, his look assured. He had been brevetted for bravery at Cedar Creek under Sheridan during the war, and to brigadier general for gallant and meritorious services. He was currently under suspension from active duty as the result of a court-martial over alleged misconduct with another officer's wife at Fort Abercrombie, where he had been commanding officer at the time. Seated with him was his civilian counsel, Mr. Lyman P. Gilbert, a pleasant young man who was assistant attorney general of Pennsylvania.

It was the twelfth day of the court.

Vandiver turned around and glanced at Whittaker. Frederick Whittaker, British expatriate and dime novelist from Mount Vernon, New York, was Custer's self-proclaimed defender. Following the so-called massacre at the Little Bighorn, Whittaker had written and published a biography, *A Complete Life of General Custer,* in just six months; and how it did laud the freewheeling cavalryman! According to Whittaker, the heroic Custer—the American Siegfried, the whitest of knights—traipsed boldly like Lancelot along the gauntlet of crooked politicos, arrogant superiors, and jealous subordinates. Whittaker had written even flowerier prose about his hero in *Galaxy* magazine, using phrases such as, "the modern Murat," and "the last cavalier" in his raves.

On May 18 of the previous year, Whittaker had written a long letter to W. W. Corlett, a congressman representing Wyoming Territory. In it, Whittaker accused Reno of gross cowardice, disobedience, incompetence, and willful neglect, and blamed the major for the tragic results of the battle. He also requested that Congress initiate an investigation into the conduct of the battle to clear Custer's name.

Reno had reacted, requesting the court of inquiry to clear his own name. Vandiver had been watching Whittaker, observing his overly done facial reactions to the ongoing testimony—contempt, disgust, impatience, or smiling approval when a witness seemed to bear out his accusation, as in the case of Lieutenant De Rudio. There was no doubt in Vandiver's mind that the biographer was milking the event, getting the most out of his time on center stage. One thing was certain, Whittaker was the catalyst who had gotten this damned court going.

There had been some argument about the admissibility of Whittaker's accusatory letter in the court, but Reno had quickly acquiesced—a good move, since its contents were common knowledge. Now Whittaker was reacting angrily to the testimony of Captain Myles Moylan, who he apparently thought should be vilifying Reno. Vandiver turned his attention to the officer on the witness stand.

The forty-year-old Moylan, a large, husky man in civilian clothes, explained to the court that he was on leave and had no uniform with him. He had graying brown hair, heavy eyebrows over rather intense eyes, and a big bushy mustache that drooped over his mouth. He was a "ranker," having been commissioned from sergeant major by Custer in 1866. He had served as the regimental adjutant from 1867 to 1872, when he was given command of Company A so he could be promoted to captain. He had always been part of Custer's inner circle.

Captain Moylan was the sixth witness to appear before the court.

The recorder was hammering away at Major Reno's actions following the initial charge by his troopers and scouts on the huge Sioux camp. Lieutenant Lee was particularly interested in why Reno had pulled back into the nearby woods when his advance was stalled by the counterattack of several hundred Sioux. Reno had subsequently ordered a withdrawal that turned into a scramble back across the Little Bighorn River and up the slope to the comparative safety of what later became known as Reno Hill. Lieutenant Lee asked, "Now please state, Captain, what was the object of getting out of the timber?"

Moylan pursed his lips for a moment before quietly replying, "I rather think the object of getting out of the timber was to save the command."

A titter went through the audience.

Lieutenant Lee clasped his hands behind his substantial back and turned away briefly before asking, "Do you not think it would have been more judicious for the command to have remained in the timber than to have exposed itself to fire at the river?"

The witness frowned as he said, "I believe that in view of the uncertainty of getting support from General Custer or Captain Benteen, the retreat was less injurious than it would have been to remain in the timber; for the command simply could not have stayed there thirty minutes longer without losing many more men than it did in the course pursued."

Vandiver turned again to observe Whittaker. The man was scowling and shaking his head. He heard him mutter loud enough for nearly everyone to hear, "Sheridan got to him."

Reno's expression was sober as he nodded his head slightly and made a note on the tablet in front of him.

The courtroom erupted.

Colonel King's gavel came down. "Order!"

Lee continued this line of questioning for a couple of minutes before asking, "In your opinion, Captain Moylan, what was Major Reno's conduct down by the river? Was it, in short, brave or cowardly?"

The witness stroked his chin, answering slowly. "Well, at times Major Reno rode at the head of the column, and when he gave me orders, he seemed self-possessed. I saw nothing in his conduct indicating cowardice."

"I tell you it's a goddamned whitewash!" Whittaker snapped, slamming his fist down on the table. "That lying Moylan has been ordered to give that testimony, sure as I'm sitting here. Why, he was one of General Custer's favorite officers. It's *impossible* that he would defend Reno of his own accord."

Vandiver had corralled the writer and ushered him into the noisy hotel saloon for a beer. They were sitting at a corner table. "Does seem a little strange," the reporter replied, pursing his lips.

"I tell you every one of those witnesses has been told what to say. And not only that, the goddamned officers on the court are rigged too!"

"How do you account for that?" the newspaperman asked, offering Whittaker a cigar.

The writer had a scrawny dark mustache and eyes that bored into you one moment and flitted around the room the next. He was a small, precisely dressed man who spoke rapidly with his British accent. "Bloody easy," he replied taking the cigar and striking a match. "From Sherman on down, they want the Custer massacre to be forgotten. Probably comes from Grant. Even though he's out of office, he's still a goddamned general. And you know how he hated Custer."

In the two weeks he'd been around the Palmer House, Vandiver had heard most of the gossip. But he wanted to get a good dose of Whittaker's slant. "You don't like generals, or you don't like Grant?" he asked, lighting his own cigar. Coincidentally, it was one of those triangular kinds that he'd heard Grant liked to smoke.

"Both," the biographer replied. "But since Grant blamed the massacre on Custer, he has to be the arch villain. And you know Sherman and Sheridan are his yes-men."

"I don't think Sherman's anyone's yes-man."

"All right, maybe it's Sheridan. The whole Little Bighorn campaign was his doing."

Vandiver decided to goad the man a bit. "But Lieutenant De Rudio, who had no use for Custer, testified against Reno. That doesn't fit your theory. Do you actually think all of those people would perjure themselves? And Custer was in command."

Whittaker slammed his beer mug down too hard, spilling some of its contents. "If Reno hadn't shit his pants in fright, he could've saved Custer, and together they'd have licked those damned savages!"

"So why would these generals want to set up a crooked court of inquiry?"

"Because they have to have a scapegoat. The American Army was supposed to be the best in the world. And the Seventh Cavalry was supposed to be its crack regiment. They can't admit that a bunch of savages wiped it out, that's why!"

"And Custer is the scapegoat?"

"Positively."

"Then you are positive Sheridan has rigged this court?"

"Without a doubt."

"How can you be so sure?"

Whittaker's eyes gleamed as a small smile touched his lips. "I have proof."

THE RIVER
AND THE
HORSEMEN

History: an account mostly false, of events mostly unimportant, which are brought about by rulers mostly knaves, and soldiers mostly fools.

—AMBROSE BIERCE

1

God help the man who won't marry until he finds a perfect
woman, and God help him still more if he finds her.
—BEN TILLETT

CHICAGO
JUNE 3, 1875

"I now pronounce you man and wife."

The army chaplain closed his Bible and nodded to the couple standing
before him. Everyone smiled as the general kissed his young bride.

"I never thought he'd do it," Libbie Custer whispered in her husband's
ear from back in the corner of the large living room where the ceremony
was being held.

He chuckled. "It's the only thing Little Phil ever took his time doing."

Libbie leaned up and kissed her famous husband on the cheek. "I think
it's so romantic," she whispered. "Think we can consummate his wedding
before he does?"

George Armstrong Custer grinned as his hand pressed firmly against
her well-clothed left thigh. "You are uncommonly wanton, Madame."

Her blue-gray eyes danced as she pushed against his hand. "I like that
term, you handsome devil, but you didn't answer me."

He bowed his head slightly. "I'll meet you in the carriage house at
sunset."

They both laughed merrily as the small crowd began to mingle and
chatter noisily. As the small group of musicians from the local army band
struck up a popular air, Libbie pressed her hand to his and their fingers
intertwined.

Lieutenant General Philip Henry Sheridan, forty-four years old and
the most eligible bachelor in the army, had just married an attractive
blonde exactly half his age. The new Mrs. Sheridan was Irene Rucker, the
daughter of Brigadier General Daniel Rucker, the officer who was soon to
become the quartermaster general of the army. The wedding was taking
place in the Rucker home and was somewhat subdued because of the

recent death of the bridegroom's father. As it was, the hierarchy of Sheridan's command was there, plus the commanding general of the army, William Tecumseh Sherman. The only one missing was their wartime boss, Sam Grant. Both Sheridan and Sherman owed their high rank to that quiet man, and Grant owed his victory during the Civil War very much to them. The president had been unable to attend because he was too busy coping with the Whiskey Ring scandal. It seemed like every time Grant turned around, somebody was trying to pull off something crooked.

Other generals in attendance were Terry, Crook, Augur—whom Crook was replacing—and Pope. Lieutenant Colonel Custer was the lowest ranking officer there, except for one of Sheridan's aides, but Armstrong was a brevet major general, and—as was the custom—was normally addressed by that rank if he so desired, and George Armstrong Custer *definitely so* desired. He noticed General George Crook speaking with Sherman near the large refreshment table, and headed for them. He knew that Crook, who had recently gotten his star back for his remarkable success with the Apaches down in New Mexico Territory, was also in town to get a briefing on his assignment as the new commander of the Department of the Platte.

Both generals nodded and smiled as he walked up. "Armstrong," Sherman said. "Pull up a glass of this fine champagne."

Custer shook his red-blond locks. "I don't imbibe, sir."

Sherman nodded. The commanding general's unkempt red hair was thinning and partially turning white. The parchmentlike wrinkles that had begun prematurely during the war were now more pronounced, but his alert brown eyes were merry. "Oh, yes, I'd forgotten. Sam Grant did the same thing, but it took his mother hen, Rawlins, to keep the grape away from him." He chuckled as he glanced across the room at Libbie. "But your mother hen is much prettier."

Custer loved a joke. "And much nicer in the nest, without a doubt."

They all laughed and Custer poured himself a cup of fruit punch before moving on. Stopping to watch the few couples who were dancing, he noted with pleasure how the army looked when it dressed up. He was wearing his best uniform, which conformed to regulation for a lieutenant colonel. It was during the time when he was wearing stars that he'd designed ostentatious, flamboyant ensembles that set him apart from the everyday flag officer—general officers had that option. Naturally, the women were in the finest silk gowns they could afford on the limited pay the army afforded its officers. He smiled, thinking he'd have to recall all of this to put it in his next book . . . *"bold midnight-blue uniforms with a flash of bright medals on brass-buttoned chests; ruffled, swirling chromatic gowns of the beautiful ladies dancing in the soft light that satin and silk cast off . . . stimulating music played by uniformed bandsmen of the same clan as the assembled military heroes . . ."*

He could see it in print now.

Moving to the head bandsman, he leaned close and asked, "Do you know "GarryOwen?"

"Yes, *sir!*" the sergeant replied. "We'll play it right away."

Custer smiled. "Thanks." He was at Libbie's side before the first notes of the Irish song he'd adopted for his regiment filled the air. Everyone stopped to watch as the Custers began to whirl around the small dance floor to the jaunty air.

"You'd think it was *their* wedding," George Crook remarked.

Sherman shook his head and chuckled. "That's Custer."

Suddenly the dancers stopped in front of the bride and groom. Bowing low, Armstrong asked Irene Sheridan for the pleasure of a dance. She smiled brightly and entered his arms. A rather tall young woman, she was a good dancer, and complemented the six-foot Custer well. A moment later, Libbie curtsied in front of Little Phil, smiled, and asked, "Will you dance with a poor deserted cavalry wife, General?"

Sheridan laughed as he took her in his arms. "You sure that wild husband of yours will let me dance to his private song?"

She chuckled. "Only on this special occasion." She squeezed his hand. "Congratulations, Uncle Phil."

As the two couples swung around the floor, a colonel's wife inclined her head toward another wife, raised her fan, and asked softly, "I wonder if there's anything to those rumors about Libbie and Sheridan?"

The other woman shrugged slightly. "I don't know. He bought her Grant's round table at Appomattox, you know. The one that was used for the surrender signing. I heard he paid plenty for it."

"Yes. And she stayed in his house at Leavenworth when Custer got court-martialed."

Both fans were now in use. "It was probably just friendship."

The colonel's wife's eyes glinted. "Of course."

Two hours later, after some of the guests had departed, Cump Sherman asked some of the remaining officers to come into the study. More champagne was served and cigars were passed around as Generals Sheridan, Rucker, Terry, and Crook got comfortable. Custer, who also abstained from tobacco, straddled a straight-backed chair in the corner and leaned on its top. The commanding general looked around briefly to get their attention, then went quickly into his brisk, staccato delivery. "Phil, I hate to talk business on this festive occasion, but we won't all be together like this again, and I want to tell you folks what's going on with the goddamned Sioux. As you know, we simply can't stop the flow of gold-hungry miners streaming into the Black Hills, or the *Paha Sopa,* as the Indians call it. It's like sticking the proverbial finger in the dike. There are far more holes than fingers, and it's going to get worse. And the Sioux claim it's their sacred ground. As you know, the government has been trying to buy or lease the area from them, but they aren't cooperating. I don't know whether they're trying to hold us up, or if it's just plain meanness. You know how those damned Indians are."

Heads nodded. Everyone remembered how Sherman had wanted to retaliate following the Fetterman disaster—or massacre, as it was deemed—in 1866. He had ordered the local general to punish Red Cloud's Sioux "until at least ten Indians are killed for each white life lost." But Congress had rejected his vengeful approach and had set up a commission that recommended negotiations with Red Cloud and his Oglalas, instead of warfare.

Sherman blew out a small cloud of smoke and went on. "We're pretty sure Sitting Bull is pulling the strings, and the story is he'll never quit spiting us. And he'll never come in and be an agency Indian. Isn't his cut. Now, the president wants this settled as peacefully as possible, but he just doesn't understand a goddamned Indian like Sitting Bull. So he's between a rock and a hard place. In short, gentleman, unless something breaks in the next few months, you're going to be leading troops into the field."

Custer drew in a quick breath. A *campaign!*

Sheridan asked, "What will be the mission, General?"

Sherman's brown eyes narrowed. "To catch those bastards and chase them onto the proper agencies."

"That wont be easy," George Crook said. "It can be like pouring water into a sieve, unless we have Sioux scouts. As you know, that worked effectively for me with the Apaches."

Custer spoke up. "I don't think we can get any Lakotas to scout for us. But we've got some good Crows and Rees. They're blood enemies of the Sioux. Oh, and I have a Ree named Bloody Knife who grew up with them."

Crook nodded. "He might be just the ticket."

Terry said, "I agree with General Crook. Those unceded lands where they like to roam are spacious. If we go after them, it'll require some luck to catch them."

Custer interrupted again. "That's where I come in, gentlemen. Remember Custer's Luck?"

Sherman nodded his head. "I agree that it won't be easy." He went on to sketch some different possibilities if the situation were to require a war stance later in the year. If Grant's peace efforts didn't work, it was certain the generals would be waging a campaign that would once and for all end the stubborn resistance of the recalcitrant Lakotas and their allies. The settlement of the interior West was at stake.

To some, Philip Henry Sheridan's life was a paradox. His scrappy nature had led him to attack an upperclassman, and the bandy-legged little Irishman from Ohio had been required to spend an extra year at West Point. Then, although he served well in Indian campaigns in the period after his graduation, it took him nearly eight years and a brewing war between the states to get promoted to first lieutenant in the spring of '61. Rising quickly to captain, he was soon given a Michigan regiment of cavalry and promoted to colonel. The Civil War and a general in chief by the name of Ulysses S. Grant who believed in him, presented Sheridan with a rich opportunity to prove himself. And prove himself he did—in spades. He was soon a brigadier and in the forefront of battles such as Missionary Ridge at Chattanooga. He arrogantly fought with his commander, George Meade, on the march to Richmond in '64, then single-handedly gave Lincoln the victory he needed at Winchester–Cedar Creek for the president's shaky '64 re-election. He was a dynamic leader of Grant's cavalry corps in the final battles of the war.

But it had taken him all of his forty-four years to find a bride.

There had been a few flings, including a rather long affair with Sidnayoh, who was known to her white friends as Frances. The attractive Indian girl was the daughter of Chief Quately of the Willamette Klikitats. She had begun living with him in 1856 during his extended assignment on the West Coast, and had even journeyed to Washington to see him after the Civil War. But, as one of the most visible and important generals in the army, he could no longer fit her into his life. She returned to Oregon and married a fur trapper from Canada.

Irene had heard the stories about Frances, and had apparently been satisfied with his answers. After all, nearly two decades had passed since the young officer had exerted his manhood on an Indian blanket in the distant Willamette Valley. Besides, as the daughter of a regular army officer, Irene was well aware of the needs and desires of young officers. She'd pushed off more than one bold hand since her lovely figure had filled out. And she delighted him, absolutely delighted him. With good humor and the bearing of a woman of the world, she had caught his eye when she was just seventeen.

Damn, he was as nervous as a cat. How could a man who had turned a whole army around and snatched a gigantic victory at Winchester be *nervous?*

He knew there was some talk. And he knew he was getting a bit fat, but he was a long way from old! Hell, right now he had half an erection as he waited under the covers for her to come out of the bathroom. It was hotter than a sweat lodge in the main bedroom, but he kept the sheet drawn over him. *Damn,* what was taking her so long? They'd be departing on their honeymoon trip in the morning, but tonight . . . Speaking of pawing young officers, he'd always assumed she was a virgin. They hadn't even talked about that, not even about lovemaking. Proper people didn't do that sort of thing. And no gentleman asked a girl such a question!

He looked up as she came out of the bathroom. God, she was lovely in her sheer nightgown.

They looked quietly at each other for a moment, then she came to the bed and lowered the wick of the oil lamp on the night stand. Her voice was soft as she smiled and said, "I forgot to ask. Do I call you Phil or General when we're in the bedroom?"

It broke the ice. He laughed. "'Darling' will do."

She smiled in the faint fight, her eyes dancing. "Are you warm enough?"

"Uh huh." He was *drenched*.

She lay beside him, facing him. "May I ask you a question?"

He turned on his side, touched her thigh with his tentative fingers. "What question?"

"Did you ever make love to Libbie Custer?"

He blinked, surprised. "No. Why do you ask such a thing?"

She moved close to him, touching his cheek. "She's a beautiful woman. I just wanted you to tell me, that's all."

"She's always been like a younger sister to me, a good friend."

Irene moved closer, putting her finger on his lips. She came into his arms, her eyes wide. He could feel her breasts against his chest, savored the light touch of her perfume as she whispered, "I love you, darling."

In a downtown hotel, Libbie and Armstrong reached the second floor landing and started down the empty corridor toward their room. Suddenly Libbie grabbed Custer and kissed him soundly. Gyrating her pelvis against him in a provocative manner, she scowled and said, "Liar!"

He shook his head, smiling. "About what?"

"You said you'd make love to me before Sheridan got to his bride."

"But Sherman—"

"In the carriage house."

"Sherman ordered us—"

She took his hand and pulled him the few feet to their door. "I don't care what Sherman said. You promised me, Autie Custer!"

He laughed as he fumbled with the key. "You'd think *I* was the bridegroom."

She rubbed against him again. "You *are*."

As the door opened, Armstrong turned and picked her up. Kissing her as he carried her inside, he went right to the bed. In spite of her silk gown, he crawled on top of her like a panther, kissing her passionately. When they finally broke, she whispered, "The door. Everyone can see—"

He disentangled himself. "Who cares? We'll charge admission and tell it's for Little Phil's hospital fund, 'cause that's where he's going to wind up if I read the passion right in his bride's eyes!"

Her laugh was merry as he unhooked the back of her dress. "You crazy man."

He locked the door and swung back to her, his uniform coat hitting the floor as he stepped forward. "Yes, I'm a crazy bridegroom. You said it. And I'm going to ravage my frightened little bride!"

She bared a breast, cupped it with her hand, and faked an evil grin. "Ha, ravage me if you must, you wild man. "A petticoat flew off. One of his boots was kicked toward the dresser, the other following. Her undergarments fell away. And in moments, two of the most vivacious lovers in North America were moving in energetic, zestful copulation.

Sometime later, spent from their ardent lovemaking, the Custers lolled in their sweaty bed. "You didn't tell me what Sherman had to say," Libbie said.

Armstrong shrugged. "Mostly the same old music. Grant wants to go easy on the hostiles and maybe buy the Black Hills from them. But Sherman doesn't think Sitting Bull and company will come around, so there may be a campaign."

He smiled as her eyes widened. "Oh, Autie," she said. "Do you think it'll really come to that?"

I sure hope so."

She pursed her lips. "Will the Seventh get in it?"

He grinned. "They couldn't do it without us. Nosiree! Our Seventh Cavalry is the best damned regiment in the army, and if they're going to catch Sitting Bull and teach him a lesson, they have to include us."

"How dangerous will it be? Just before we left Fort Lincoln, I heard that Sitting Bull and Crazy Horse would fight."

Custer snorted. "Now who told you that?"

Libbie arched an eyebrow. "Our *maid,* that's who. She got it from her laundress friend, who got it from her sergeant husband, who got it from two scouts, one Ree and one Crow."

"Nonsense. The only way an Indian will fight is if he's got about ten-to-one odds on his side. And these damned Sioux aren't any different."

"Well, I thought you ought to know."

He reached over and kissed her bare shoulder. "Libbie girl, there isn't a pack of Indians alive who can stop George Armstrong Custer."

2

We are all tattooed in our cradles with the beliefs of
our tribe.
—OLIVER WENDELL HOLMES

Since before the rocks were hard, the people who would one day be known
as Sioux had lived in North America. And always they had wandered.
Sometime during the eighteenth century, the powerful Chippewas chased
them west onto the Great Plains. They were the last major Indian group
to arrive there. The western part of the Sioux, who became great buffalo
hunters, were known as the Tetons, or Lakotas. They fashioned themselves as a warrior nation and began to strongly assert themselves. Their
arrival on the Plains coincided with two major additions to life there—the
horse and the gun—and soon the pinto pony greatly enhanced the ways of
the Lakotas as well. Because they could range far, strike quickly, and hurry
away, they became far better hunters and warriors than they had been on
foot. Their firearms, acquired from traders, merely added to their arsenal.
Ironically, it had been the firearm, first in the hands of the hostile
Ojibwas—also known as Chippewas—that had pushed the Lakotas west
out of Minnesota. By the mid-nineteenth century, the fierce Sioux,
abetted by the sheer size of their numbers, ruled wherever they wished.
Many other tribes were their enemies. But the primary lands in which the
Lakota roamed were west of the Missouri River in Dakota Territory and
in much of eastern Montana.

The Sioux were arrogant and vainglorious in their demeanor, but their
vanity was understandable. They were well aware of their great power and
knew they could meet the challenge of any Indian tribe within their considerable scope.

True to their origins, the Lakota were nomadic. Their ponies needed
grass in the summer, as did the buffalo herds on which the tribes subsisted.
As the game moved, the Lakotas followed. During warm months a band
relocated at least once a week. In the winter, however, they generally settled
down into a secluded and sheltered cottonwood valley to wait for spring.

The sacred core of Lakota life was the buffalo, or *pte*, as they called them. Virtually all parts of the buffalo's body from its tail hair to its penis were used in some manner in the daily life of the Lakotas. And when they killed, they made offerings to the Buffalo spirit so he would continue to be generous with them. The great hunters among the Lakota were nearly as revered as their great warriors.

No one knows when the Lakota Way began. But it was generally believed that it coincided with the arrival of White Buffalo Woman and her Sacred Calf Pipe. This may have been in the days of the Chippewas' problems, or maybe before, or perhaps even afterward. Time and dates mattered not to the Lakota. What was vital was that she came and gave Lakota life meaning and direction.

It is said that she was a remarkably beautiful maiden, actually the Goddess Whope, wife of Okaga, the South Wind. Her figure was shapely, her face pale and lovely. She first appeared to two warriors returning from a hunt wearing exquisite white buckskin. One of them was overwhelmed by her beauty and lusted after her. She beckoned him, and when he neared, a thick white mist shrouded them. It soon faded, leaving only the other warrior on his feet; the lustful one was a pile of bones, swirling with slimy snakes. The Goddess ordered the remaining hunter to hurry to his village and prepare the people for her coming.

The excited villagers quickly changed into their best ceremonial attire and waited with keen anticipation. When the beautiful woman arrived, she removed a bundle from her back and spoke to the chief. The people pressed forward to hear her wondrous words. Inside the wrappings were a round stone and a long-stemmed, richly adorned pipe. Some of the villagers later claimed they could hear flutes playing in the sky as the beautiful visitor held the pipe aloft and proclaimed, "This is the Sacred Calf Pipe. Its red stone bowl stands for Mother Earth, the buffalo calf carved on its outside stands for all four-legged creatures, its bird skin–sheathed stem represents all growing things, and these twelve ornamental feathers stand for the great eagle and all other birds of the sky.

He who smokes this pipe speaks to all who breathe and walk on the earth and in the spirit world. He is heard by Wakantanka, the Great Mystery, and he is one with all." White Buffalo Woman raised the pipe high again. "This pipe will let you walk on Mother Earth, who is also your sacred Grandmother. It binds you to your father and grandfather, and to all your other relatives. And this stone will teach you the order of your lives henceforth."

The beautiful woman then walked a few steps and turned into a red and brown buffalo calf that moved a few steps farther and rolled in the grass while becoming a white buffalo calf. By the time the calf reached the brow of the nearby hill it had become a black buffalo that bowed solemnly to the Four Winds, then disappeared.

The White Buffalo Woman not only brought the Stone and the Sacred Pipe, she gave the Lakotas a sacred oneness with nature and family, and a rich spiritual and ceremonial life that embraced Wakantanka in all its forms.

It was the Lakota Way.

Gall was steeped in the Lakota Way. Born in 1840, he was a Hunkpapa.

There were seven groups within the Lakota nation: the Black Kettle, Oglala, Brule, Saris Arcs (Without Bows), Miniconjou, Blackfeet Sioux, and the Hunkpapa. These groups followed their own prerogatives, often loosely banding together with others. But they generally acted in concert, which gave them their powerful numbers. The Hunkpapas, one of the smallest tribes, usually camped with the Sans Arc and the Blackfoot Sioux.

Gall had been named *Matohinshda*, or Bear-Shedding-His-Hair, as a small boy. At a very young age, he'd exhibited signs of bravery and had never stopped. Later, when hard times were upon his camp during a particularly bad winter, he was found eating the raw gallbladder of an animal carcass. Thus his adult name became *Pizi*, or Gall.

He quickly passed through the apprentice stage of his warrior training, and in his midteens he distinguished himself so well in tribal battles he was taken into the prestigious men's society, the Strong Hearts. In the late 1850s, he and the redoubtable Sitting Bull, along with several other leading warriors, formed the Midnight Strong Heart Society, an ultra-elite group that met late at night. And now he was the strongest war leader of the Hunkpapas. His tribal brothers liked to follow him on raids because he was always successful. Like Crazy Horse of the Oglalas, Gall wore the mantle of good fortune in war, and since he mixed his fearlessness with shrewd leadership, a warrior could count on bringing back both fortune and fame when he rode with him.

In his thirty-fifth year, Gall was a powerful man. Tall, with a barrel chest, he could lift two times his own considerable weight. He was a handsome man with pronounced cheekbones, a broad face and square jaw, thick lips, and dark, intense eyes. Power seemed to emanate from him, yet he could be open and of good humor. While he practiced the Lakota custom of extensive charity, he so readily replenished his horse herd that he was considered a wealthy man.

The exuberance of Sioux youth and the freedom of Lakota life required a rein, a hobble, to ensure the survival of the clan. This restraint came in the form of policing societies, *akicitas*. Sort of a cross between a men's social club and an auxiliary police unit, each *akicita* within a village took turns enforcing order for the period of one moon. They kept discipline in camp when the clan was on the move, and particularly during tribal hunts and on war parties.

They beat those who would violate their order, and sometimes expelled them from camp. They were the law. They also provided a place for their members to eat, sleep, dance and sing, and generally while away the time when they weren't doing something more important. Each club had its traditions, insignia, and songs.

The role of the *akicita* also related to war.

Gall was a member of the Kit Fox *akicita* of his Hunkpapa village, and on the white man's June 8 a member of the society was killed by a Crow war party while he was on a buffalo hunt a few miles from the village. The dead warrior had seventeen summers, and was the son of Bow Dog, a tribal Big Belly—a *Naca Ominicia*. The *Naca* was an honored assembly of distinguished leaders, warriors, hunters, and shaman who had reached an age when their value to the tribe lay mostly in giving advice. Since many of them had also reached a stage of advanced girth, they were fondly called "Big Bellies." At the *wacekiyapi*, or memorial ceremony for the dead son, Gall had pledged to avenge the death of the warrior as a favor to the gout-ridden father—who himself had been a Kit Fox.

Gall proclaimed that he would lead a war party of Kit Foxes against the Crow.

Three days later, Gall carefully packed his saddle bags with the accoutrements of war. Everything had a specific purpose: otter skin braid wraps, spare moccasins and leggings, a carved wooden bowl, the bone breast plate he'd so carefully assembled, spare bullets for his Henry repeater rifle, his smoking pipe, tobacco, buffalo bladder food bag with enough pemmican to last him several days, and his vitally important war paint kit with its elk grease and containers of paints.

It was hot, but he wore a scarlet robe over his breech clout. Of course, it could snow before they reached their objective in this mammoth country; in that case, it would come in handy. But mostly he was wearing it because it was the Way. He saddled both horses, one for riding as well as his fast warhorse, Hurry, who would be led. The folded eagle feather war bonnet was attached to Hurry's pommel. The Henry rifle went in a holster by the saddle of his travel horse. The broad-bladed knife that he had honed to a fine edge was in its scabbard on his hip, and his favorite killing weapon—the stone axe—was within easy reach on his saddle, as was his bow and three dozen of his special arrows. The bright shield depicting his most important first coups was also attached to his warhorse, as was his coup stick and one other weapon, his lance. Attached to it were the feathers of his office in the Kit Fox as well as his sash. As a high-ranking sash bearer, he carried a picket pin and rope. In battle he could drive his lance into the ground and attach himself to it. He would be bound to stay there and fight until released by a fellow warrior or killed by the enemy.

But this battle would be different, if his plan worked.

With everything ready, he knelt beside his tipi and spoke to his wide-eyed son, Little Hawk. "My son, you must guard your mother and sisters while I'm gone. Do you have your arrows?"

The grave five-year-old with a bow slung over his shoulder nodded, holding out two small arrows. "I have more, Father."

Gall nodded, smiled. "Good. Be brave."

"I will, Father."

As the first two warriors for his party rode up, Gall turned to the tipi and nodded to his two wives and to his two daughters. He had said goodbye to them earlier. All of them nodded in return as was the custom when a warrior departed on a raid. Afterward they would join the other warriors' women in crying and wailing.

More warriors from Kit Fox arrived, and soon the entire twenty-eight were on hand.

The bright, hot sun—Wi—was high.

It was time.

Gall and the small column rode out of the village.

Red Elk was fifteen, the son of Bald Wolf. This was his sixth raid, and he hoped to count his first "first coup" this time. He had a second coup, and a fourth coup. For the second coup, he was permitted to wear an eagle feather tilted to the left. Counting coup was mostly the touching of an enemy. It could be done with one's hand, a lance, bow, musket barrel, a special coup stick, or anything else. It could be done when the enemy was alive or dead. It was more important than just killing, although an enemy scalp was powerful evidence of a coup. How did one get a *fourth* coup? Easy—if he were accompanied by three other warriors and was the last to touch an enemy, he got fourth coup.

Red Elk was tall and spindly for a Lakota, but had great strength and hadn't been beaten in a foot race in two summers. His nose was hooked, like his father's, but he was considered handsome and had been taken into the warm blanket of a pretty Sans Arc widow just a week earlier. Before joining Gall's war party, he'd consulted the shaman, Crooked Tree, about his strength. The medicine man had assured him that seven days after intercourse was enough to build his reservoir of power back to a fighting level.

He was young to be accepted in the Kit Fox. His father, Bald Wolf, had been a highly regarded Kit Fox before being killed on a Shoshoni raid. And Red Elk himself had killed a lion with an arrow when he was eleven. Now, with the highly respected Gall, Red Elk needed that first coup so he could forever wear the eagle feather straight up and be the envy of every young Lakota! He was fired by the old Lakota saying, *It's better to die on the battlefield than live to be old.*

He had his father's wolf hide, the one he always wore on raids, in his saddlebag. It was his most powerful medicine. His second pony had turned up lame just three days before departure, and he hadn't been able to borrow a replacement. Gall had nearly turned him down for that reason, but Red Elk had looked into the piercing eyes of the great war leader and said, "My pony is stronger than any in the village. He can get me there and fight too!"

Gall had looked at him for a moment and acquiesced.

Red Elk looked forward a few paces in the column to where the *blotahunka*—war leader—rode on his brown-and-white spotted pony. He dreamed of being like Gall! He wasn't a full chief, but he was the best *blotahunka* in the Hunkpapa tribe, probably the best in all of the Lakotas, next to Crazy Horse. Sitting Bull had previously been the greatest one, but now he was devoted to his spiritual medicine. Wakantanka had moved the entire Lakota nation to this great land of the huge sky to fight and rule over all the peoples, and its greatest men had always been its best warriors. At the age of six Red Elk vowed to be one of its greatest leaders.

He rode beside Black Ash, his *kola*. Most Lakota boys had a *kola*—a close friend with whom one grew to manhood. Black Ash was four inches shorter and thickset, the same age as Red Elk. He, too, was a good young warrior. But ever since they were small boys, he had been content to tag along with Red Elk—which made their relationship work.

They camped that night without posting guards. But that was because they had been safely in Sioux territory, and also because all warriors were trained to sleep lightly and awaken at the slightest disturbance. The next day, after stopping for a midday meal of pemmican, they were riding more carefully through the rolling, lightly wooded countryside. Suddenly, Gall's hand shot up and the column halted. A small herd of buffalo was grazing in the near distance. The war leader called up his best hunter, Angry Bear, and told him to kill one.

Angry Bear held a single arrow aloft, signifying that he would use just one to make his kill. Hurrying forward on his bareback warhorse, he stopped near the edge of the herd to select his quarry. Moments later, reins in his teeth, he rode close to the fat cow he'd selected and fired the draw deep into her heart. The buffalo stumbled, dead by the time she hit the ground. Angry Bear let out a whoop and waved his bow.

Everyone in the party but Red Elk took up yelling as they hurried in to help butcher the cow. It was his job to get the fire going down by the nearby stream. The meat was quickly cut, and it was soon time for soup. Stones that would go in the cow's paunch were piled around the blazing fire as the big bag was filled with water. There were pieces of tender meat from the rump, but the choicest parts of the cow were her kidney, liver, and tongue. When the stones were hot they were picked up with sticks and dropped sizzling into the water. Soon the water was boiling.

Red Elk served Gall first, first a center cut from the tongue, and then a piece of soft and flavorful kidney. The *blotahunka* nodded with approval, and the rest of the warriors joined in devouring the rich meat. Afterward they filled their cups with the steaming soup.

They slept later in the day, then rode several miles under cover of darkness. They were no longer in Sioux country and had to be more wary. They journeyed this way for two more nights, and each night when they stopped, Gall sent out the scouts to look for the enemy. After the third night, Angry Bear and another scout hurried excitedly into camp shortly after sunrise. Gall quickly lit his pipe, offered it to the Four Winds, the Earth and the Sky, and solemnly handed it to the scouts. The Crow camp, a midsize village, was nearby. The two scouts would get the first honors for finding it.

Red Elk could hardly contain himself! Everyone could now pull the trappings of war from his saddlebags and begin preparing in earnest for battle. He touched the *wotawe*, the special amulet on a thong around his neck. It was a small irregular stone, shaped something like a flint arrowhead that he'd found beneath the head of a mountain lion he'd killed with an arrow when he was younger. On it, he had imbedded a tooth from the lion's mouth. The tooth would help the brave heart of the lion, the *manaza*, to sustain him. From his saddlebag, he withdrew the fine buckskin leggings his sister had made for him, and a quilled armband the color of the morning sky that his mother had made. He removed his paint containers and the porcupine brush with which he would apply them—that would come last.

A warrior had to look his best on a day he might die.

Gall was pleased as they approached the peak. This was the way a war party was supposed to go. The scouts had shown everyone exactly how the enemy camp was situated, and every warrior knew what he was to do. The experienced war party had only six young members, so he felt confident. They had been riding quietly single file since shortly after dark as Angry Bear led them toward the camp. Now, thirteen miles along, they were less than two miles from the enemy. He had left two warriors behind to guard their camp and extra horses, men whose ponies had seemed the most tired. He'd nearly kept the young Red Elk back, but the boy showed such promise that he couldn't. And he knew how the young man felt—he'd been the same at his age. This raid would be good for him.

He was pleased that Angry Bear had come along. Any experienced *blotahunka* needed a top warrior in his party, one who could assume control if something bad happened. Angry Bear was dependable. They had been friends since childhood, and at times Angry Bear acted as a war leader himself. They worked well together.

Gall touched his *wotawe*. It was a piece of riven bark torn from a tree struck by lightning. It had happened in his twelfth summer, when he was on his first war party as a water boy. A huge storm had come up, with the Gods of Lightning and Thunder making great medicine. He had been standing under the tree at the time and was dashed to the ground like a rigid, cracking branch. But in only a short time, he had returned to normal—nearly normal, because from that moment on, he'd been stronger—stronger than any other Lakota youth his age. He'd never since been defeated wrestling or in any other contest. As he rubbed the *wotawe* it seemed to glow in the moonlight. Softly, he whispered, "Wakantanka, give me the power to lead well this morning. Save my brave ones as we avenge an unholy death."

He checked his weapons as they neared the peak. Everything was ready.

He gave the signal to dismount. They silently walked their horses the last mile, then removed the saddles. Man and pony would rest awhile. Those who couldn't sleep might paint their ponies, or tie colored cloth in their manes and tails. The battle was approaching.

No one spoke.

The enemy village was located nearly a mile away by a swiftly flowing stream. When the first gray touches of light brightened the eastern horizon, everyone was fully awake with anticipation. Last minute adjustments to equipment and attire were made. Gall fitted his long war bonnet of eagle feathers to his head.

Angry Bear pointed out the flats where the enemy ponies would be grazed. And as everyone watched, they suddenly appeared! The Crow horse tenders were turning their herd out to eat. The animals ran along the river bank, heading straight toward the war party, stopping here and there to drink. A few who weren't too thirsty turned toward the grassy flats for their morning meal.

The horse tenders headed lazily back to their village, probably to return to their blankets.

Gall held up his hand, turning respectfully to the north, east, south, and west before giving the signal to start the attack. Quietly, the warriors rode down to the river and into a copse of willows along its bank. When they reached the first of the drinking ponies, they herded them onto the flats, and then rounded up the whole herd. Moving away rapidly toward the peak, they gave up any attempt at silence. Speed was now essential—and battle. They hadn't come here just for horses.

The son of Bow Dog had to be avenged.

Gall watched the edge of the village closely. The Crows were alerted. He guessed the pony herd had well over a hundred head, but he knew the Crows had other horses, and that they would surely try to retrieve their prize possessions. But first, they needed to get some paint on their faces. Wouldn't be long. *There,* the first Crows were galloping out of the trees! Gall gave a signal and his warriors began to whoop and push the pony herd even faster. When the Crows drew within shooting range, Gall gave another signal and the Hunkpapas hurried away from a cloud of arrows.

No one was hit. The herd thundered on amid the howls of the Sioux. After some three more miles, Gall gave another signal and suddenly the Kit Fox wheeled their ponies. Slipping to the side to use the animals as a shield, they fired arrows at the pursuing Crows. They then swung their ponies in another circle, and unleashed a second volley of arrows as they closed fast on the enemy. Gall shot the nearest Crow, then whirled back to knock him from his horse, counting a first coup. He also slapped the horse with the lance, claiming it. As his warriors slammed into the other Crows, he jumped to the ground and grabbed the hair of the brave he had just shot. With a series of deft slashes with his knife, he severed the dying Crow's scalp and held it aloft. Moments later, he was back on his warhorse, joining the melee. He killed one more Crow and took both the warrior's scalp and his horse.

Red Elk caught a Crow with a vicious swipe of his battle-ax a moment later. Blood spurted from the large neck wound as the enemy warrior's eyes glazed over and he slid slowly from his pony. Red Elk thrust the ax high in exultation. First coup! He reined his pony around to get the scalp. *First coup!*

The enemy was routed; those who were not killed fled toward the village. Gall broke it off. There were twenty-two dead Crows, and only one Hunkpapa had received a serious wound—an arrow in the arm. Two others had minor cuts. As his warriors raided the dead for spoils of war, they scalped and cut off genitals. Some counted first coup; all counted lesser coups.

They finally rounded up the horses won in the battle, added them to their herd, and started back to Lakota country. Along the way, they would divide up the animals. And that night twenty-two Crow scalps would be treated with grease and red paint before being hung on long poles.

Three days later, reaching a point four miles from the main Hunkpapa camp, Gall ordered an overnight stop that would enable them to get ready for their triumphal return. A scout was sent to the village to alert the people.

At dawn the following morning, Gall led the war party to the village. Each member was stripped to his loincloth, with his bare body painted and his face blackened. He was the first to gallop into the village, leading the first pony he'd captured and waving the pole with its attached scalps. He sang out the customary, "I'm Gall, the war leader! I've made kills and taken their horses. All the warriors have returned!" Everyone in the village was gaily dressed and noisy. Dogs barked, drums were beaten, rattles shaken. The women and children cheered.

The rest of the warriors rode in and bragged about their conquests. It was the Way—not to brag was disrespectful. As the last one rode by, Gall raised the first scalp he had taken and called out, "Bow Dog! I have brought the hair of your son. The Kit Fox have avenged him. And here is his horse. Take this horse and ride him. Blacken your face and join us!"

Everyone cheered and laughed as a *Naca* came to Gall with a sacred pipe. Offering it first to each of the Four Winds and then the Earth and Sky, he presented it to the war leader to share with his warriors. And then Gall, in his deep, booming voice told the now quiet crowd the details of the battle. When he finished, there was a great burst of noise, and then the warriors' sisters and female cousins took the scalp poles and started the victory dance. Bow Dog could stop mourning, for his son had returned in the form of the scalp.

The feasting began. The new horses would be distributed between sisters and other female relatives. The "Dance Until Morning Dance" would begin, the scalp dance that would last for four nights, with black-faced warriors singing about their coups.

Gall was quite pleased. The Kit Fox had been avenged, and in five days life would be back to normal. As he watched the younger warriors dance, a taller man wearing the upright feather of first coup approached.

"Well done, my brother," Sitting Bull said.

"The warriors fought well, my brother."

"You always lead well."

Gall nodded, smiled. Custom or not, there was little point in bragging to a man who had counted sixty-seven first coups.

3

'Tis the gallant Seventh Cavalry
It matters not where we're goin'
Such you'll surely say as we march away;
And our band plays, 'GarryOwen.'

FORT ABRAHAM LINCOLN, DAKOTA TERRITORY
AUGUST 2, 1875

"How died my master, Strato?" Messala asked.

"I held the sword, and he did run on it," Strato replied.

"Octavius, then take him to follow thee," Messala said. "That did the latest service to my master."

Marcus Antonius shook his head sadly. "This was the noblest Roman of them all. All the conspirators, save only he, did what they did in envy of great Caesar. He only, in a general honest thought, and common good to all, made one of them. His life was gentle, and the elements, so mixt in him, that Nature might stand up and say to all the world . . . 'This was a man!'"

Waiting a moment to build up to the finale, Octavius Caesar said, "According to his virtue, let us use him, with all respect and rites of burial. Within my tent his bones tonight shall lie, most like a soldier, ordered honorably." He paused, looked again at the audience, and intoned, "So, call the field to rest, and let's away, to part the glories of this happy day." The jury-rigged curtain was squeakily drawn together and this 1875 rendition of the commanding officer's favorite Shakespeare play, *Julius Caesar*, was over.

After a hushed moment, Libbie Custer was on her feet applauding. "Bravo! Bravo!" she shouted from the first row of benches. The rest of the audience seated in front of the Custer house followed suit, filling the hot Sunday evening with exuberant applause. With Tom Custer bowing deeply and grinning from ear to ear as Marcus Antonius, the rest of the cast crowded out the front door onto the huge veranda that served as the stage. Captain Tom Weir nearly touched the floor with his head as he bowed; he played Octavius Caesar. Miles Keogh had been the dastardly Brutus. And of course George Armstrong Custer had portrayed Julius Caesar.

When the clamor settled down, Libbie announced, "Mary will have refreshments ready in a few minutes in the backyard!" Mary Adams was the Custers' black cook, a genius at producing remarkable dishes from whatever meager ingredients she might have on hand. On this pleasant summer evening, the result was a delicious cherry cobbler and spiced coffee that only she could brew.

Most of the regimental officers and wives were present for the entertainment. Custer had ordered a regimental officers call for the following morning, and only one lieutenant, serving as duty officer, had been left at Fort Rice, twenty-five miles downriver.

Actually, the regiment—the famed Seventh United States Cavalry—had never been completely together. Authorized by an act of Congress in July, 1866, the Seventh was organized as a number of scattered cavalry troops with headquarters at Fort Riley, Kansas. Rather than a cohesive regiment, these troops were more readily identified by the names and reputations of their commanders. Even now, a few of the companies of cavalry were scattered far away from the main body. A, E, and F Companies had arrived in Dakota Territory from the Department of the Gulf in May.

Stationed at Fort Randall, way down by Yankton, A and E Companies were temporarily in the field ejecting miners and other unauthorized persons from the Black Hills. All troops had been redesignated "companies," even though the size of the unit was the same. But Custer had most of his "royal family" with him at Fort Lincoln, and that was what made life and duty pleasant there.

The so-called royal family was made up of the commanding officer's actual family and other insiders. The most flamboyant and fearless of these was the rambunctious First Lieutenant Thomas Ward Custer, Autie's younger brother. The general's youngest brother, Boston, was serving as a civilian quartermaster. Another family member was Autie's brother-in-law, the good-natured Jimmi Calhoun. Married to Autie's sister, Margaret, Calhoun was often the butt of the ever-present Custer jokes.

As everyone sipped the spiced coffee and punch in the backyard, Captain Fred Benteen and his wife, Cate, stood off near a recently transplanted rosebush talking to Captain Tom French. French, the commander of M Company, was stationed at Fort Rice, where the white-haired Benteen was the commanding officer. French poured some brandy from his silver flask into Benteen's cup of punch and offered it to Cate Benteen.

"No, thanks," she said.

"Well, I see General Caesar is in his glory, as usual," Benteen said sarcastically.

French shrugged. "I guess it's better than just sitting around reading. Actually, I sort of enjoy these things. Anything to get away from Rice and see some pretty ladies once in a while." "That's a fine thing to say in front of me," Cate said, feigning affront.

French grinned. "Aw, you know what I mean." There were two officers' wives, three enlisted wives, and four rather fat laundresses at Fort Rice. The only other women were a few Rees living a short distance away, and none of the ones who weren't married were worth a second look. French was thirty-two and single. He was also the best shot in the regiment. He had been brevetted captain during the war in late 1864 and had been quite fortunate to get a captaincy in the regular army afterward.

Many regular officers had attained high rank in the Civil War, but had been forced to go back to a much lower rank in the greatly reduced peacetime army. Custer was a prime example: brevetted major general at the age of twenty-five, he was actually serving as a lieutenant colonel. In several cases, officers who had served as generals during the war had had to revert to as low as major, some even to captain, in order to remain on active duty. In one of the most extreme cases, W. H. McCall, who had been brevetted brigadier general, reverted to sergeant after the war and served for a time in Sheridan's special rangers.

As one of the half-dozen most famous Union generals during the war, even the dashing and heroic Custer had been forced to scramble for peace-time rank. He had accompanied President Andrew Johnson on a speaking tour, ostensibly as the president's bodyguard, after the war. From this association and also based on his remarkable performance during the war, Custer was offered the colonelcy of one of the two black cavalry regiments being formed along with the Seventh and Eighth white regiments. But due to his Southern sympathies, Custer declined. Then the lieutenant colonelcy of the Seventh was offered. Since the colonels of regular regiments were often away serving on boards and such, the lieutenant colonel performed the actual command. Autie Custer assumed this rank and assignment at Fort Riley, Kansas, in November 1866. But *no one* would ever have any doubts about his brevet rank.

Fred Benteen also had an illustrious war record, rising to the rank of colonel and being recommended for brigadier general. After the war he had received another brevet—to colonel for heroic action against the Cheyenne on the Saline River in 1868—while Custer was undergoing the punishment imposed by his court-martial. At age forty, the gritty Benteen had the wide open look of an owl. His pale-blue eyes often seemed to carry a touch of whimsy, but they could harden quickly when his anger took hold. He was a fearless, capable officer.

And Fred Benteen had no use for George Armstrong Custer.

It was like that in a small army. One officer could serve with or under another for years, and hate his guts. And it could be a two-way street. Somehow professionalism permitted such an illogical relationship to function. Space helped. Custer, who returned little of Benteen's dislike, simply kept the white-haired officer at a distance as much as possible—which was why the captain commanded Fort Rice.

Benteen drained his cup and pulled out his own flask. Pouring some mash whiskey into it and into Cate's cup, he shook his head as he looked at members of the royal family clustered around Custer. "I have trouble breathing their smug, superior air," he said. I wonder if any of those ass-kissers ever get their noses broken when Caesar makes a sudden turn?"

French shrugged, smiling. "Strong possibility. I'll check with the surgeon."

As if Custer's ears had been burning, he abruptly headed for the officers from Fort Rice. Benteen nodded coolly as the general ambled up in his white Roman toga.

"Enjoy the Shakespeare?" Autie asked casually, touching his brow with a finger salute of greeting to Cate.

"Oh, yes!" she replied enthusiastically. "Theater at Fort Rice is rather limited."

Custer grinned. "As in nonexistent."

"Right. Totally nonexistent."

Custer nodded to the two captains. "And how are you gentlemen tonight?"

"All right," Benteen replied. He seldom used "sir" when he spoke to Custer.

"Just fine, General," French answered. They both knew Custer didn't drink, so neither offered him any. French didn't particularly care for his commander, but he hadn't joined in any palace revolt either. Actually, there was no revolt. A few other officers resented some of Custer's ways, but commanding officers since the beginning of armies have been less than popular. Tall and fit, with remarkable stamina, and equally remarkable vanity, Custer just happened to be a lightning rod. It was difficult to take him casually; he was too much of a presence.

"Your quarters okay?" Custer asked Cate.

"Just fine," she replied.

He smiled. "Good." Turning back to the other two officers, he again touched his brow in a finger salute and said, "Enjoy yourselves. See you in the morning."

As he walked away, Benteen frowned. "I wonder what's on his damned mind now?"

French shrugged. "One thing's certain, we'll find out."

Elizabeth Bacon Custer was, at thirty-three, a most attractive woman. With dark-brown hair and deep-set gray eyes that would cause most men to take a second look, the slender but shapely native of Monroe, Michigan, had been the target of men's desires and affections since she was thirteen. At that age, she'd been forced to slap a doctor's face when he kissed her. Her mother had died when she was twelve, and she had been placed in a number of girls' schools while her father, Judge Daniel Bacon, searched for a second wife. Vivacious and adventurous, the young Libbie Bacon had been mostly bored by her suitors until the war began, when a rather wild, romantic young West Pointer with red-blond curls began to pursue her while spending leave time in Monroe. At first she wasn't overly attracted to him, but his attentions to her girlhood rival, Fanny Fifield, soon increased his desirability. When he came back again on leave as a captain, he began to attract her in earnest. But it was when he returned as a twenty-three-year-old brigadier general commanding all of the Michigan cavalry regiments that she had finally fallen for him. "Boy General," "Fearless National Hero." Newspaper phrases like these captured her romantic imagination, and she finally agreed to marry the dashing cavalry leader.

That had been nearly twelve years earlier.

She had climbed on the flamboyant Custer bandwagon, and what a trip it had been! The young Monroe girl who had become enamored of Shakespeare's *Macbeth* and *King Lear* on her way to becoming her class valedictorian (edging out Fanny) soon became one of the most famous and glamorous women in America. She employed military touches in the clothes she designed—and set as style—and went wherever she could with her celebrated husband. And that included into the field, where she often suffered privations seldom experienced by officers' wives. She loved to entertain as the "general's lady" and play mother hen not only to the bachelor officers, but to the women on the posts where her Autie took her. She loved his scads of hounds and his horses, and most of all, she loved him.

Tonight was another of those pleasant entertainment nights. The play had been fun—*Julius Caesar* was always enjoyable—and more of the officers and wives from the outlying posts were on hand. She paused to dab at her moist brow. Fort Lincoln could surely be hot this time of the year!

Tom Custer walked by, giving her a little pat on the fanny. Grinning back over his shoulder, he said, "Nice little shindig, Mrs. Custer."

She feigned a scowl. "Go take care of our house guest, young man!" she said, then smiled. She didn't think he'd *ever* marry any of these lovely young women she occasionally brought in from Monroe. He was just a hopeless *rake*. She smiled to herself. Good word, most appropriate for an evening of English drama.

She swatted a mosquito on the back of her neck. Darned things! A person couldn't *wear* enough clothes in this blessed heat to keep them away. But they weren't as bad as last year. And the grasshoppers weren't everywhere this year. Those jumping, spitting characters had been quite frightful! She caught John Burkman's sleeve as he carried a fresh tray of cookies toward the serving table. "Burkman, will you fill up that punch bowl, please?"

Custer's orderly nodded his head. "Yes'm."

Private John Burkman was the same age as his master, and that was the way many of the enlisted men in the regiment viewed their relationship. But Burkman, in his slow way, liked to think the general was his friend. Oh, Custer growled at him in quick anger now and then, but that was the way the sometimes hot-tempered commander was. And he usually came around a short time later and apologized—like when the hound bitch, Lulu, one of Custer's favorite dogs, jumped off the troop train and got lost forever. The general had climbed all over him for opening the door, but it wasn't too long—even in his grief at losing her—that he had put his arm around Burkman's shoulder and forgiven him.

Being the general's orderly gave Burkman purpose. Some of the troopers called him "dog-robber" and worse, and sometimes when he'd had a bit too much to drink, he got into a fight over it, but all in all, he loved the general, and most of all, he adored Miss Libbie. Do anything for her. He liked to think that the Custer household couldn't operate without him. And maybe "dog-robber" did fit. In addition to taking care of the general's horses, he tended to Custer's huge pack of hounds, exercised them and tried to keep them out of trouble. He liked to say there were eighty of them, but it was more like a third that number. All over the place. Always hungry. He fed them scraps from the mess hall after meals. Took care of their pups, and fetched them when they wandered off. The general favored Tuck, and Miss Libbie liked Bleuch the most.

Miss Libbie wanted to fatten him up, so Burkman started eating in the Custer kitchen. And that was some eatin'. A trooper even hung a moniker on him for his eating prowess—"Old Nutriment." Mary Adams, the Custer maid, had to be the best damned cook west of the Missouri. And there was that time when the maid's sister, Maria, visited, and she and Burkman wound up one night out on the grass behind the house. Only time since he first went to war that he ever laid with a woman other than whores in town. Or one of them unmarried laundresses.

Nope, being the general's striker wasn't all that bad.

Margaret Calhoun, Custer's younger sister, came up to the serving table bearing a bottle of wine. "Care for a bit of the grape?" she asked Libbie.

Maybe Autie didn't drink, but Libbie liked her spirits in certain moderation. In fact, she'd had a good sized portion of bourbon shortly before the curtain went up, courtesy of Tom Weir's flask. She held out a clean cup and her sister-in-law poured. It was a cheap wine, purchased in Bismarck, but Fort Abraham Lincoln wasn't exactly Paris. She sipped, shrugged, and said, "I like its rich body and dry perfume, Maggie."

Maggie laughed. "Missouri River, '74. A good year."

They touched glasses and raised them. "To Julius!" Libbie said.

"To Julius," Maggie echoed, and they drank.

Libbie reached down to rub the long, velvety ear of Bleuch, who had just plopped down at her feet. Seven other hounds were hanging around the serving table, waiting for crumbs to drop. She wondered where the rest were. Probably in some kind of mischief, if they were passing up an outdoor party. She knew Tuck was with Autie.

"Want another little shot of the best bourbon in Dakota Territory, Mrs. Custer?"

Libbie turned to face a broad grin on Captain Tom Weir's slightly round and somewhat flushed face. "No, thanks, Tom. I'm having a bit of wine." She could tell by the slight slur in his words that he'd imbibed rather heavily, but that wasn't anything new for Tom Weir. The captain had played Mark Antony in the production, and well. He was an entertaining fellow who usually made her laugh. In fact, he'd had a crush on her for some time, and had tempted her when the story about Autie and that Cherokee girl had circulated. She'd toyed with getting even with Autie at that time. More than one army wife had done so when her husband strayed.

There'd been that period when Autie had written her letters about the women he was seeing in New York, and the report that he'd been in a brothel at Leavenworth, and about an affair he'd had with a certain captain's wife, and on and on. That was when her ardor had cooled. But one day she'd just sat herself down and told herself that he was one of the most famous and desirable men in the country, and women were always going to chase him.

And at times he was still a willful child.

It had taken a while for her to get fully out of her resentful frame of mind, but all at once she'd decided to start having fun again. And she did love sleeping with him. He was so vigorous and adventurous! She looked over to where he was laughing full tilt at some joke with Tom and Boston. How those boys did carry on! You would never know one was a general and another one a brevet lieutenant colonel.

She smacked another mosquito, this one on her arm. A person just couldn't get away from them! And they went right in the house. Still—she smiled. The army was good to her. And being a general's wife, even on lieutenant colonel's pay, certainly had its points.

There weren't many single women around Fort Abraham Lincoln, except in the "hog ranches" across the river. A single, not-too-ugly laundress passed through now and then, but if she wasn't too lewd or too much of a drunk, someone married her. In fact, one frontier general had said "post surgeons had little to do except confine laundresses and treat the clap."

On this particular Sunday, the last day of payday weekend, there was a little money left in a soldier's pocket—that is, if he hadn't lost it gambling in the barracks already, or if he didn't owe it to the loan sharks, or for fines, or for the other myriad reasons that kept a poorly paid trooper broke—or a poorly paid non-com, or a poorly paid officer, for that matter. When it came to low wages, the army was quite democratic—in a comparable sense. Of course, the officers had to stay out of the hog ranches. That was enlisted country.

My Lady's Bower was the favorite of several of the non-coms, but that didn't keep the privates out. The new owner, "Lady Jane" Dauveraux, fresh from New Orleans with an affected accent to prove it, had bought the large, two-story house after the Missouri River had gone back down to a decent level in the spring. The previous madam had tired of the capricious river and her troublesome clients, had thrown her hands up in resignation, and had sold out the very moment the visiting "Frenchwoman" made an offer. Lady Jane had renovated everything on the damaged bottom floor, and had even sent down to New Orleans for three new girls, one of them reputed to be a "high yellow" who had learned her specialties in Paris. Cheri, they called her.

A total of seven girls worked at the Bower, although to call two of them girls was stretching it a bit. Neither Emmy Lou nor Sadie would see forty again, and the only thing that wasn't worn about them was their latest eye paint. Victoria and Elizabeth had each broken a bottle of cheap wine over the prow of a ferryboat when it was launched—ferryboat meaning the flatbottom that brought people from one shore of the often swift Missouri to the other. It had been a fitting performance for royalty. The three new girls, including Cheri, looked as if they were still in their twenties.

But everyone who came to the Bower didn't visit just for a woman. It was a good place to drink. Lady Jane didn't water the whiskey much and she didn't charge very much for it. A married man who didn't want to take a chance on getting the old *clapoir,* as the French called it, could just come for a drink. Several Civil War lithographs decorated the walls, but its main piece of art was a huge painting of a buffalo behind the elaborate mahogany bar. On this Sunday night, the large parlor was full. A piano player, a private from the regimental band, was banging out the old favorites such as "Jeannie with the Light Brown Hair" on an aged upright, and the place was noisy with loud, boozy voices. Two of the whores were sitting with sergeants, one with a corporal from M Company. Two were dancing with awkward privates, and two were elsewhere, probably upstairs earning an honest living.

After two and a half days of drinking since pay call on Friday, no one at the Bower was sober.

Sergeant Daniel Kanipe was talking to his friend from C Company, Ygnatz Stungewitz, at the end of the bar. Kanipe was a twenty-four-year-old platoon sergeant from North Carolina. At five feet, eleven inches he was a few inches taller than the average cavalryman. He was a little drunker than Stungewitz because he was feeling sorry for himself. For two months now he'd known that he was totally, unconditionally, in love with Missouri Ann Bobo, the wife of First Sergeant Edwin Bobo. There was no mistake about it. He had been attracted to the lively North Carolina girl as soon as he joined C Company, but it was only when he started taking his laundry to her personally after he made sergeant that it had become more serious. The bad part was that Ed Bobo was his first sergeant—the man who had gotten him his sergeant's stripes. At least he'd talked Lieutenant Tom Custer, his company commander, into it.

He shook his head as he poured some more cheap whiskey into his glass. "I guess all them laundresses know about it."

Ygnatz Stungewitz shook his head. In his slight Russian accent, he said, "You go down there on Suds Row with the big eyes of a little foal, who don't know?"

"You think Ed knows?"

"Is he blind?"

"He don't say nothin."

"He likes you, and don't want to have to shoot you."

A sad look fell over Kanipe's face. "Don't say that."

"Iggy" Stungewitz was the only Jew in C Company. Four years older than Kanipe, he had come to New York from his birthplace of Kuuno, Russia, in 1873. But there hadn't been many jobs that appealed to him in the big city, and since he'd served four years in the Czar's army, he'd enlisted for what the recruiters called the "elite Seventh Cavalry." Besides, he'd always wanted to see the famous American West. He was a quiet man of medium height, with black, intense eyes, tightly curled dark hair, and a bushy black mustache. He'd suddenly, for no particular reason than the fact that the odds were against his fellow cavalryman, stepped in beside Kanipe in a barroom fracas in the Deadwood Gulch saloon the previous year. It was during the Black Hills expedition, when some miners had picked a fight with Kanipe, calling him a "yellow-bellied Confederate traitor."

The two troopers had lost the fight, but they'd gained a friendship.

Kanipe liked Iggy's laconic humor and the soldierly way he went about his duties. He was also drawn to the Russian's interest in books. As a farmer who had managed to stay in school in a rural Reconstruction community until he was fourteen, Kanipe was far from illiterate, but largely unread. A handful of dime novels—and now and then a thumbed-over magazine—had been the extent of his literary fare.

"Ya know, Iggy, maybe I oughta just go right up to old Ed and tell him."

Iggy shook his head. "I told you. He have to shoot you."

Kanipe shook his head. "I'd be better off."

"Naw you wouldn't. She's just a woman. You'll get . . ."

"I see you're still drinking with Christians, *Slugwitz.*"

Iggy turned at the familiar brogue of his nemesis, Michael Martin. The stocky Dublin native and first sergeant of D Company, not only turned surly after a certain amount of whiskey, but usually made life difficult for non-Irish troopers. He didn't like Jews, and he particularly didn't care for Iggy. The way he spat out *Slugwitz,* his private corruption of Iggy's last name, was almost like swearing.

It was all part of the ethnic divisiveness of a regiment that was roughly one-quarter Irish immigrants, one-quarter German immigrants, and one-half American born.

"Ya, Sergeant, I am," Iggy replied quietly, going back to his glass.

"Sure, and I just think you oughta get on outta here and find yourself a goddam *synagogue,* little Jew boy."

The burly forty-year-old Martin had a reputation for pushing men until they wanted to fight him, and then hurting them. He made no bones about it—he *liked* to hurt people. If he met one who was his match, he got him court-martialed. Dan Kanipe had never liked the man. He turned, stepping between his friend and the first sergeant. "Leave him alone, Martin."

A slow grin spread over Martin' s face. "Well, well. So the Reb's going to interfere, huh?"

"Just leave him alone."

"I can leave," Iggy protested, catching Kanipe's arm. "Or Martin can come outside with me alone."

"Tell you what," Martin said harshly, pulling out some brass knuckles and putting them on his right hand, "Why don't I just settle this little problem with both of you?"

A hand came to rest on Martin's shoulder. "No, why don't you settle this with *me,* arsehole!" First Sergeant Ed Bobo said coldly. "Those are *my* troopers you're messing with!"

Ed Bobo was thirty, a swarthy Ohioan who had spent three years fighting in the Civil War, and he knew how to put away his share of whiskey. He weighed at least thirty pounds less than Martin, but he was the best bare-knuckle fighter in the regiment—which was a good way to get those stripes in the Seventh, or in any other regiment, for that matter.

Martin shrugged off his hand, adjusting the brass knuckles. *"Arsehole is it"* It's about time you learned a little respect, Jew-lover.

Bobo sprang back, raising his fists.

"C'mon, Sarge," Kanipe interjected. "This is my fight!"

"No, it's my fight, if it's in here!" Jeremiah Finley waved a sawed-off shotgun at them. He was the provost sergeant of the post, but off-duty he sometimes worked as a bartender in the Bower. "You fellas want to draw blood, do it outside," he said. Finley was alleged to have killed a Protestant back in his native Ireland, escaping to serve in a Canadian regiment before landing in the Seventh. He was also good with his fists, and one of the best shots in the command—which is why Custer made him the provost sergeant. "But you know what Old Ringlets will do if he hears two of his first sergeants was in a brawl."

Martin glared at him, then shrugged. Turning back to Bobo, he growled, "Some of these days you ain't gonna be around to nursemaid these little pricks, and they'll be all mine."

There was one hog ranch where an officer could go discreetly, because enlisted men weren't allowed on the premises. It was in town—Bismarck—and was run by a quiet woman with soft, honey colored hair named Geraldine Gentle. At least that was the name she used, and since it fit, no one questioned it. She did her own bartending, paid a civilian to plunk a guitar off in a corner of the parlor, and employed three girls. The large, two-story clapboard house was also a place where Bismarck's mayor and the few other respectable citizens could get a quiet drink or spend an hour with a comely girl who got checked for disease once a week by one of the town's doctors—who, in turn, got paid in trade. She'd gotten the girls from a big chain out of San Francisco, and while she had them dress like dance hall girls to stimulate the men, she insisted that they keep their drinking to a minimum and conduct themselves as much like ladies as possible.

She had a fourth girl who had recently married a passing railroad engineer, so she was expecting a replacement any day. Years before, it had been said that most of the small town's women were prostitutes, but actually new families were moving in every day—most respectable. Bismarck even had a newspaper now, the *Tribune*.

Tom Custer liked Geraldine and was one of the few men she personally took to bed. She liked his good looks, his ever-present humor, and his passion—both as a lover and for life. She was also drawn to his devil-may-care attitude. Handsomer than his older brother, the thirty-year-old Tom was every bit as wild and fearless in battle. He'd won the Medal of Honor *twice* after being commissioned late in the war, and enjoyed being a sort of crown prince of the regiment. He and Autie had constant good times together. The general had gotten him brevetted to lieutenant colonel back in the spring of '67 for his bravery at the Battle of Sayler's Creek during the war. It sure didn't hurt an officer's career to have Autie for an older brother. An officer could stagnate in a rank for years until a vacancy occurred, but Tom's active duty captaincy was expected to come along in a few months.

Since he commanded C Company, it had been his men who'd almost gotten in trouble over at the Bower. C was a pretty good company as far as the regiment went. A bit larger than most, with fifty-one men present for duty, in the hospital, or on leave.

Once, while on a drunken leave in Chicago, Tom had visited a tattoo parlor on a dare. The artist had needled "TWC," for Thomas West Custer, on his arm, and a patriotic eagle on his chest. He was indifferent to the tattoos, but Geraldine liked the eagle and sometimes rubbed her breasts against it in a little expression of wickedness.

In the meantime, life at Fort Lincoln was fun. Lots of parties. Sweet Libbie kept bringing pretty girls out to visit, and he highly enjoyed them even if they always wanted to play the innocent virgin role. Hell, they had to catch a husband somehow, he knew that. But not him, *nosiree*, he wasn't the least bit interested in being hog-tied yet. Besides, Geraldine Gentle was all the woman he wanted. Gorgeous little thing. Hell, he might even take her out of this saloon and whoring business and marry *her* some day . . . if he ever lost his mind.

Two other officers had come over with him after leaving the Custer party. No, actually only one was an officer, but the other man had that status, having been a contract surgeon with General Crook down in Apache country. Doctor Henry Porter was seriously considering taking on a new contract, this time with the Seventh. In the meantime, the general liked him and he was sort of an honorary surgeon with the regiment. Twenty-seven years old, with balding blond hair and a sweeping red mustache, the good doctor also liked a good time. He was the physician who inspected Geraldine's girls each and every week.

The real officer was Captain Myles Keogh, the handsome Irishman who commanded I Company. Keogh had an illustrious background, having been commissioned in the Battalion of St. Patrick, Papal Guards, in Italy when he was twenty. After being awarded the Cross of the Order of St. Gregory the Great and the *Medaglia di Pro Petri Sede,* he hurried on to the great American Civil War, where he took part in thirty engagements. He was an aide to General John Buford at Gettysburg and held other staff and command positions. His brevets for gallantry in action reached to lieutenant colonel. Following the war, the dashing Keogh was commissioned captain in the Seventh and had commanded Company I ever since. He was a well-liked member of Custer's royal family who shared Tom's taste for lusty women after he'd had a couple of drinks.

Keogh's favorite at Geraldine's was Molly O'Brien, who was about as Irish as Polish sausage. Her story—all prostitutes had some kind of a story—was that she had been raised in a wealthy family in Philadelphia, but her father had beaten her when she wouldn't give him sexual favors, and she had run away from home at the age of sixteen. Actually, her father had been a laborer who had caught her in bed with a neighbor boy when she was fourteen. But she had run away from home at sixteen, and her Irish brogue had become almost perfect.

But at the moment, while Keogh was having a drink with Molly O'Brien, Tom was involved in a poker game in the corner of the parlor. Being Sunday night it was quiet in Geraldine's, but there were four other poker players in the game—the police chief, a railroad man, a grocer, and a man Tom didn't know. They were playing dollar limit, three-card draw, with a ten-cent ante. Pretty stiff on army pay. Tom loved the game because everyone knew he was reckless and they couldn't play him tight. He could bluff and bull the game pretty much as he saw fit, as long as he caught a good hand once in a while—which he did rather frequently.

Five years and four months younger than his famous brother, Tom had been a wild one growing up in Monroe, Michigan. With his blond good looks and carefree laugh, he'd started having his way with girls in his early teens. One, a livery stable owner's daughter, had kissed and told, getting him into hot water with her father and his own strict father. "You keep that thing in your pants," his father had thundered, "or we'll see what a horse whip will do to it!"

He worshiped Autie and had roughhoused and played tricks with him almost since he'd learned to talk. When Autie went off to West Point in 1857, it seemed as if his life stopped. But he picked up what his brother had fantasized about—being a soldier. A month after his sixteenth birthday, Fort Sumter was fired upon and the Civil War began. He ran away from home and enlisted as a private in the Twenty-first Ohio Infantry, and saw action in several big battles during the next three years. In 1864, Autie used his influence to get Tom commissioned as a second lieutenant and assigned to his staff. Fearless, the young Captain Custer twice captured enemy flags as he led wild attacks on rebel positions in the final phases of the war. For these acts of gallantry, he received brevets to major and lieutenant-colonel, and was the only one to receive two medals of honor in the entire war.

"Dang me, if I didn't catch another spade!" Tom laughed aloud as he pulled in another pot, winning with a flush. "You fellas are more fun than Christmas!"

Over on the green velvet sofa, Myles Keogh chuckled. "By the Lord Harry, that Custer lad is the luckiest chap I ever met!" He squeezed Molly's mesh-stockinged knee. Her unblemished ivory skin always excited him, particularly when she was wearing those black stockings.

"No, *you* are, love," Molly replied, kissing his cheek. "You're the one's got me."

The captain chuckled. "Right you are, lass. And we've wasted enough time down here with these boring folks." He jumped to his feet, pulling her along, and, as she laughed, headed for the stairway. At that moment the guitar player started to pick away at *La Paloma*.

"Disgusting, cheap, carnal behavior," Doctor Porter said to Geraldine as he watched the couple disappear up the steps. He leaned his elbows on the bar and shook his head. He was beginning to feel quite drunk. "Some of these days I'll have to fall in love."

Geraldine smiled as she poured more whiskey into his glass. "You are. You love all of the women in the world."

Doctor Porter's expression turned sad. "I know. I think I'll become one of them new-fangled gyna, gyno, gyne*cologists!*"

Back at the fort, Dan Kanipe and Iggy had just returned from the Bower. As they reached the C Company barracks, Dan said, "I'm gonna go down to the stables and say 'good night' to my horse." He'd been thinking about that excuse on the boat all the way across the river.

Iggy shrugged as he turned toward the steps. "Say 'good night' to mine too." He hiccuped and disappeared through the screen door.

Dan didn't like what he was doing, but he couldn't help himself. His gait wasn't too steady after all the drinking, but he headed directly for the non-commissioned officers' quarters. The yellow moon was about three-quarters and still bright, giving the landscape a bluish gray tint. As he got close to the front of No. 8, his heart jumped. The curtains were open and a lamp was burning in the front room. More than he expected. He edged closer. *Would she still be up, maybe sitting where he could see her?*

He moved nearer, straining to see inside. It was quiet as a church on Monday, except for the faint sound of a flute coming from the band barracks. Then that stopped. All he wanted was a glimpse of her—

Her soft drawl startled him! "You lookin' for somethin' special, Danny Kanipe," Missouri Ann Bobo chuckled from the shadow, where she was sitting on the stoop, "or are you lost?"

"Oh, uh, I was just going to say 'good, uh, night' to my horse."

"Yes, of course, your horse."

He could see her lovely smile, even in the shadow. He mumbled, "Uh, he gets, uh, lonesome this time of night."

Her light laughter was tinkly, and directed at him it was embarrassing. "He really does, you know."

"But you passed the stables, Danny. They're over there, remember?"

He looked around, feigning surprise. "I'll be dogged."

"You had a lot to drink, honey?"

She called him that once in a while, usually in a teasing way. But it always warmed him.

"Some," he replied.

"That's what my husband says. You see him tonight?"

That really made him feel guilty. "Uh, huh."

Missouri Ann had been eighteen when she married Ed Bobo, two years and two children earlier. He was ten years her senior. "Want to sit down with me?" she asked.

It was as if someone had jabbed him with a bayonet. "No!"

"I know you want to."

"Ain't got nuthin' to do with it. You're a married woman."

I won't bite, you know."

"Uh, nope. I gotta go."

Her laugh tinkled again. "Yes, your horse. He's lonesome."

"Uh huh." He turned and headed for the stables, trying not to hurry and wanting to go back.

4

Men grow tired of sleep, love, singing and dancing sooner
than war.
—HOMER

Fort Abraham Lincoln, D. T. was one of the army's finest new western posts. Started in 1872 as a small infantry fort behind a log palisade, the post was enlarged considerably the next year to accommodate the Seventh Cavalry. That original cluster of buildings on the north hill still housed the garrison's infantrymen, whose mission it was to protect the post from marauding Indian bands while the cavalry was away on whatever missions Sheridan might prescribe for it. Slightly more than a mile separated the center of Infantry Post from that of Cavalry Post, which was located on the plain to the west of the Missouri River. Cavalry Post was open, with no wall. It's main buildings formed a rectangle with the barracks on the east side, the hospital and post headquarters on the north, the storehouses to the south, and the officers' quarters on the west side. The granaries, dispensary, and guardhouses were in the center and just north of the parade ground. The stables were behind the barracks as were the scouts' quarters, and also Suds Row, where the laundresses lived and plied their washboards.

In the center of officers' row, the three-story Custer house stood like a majestic palace. Said to be the finest house on the frontier, it was a copy of the original—which had caught fire, supposedly due to some highly regarded "warm paper" insulation—in February of '74. The replacement, with its wide veranda, had been constructed immediately. The Custers had salvaged most of their belongings from the fire, so their loss wasn't nearly as bad as it could have been.

Even in the disagreeable condition caused by days of excessive drinking, the men of the Seventh Cavalry Regiment tumbled out into the awakening August morning for reveille with a certain casual air. Some of them were still a trifle drunk, others who were fortunate enough to have some spirits on hand had nipped some hair of the dog before standing half-asleep in ranks. But reveille seldom took long, so they were soon back inside. At this time of the year it was not an unpleasant formation. In the harsh Dakota winter it was another matter.

After breakfast, the twenty-seven officers present for duty assembled at post headquarters for the officers' call the commander had set up. At one minute after eight, the adjutant, Lieutenant William Cooke, called *"Attention!"* Custer strode into the conference room.

"As you were!" Custer barked, going to a small podium. All business, he looked around briefly as they took their seats, and said, "Good morning, gentlemen. I've called this meeting so some of you officers from outlying posts could come into headquarters and get a little taste of civilization, at least what we have."

A few chuckles were heard in response.

"The other reason," Custer continued in his rather high pitched voice that now and then contained a slight stutter, "is to apprise you of what I learned in Chicago in June, and what has transpired at higher headquarters since then." A brief smile touched his lips, his eyes suddenly glowed. "It's what we want, gentlemen, a chance to bring some more glory to the Seventh Cavalry. General Sheridan is certain that Sitting Bull and Crazy Horse will not bring their hostiles into the agencies as ordered. Furthermore, the Sioux will not accept any kind of terms to sell or lease us the Black Hills. As you know, the hostiles consider that area sacred and resent the presence of miners and other white people. Since the army simply can't keep civilians out of that area, there will be conflict."

Custer smiled again. "And that's our middle name. General Sheridan is thinking about a winter campaign if the need arises. And I want us to be ready. That means I want you company commanders to step up training in the next few months. Lieutenant Cooke, how many new recruits do we have in the regiment?"

The adjutant, a tall thirty-year-old first lieutenant with a massive set of dark sideburns—Dundrearies, as they were called, referring to the arrogant Lord Dundreary in the play *My American Cousin*—came from a wealthy Canadian family. A bachelor, he was brevetted lieutenant colonel in the war. He was also, naturally, one of Custer's royal family. He replied, "All told, sir, with the arrival of the latest recruits at all posts, ninety-three of them with less than three months' service."

"How many losses do you project among seasoned troops in the next five months?"

"With expected desertions and the end of enlistment of men who fail to re-enlist, sixty-five, General."

Custer scowled. "I don't like that word, desertion, but it's a fact of life. That means some one-fourth of this regiment will be new troopers come winter. You gentlemen have your work cut out for you."

Captain Benteen held up his hand and spoke. "You expect us to give them target practice with these new rifles, Colonel?" He never called Custer *General*. He was referring to the M-1873 Springfield .45-.70 carbines that had recently arrived in the command. "Where are we going to get the ammunition?"

"I've put in a special requisition." Custer replied.

"That's fine, but when's it going to get here?"

"Within two months, I hope. I'll write to General Terry and have him expedite it."

Benteen shrugged, replying sarcastically, "Yeah, that means they'll hurry up and get it here just before I retire."

Everyone smiled, several of the officers laughed. "Correct," Captain French said.

"No, Terry promised me this would be different," Custer insisted.

"What about mounts, General?" Captain Yates from F Company asked.

"We'll be getting some replacement mounts in sporadically over the period. I expect we'll have plenty of good horses by the time we ride out of here next winter."

"Do you think the hostiles will fight this time, General?" First Lieutenant Tom McDougall, the CO of Company B asked.

Custer shrugged. "Who knows? My scouts tell me Crazy Horse and Gall have been pretty frisky lately."

Tom Custer had the most serious hangover in the room. He hadn't left Geraldine's bed until two-thirty in the morning, and it had cost him part of his poker winnings to get a ride across the river at that hour. "I'd like to get that spotted little bastard in my sights just once."

"Hear, hear!" several of the officers echoed.

Armstrong smiled. "We *all* want him in our sights. Now, another thing. As you know, the men are complaining about the sutler robbing them. Well, I've checked the prices at the sutler's store and sure enough, he is. Most of the stuff is cheaper in town. And, as you know, I can't throw him off the post because he's not under my control. But we can do something that may change his outlook. Each of you company commanders has a company fund. Now this may not be legal, but I want you to begin buying the things the soldiers need the most . . . tobacco, soap, candy—you can figure it out—in town. Have your first sergeants lay in a supply and sell it to the troops for cost."

Myles Keogh grinned. "Of course. That bastard will change his tune if we hit him in the pocketbook. Good idea, General!"

There was a murmur of agreement as Custer nodded his head. He looked around for a moment before saying, "All right, gentlemen, Lieutenant Cooke has some other information for you. Thanks for coming." As he strode from the room, all of the officers scrambled to their feet and stood at attention.

To a casual observer at Fort Lincoln it would seem that the Seventh was full of drunks on this Monday morning. Major Reno sipped from his flask. Captain Weir had tipped a jug back in his quarters before breakfast. One lieutenant, seven sergeants, three corporals, one farrier, one trombone player, and twenty-two privates had also consumed some hair of the dog in one form or another. It *seemed* as if there were a lot of drunks in the Seventh, but this wasn't a very heavy attack on distilled spirits for a Monday morning right after payday for a regular army regiment. It would be a long, hot summer and there hadn't been much to do for some time.

Drinking was a common pastime on the frontier and particularly in the army. Many officers, including some of those in the Seventh, drank to excess. So did most of the NCOs. The insidious, addictive nature of excessive alcohol intake respected neither rank nor background. Ulysses S.

Grant knew what it could do, as did many others. But George Armstrong Custer wasn't one of them. He had taken the temperance vow during the war and didn't touch a drop, as the saying went. Normally he looked the other way about drinking because it was so prevalent, and because many of his officers put away their share.

But recently there had been just too much whiskey in the barracks. Upon finding one trooper drunk in a squad room a few days earlier, Custer had decided to resort to his "barrel punishment" to make an example. The trooper was offered his choice of a court martial or "wearing the barrel."

It was an easy choice: the barrel would last for only ten days. A court-martial could lead to prison. And that particular trooper was most highly qualified to make the decision.

Private Lucien Burnham of F Company had been wearing the barrel since the morning after payday when Custer encountered him drinking by the rifle rack in his barracks. Lucien Burnham was a twenty-four-year-old redhead who was an oddity in the regiment. He was a real lawyer, having graduated from law school, and quite possibly would have been able to get a commission, had he applied. But for reasons known only to himself and one friend, he had opted for the anonymity of being a private in the Seventh Cavalry. Normally his drinking was quiet and unobtrusive, but on the day Custer caught him he had not sobered up since the night before.

His adornment was an empty vinegar barrel with shoulder straps at the top. It had to be worn during all waking hours, except when eating or relieving oneself, and became more and more uncomfortable as the days passed. At first, Burnham had merely been the object of derision from the troopers—which he managed to ignore—but the discomfort of toting the heavy barrel everywhere had become nearly unbearable.

On this day, his last in the keg, he had been ordered to walk back and forth by the manure pile, "guarding it," as a final admonition to others who might bring spirits into the barracks.

Private Iggy Stungewitz was the friend in whom Burnham confided. Finding the educated Burnham reading a book he was familiar with one day, Iggy had struck up a conversation. And their association had blossomed. At times, Burnham's longing looks were a bit disconcerting, but Iggy enjoyed the man's intellectuality. He walked up as Burnham who had paused on the shady side of the dung pile. "Last day, huh?" the Russian asked.

Burnham nodded, making a face. "Yeah, and they had to give me the shit pile to further ridicule me."

Iggy shook his head, removing his hat and wiping the sweat from his brow with a big red bandanna. "Makes you smell just great."

Burnham found a chuckle. "But you notice no one's stealing any of this shit while I'm guarding it, right?"

Iggy laughed. "I haven't seen a single wheelbarrow being toted away. Damn, it sure is hot. I think I must be sweating pure Bower whiskey."

"You went over there last night, huh? Any excitement?"

Iggy told him about Martin accosting him and Kanipe.

"Martin's an ass. One of these days someone's going to run him through with a hayfork.

Iggy waved the wet bandanna to air it out. "That's too quick."

"What would you do?

"I have my special ways."

Burnham looked at him admiringly. "Have you ever killed anyone?"

"There was once a very bad man in the Cossacks who didn't like me."

"And you killed him?"

Iggy shoved his hat back on his head. "Let's say he met with an unfortunate accident. They found him with a broken neck."

Burnham's eyes were still wide. "Think you could do that to Ol' Ringlets?"

Sergeant Danny Kanipe had gone through the morning with only minor suffering from the night before. Drinking seldom bothered him. The only thing that troubled him was his heart—which belonged over in NCO quarters No. 8. But it didn't *really* belong there because that was Ed Bobo's home.

But she had been friendly the night before.

She knew he cared.

And he knew she didn't object to his attentions.

Ed Bobo was a good first sergeant, he knew that, but he couldn't be much of a father *and* be over there in the Bower drinking when he should be home with his wife and children. *Nosireee!* Still, this feeling he had for Missouri Ann made him feel so damned guilty.

He shifted the laundry bag to the opposite shoulder as he walked along. If he were married to her, she'd never be a laundress, that was for sure. Why, he'd—

He saluted Major Reno in passing and said, "Good morning, sir." One of the general's hounds was following the major at a short distance. He wondered about the latest Reno story, the one in which the major was seen in the stable one evening about dusk with a trooper on his knees in front of him. The rumor had it that the trooper had looked like that lawyer private over in F Company, but it had been pretty dark in the stable and the bearer of the salacious tale had said the man who observed them wasn't sure about anything.

But it was a hell of a story! With a *private!*

Couldn't be true. No, Major Reno had been a hero in the war—a *general!* And he had been married. Wife had died. No, someone had made the story up. Although that lawyer trooper was kind of a strange duck. He'd have to ask Iggy about it.

He was about to turn the corner toward Suds Row when he just missed running directly into First Sergeant Martin. The bullnecked Irishman stopped. "Can't you see where the hell you're going?" he snapped in his Dublin brogue.

"Sorry, First Sergeant," Kanipe replied.

He started to go on, but Martin stopped him. "Where's your little Jew bunkie?"

"If you mean Stungewitz, he's over at the farrier's. And he's not my bunkie."

"Of course not. You just bugger each other out in the weeds."

Kanipe felt the anger rising. "I resent that, First Sergeant. And you know it isn't true."

Martin slapped his thigh with the leather riding crop he always carried, and laughed loudly. "Sure and wouldn't that be a funny one though." He pointed to the laundry bag. "Here you are panting like one of Ringlet's hounds for Bobo's slut laundress, and you're buggering a little Jew. Ain't that a case!"

Before Kanipe could respond, the first sergeant had turned away and moved on.

☆ ☆ ☆

Drinking wasn't confined to the soldiers, nor was boredom. Scouts drank and were always bored between campaigns. Living in the middle world of the scout—between the hunter warrior's life and the often sedentary life with the army—could be destructive to the more restless type of Indian. In fact, boredom could be as destructive as firewater itself.

Bloody Knife was one of the restless types. Arikaras or "Rees" as they were most commonly called, seemed to have a higher tolerance and lesser need for alcoholic spirits than most other tribes. And he was only part Ree. His father had been a Hunkpapa Sioux, and he blamed his need to go on a drinking spree now and then on that part of his blood. Not that he cared why he did it. Being drunk also allowed him to vent his rage about his enemy. He very much liked how whiskey made him feel while he was drinking it.

This morning Bloody Knife had enough alcohol left in his blood from two days of drinking that all he could do was sit out behind the scout quarters on a rock and clean his Winchester carbine. He felt lousy. Sweat was pouring out of him, flies were bothering him, and his wife, She Owl, was acting mad. *The woman needs a good beating.* The children had pestered him, but he had chased them away. *Too many children around.* He figured there must be twenty-five of them, offspring of the scouts and their wives. The Indian scouts' quarters were one-story barracks, flimsily partitioned to afford the different families only a semblance of privacy. Not much, certainly more private than a tipi, but they kept the glaring North Dakota sun away, and shielded them from the fierce blizzards that could howl as late as June.

The flies, mosquitoes, and bugs just came inside.

Still, it was part of what made army scouting attractive, that and the rations. The uniform of an enlisted scout was appealing, and a private's pay of thirteen white man's dollars every month traded out for more than most skins or whatever else a warrior might have to exchange. He'd enlisted so many times—for different lengths of time: weeks, months, years—that he couldn't remember the number. He'd even been a lance corporal for a while—until he got drunk and took the "Grand Bounce," as the troopers called going missing for a few days. He liked that term. In fact, he liked many Long Knife words, but he never spoke them, not even with Custer—and he was Custer's favorite scout, his best Indian friend. He spoke only Ree, Lakota, Cheyenne, or Mandan, maybe some Assiniboines now and then. The rest of the time, he signed. It was the everyday language of Indians almost everywhere. And traders. And he was skillful at it.

His mother, She Runs High, had been captured in 1836 on one of the numerous raids the Sioux made on the Arikaras. She soon became the wife of his father, Hail-Storm, and settled into life as a Hunkpapa Lakota and gave birth to her first two sons. He'd been born in the white man's year of 1840 in a Hunkpapa village on the edge of the Black Hills. They named him Tamena Wayway when he was little, and later Bloody Knife, which had been the name of a successful warrior uncle. As he grew into boyhood, competing with the other young Hunkpapas in warrior training and games, he quickly found that being of mixed blood carried a strong stigma. His rivals, led by a strong youngster his own age, seldom stopped teasing him. Overly sensitive, Bloody Knife's quick anger did nothing to abate this minor persecution. The other boy's name was Bear-Shedding-His-Hair—Gall.

Soon the maturing Bloody Knife centered his anger on Gall, and grew to hate him. When he was about twelve, his mother fled back to her own people, taking him along. But he had been an apt pupil during those years of training to be a Lakota warrior, and he wanted nothing more than to use those skills to become a rich and famous fighting man. And since the Rees had turned mostly into a trader tribe, a good hunter and warrior was someone quite out of step. In his twentieth year, he went back to his father's village on the Rosebud River for a visit. But what he hoped would be a pleasant reunion with his relatives and the few young men who had befriended him turned into a nightmare. Once more he was derided and scorned as a worthless trading Arikara, not worthy to carry the moccasins of a Sioux warrior. He finally challenged Gall, now a war leader, to a wrestling match that turned into a battle almost to the death. Only the intervention of the young chief, Sitting Bull, ended it before further blood was shed. Following this, Gall's Kit Fox *akicita* humiliated Bloody Knife further and threatened to kill him if he didn't leave their camp.

Seething, Bloody Knife returned to the Rees and became a scout for the Long Knives. During the intervening years, his two brothers had been killed by Hunkpapas, and he was convinced that Gall was to blame. Just once, he had come close to the vengeance he never stopped dreaming about—so close that he couldn't believe his enemy had survived.

The stocky Bloody Knife looked up as Bob-Tailed Bull, sporting his new corporal's stripes, asked, "That gun dirty again?"

"Always dirty," Bloody Knife replied in Ree. "Trouble with you stupid Indians, you forget."

Bob-Tailed Bull snorted. It was an old joke between them. "You got any whiskey?"

"If I did, I wouldn't be cleaning this rifle."

"Want to go hunting?"

"No. I want to stay right here."

The corporal wandered away as She Owl came back from washing some clothes in the nearby river. She was thickset and quite dark for a Ree. She had become his wife nine years earlier and had given him a son, Red Knife. "Why don't you hunt?" she asked. "The soldiers still have money to buy meat."

"Be quiet, woman, I'm sick today."

"You're always sick from whiskey," she grumbled.

Bloody Knife scowled. "Go away!"

She turned to go inside as a man in a spotted vest walked up. Mitch Boyer was the son of a Santee Sioux woman and a French Canadian blacksmith and frontiersman who had stretched his luck and had later been killed by Indians while trapping. Like Bloody Knife, Boyer was a linguist. He was one of the most respected of the frontier guides and interpreters, even though he usually spoke softly and slowly as if he wasn't sure of himself. At thirty-eight, he was the same age as Bloody Knife. His trademark black-and-white calfskin vest he wore much of the time. In fact, one of his Indian names was Man Wearing Calfskin Vest. Others were Chopper and Hammering Out.

With him was Young Hawk, the twenty-six-year-old nephew of Bloody Knife who sometimes cooked for Custer. He was the best drummer among the scouts.

"The Crows want to start a Moccasin Game," Boyer said. "They've challenged the rest of us. You got any money to bet?"

Bloody Knife nodded. He loved to gamble more than drink whiskey. "Enough." The dumb Crows never quit trying. He and Mitch Boyer were two of the best Moccasin Game players to ever serve the Long Knives, but the Crows never learned. The troopers had a word for them: suckers. He shrugged, stuffing the rag in his belt and getting to his feet. "Might as well. My rifle's clean."

5

Who will watch the watcher?
—JUVENAL

"General, there's a reporter from the New York *Herald* here to see you."

Custer looked up from his desk at Lieutenant Cooke's interruption. "The *Herald?* What's he doing out here?"

"Claims to be investigating graft in the Indian traderships, sir."

"Show him in." Custer frowned. He was in pretty thick with the publisher of the *Herald,* James Gordon Bennett, Jr., so why hadn't he been informed that this reporter was coming? He glanced at the doorway as his adjutant ushered in a plumpish man in his late thirties. His hand was outstretched and he wore a broad grin under a bushy red mustache.

"I can't tell you what a pleasure this is, General Custer!" he said. "You've been my hero ever since Gettysburg. Name's Ralph Meeker, but I'm using the nom de plume J. D. Thompson."

Custer got to his feet and shook hands. "You're here to investigate Indian traderships, Mr. Meeker?"

The reporter's grin faded into a scowl. "That's right. There's a lot of chicanery going on, and I'm going to get to the bottom of it. It reaches right to the top, you know."

Custer had heard a couple of rumors, and he, of course, knew how his own trader tried to take advantage of the troopers. He'd also read the exposé the local newspaper had printed. "Is that a fact?" he asked.

"Yes. Goes back to when Secretary of War Belknap converted the traditional army sutler to a post trader. As you know, a board of local officers used to appoint a sutler, and a commander such as you could supervise his operation."

Custer nodded.

"And then the Secretary of War started making the appointments and the new traders were answerable only to his office. Then a couple of years ago Belknap issued a gag order forbidding officers from speaking out on such crooked dealings, right?"

"In effect, yes."

Meeker smiled. "And that's why you published articles in the *Herald* under an alias."

"Officially, I've never done that."

"But we know better, don't we?"

"Why are you here at Fort Lincoln, Mr. Meeker?"

"As you know, there has also been a tendency to lump post traderships with Indian agency traderships, opening another chance to steal. And Orvil Grant, our dear president's crooked little brother is in it right up to his arse, General. The Bismarck *Tribune* has chronicled this graft assiduously. *That's* why I'm in Bismarck."

Custer stroked his chin. He'd read with interest the *Tribune's* allegations, but hadn't believed all of what he'd read. Supposedly all of the Indian trader licenses on the upper Missouri had been revoked rather suddenly. And Orvil Grant had purportedly traveled from one post to another, peddling influence for a price to get the licenses reinstated. The *Tribune* had referred to him as "the Christian Capitalist." He said, "How can I help you, Mr. Meeker, or Mr. Thompson, if you wish?"

"Tell me all you know about crooked traders and particularly about Orvil Grant."

"Frankly, I can tell you only that our local sutler or trader overcharged and I found a way to get him in line. As far as Orvil Grant goes, he hasn't been here, nor at Fort Rice. In fact, I've never met him."

Meeker scowled again. "I was hoping you'd have some direct information about him. Will you tell me how you got around your own trader, and help me with this matter? Mr. Bennett will be most grateful, I'm sure."

"You're welcome to anything I know."

"I'm simply not going to cater to him," Custer said.

Libbie looked at him over her after-dinner coffee. "It's not a matter of catering to him. He's the secretary of war and he's your superior. Being rude to him will net you nothing, Autie Custer, and you know it."

"I told you, I'm convinced that he's in this trader graft right up to his ears and I can't put on a big smile and act like everything's okay. I can't do it." It was September 2 and Secretary of War Belknap and his party were due to arrive in Bismarck from an inspection tour on their way to a holiday at Yellowstone National Park. Custer had been notified that the secretary's party would visit Fort Abraham Lincoln for a few hours the next day.

"You told me yourself that he hasn't even been charged with anything. You're just enamored of that nasty *Herald* reporter, who as far as I'm concerned has overstayed his welcome. You know that most of what he has written is filled with innuendo and rumor."

Custer frowned. "I don't care. This graft couldn't be going on if Belknap weren't in on it somewhere."

Libbie wasn't giving in. "What if you're wrong? He's still the head of the army. Do you think you'll get your star back by being rude to him?"

Custer had learned a long time ago to respect Libbie's opinions, because she was usually right. She had good instincts and that famous woman's intuition, but he simply wasn't going to shine up to Belknap. "All right, if anyone asks, I'm sick with dysentery."

"That will reflect on the sanitation of my kitchen."

"No, it won't."

Libbie just shook her head.

Just as he intended, Custer refused to meet Belknap and his party the next day. Instead, his brother Tom greeted them at the landing when their boat brought them over from Bismarck. One of the members of the group was Lieutenant Colonel James Forsyth, longtime aide to General Sheridan, who had accompanied the secretary as his aide on the outing. But the main attraction was Brevet Major General, USV, William Worth Belknap. The former lawyer had an illustrious war record, having come into the war back in '61 at age thirty-two as a major. He'd fought at Shiloh, Corinth, and in the Vicksburg campaign. As a volunteer major general, he'd commanded a division at the end of the war under Sherman. He'd been appointed secretary of war after the death of his predecessor, Grant's close friend, John Rawlins. Seven other men, civilian guests of the secretary, completed the party.

Tom Custer took them on a tour of the post, stopping at the stables, where he showed them Armstrong's mounts. He gave them a cock-and-bull story about how the two horses had run a match race against the fastest ponies Sitting Bull owned, and how they had won. The bet, Tom fibbed, was the horses. His audience, slightly wide-eyed throughout the story, bought it, while Tom could barely keep a straight face.

"What did the general do with them?" one of the members of the party, a railroad executive, asked.

"Shipped them off to New Orleans, where they are the top brood mare and stallion on his French breeding farm. He expects to develop a blood line of pintos."

The next stop was at the barracks of the regimental band, where the secretary was honored with a sprightly rendition of "GarryOwen," "Yankee Doodle," and "The Battle Hymn of the Republic." Then it was on to the Custer house, where a gracious Libbie met the party on the piazza.

"Welcome to Fort Lincoln, Mr. Secretary," she said brightly. "General Custer has been under the weather, but he'll be along shortly. Will you be able to stay for lunch? The officers' wives would very much like to meet you.

Belknap gallantly kissed her hand. "It's such a pleasure to meet you, Mrs. Custer, you're every bit as lovely as I've heard. No, I'm afraid our schedule requires us to be back in town early this afternoon. But I thank you anyway." He looked around. "Seems to be quite a nice house you have here."

"Yes, it is," Custer said, coming out the front door. "The best on the frontier." His tone was cold. "Is there some particular reason why you are making such a brief visit, General?"

Belknap glanced at Colonel Forsyth, who replied, "Yes, General Custer. Since this is an informal stop on a non-official mission, it was thought best not to intrude on your normal training. And the secretary is scheduled to meet with the mayor of Bismarck and some of their leading citizens this afternoon.

Custer didn't bat an eye as he said, "I'm sorry that those people are more important than the soldiers of one of the secretary's finest regiments."

Before anyone could say anything else, Libbie broke in with a warm smile, "Maybe you don't have time for lunch, but my cook has prepared the most delicious tea cakes this side of Philadelphia, and the teapot is on. Please come in so I'll have a chance to show off my best china."

Belknap drew his eyes away from Custer's hostility and smiled. "It would be a distinct pleasure, Mrs. Custer." He crooked out his arm. "Will you lead me to table?"

Libbie took his arm and they led the way inside to the parlor, where Mary and Private John Burkman were standing by the long table, ready to serve the refreshments.

Tom said, "She isn't joshing, gentlemen. Her Mary is the finest cook the army has ever seen."

Inside, Custer was introduced by Forsyth to the other members of the party. As tea was poured and everyone stood around the table, Custer walked up to Belknap and said, "I'm afraid I don't feel too well, General, so if you'll excuse me, I'll leave you in Mrs. Custer's capable hands."

The secretary searched his cool expression briefly, then slowly nodded his head and found a smile. "Of course, General." He extended his hand. "I'm sorry we can't talk. Some other time."

Custer nodded to Forsyth. "Give my regards to General Sheridan." And with that he turned and left the party.

The next day at shortly after two o'clock in the afternoon, the publisher of the Bismarck *Tribune*, Clement Lounsberry, came to Custer's office at the post. The newspaperman had come to the town and bought the little paper about the same time that most of the regiment arrived. His newspaper coverage of the post had been fair and as unbiased as possible, Custer thought. An army town newspaper could be pretty hard on the military and the foibles of its soldiers if it wanted to be. As he took a chair by Custer's desk, Lounsberry said, "I've come to apologize for the rudeness shown the army in town yesterday afternoon and this morning."

Custer raised an eyebrow. "What rudeness?"

"I thought you might have heard—the handbills?"

Custer shook his head. "Nope. Don't know anything about them."

Lounsberry, a slender, balding man, pulled a sheet of paper out of his inside pocket and handed it over. It looked like a circus program, billing "Bilk-knap, Grant & Co." and their collection of "acrobats." Each character was decked out in rich jewels and costly Indian rings, and was pushing a wheelbarrow full of money. "They were posted all over town and practically shoved in the secretary's face at every turn."

"Did you have anything to do with them?"

"No, they were run off in my newspaper job-shop in my absence. Had I known about them, they'd never have been printed."

Custer didn't like the idea of the secretary of war and Sheridan's aide being openly insulted, but part of him liked the affront. *Serves the damned crook right*, he thought, suppressing a smile. "Do you know who did this?" he asked.

"No, but I'll find out. In the meantime, next week's issue will carry an apology."

Custer stood up and clapped him on the shoulder. "I think that's downright decent of you, Mr. Lounsberry. C'mon along to my house. I want you to meet my wife and have some tea."

The newspaperman's eyes widened at bit. "Uh, yes sir, that would be a pleasure."

Custer jammed his hat on his red-blond curls and told the adjutant that he'd be in his quarters. On the way out the door, he smiled to himself.

George Armstrong Custer never passed up a good newspaperman.

6

ON THE YELLOWSTONE
SEPTEMBER 20, 1875

The sky was yellow with the hot sun at midday, and even in the shade of a large and twisted Jeffrey pine, Gall sweated as he finished rewrapping his favorite stone battle-ax with new leather thongs. He regarded his handiwork for a moment, then swung it about, as if he were smashing enemy skulls.

"Why do you like the ax, Uncle?" Uncle was a normal title of respect.

Gall turned, surprised at the intrusion. It was Red Elk, impolitely interrupting him. The young man's eyes met his, as he waited. That, in itself, was rude, for custom required that his gaze should always be downcast. But he liked the young man, and saw a bit of himself in Red Elk's brashness. "It's a perfect weapon for counting coup," he replied. "Striking with it from close in enables a warrior to kill at the same time."

Red Elk smiled. "And it's a brave man's weapon."

"Yes, again only one who is willing to fight in an enemy's face can use it."

"And it takes strength to be good with it." Red Elk smiled again. "I'm strong, Uncle."

"Can you use the ax?"

"Not like you."

Gall nodded. "And you wish to learn."

"Yes, Uncle, but I'm interrupting you because you once offered your advice, should I ever need it."

Yes, he'd done so; it had been after the big, successful Crow raid two moons earlier. He had made the offer because Red Elk showed certain headstrong tendencies, and he wished to subdue them enough that the young man could live up to his potential as a war leader. "What do you wish to know?" he asked.

"Hard Bear, a warrior over in the Sans Arc village, has a special gun for sale. He says it will kill a buffalo or a man at twice the distance of a Long Knife Springfield.

"What's its name?"

"Sharps."

"Does he have bullets for it?"

"Yes, Uncle, many."

"Why does he want to sell it?"

Red Elk smiled again. "He's a small man, and it's a big gun. But I think he just can't hit anything with it."

Gall raised an eyebrow. "What do you want from me?"

"Should I buy it?"

"How much?"

"Three horses, one a fine warhorse."

Gall raised an eyebrow. "For a gun?" He remembered when he'd have given more for a gun, but that was long ago. Now the Lakota had all kinds. "No other Lakota has a gun like this, Uncle."

"Do you have the horses?"

"I have to get the warhorse, because I won't give him mine. He's too good an animal. May I have your permission to go on a pony raid at the Long Knives' Fort Rice to get one?"

It was just what he'd have done at that age, Gall thought. But the risk of a few young braves going brashly out alone was too big. "No, my son, I have two extra warhorses. I'll give you one for him. You can repay me later."

"But I can get one myself."

Gall frowned. "That is my decision. Come." He headed off toward the pony herd.

The next day Red Elk was back with his big rifle. He didn't know the nomenclature, but it was a Sharps. This one was a falling-block, single-shot, breech-loading model that used brass cartridges and could be fired pretty fast. With its long barrel, it weighed some twelve pounds—so heavy the shooter had to rest it on something to aim it. Of no interest was the ornate carving on the stock. He had a box of one hundred large shells and another that contained seventy-two unfired rounds, plus the spent cartridges of the other twenty-eight. The special cartridges would be hard to come by, so he would have to be selective in their use.

Gall knew about the rifle. He'd seen one before. And he'd seen one of the old muzzle loaders that could drop a buffalo from what a half-breed told him was "one thousand yards." That meant nothing to him, but he knew it was a long way. The boy was right—no Hunkpapa had ever had one of these rifles that he knew. If so, no Hunkpapa ever had enough ammunition to learn how to shoot it. Besides, a warrior couldn't count coup from that far away. But young Red Elk was pleased, and who knew what good the strange gun might be some day?

Gall lifted it and grunted, sighting it. It had a strange rear sight that stood up. He shook his head. "*Three* good horses?"

Red Elk grunted. He admired the gun. It set him apart from the other young warriors. "Come, Uncle, I'm going to shoot it."

Gall followed him to a place not far from the edge of the village where Red Elk had stuck a thick forked stick into the ground. Some six hundred yards away he had placed a white horse's skull up against a small knoll. At that distance the skull was a blanched dot against the sienna-colored grass, hardly something that could be hit. Resting the rifle barrel in the fork of the stick, the young warrior slowly took aim and fired. The Sharps roared and kicked, knocking Red Elk's shoulder back. Gall squinted, watching the target. In what seemed a long time but was really less than two seconds, the big slug kicked up some dust several feet to the right and above the skull. As the disconcerted Red Elk put another shell in the chamber, the war leader chuckled. *"Three horses?"* he asked, and walked away shaking his head.

The Yellowstone was the white man's name for the usually swift-flowing river that watered a broad grassy valley set off by the often snowcapped and imposing peaks of the Bighorn Mountains. Here and there thick groves of willow and cottonwood trees accented the river's edge or other places where seeds had fallen long before the arrival of the *wasicus,* or whites. Broad and rolling plains on either side could range from hunter green to burnt ginger, or to crackling hip-deep alabaster in mid-winter. Off to the south, the Tongue, Powder, Rosebud, and Bighorn Rivers fed the Yellowstone and provided the water for the buffalo and other game that thrived there. It was the heartland of the Lakota.

They called the river the Elk.

It was the domain of one of the most powerful men to ever stride the American stage, a Lakota whose name could demand ink on the front page of any newspaper in the country and strike fear into the hearts of traditional enemies he might face.

He considered himself invincible, truly immune to enemy weapons.

He was Sitting Bull.

Now he was forty-four years old.

Going by his boyhood nickname of "Slow," he'd counted his original first coup at fourteen, when he killed a Crow warrior with a tomahawk. He was later named for his father, a wealthy and important chief. Imbued with the four virtues: bravery, fortitude, generosity, and wisdom, he'd become the foremost warrior and most respected war leader in the Lakota world.

He was the main chief of the Hunkpapas—tall, and every inch a man who was used to the mantle of authority. He had a heavy, muscular build, a big chest, and a large head. His face was broad, with a prominent hooked nose, and his half-bloodshot eyes gleamed alertly from beneath arching black brows. His dark hair, braided on one side with otter fur and hanging loose on the other, was thick and reached down to his shoulders. It was severely parted in the middle where it glistened with a heavy streak of crimson paint. A superb horseman, he was nearly as noted a hunter as he was a warrior. Since his early war years, he had been a member of the best warrior societies, and had long been qualified to wear the long eagle feather headdress of a great war leader. He was a master of all arms but preferred the lance. By always being in the forefront in battle, and seemingly impossible to hit, his name struck alarm and fear in the enemy. His horsemanship in battle was legendary; without using a bridle or saddle he could flatten himself on one side of the animal or the other. Gripping the horse's mane, he was amazingly accurate with a firearm.

When possible, though, he carried his famous shield, a gift from his father believed to possess remarkable powers. The design on its tough buffalo hide had appeared in one of his father's visions, and a holy man had painted it on the skin. The colors were rich, suggesting a bold manlike figure, though some said it was birdlike. Hanging from its circular frame, four eagle feathers signified power in all four directions.

In war he was invincible.

But now he had assumed the role of spiritual leader, and had put away his lance.

The Lakotas loved their Elk country, even though many of the buffalo herds had been depleted and life there could be hard. They had won it, and they would give it to no one. They had, in no uncertain terms, told the *wasicus* this. When the Northern Pacific surveyors were escorted by U. S. Cavalry into the region in 1871, the Lakotas had again protested, stating they would fight forever to keep a railroad out of their heartland. Finally, in the late summer of 1872, the shooting began. The Sioux had brought together a large number of people in a massive encampment and were planning a major attack on the Crows.

But they changed their minds.

Finding a Long Knife base camp on the north side of the Elk, the chiefs met in council to determine if they should attack it. But before they could do so, hot-headed young warriors and their leaders had broken through the *akicitas* and started to harass the twenty surveyors and their cavalry escort. By daylight, both sides were in position for a pitched battle, and firing had begun. But just as the salmon sun broke over the horizon, Sitting Bull, carrying his pipe and rifle, plus his bows and arrows, strode nonchalantly into the flat by the river. Calmly seating himself, as if he were going to have a friendly chat, he began filling his pipe. He was dressed plainly, with only a first coup, and a red "wound by an enemy" eagle feather in his hair. Holding his pipe high, he called out to his tribesman, inviting them to smoke with him. Soon he was joined by four of his party. They nervously puffed and passed the pipe as cavalry bullets whistled around them. Shortly, Sitting Bull got to his feet, and while the others scurried back to safety he walked slowly to the bluffs and loudly ordered the warriors to break off the battle.

It was an act of courage that would be recounted around council fires for years to come.

And it was but one of the heroic acts that constituted Sitting Bull's great fame.

Naturally, the war chief had great means at his fingertips. His warring brought many spoils, particularly in horses, the measure of a Lakota's wealth. Even though in his famed generosity he had given away more ponies than anyone could remember, he still owned several. He loved the animals, and had gloried in a very fast sorrel named Bloated Jaw that he usually rode in battle or in a hunt. But in 1872, while going through family turmoil, he had swapped the fine animal off. His first and beloved wife, Light Hair, had died in childbirth many years earlier. He then took in two wives, Red Woman and Snow-on-Her, but they bickered constantly, and he finally divorced Snow-on-Her. Then Red Woman died in '71, and the great chief once more searched for a mate. A beautiful woman named Four Robes attracted him, and he brought her into his lodge at the cost of four of his fine ponies. Soon after, following their lovemaking under their fine marital buffalo robe, she talked Sitting Bull into marrying her older sister, a widow by the name Seen-by-the-Nation. The chief gave the brother of the two women, Gray Eagle, his famed warhorse, Bloated Jaw, for her hand.

Shortly thereafter, Sitting Buffalo had laughed aloud, saying he was glad Gray Eagle didn't have any more sisters, or the man would be the richest Hunkpapa in the world!

To rise to Sitting Bull's exalted position was nearly impossible in the Sioux world. Democracy and decision by council limited the powers of a leader. Self-determination began in the home tipi, where the basic family, or hunting group, was called the *tiyospe*. In it, the family was the core. And a strong family ensured the manpower necessary for survival. A warrior did not turn his spoils of war over to his wife, he gave them to his sisters and sisters-in-law, for sibling relationships were more important than marital ones. A family lived within a village, according to its heritage. There were noble, or quality families in the social order—aristocrats headed by powerful and wise chiefs or war leaders—and lesser families. However, life still held much opportunity, because a son from even the lowest family could rise through heroic and successful warmaking to leadership, wealth, and social standing. Thus, a young boy in this warrior society could dream of such success, and usually extended himself to the limits in his training.

A warrior such as Gall sometimes emerged. His family held no particular distinction and his father had died when he was young. Of course, being under the wing of his older friend, the mighty Sitting Buffalo, hadn't hurt him, but Gall's ferocity and cool leadership in battle would have propelled him to the top in any band. He was a war chief, but he wasn't a true noble. And a certain unspoken snobbery existed in Sioux culture.

Sitting Bull was different. To a manor born, as the white man might say, this brilliant leader had no trouble in following in his father's tracks, and going far beyond them. In a sense, he was also a politician, because he joined many societies. Besides the Kit Fox, he belonged to the Strong Hearts *akicita*, and the secret elite Midnight Strong Hearts that met in the middle of the night. He also belonged to the social societies. He was a Dreamer, one who had meaningful visions and dreams, so he belonged to the Dreamer societies.

Sitting Bull was also a holy man, a *wichasha wakan*, and a Dreamer who could prophesy. He understood all nature, and felt that he was close to Wakantanka, the Great Mystery. His spirituality was intense—driving his insatiable desire to understand all, and to translate his powers to the good of his people—for his people were his meaning, his reason for being.

He was captivated by birds and imitated their songs, believing he understood the language of the meadowlarks. Once he interrupted a ceremony to give aid to a wounded meadowlark, and directed that thereafter small boys be instructed to be kind to them. He fiercely believed he was related to them.

Smoking the pipe invoked spirituality, and the memory of White Buffalo Woman. All important men owned a replica of the Sacred Calf Pipe, and brought it out of its wrappings in their tipis only on important occasions. The pipe was to be smoked prior to any vital matter, summoning Wakantanka to guide in decisions. It signified peace, mutual trust, and truth. It was the most sacred of Lakota customs. *Wichasha wakan,* in particular, were great pipe smokers.

As much as anyone, Sitting Bull treasured his pipe and smoked it often. But there was another side to Sitting Bull, that of independence and pride. Many years earlier he had stated, "I want nothing to do with those who make one carry water on the shoulders and haul manure. The whites may get me at last, but I will have good times 'til then. You Lakotas are fools to make yourselves slaves to a piece of fat bacon, some hard-tack, and a little sugar and coffee."

This was Sitting Bull, holy man, intractable and intransigent enemy of the Long Knives, and the most revered chief in the Lakota nation.

He was brushing one of his favorite horses, a beautiful bay, when Gall approached him and spoke quietly, "Uncle, the boy, Red Elk wants to join the Midnight Society. As I told you, he was very good on that Kit Fox raid against the Crows. Now he has one of those big guns that kill the buffalo from a thousand steps. He shows promise."

Sitting Bull frowned. "We've never had one so young."

"It might be an encouragement for all the young men."

Sitting Bull whispered softly into the bay's ear. It was part of his way with animals. After a moment he said, "Yes, it could be something for boys to talk about."

"Should we invite him?"

"Tell him the way may be open, but we must think on it."

Gall smiled. He knew the wait would be difficult for the eager Red Elk.

That day at sunset, Sitting Bull was scheduled to conduct a *Kici yuksa pi,* the Untying Each Other ceremony. Thunder-in-Face, a Hunkpapa with twenty-three summers, had won a horse in a race with a slightly older warrior, High Hoof, and had been accused by the loser of cheating. Thunder-in-Face had become so angry that he had stabbed High Hoof in the back and killed him. He was now a murderer, and could leave the camp, or cleanse himself repeatedly in a sweat bath and hope High Hoof's relatives did not avenge the killing. He had now been in his small sweat lodge outside the camp for three days.

It was time for the families to make peace.

As the huge orange sun settled over the western hills, several old *nacas*, the Big Bellies, gathered at the Red Council Lodge, the great tipi in the center of the village circle that was the heart of all events and matters of importance. Several of them led ponies. Sitting Bull, accompanied by the dead man's parents, Bald Bear and Water Woman, strode to a place in front of the entrance. Shortly, Rain-on-Hawk, the murderer's father, led a beautiful black pony up to the chief. His tearful wife walked on the other side of the horse. As everyone grew quiet, Sitting Bull withdrew his ceremonial pipe from his robe and lit it with a buffalo chip. Handing it to the bereaved father, he said, "Take this pipe, and in smoking it, have no ill feeling toward another."

The victim's father puffed on the pipe grimly and handed it back to the chief, who then presented it to Rain-on-Hawk with the same admonition. The murderer's father puffed sadly and returned the pipe. Sitting Bull signaled to the watchful members of the *akicita* that was in charge of policing, and they took the reins of the ponies the *nacas* had brought. Sitting Bull took the hand of the victim's father, Bald Bear, and led him to the beautiful black pony the murderer's father had brought. In a quick and powerful motion, he placed the father astride the animal and led everyone to Bald Bear's tipi.

The rupture had been sealed. The smoking of the pipe together in the *Kici yuksa pi* had bridged family differences.

Whether vengeance would be taken against Thunder-in-Face would remain to be seen, because sometimes the forgiveness of the ceremony faded into some form of reprisal. But not often.

From a distance, Red Elk had observed the whole ceremony, and had felt deep sadness. He turned and walked slowly to the river. Reaching it, he looked up into the red dusk and said softly, "Oh, Wakantanka, Great Spirit, help me to hold my anger, and make me wise in judgment. Let me kill only our enemies, and be as generous as my chiefs."

Red Elk had turned sixteen three days after his successful Kit Fox raid with Gall during the Moon of the Ripe Juneberries, or the white man's month of June. And all of the juices of growing manhood coursed through his veins. The first coup he'd counted on that raid had elevated him above all of the young warriors near his age, and the Sharps rifle that he was slowly mastering gave him added pride. He walked tall, always wearing his first coup eagle feather straight up.

He had been to see the Sans Arc widow twice, and she had taken him into her blanket. After his explosive, uncontrolled lovemaking, she had pleased him by crowing about his manhood, the crowning glory to his coming of age. It had given him even more to brag about to the other young warriors. He was as full of himself as a young Lakota could be. The only flaw in his glorious life was Late Star. He loved her so much it pained him, but she seemed to enjoy ignoring him.

Red Elk couldn't remember a time when he did not love Late Star. It had been at least since the time when he killed the lion. She'd been skinny then, but always she'd had those big soft eyes that seemed to be forever holding back something humorous. They could also mock him if he made too much of himself, which puzzled him, because it was the Way. Warriors always bragged. It was how everyone knew of their accomplishments. A warrior who did great things in battle could speak of it around campfires the rest of his life.

Now, after walking over to her father's camp, he stood outside of her family tipi, hoping to see her. It was a breach of etiquette for him to do this, but this morning he didn't care. The tipi was large and relatively new. The bottom was rolled up, the custom in hot weather. One of the best artists in the village was decorating it on the outside with bright paintings telling of Running Antelope's victories as a younger man, and of his wisdom and his rise to Shirt Wearer status. With deep lines in his face at age fifty-six, Running Antelope seemed elderly to Red Elk, but he knew the older man was a close friend of Sitting Bull's and was highly respected among not only the Hunkpapas, but with most of the other Lakotas. He was also the greatest orator among the Lakota leaders. At that moment he came out of the tipi and walked directly up to Red Elk. "Do you have reason to be staring into my lodge?" he asked brusquely.

Red Elk immediately look down to the ground. "No, Great Chief."

The Shirt Wearer nodded and walked on.

Red Elk looked back at the tipi, but it was no use; Late Star was elsewhere. He strolled down toward the river. Seeing Crooked Tree, the old medicine man, he hurried to meet him. "Grandfather," he asked, "is my flute finished?"

Crooked Tree nodded. Suffering with arthritis, he hobbled bent over a gnarled cane of cedar that had been in the river a long time. It was one of his private identity badges, and he never ventured from his tipi without it. The shaman had suffered a stroke a few years earlier that had rendered the left side of his face partially paralyzed, so the lower lid of his eye hung down, exposing the bottom of the ball, and only the right side of his mouth moved when he talked or smiled. And he liked to smile; it went with his frequent cackle. Today he was wearing a hat of black bear fur, from which hung the teeth of a grizzly bear that had died giving birth. To make the teeth even more powerful, they were strung on a string of gut from a bobcat that had been struck by lightning. The dried testicles of the same cat hung over his right ear. Crooked Tree had so many summers that no one, not even the ancient and sightless Antelope-Woman-in-River remembered how many. And she was the other oldest Hunkpapa, believed to have well over ninety summers.

Crooked Tree had often demonstrated his powerful medicine, once bringing the chief, Slow Rain, back from death caused by a severe battle wound. He was also a *wichasha wakan*, a holy man, and as such was versed and trained in the knowledge of the universe. And he knew intimately all of the gods, major and lesser. He was particularly familiar with Hunopa, the Bear, who was the patron of medicine and powerful wisdom, and his personal guardian. His attire always included some element of a bear's body.

It was also Crooked Tree's charge to teach the essence of the Sioux.

And it was complex. In it, *everything* was four, even Wakantanka, the Great Mystery. He was Chief God, the Creator, the Executive, and the Great Spirit. Below him were the four Superior Gods: the Earth, the Sky, the Rock, and Wi, the Sun.

Next came the Associate Gods, who were closely identified with their superiors. Tate, the Wind, Associate of Sky, controlled the seasons; the Winged, who was the Associate of the Rock, was the patron of cleanliness, the voice of thunder and the glance of lightning; Hanwi, the Moon, was the wife of Sun and set the time for all that was important. And then there was Whope, the Beautiful One, who was the daughter of the Sun and the Moon. She was the patron of harmony and pleasure.

At the next level were the Bear, the Whirlwind, the Buffalo, and the Four Winds. And finally, to round out the fourth level, were the Spirit, the Ghost, the Ghostlike, and the Potency.

The people themselves incorporated all of the essence and were a part of Wakantanka.

They were also the people of the Sun.

But the Gods had competition. Iya, the Cyclone, was the chief of all evil. Iktomi, son of Rock, was a deposed god also known as the Trickster. Other evil spirits were the Old Man, his wife, the Witch, and their daughter, the Double-Faced Woman. There were, as well, many lesser gods in the demon world, so a Lakota had much to learn and respect—if he was to stay out of their grasp.

Crooked Tree respected the trust of his responsibility, and served as a severe reminder of the Way. He sometimes scolded, and was not averse to speaking out to the leaders. He, of course, had his own weaknesses, primarily that he was jealous of Sitting Bull. He saw the younger holy man as a growing threat to his position as the wisest and holiest of the tribal *wichasha wakan.*

Crooked Tree had a special feeling for Red Elk. He saw in him something unique, and sensed that he might become a great war chief. If the young warrior could achieve such fame at an early age, and he were regarded as the protégé of the wise Crooked Tree, it would be powerful medicine in his lodge. Now it was the matter of the Big Twisted Flute that the boy was asking about.

"Come with me," the shaman said, and began making his labored way toward his tipi.

Red Elk smiled as he followed the old man. As in the case of most shamans, Crooked Tree was skilled in aiding the lust drive of young men. He prepared love potions, and created medicine that was supposed to give these stricken young men power over the girls who attracted them. The most powerful of these love aids was the Big Twisted Flute. Properly made by a skilled shaman—and he had to be one who had dreamed of the Buffalo—such a flute could be so powerful that its melody could mesmerize a girl, and draw her away from whatever she was doing to follow its music wherever it led. In other cases, the flute blower would touch the girl with the powerful flute and she would follow him anywhere.

Reaching the shaman's tipi, Red Elk waited until the old man came out with a burnished cedar flute. Handing it over, Crooked Tree cackled and said, "I will teach you the music to play." The melody had come to him in a dream, and it was part of the deal. "I have also prayed to Whope, the Beautiful One, and she appeared in the dream when the music came to me. She promised the owner love and harmony." He cackled again. "The girl will be helpless."

Red Elk looked admiringly at the Big Twisted Flute. Carved on it was the effigy of a horse, the most ardent of all animal lovers. The instrument was the end-blown variety with five finger holes and an air vent covered by an adjustable block for changing pitch. Phallic in form, it was a powerful instrument of love. When not used for that purpose and played by someone with talent, it was the most advanced Sioux musical instrument. Red Elk played the flute well, having begun at the age of six.

His eyes shone as he examined the beautiful instrument, then placed it to his lips and blew a long sweet note. "It's beautiful, Grandfather," he said softly. He was afraid he wouldn't be able to pay for it. "What is the cost?"

Crooked Tree squinted up at him and cackled. "A fine white horse."

A troubled look crossed Red Elk's face as he handed the flute back. "But I have none."

The old shaman cackled again. "When you get one, bring it to me."

Now Red Elk was in debt for two special horses.

Late Star's mother had died in childbirth, and the girl had been raised by her father's young second wife. But she had been independent for as long as she could remember. She was known throughout all three of the tribes that banded together—the Hunkpapas, the Sans Arcs, and the Blackfeet Sioux—as the strong-willed, only daughter of Running Antelope. For two years she had spurned the many suitors who had asked for her hand, and had three times defied her father when he found an offer acceptable. And not many Lakota daughters resisted a father in such a matter, let alone a Shirt Wearer. She was a lovely young woman. She had high cheekbones and long silky black hair that reached to her shapely buttocks. Taller and thinner than most Lakota girls, her white teeth flashed in her dark face when she laughed. She was a year older than Red Elk.

They didn't see each other frequently because her father was a "fence sitter," a chief who took his band to the agency for the White Father's food part of the time, and at other times joined the main Hunkpapa village. The latter was usually in the warm months. Just four moons earlier, he had taken them to the Long Knives fort by the Big River to tell its chief, Long Hair, about how the Indian agent was cheating them on their rations. They called the place *Lin-cun*.

She had been excited when her father told her he was taking her along to the fort. She vividly remembered following him and his headmen into the cluster of big buildings with all of those Long Knife soldiers around. She knew her eyes had been wide. The place was so much bigger than the agency. She'd never seen a lodge so *tall*, and when she was told that Long Hair and his wives lived in it all by themselves, with *seven* fires in the winter, she was astounded. Long Hair, a tall chief with hair the color of sunset, had been most friendly and had invited them to eat in the big lodge. His pretty wife and the second wife, the black one, had given them delicious roasted deer meat that Long Hair had killed. And later, the black wife had served a fine sweet crumbly bread she called *choc-o-lut* cake. And the headmen had talked. And smoked. Her father had brought his sacred pipe. Long Hair had smoked and said he would fix the bad thing with the agent. She had been the only Lakota woman there, an honor few Sioux chiefs ever accorded their women. She had watched quietly from behind her father, stealing a glance at Long Hair now and then. She had heard that he also had a Cheyenne wife, a certain Monahsetah. But if it were true, why wasn't the Cheyenne living here as well? She had liked Long Hair. Also his wives, although the black one had said very little. The white one had pale skin like soft new snow and a pretty dress the color of fresh juneberries.

She would never forget going to *Lin-cun*.

Today she was excited as she waited for Little Blackbird to appear.

Late Star was very good in the craft of quilling, the art of sewing multicolored porcupine quills on the edge of a garment or other item as a decorative fringe. Her "quilling count" was already started on the dew cloth of the Red Council Lodge, where a woman's marks correlated to a man's war honors. Quilling and the making of beautiful cradles were the most respected of the female arts, and even one her age could get recognition for doing it well. Tanning required a certain amount of brawn, and Late

Star was quite good at it, but porcupine quillwork demanded dexterity and a feel for beauty. Usually those who were best at it had dreamed of *Anogite*, the Double-faced Woman, or of Deer Woman, a beautiful woman who always disappeared as a deer. Late Star had dreamed of both in her twelfth summer.

Little Blackbird was the best quiller in the village. And today she was holding a contest, an event she had announced throughout the camp well beforehand. Since such a contest was always a special affair, many of the women, and particularly the younger ones, had anticipated it with excitement. Late Star had worked furiously to finish several items she had started and put aside, sewing from first light until dark for several days.

Shortly after the sun reached its bright zenith, Little Blackbird walked slowly and somewhat regally to the center of the village, where she placed her finest decorated cradle at a point that would represent the door of a make-believe lodge. It was the signal. Quickly women and girls began to appear from their tipis, most carrying examples of their quilling work. There were men's and women's knee-length moccasins; several pipe bags; fancy shirts; doeskin dresses, one of elk skin; men's leggings; and robes— garment robes of buffalo skin mostly—long fur for the cold season, and with the fur scraped away for the warm season; painted ones, and those with brightly colored quilling only.

The participants took places around the imaginary lodge, seating themselves and placing their handiwork before them. Late Star sat directly opposite Little Blackbird. Her pile consisted of a new pipe bag for her father, two pairs of moccasins, a soft doeskin dress for herself, and a robe that she had painted with rich scarlet and bright yellows. In the part that would be worn over the owner's shoulders, she had quilled a red sun setting under a full yellow moon. The yellow moon was her special symbol. The submissions were neatly piled in front of her.

Two of the other participants who had been invited were within a year or two of her age; one was her lifelong friend and competitor, Blue Feather. The rest were older women ranging up to one who had over forty summers. Other women of the village gathered around the circle to watch, laughing and making remarks behind their hands. Young girls also watched, wide-eyed, knowing that someday they would have a chance for such recognition. It was a festive occasion, and fortunately it was a calm, overcast day that foretold the possibility of rain that evening. No wind should disturb the ceremony. But in the Moon of the Yellow Leaves, any kind of weather could visit Elk country.

At last, as someone shook a rattle, Little Blackbird raised her bag of sticks high and intoned the blessing of Whope, the Beautiful One. That done, she went to the closest woman and examined the objects she had brought. She then asked when they had been completed, and questioned the woman about other finished works, allotting small thin sticks from her bag. For work done prior to puberty, she placed the sticks on the left. For that work done after the first visit of the menses, the sticks went to the right. The contestant smiled as everyone chattered with comments of approval.

Little Blackbird moved to the next woman and repeated the awarding of sticks, then to the next, finally arriving in front of Late Star. Examining the robe, she nodded her head emphatically, saying, "Your work is beautiful, my daughter. And how many pieces have you finished since your becoming a woman?"

"Sixteen, Mother."

A murmur went through the crowd. Little Blackbird placed sixteen sticks beside Late Star's right knee. "And how many before?"

"Six."

The sponsor withdrew six thin sticks and with a smile put them on the blanket next to the girl's left knee.

Late Star smiled and bowed her head in thanks as the older woman moved on. In another fifteen minutes it was over, and it was time to count sticks. Late Star tried to remain calm, but she noticed a tiny tremor in her hand. A woman named Buffalo Knee rose as Little Blackbird announced that she had the fourth most sticks and led the finalist to a place of honor in the middle of the circle. The hostess then pointed to Blue Feather and announced that she had won fourteen sticks. Late Star's friend got to her feet, smiling, and was led to sit in front of the other winner. The sponsor then looked around a moment before announcing, "And for *twenty-two* quillings, we congratulate Late Star!"

The Shirt Wearer's daughter arose amid much approval and was led to a position in front of her friend. She felt warm, proud, as she kept her eyes downcast and heard the name of the winner being announced. Coming in second would put her name and her marks on the wall of the Red Council Lodge to be seen throughout her life! Her friend touched her back and giggled as the last woman, with twenty-five quillings, sat in front of her. The laughing women in the crowd moved close, congratulating the winners, serving them food in the order of their finish. And then everyone had a good time. Especially Late Star.

7

Military glory—that attractive rainbow that rises in showers of blood.
—ABRAHAM LINCOLN

FORT ABRAHAM LINCOLN
SEPTEMBER 26, 1875

One of those storms that builds and snarls across the plains like a great wet beast had struck Bismarck the day before, and now the dark undercast clouds of the aftermath were roiling overhead. Some two inches of rain had fallen from the crashing and flashing thunderheads, and on the post, large pools of water splotched the ground like huge haphazard mirrors. A piece of roof from the stable had been ripped off, and one gelding, noted for his skittish nature, had so injured himself tearing wild-eyed into the wooden corral fence that it had been necessary for the veterinary sergeant to destroy him. Nevertheless, Saturday was inspection day, and the Seventh Cavalry was holding theirs in the barracks. Normally, George Armstrong Custer didn't participate in these routine inspections, but he'd decided it was time to show the troops his personal interest, so he had decided to make a walk-through. He knew, of course, the company commanders would have conducted a rigid previous inspection, so everything would be in excellent condition. It was just one of those parts of military procedure. Accompanied by the adjutant, the Dundrearied Lieutenant Cooke, he entered the barracks of C Company at ten o'clock sharp. Waiting at the door was the company commander, who saluted and said crisply, "Lieutenant Custer reporting, sir!"

"Accompany me on the inspection, sir," Armstrong replied.

Tom Custer followed his brother and the adjutant as they stopped in front of First Sergeant Edwin Bobo, who snapped to rigid attention.

"How are you this morning, First Sergeant?" Armstrong asked pleasantly.

"I'm *fine*, Sir!"

"Good. Accompany me on the inspection."

Each NCO was standing inspection with his troopers, who were standing at parade rest by their bunks. Custer stopped in front of Sergeant Daniel Kanipe, who came sharply to attention. Custer gave him a quick once-over and nodded. "How are your men, Sergeant Kanipe?"

"They are well, sir!" Kanipe replied.

Custer nodded approvingly. "That's excellent." He led the entourage down the line of troopers, stopping frequently to ask questions as he looked at them and their equipment. The next to the last private was Iggy Stungewitz, who stood solidly at attention. "What's your name, Trooper?" Custer asked.

"Stungewitz, Sir. Ygnatz, private."

Custer frowned. "Hmmm. Are you new, Stungewitz?"

"Somewhat, sir."

"I don't recognize your accent. Where are you from?"

"Russia, sir."

"Ever do any fighting for the Czar?"

Iggy's answer was emphatic. "Sir, there is *always* fighting for the Czar."

Armstrong smiled and turned to his brother. "Hear that, Tom? If we can't catch up to the damned Sioux, maybe we can take the Seventh to Russia."

Everyone laughed as they moved on to the next man.

"What are you doing, Sweetheart?"

Custer looked up from his writing table and put the ink pen in its well. "Writing to Russia."

"To Russia?" Libbie asked.

"Yes, to the Grand Duke."

"Any particular reason?"

"Yes. We have a trooper from Russia in C Company. During inspection this morning, I got an idea." He smiled, eager to share his enthusiasm. "As you well know, my financial ventures aren't working out too well, and the Lord only knows when that promotion is going to come through. Soooo, Little Standby, I'm going to test the foreign waters."

Libbie's eyebrows shot up. "You really mean it? Russia?"

"Alexis told me when he departed that there would always be a place for me in their army." He was referring to the Grand Duke Alexis, son of Czar Alexander II, whom he had guided on a buffalo hunting trip to Nebraska and had accompanied on a tour through the South. The nineteen-year-old prince had so enjoyed being with both Libbie and Custer that he had taken them to New Orleans, where he treated them grandly.

Libbie put her hand on Custer's shoulder. "You can't be serious."

"They are headed for war with Turkey, and are eyeing the belligerent Germans. I'm sure his papa would make me at least a major general of cavalry—who knows, possibly a *lieutenant* general! And he might throw all kinds of extra money into the hat."

She kissed his cheek and chuckled. "You don't even speak Russian."

"They've got interpreters. Besides, I can learn."

She pulled away, her gray eyes dancing as she twirled around. "I can see myself at one of their imperial balls, beautifully gowned, hair piled high, the object of all those royal women's jealous eyes. All of those rich aristocrats bowing over my hand, flattering me, and suggesting assignations. When do we leave?"

Custer frowned. "Go ahead, laugh. But I'm also writing to each of my British friends, Lord Waterpark and Lord Paget. There may be something interesting available in their army—probably not in the illustrious home army, but their colonial armies are vast."

Libbie bowed low and feigned a British accent. "Oh, I'd love *Injia*, m'lord. And we wouldn't have to learn Russian."

Custer pursed his lips as he pulled the pen from the well and dipped it. "I'm sure they could arrange for me to be a brigadier as a starter."

Libbie headed for the door. "Well, give me some advance notice, so I can pack my sea trunk, Nomad." Nomad and Standby were two of the many nicknames they had for each other. Nomad was also the pseudonym he often used for the magazine or newspaper articles he wrote.

"Speaking of that, are you about packed for our trip east?"

She smiled over her shoulder. "Almost."

He got up and stretched, looking around at the memorabilia hanging on the walls of his comfortable study. He was dead serious about the foreign possibilities. He simply was not going to spend the next twenty years as a U.S. Army lieutenant colonel, he wasn't going to do it! If this coming campaign didn't produce a promotion, he was certainly going to look at the alternatives.

He had to admit that being at Fort Lincoln wasn't too bad. Boring, but he was the commander, and he loved this house. As Late Star remembered, it had seven fireplaces. It also had a huge parlor, thirty-two feet long with a large bay window, and a billiard room. The large dining room, where Libbie could utilize her Haviland china and extensive silver settings, could accommodate several guests, and was often used for that purpose. As the social center and unofficial officers' club of the post, the house was seldom still.

Custer sometimes locked himself away in his study, even when he had arranged an entertainment in the house. On more than one occasion when guests were dancing, he had sent for Libbie to come into his study to dance with him behind closed doors. And usually while he was writing, he wanted her there, sewing or reading. His high-ceilinged study was truly his castle. Hanging over the outside of the door hung a sign with Dante's famous caveat, *Lasciate ogni speranza, voi ch'entrate—All hope abandon, ye who enter here.* He pictured himself as a scholarly general, and quite frankly, he was now much more literate than when he was the poor student who graduated last in his class at West Point. Naturally there were plenty of books on the shelves. Stuffed animal heads stared balefully back at visitors—high up were two antelope, a rack of blacktailed deer horns on which perched a horned owl; a mountain eagle and foxes joined a huge grizzly and a craggy buffalo head. Custer had taken up taxidermy a few years earlier, and these were some of his trophies. Pictures of two generals hung above his writing table: Phil Sheridan and himself. In between was a photo of Libbie in her lovely white wedding gown. On another wall was a photograph of his best friend, the actor Lawrence Barrett, and one of his first benefactors, General George McClellan, the western Napoleon who had been the emperor of the American procrastinators.

He glanced at Lawrence's picture and a smile touched his lips; he'd be seeing his good friend soon.

Picking up the leather-bound copy of his recently published *My Life on the Plains,* he thought of how good it felt. It was his creation, and tangible proof of his immortality. No matter what happened, someone would always have a copy of his work a century hence, maybe two—maybe forever. He smiled and opened it, read a paragraph and remembered how he'd labored over that particular part. Good writing, the public needed to know this sort of thing. He nodded his head. Immortality. Without it, George Armstrong Custer might be forgotten.

He put the book back on its pedestal and leaned down to pet one of the three hounds at his feet. No, there were too many battles to be fought for him to be soon forgotten, book or no book. . . .

He picked up a letter containing the bank draft for the Stevens Mine stock. Two hundred forty-six dollars. It was far from what he had expected, but it would pay for some of his upcoming leave in the east. With Sheridan's winter campaign delayed until sometime after the first of the year, he'd given in to Libbie's wish for a vacation. He frowned, thinking back to 1871. He had been connected with the people who were developing this Colorado mine, essentially so they could use his name. The sales brochure stated that he had subscribed $35,000 of the $100,000 the company wanted to raise. George Armstrong Custer had never seen a quarter of such a huge sum, let alone invested it. The stock he wound up owning was what he had earned in sales commissions on the certificates he'd peddled among wealthy acquaintances in New York.

He shook his head as he looked at the draft. The Stevens Mine venture was supposed to make him rich—just like some of the other schemes he'd gotten into. And here he was, still so damned poor that he'd look like a pauper when he got to New York. If it weren't for the royalty advance from his book, and this stock check, he wouldn't even be *going* to New York!

But this was the famous Gilded Age, where shenanigans were winked at and the sharpers like Jay Gould could do almost anything and get away with it. And Belknap—imagine a *secretary of war* in on the graft! Yup, nearly anything was possible. He reopened the letter from Rufe Ingalls, the president's one-time roommate at West Point who was now the acting quartermaster general of the army. He'd become acquainted with Ingalls right after the war when he got in a poker game with him in Washington. *That* had been a mistake. Ingalls, then the quartermaster general of the Army of the Potomac, was reputed to be one of the best poker players in the army, and it had cost him over three hundred dollars to find out it was true!

Now Ingalls was apparently in bed with Ben Holladay, the stagecoach magnate who had his fingers in all kinds of pies relating to the army. The words in Ingalls's letter were quite frank:

> *We want to do a big thing in the Black Hills and surrounding territory. Ben wants to put in stages and be the sutler for new posts that are going to be opened. The Department of the Interior has promised him a big chunk of the Indian trade when things are more settled. If Ben knew where these posts were going to be built, he could buy in before other would-be traders run the price up. He thinks highly of you, Armstrong. And all he wants to do is be in the* right place *at the* right time.

There was more about procuring horseshoes, and about the possible board, of which he, Armstrong, would be president. That, too, smacked of collusion.

Custer shook his head. The Gilded Age. He might not have to go off to fight foreign wars after all. And why shouldn't he get in on a little of the largesse? It reached all the way to Grant, he'd heard. At least to the president's brother, Orvil—

He sighed. No, he wouldn't do anything corrupt.

The Belknap thing still rankled him.

On the other hand, it might not hurt to let them *think* he was interested. And he *did* need some money. He sat down and penned a quick note to General Ingalls, stating that he *might* soon be privy to information about new posts, and that he would also be interested in being the president of the horseshoe procurement board, "to ensure that the right shoe is selected for purchase."

He moved on, going to the gun case and pulling out his Remington sporting rifle. Absently, he wiped the octagonal metal barrel with his sleeve and held it up to sight on an imaginary dove. Squeezing the trigger, he pictured the dove crashing to the ground. Replacing the Remington, he pulled out the gun belt that held his favorite pistols. They were double-action .45 caliber Webleys, with white bone handles and lanyard rings dangling from the butts. Officially named Royal Irish Constabulary revolvers, or RICs, they were his favorite handguns. The green velvet-lined oak case in which the Englishman had shipped them bore the inscription: *Presented by Lord Berkeley Paget to Major General Custer as a token of a sincere regard and in rememberance of the very happy time spent at Fort Hayes while Buffalo hunting in Kansas in Sept. 1869.*

He pulled one out of its holster and aimed it at an imaginary target, then checked the cylinder. His instructions to his orderly, John Burkman, were precise—after periodic cleanings, always leave them with a very light coat of oil, the cylinders full, and the chambers empty. That way, if he ever needed them in a hurry, they were ready for use. The gun case also held his other hunting weapons, including the Winchester sporting rifle that had been a gift as well.

Turning back to his writing table, he nodded his head. Life was good here at Fort Lincoln, but he was treading water, and his proud mane of luxurious red-blond locks was beginning to recede . . .

8

Sergeant Danny Kanipe squared away his hat as he checked himself in the small mirror on the back of the door. He turned around and regarded the room that he shared with another platoon sergeant who was on leave. He was getting away from the torment. He'd saved a few dollars from the stake he'd won in the poker game payday night, and he was going to the livery in town to rent a horse for the afternoon. Ride out to some quiet place, be alone. Then come back to the Bower and probably get a little drunk. It was always better to go out late in the month, when nearly all the privates were broke. Except the handful who were the big gamblers and money lenders—the usurious bankers, who loaned out money at two-for-three, or sometimes at *even money* if the borrower was really hard up and it was quite late in the month. There were always some of them on any army post—professional privates who were the takers, the leeches. They usually paid other off-duty troopers to pull their guard duty and kitchen duty. Sell a soldier anything. Couldn't be NCOs or they'd get court-martialed for doing what they did.

He picked up the red clothbound book Iggy had loaned him, Sir Walter Scott's *Rob Roy*. It had been published some twenty-five years earlier—its fifth printing—and showed its heavy use. But he was enjoying it, and all the more so when a trooper from Virginia told him it had not only been a favorite of the pre-war aristocracy in the South, but had been one of General Robert E. Lee's most treasured books. It gave him a connection to his Southern roots—which reminded him of that most desirable North Carolinian he knew.

She was never far from his mind, her dancing blue eyes smiling, maybe even encouraging him. At least that was what he wanted to believe. Missouri Ann, Missouri Ann . . .

He shook his head. That damned lovely, *wholesome,* winsome, *appealing* woman! His pet name for her was Abra, Missouri Abra. He opened the book to the page marked by a thin yellow bookmark. The familiar words, underlined in pencil, leaped out: ". . . Her name was written in every book I attempted to peruse; and her image forced itself on me in whatever train of thought I strove to engage myself." It was like the officious slave of Prior's *Solomon:*

> Abra was ready, ere I named her name,
> And when I called another, Abra came.

"Abra, you witch," he said aloud, closing the book and leaving the room.

It was nearly quarter to two when Danny Kanipe went into the Mangan hardware store in Bismarck. He wanted to buy some good brass cartridges for his Colt revolver. The issue copper shells were often faulty, too soft, and they could hang up. He was a good shot with the pistol, even on a moving horse, and he wanted to make sure he was as well-equipped as possible. He would make his own loads and be able to use the cartridges over and over in practice.

After waiting for a couple of minutes, he completed his purchase and was about to leave when a familiar voice said, "Aren't you a long way from Carolina?"

He whirled to find Missouri Ann Bobo standing with her hands on her hips just four feet away. "Uh, yes, I guess I . . . we are," he replied jerkily.

She was wearing a light-blue gingham dress that was perhaps a bit out of season, but Missouri Ann wasn't the type to worry about what *Godey's*

Lady's Book recommended. Besides, the aftermath of the storm had broken up about noon to let the sun back in, and the rest of the day promised to be nice. But he never noticed, or even thought that she had but few dresses to choose from. The gray shawl over her shoulders, and a small dark-blue hat that sat on the back of her dark tresses completed her ensemble. Along with a broad smile. She looked down at the paper sack in his hand. "What did you buy?"

"Some, uh, bullets." *What is she doing here?*

She kept smiling. "You going to shoot someone?"

"Uh, practice. They don't have the right kind of cartridges, issue, that is. The army doesn't buy what they should, and since I want to always be ready to fight good . . . well, you know. I didn't know you came to town by yourself."

She shrugged. "Oh, I get out once in a while. I get a pass like all good soldiers."

He looked at her large paisley bag. "What did you buy?"

"Some cloth for a new dress and some for trousers for the boys."

He couldn't believe she was here like this!

"What are you going to do now?" she asked.

"Now?"

"Yes, after you leave the store?"

"Oh, I was going to rent a horse and go off for a long ride by myself."

"Can I come along?"

He looked into her eyes as she moved closer. *She can't mean it!* "How can we? I mean, you can't ride in a dress, and . . . someone will see us."

She shook her head. "No, you get a horse and buggy, Daniel. And I'll meet you behind the livery stable, and we can ride out of town that way and no one will see us."

"I don't know—" *God, how I want to!*

"Besides," she went on, "a little danger just adds fun! You got enough money?"

He was still looking into those smiling blue eyes. "Uh huh."

"Then, damn it, Sergeant, get going!"

Iggy Stungewitz was reading a book of Sir Walter Scott's poetry while finishing a half-cold cup of coffee in the regimental mess. Saturday was a day when one could linger a bit after the noon meal without the mess sergeant growling, and after discussing Scott's works with Danny Kanipe, he decided to read some more of the Scottish author's works. He preferred the warrior ballads, and was just finishing "Lullaby to an Infant Chief."

> Oh, hush thee, my babie, the time will soon come,
> When thy sleep shall be broken by trumpet and drum;
> Then hush thee, my darling, take rest while you may,
> For strife comes with manhood, and waking with day.
> *O ho ro, i ri ri, &c.*

Iggy liked Scott's work; in fact, he liked anything romantic that involved war and warriors. Being Jewish in Russia had been a somewhat warlike existence, even when he wasn't in the army. Of course he hadn't used his own name when he enlisted in the Hussars, they were too elite to accept a Jew. He had dyed his hair blond and worked assiduously on his English to affect a British identity that the average Russian Cavalry recruiter would never be able to fathom. Plus, he'd shipped out as a cabin boy on a large sailing ship based in St. Petersburg when he was thirteen, and had jumped ship in Southampton, England, for a year. But all of that was behind him. He was good with languages and was now working on signing, the universal language of the American Indians.

O ho ro, i ri ri, &c.

"What the hell d'ya think yer doing, Jew-boy?"

He looked up at First Sergeant Michael Martin's taunt. The bull-necked Irishman was standing a few feet away, hands on hips and glowering. "Reading, First Sergeant, and finishing my coffee," Iggy replied.

"And holding up the cleaning of the mess. Well. I can fix that!"

Iggy got slowly to his feet, closing the book.

"You'll just by God start helping them. Report to the first cook!"

The two soldiers who were cleaning the tables were the only other persons in the large room. They both stopped what they were doing and watched. Iggy picked up his cup and started for the kitchen, with Martin following a few steps behind. A cook in his whites, looking in through the big serving window from the kitchen, also stopped to see what was happening. But he went back out of sight. Iggy quietly put the cup in a tray of dirty dishes and turned toward the door.

"*Trooper!*" Martin barked, "Just where in the hell, are you going? I just gave you an order!"

Iggy stopped, turning slowly. "It was no legal order, Sergeant."

Martin was quickly getting livid. "What the hell do you mean by that?"

Iggy took a deep breath. "You know what I mean. You aren't my first sergeant and you can't order me to perform such duty."

"By God, I'll show you who can give you a bloody order!" He moved toward Iggy, cocking his right fist. Iggy's dark eyes narrowed as he looked into Martin's hate and spoke softly, "You even touch me, Martin, and I'll prefer charges. We have three witnesses, so go ahead."

Martin turned around and laughed. "Those men are mine, Jew-boy. You think they're going to put their arses in a sling for you?" With a roar, he lowered his head and slammed into Iggy, smashing him back against the wall. Grabbing Iggy's shirt front, he twisted it and leaned right into his face, his mouth twisted in hate. A straight right jab slammed into the side of Iggy's cheek as Martin snarled, "You yellow Jew *son-of-a-bitch!*" and tried to ram a knee into his groin. Iggy managed to turn in time to avoid injury, and twist out of Martin's grasp. Taking two quick steps away, he picked up a chair, holding it in front of him. Without looking at the two privates, he said, "You both saw this. I'm preferring charges against this NCO."

With that, Iggy slowly backed toward the door.

Martin roared after him, "They didn't see *nothin*, Jew-boy! You won't live long enough for it to matter anyway!"

Private Lucien Burnham was almost as broke as anyone else at Fort Abraham Lincoln, so he had decided to approach Mitch Boyer about learning Indian sign language. He had gotten the idea from Iggy Stungewitz—it would further his practical education, and might be of value if he decided to get out after his enlistment ended and start a business career in the Territory. Might even help if he were to go into law practice. Rounding the corner of the barracks, he saw several of the scouts squatting in a circle close to the entrance, noisily involved in a game. He knew about the game—several of the troopers had tried it with the scouts, but they'd never been able to win. It was called Shooting Dice with a Basket, and although it was a Sioux women's game, it lent itself readily as a good gambling game for the men. And how they loved to gamble!

Bloody Knife looked up and laughed, saying in Ree, "Here's 'Trooper-in-Barrel.' Let's see if he has any money?" The other scouts, seven of them, laughed out loud.

Mitch Boyer, wearing his black-and-white calfskin vest, was one of the players. When he had money he sometimes played in the enlisted poker games, and at other times he played in the Indian games with the scouts. At this time of the month, the Indians played for trinkets or "jawbone" money—meaning, in essence, IOUs.

Shooting Dice with a Basket was played with a small basket of shredded cattail leaves or woven willow shoots that was about six-by-eight inches in size. The dice, thrown from the basket, were three pairs of plum seeds, one pair painted with the image of a swallow, another pair with a buffalo, and the third pair just plain black. Different combinations scored various amounts of points, for example, a pair of buffalo with the reverse side of the four remaining dice counted ten points. Other combinations were worth more or less, but tossing all six reverse sides was worth thirty-two points, plus everything that had been bet.

It was a fast game with lots of excitement.

The players all looked up as Boyer asked, "You got any money, Trooper?"

"Or any whiskey?" Bob-Tailed Bull asked.

"A little, but I don't want to play, I just want to talk to you—privately, Mr. Boyer." The half-breed shrugged and got to his feet, following Burnham several paces away from the game. The soldier held up a dollar. "I'll pay you this today if you'll get me started on the Plains sign language. Give me five lessons and make sure I can get by, and I'll pay you two more dollars on payday."

Boyer pursed his lips. He was fluent in English and could easily live in either world. He also knew this soldier was educated. And he had nothing more to do than play Shooting Dice with a Basket. A whole dollar at this time of the month would buy a gallon of whiskey, maybe more. "Okay, Trooper, you got a deal."

First Lieutenant Tom Custer had just stopped by the C Company orderly room to get some fresh paper to write a couple of letters later in the weekend—that is, if he got back from town in time. He looked up as Private Stungewitz walked in and asked the charge-of-quarters if First Sergeant Bobo was around. There was a red welt brightening his cheek.

"No, Bobo's gone."

"What do you want, Stungewitz?" Tom asked.

Iggy came to attention. He seldom spoke to an officer, actually wanted Bobo to handle this since he had been involved in the small fracas in the Bower a few weeks earlier. "Sir, I want the first sergeant to authorize papers to charge First Sergeant Martin from D Company with striking me in the mess hall.

"Striking you?"

"Yes, sir."

Tom scowled. "Hmmm, that's a serious charge, Stungewitz. How'd it happen?"

Iggy gave him a quick account of the incident after Tom told him to stand at ease.

"Any witnesses?"

"Three. A cook and two privates. Actually one of them was a farrier— Vincent Charley. I think he was on mess duty as company punishment. The other private was McDonnell. I don't know the name of the cook."

Tom frowned again. "Do you know what you're getting into?"

Iggy stared straight ahead. "Yes, sir."

"Martin will coerce those two men of his to the point where they wouldn't support their own mothers. The farrier is already in trouble, and McDonnell is a fellow Irishman. And this will all happen out of earshot or sight of the company commander. You'll probably wind up empty-handed."

"I understand, Sir. I wish to prefer charges."

Tom Custer shrugged. "Can you write?"

"Yes, Sir."

"Very well. Write out an account of what happened and bring it to First Sergeant Bobo Monday morning."

"Yes, Sir."

☆ ☆ ☆

Sergeant Dan Kanipe had been able to rent one of those black one-seat buggies with a top that folded down or pulled up to protect its occupants from the weather. It also provided a bit of privacy. He slapped the reins on the small harness horse's rump as he trotted along the slightly muddy trail that ran alongside the river to the north. The fact that he didn't have a weapon in the event any rogue Indians attacked them had passed through his mind, but he was so excited at having Missouri Ann beside him that he'd quickly discarded any such worries. She sat there laughing as they bounced along, holding her hat with one hand and his arm with another. The smell of her perfume was tantalizing.

"Where are we going?" she asked.

"Oh, I don't know. For a ride."

The scudding clouds had broken and fled, leaving an open sky for the warm fall sun. Off to the left, the brown Missouri was beating its swift, swollen way southward. Here and there a jagged branch struggled in the rapid current, a remnant of a gust of fierce wind or perhaps a stab of angry lightning somewhere. The turbulent river's sound nearly blotted out the thuds of the horse's hooves, but with Missouri Ann sitting so close, they could easily hear each other. She pointed ahead to a clump of trees poking out of a stand of bushes. "Oh, what a nice place to stop and talk," she exclaimed.

He nodded, steering the horse in that direction. Moments later, he stopped a few yards from the riverbank in near seclusion. She smiled into his eyes. "Perfect. A good place for our picnic."

"Picnic?"

"Yes." She groped in her large valise, withdrawing a pewter flask. Uncapping it, she handed it to him. "Here's our picnic lunch."

He shook his head, then took a swig of the whiskey. "Not bad," he said, wiping his mouth with his sleeve.

"The best you can get on Laundress Row," she replied, tipping it up and taking a big drink.

"When does your husband expect you back?" he asked, almost afraid to find out and not wishing to think of Ed Bobo.

"Oh, on the six o'clock wagon."

Danny pulled out his watch and looked at it. "Not much time."

She gave him that disconcerting smile. "No, what are you going to do about it?"

He didn't like this, always being on the defensive, so to speak. Always reacting to her, rather than acting. But the question jolted him into action. He leaned over and kissed her. It was more of a peck, but before he could pull away, she drew him back and kissed him fully. Her knowledgeable tongue found his, explored, then became busy. "Ummm, I like that," she murmured when they ended the kiss. I knew I would."

"I've been wanting to kiss you for months," he said softly.

"I know." For once there was no tease in her tone. "And I've wanted you to. Those couple of times when we were alone in the laundry room when we touched—well, why didn't you then?"

Her eyes were so blue, so wide, so close to him. "I, well, I almost did, but you know—you being married and all that."

"Doesn't matter to me, Danny Kanipe. Ed's a nice man, and I wanted a husband. Doesn't mean I can't care for you, does it?"

He shook his head. "Makes me feel bad. But I can't ever quit thinking about you. I—"

She put her finger on his lips and kissed him again. This time, she found his hand and placed it on her breast.

It was so full and firm. He could feel her erect nipple through the fabric. Their kiss continued, getting more and more demanding. His mouth went to her neck to her ear lobe and back to her neck. She quickly unbuttoned her high-necked blouse below her breasts, then pulled his head down to her cleavage. She moaned as he soon found a nipple with his lips. Kissing the back of his neck as he continued to suck her nipple, she arched up to him. She began to rock as she leaned back against the leather cushion, spreading her legs. "Oh, touch me down there," she exclaimed. "Touch me!"

"Damned long dresses," he said.

"Don't worry about that," she replied, lifting up and hiking the long folds of her dress above her hips. Settling back, her hand found his erection and she began to unbutton his pants. "Oh, darling," she sighed, "Oh, I want you so much!"

In moments, he was inside her.

Sergeant Jeremiah Finley held the soft piece of buckskin up to the long rays of the lowering sun and inspected his handiwork. It was the best piece of skin he'd ever worked on, lighter than most, and he wanted the sewing to be the best he could produce. After all, it was for the general, and he was a particular man. He had just finished the collar, and, he decided through narrowed eyes, the stitching barely showed. The general liked his work, and would reward him well for this particular shirt. His tailoring was another of the skills that made his service in the Seventh quite pleasant. The other was his marksmanship; there weren't more than three or four men in the whole regiment who could outshoot him. And that had given the general a reason to make him provost sergeant. Add the money he made bartending over at the Bower, and he was doing okay, even before his wife's income as a laundress. All told, he was probably better off than any three-striper in the regiment, even with three little ones to feed.

He sat back down on the stoop in front of his quarters and picked up the needle.

"Hey, Sarge, you got a minute?"

Finley looked up as a frowning Vincent Charley walked up. He had known the Swiss farrier since meeting him in Chicago when they both enlisted for the Seventh a few years earlier. And since Charley was also a pretty good shot, now and then they did some shooting together. "Sure, Vincent, what's bothering you?"

"Something bad happened when I was pulling kitchen duty today." The red-haired farrier had a noticeable accent, but spoke good English. At twenty-seven, he had nearly five years service, and had deserted once. But he'd been apprehended the same day and confined for ten days on bread and water. That had been back in '72. He had a spiritual side and often kept to himself.

"You know that arse of a first sergeant of mine, Martin. Well, he got into it with that Russian, Stungewitz."

Finley remembered the night of the trouble in the Bower. "Yeah, he doesn't like him 'cause he's a Jew."

Charley told him what happened in the mess hall.

"So what's your problem?"

"Stungewitz is preferring charges and wants me to testify."

"And?"

"Martin just cornered me and told me to forget anything I *thought* I saw or heard, or my arse would be in shit forever."

"So, what's your problem?"

"I want to testify against that bastard."

The Irishman shrugged. "That *is* a problem. What about the other witness?"

"Oh, he'll go along with Martin. He doesn't like Jews either."

"What do you want me to do about it?"

"Tell me what to do. You're a sergeant and all. And the provost to boot.

Finley shook his head. "You know I can't do that, Vincent. Sure and you were in the wrong place at the wrong time, just like the Russian. And now your conscience is after you. I'll tell you one thing—there ain't a man in this regiment would hold it against you if you went along with Martin. It's hard, but life ain't always fair."

Charley scowled again. "*Ja*, Martin won't ever let up."

Finley went back to his sewing. "I wish I could help."

9

Captain Tom Weir forced a smile as Rita finished her joke. It wasn't any use; he had a bad case of Libbie Custer on his mind today, and he couldn't shake it loose. Rita was Geraldine Gentle's latest arrival at the uptown hog ranch. Supposedly from Kansas City, Rita was slender, with large breasts and skinny legs. He poured some more whiskey in his glass. "Uh, I think I'll go over and watch the poker game," he said, getting to his feet.

"You don't want to go upstairs with me, Tommy?"

"No, not today, sweetheart." She really did look skinny. And the bags under her painted eyes seemed more pronounced. *Where the hell did Geraldine get her?* Things must be bad in Kansas City.

"Won't cost much."

"No, I'm not in the mood."

Rita shrugged. "Maybe later. I'll be around."

"Yeah." Weir was feeling low. He got that way now and then, more often lately. He wanted to break something—that sometimes relieved the feeling. He watched the dealer hand out the cards. All civilians in the game today. He ought to get in, beat their asses. Maybe one of them wanted to fight or something. *Goddamn civilians.* He hated them, especially when he'd had something to drink. Not even good poker players, goddamn civilians. *Goddamn Libbie.*

He drained the glass, went back to the table, and poured some more. He'd dreamed about the little bloody faces again. But that wasn't all.

He hated what the devils did to him when he drank. He hated the anger it brought on, this *poison.* At times he even hated Armstrong Custer, hated him for being Libbie's husband.

For he loved that beautiful woman more than any man had ever loved. But he couldn't hate the general—he *loved* that man. George Armstrong Custer was his illustrious commander, the bravest, most exciting officer in all of the cavalry! But he was her husband. And he kept her from him. It was all part of his cage. That was what his life was, a goddamn cage. He *had* to drink to stand it and when he did, the morbidity, the fruitlessness, the *misery* of it all spilled over him like a flood of dark, sticky blood.

It had been eight years since he had fallen completely, hopelessly in love with Libbie Custer, back at the time of the general's court-martial. In fact, it had been an anonymous letter stating that his wife was getting too interested in Tom Weir that had made Custer come riding hell-bent-for-leather all the way to Fort Riley to see her. Actually the general had deserted his command to get there. And Custer had wanted to *kill* him! But it had all worked out, even though the general was found guilty on several counts of dereliction. It was more than dereliction—Custer had been found guilty of being "absent without leave," "of misuse of government property—in the form of horses," and, in an unrelated incident, "of ordering deserters shot." The sentence, mild in view of the offenses, was a year's suspension without pay. The lightness of the sentence had brought a caustic notation from General Grant, then head of the army. But the whole mess had only added to the romantic Custer legend.

He'd fantasized that Libbie would leave Armstrong then. He was sure she had cared for him, not just dallied with him as some officers' wives on the frontier did now and then. But she'd never told him so, he just *knew.* And he'd gotten it under control, usually keeping it under wraps all these years, being the witty hanger-on who made her and the other women laugh. But just today he'd bumped into her at the sutler's and she'd held his hand for a moment while they talked. He knew it didn't mean anything, but still . . . damn, it had brought out all those old feelings.

Maybe he *ought* to take Rita upstairs. Trouble was, he sometimes got angry with women like that and wanted to knock them around a little. And he couldn't do that. Still, it might make him feel better. He emptied the glass and poured some more whiskey into it. Felt good, burning its way down.

Colonel Sturges, the actual regimental commander, had once stated that Captain Thomas Benton Weir "became dissolute and abusive when he drank." Weir hadn't challenged the accusation. There had been that incident with the Cheyenne girl back in '68. He had knocked some of her teeth out, but she had been demanding, had shrieked at him. Still, he'd been sorry that he did it. Other officers sometimes had to discipline their Indian girlfriends. And the general and his brother, Tom, had passed that girl, Monahsetah, back and forth like a hot penny. . . .

Maybe it was the war. No, not after ten years.

Was war a cage?

Was an Indian campaign a cage?

Had to be. Didn't he dream of those dead Cheyenne children at the Washita? Like the previous night. Maybe that's why he'd beaten the Cheyenne girl. Uh huh, guilt. But he had nothing to feel guilty about; the general had given the orders to attack, to *kill*. Women and children were also the enemy, everyone knew that. If it didn't bother the general, why should it bother him?

Little bloody faces.

Somewhat round-faced with a mustache and a receding hair line, Weir was about to have his thirty-seventh birthday. He'd grown up in a small Ohio town, and after graduating from the University of Michigan in 1861 had enlisted in the Third Michigan Cavalry. He'd held all of the enlisted ranks before being commissioned and by war's end had been promoted to brevet lieutenant colonel. Then they'd put most of the flags away, squashed the army down to a smidgen, and started spitting on soldiers again. He had to accept a lieutenancy in the Seventh when the regiment was formed in 1866, but had been a captain for some time. He commanded D Company, where his first sergeant was Michael Martin.

Picking up the bottle of bourbon, he went up to the bar and nodded to Rita. "C'mon, lady, let's go somewhere private."

Rita smiled through her heavy makeup. "Yes, *sir!*"

Libbie wasn't sure when they'd get back from their trip to the east, so she had decided to have one more Sunday evening dinner party before their departure. The royal family was out in force. Ellen, her house guest from Monroe who would travel back to Michigan with them on the train, was making her last concerted effort at Tom, but she was joining the ranks of the other losers. Darn Tom! He was simply *not* interested in having a wife. And Boston—he was twenty-seven and one would think *he'd* be wanting to start a family—but he'd pretty much ignored her as well. And she hadn't been interested in any of the other single officers. What was *wrong* with these young Custers? All they wanted to do was carouse and play!

There were three civilian guests this evening. A preacher from Bismarck who had come out to perform an afternoon service, since there was no regimental chaplain, had readily accepted her dinner invitation. His wife had also come along. And Doctor Porter, the Bismarck physician whom Autie was trying to recruit as a contract surgeon, was there.

The drink table had the usual regimental punch bowl with its non-alcoholic fruit concoction, plus some assorted bottles of alcoholic drinks. Most of the guests were gathered there. The large dining table was set with the best silver and her Haviland china. John Burkman was pouring wine in the sparkling glasses, and Mary was starting to bring in the food. The menu was a cinch to please. The main dish was a spicy roast antelope that was one of Mary's most famous recipes. There were two kinds of potatoes, a dark, rich gravy, and her light and fluffy biscuits. The mock oysters—a mixture of corn, eggs, butter, and flour richly seasoned and fried in oil—were another of Mary's specialties. A large platter held the long sauce—the turnips, carrots, and parsnips coated with a sweet dressing of butter and honey. There would be an assortment of desserts.

"I don't like the way Annie is looking," Libbie said to her sister-in-law, Maggie, as they gave the table a last look before dinner call. She inclined her head slightly toward the very pregnant Annie Yates, who was laughing over something Miles Keogh had said.

Maggie Calhoun shrugged. "She always looks bad at this stage of her pregnancies. It's Tom Weir who looks like he's been to the undertaker."

Weir was quietly drinking whiskey with the other officers. He looked up and smiled briefly as Libbie glanced at him. His mood had improved since his visit to Geraldine Gentle's the day before. He'd been sipping from his flask most of the day. Sometimes it was like this; he'd reach a pleasant frame of mind and let the little nips of whiskey keep him there. Too much, and he might suddenly tip over into gloom.

"I worry about him," Libbie replied.

"You worry about everyone. You're the worst mother hen in the country."

"Mother hen of the decade," Tom Custer added as he came to the table to look for his name card.

Everyone was soon seated at the long table and grace was said by the visiting clergyman, Reverend Gale Williamson. His wife was an attractive woman with a fine singing voice and a ready smile. Miles Keogh was busy in conversation with her. Tom Weir began picking at his food, looking up at the foot of the table now and then to observe Libbie, who was being her vivacious self with Captain George Yates at one elbow and the minister at the other. Henry Porter, the disease prevention and control doctor of Geraldine Gentle's parlor house, was seated at the other end of the table next to Autie. The bewhiskered adjutant, William Winer Cooke, Boston Custer, Maggie's husband—Lieutenant Jimmi Calhoun—along with Lieutenant Algernon "Fresh" Smith and his wife, Nettie, made up the rest of the party. The dozen or so hounds watching with alert eyes to catch any wayward crumb, rounded out the group. The zestful conversation was, for a moment, slowed, as everyone fell to with gusto on Mary's fine repast.

George Yates wasn't quite his usual pleasant self—the fact that the Custers were departing on a long leave rankled him. He had applied for a much needed leave early in the year, but in spite of his closeness with Custer, Autie had turned him down. Both of the other officers in his company had been on extended detached service, a not uncommon practice, and Custer had insisted that no replacement was available to assume his command—F Company, the "Band Box Troop." Finally, just the previous Friday, Cooke had told him his six-month leave had been approved. But now it was too late because Annie was seven months pregnant and absolutely incapable of travel.

George Yates was from a distinguished New York family, and went back a long way with Custer—to Monroe, Michigan, in fact. While recuperating from wounds received at the disastrous Union assault on Fredericksburg in December 1862, the young lieutenant ran into Captain Custer, who was also on leave and busy trying to make the lovely young Elizabeth Bacon pay attention to him. Soon after, Custer wangled a position for Yates as an aide to cavalry general Alfred Pleasonton. Blond and blue-eyed, the six-foot George fought gallantly throughout the war and later, with Custer's aid, was awarded brevets to major and lieutenant colonel. Eventually Custer helped him get a captaincy in the Seventh Cavalry, and before long his Band Box Troop became the show company of the regiment. Capable and fastidious, the non–West Pointer was famous for turning his pockets inside-out every night to brush out the lint.

Yates had married a talented nineteen-year-old woman from an influential St. Louis family shortly before the end of the war, but that union had ended in divorce two years later. Then, in 1870, the dark-haired and twenty-one-year-old Annie Gibson Roberts came to spend the summer with her uncle, an infantry major, at Fort Hays—also the home of the Seventh Cavalry. And George Wilhelmus Mancius Yates fell hopelessly in love.

He looked across the table to where Annie sat between Tom Custer and Jimmi Calhoun.

They said that some women glowed in pregnancy; his lovely Annie wasn't one of them, but *God,* how he loved her!

As if feeling his intensity, Annie glanced up and tossed him a quick smile. She had fought off vigorous resistance from her straitlaced family to marry George Yates, the sinful divorced man, and she loved him with equal ardor. But then, she had always been a free thinking and adventurous girl. Her maternal grandfather had been chief justice of the Pennsylvania Supreme Court, and her father was one of America's foremost civil engineers. She was well-educated and liked to read. Years in Brazil had added to her linguistic skills. An accomplished violinist and singer, she was also a proficient horsewoman. While a bit sharp-featured, with high cheek bones, her abundance of rich dark hair and large, expressive eyes often turned men's heads. She did have trouble with her pregnancies, although her two children were thriving. Now, "with an elephant belly," as she described herself, she was disappointed that she wouldn't be going back home this year.

But this was tonight, and she couldn't go to *any* party without enjoying herself. She turned to Jimmi Calhoun, who was quietly working on his roast antelope. "James, I understand you bought a new horse."

Calhoun looked up from his plate. "I did?"

Tom Custer leaned forward and laughed. "Yeah, and you named him Sitting Bull because he wouldn't get off his butt!"

Annie joined in the laughter, as did Boston from across the table. "Oh, James," she said, patting his arm, "why do we have to tease you so?"

Calhoun shook his head good-naturedly. "Every batch of bullies has to have someone to pick on." Jimmi Calhoun was thirty years old. A native of Cincinnati, Ohio, he had been refused a commission near the end of the war, and had served as a first sergeant for two years afterward. He was later appointed second lieutenant in the infantry, joining the Seventh in 1871. That same year he met the vivacious Margaret Custer while she was visiting her brothers. It was love at first sight for both of them, and they were married the following March in Monroe. Custer had thrown in a promotion to first lieutenant as a wedding present. The fair-haired, tall Jimmi, whose nickname was "Adonis," had been Custer's adjutant for a while, but now commanded L Company.

"You're right," Fresh Smith said from down the table. "They *are* bullies, particularly the Custers. And specifically Tom, here. Before he was old enough to shave, he was bullying Rebs. Taking their flags away from them. Assuredly taking their girls any time he got a chance."

"Really?" Annie asked. "Do you mean he consorted with enemy females?"

"He consorts with *any* females," Smith replied. "He has this theory that he's creating a female spy network, and if they fall in love with him, they'll always be loyal to his cause."

"Yes, and we all know what *his* cause is," Boston said.

Everyone laughed as Tom shrugged and affected a pained, innocent expression.

Tom Weir choked as he laughed, coughed, and drained the wine in his glass. With wet eyes, he refilled it from the carafe in front of him. He wished he hadn't come. He could have made one of a dozen excuses. But then he wouldn't have seen Libbie. And besides, he had a recital to give.

At the end of the table, Autie perked up as Doctor Porter brought up the subject of Turkey. "People are fleeing the province of Bosnia in large numbers, according to the government in Constantinople. According to the newspaper, they announced they will reward the Serbs for remaining neutral, by evacuating Zwornik, and agree to a rectification of frontiers to Montenegro."

Maggie, seated at Autie's right elbow, shrugged. "I don't know why they keep fighting."

"People always fight," Autie said. "Ten years ago we finished the most violent war in history and it was all us, brother against brother. And look at the Indians—they've always had tribal wars. Right now, when they aren't fighting us, they're still fighting each other. It's the nature of things since the beginning. Those people over there in the Balkans, like the Serbs and the Bosnians, have probably had tribal enmities just as long as the Indians, and they all hate the Turks. Read the Bible if you want to learn about tribes fighting each other."

"Speaking of brother against brother," Tom Custer said, "did you read about Jefferson Davis drawing twenty thousand to hear him speak in St. Louis? The dirty traitor revolts against the Union, starts the worst war in history, and now everyone wants to hear him lecture. Doesn't make sense."

"That's America, Tommy-boy," Nettie Smith said. "We're out here so you can fight Indians, but a lot of people in this country think we ought to quit."

"Not the Indian agents," Jimmi Calhoun said. "You know what the newspaper said about the Red Cloud Agency investigation back in Washington. That fellow, Bishop Hare, confirmed Professor Marsh's charges against that snake, Agent Saville. The crook was certifying that eight-hundred-fifty pound cattle weighed a thousand, and that wasn't the only place he was lining his pocket."

"And the agency Indians don't get enough to eat," Annie Yates added. "No wonder they run off to join the likes of Sitting Bull and Crazy Horse."

That started an animated discussion about Indians and fighting them that lasted until Mary and Private Burkman brought in the dessert trays. Mary had outdone herself, providing a choice of dark, moist chocolate cake, a spicy brown betty, peppermint cakes laced with brandy, and cherry cheesecake.

Later, when more coffee was served in the parlor, Nettie Smith went to the piano and accompanied Annie Yates while she sang a rousing medley of Civil War songs in her clear soprano. After "Tramp! Tramp! Tramp!" she asked everyone to join in on the finale, a spirited rendition of

"The Battle Cry of Freedom." Enthusiasm shone on everyone's face as they reached the final chorus and with gusto sang, "Up with the star; while we rally round the flag, boys, rally once again, shouting the battle cry of *free-dom!*"

As soon as the applause faded, Tom Weir took center stage and announced that he would recite a poem. He walked with his legs slightly wide apart and slightly slurred the word "recite." But from that point on, one would think he hadn't touched a drop of spirits all day. The room fell silent, as he softly began in his firm voice, "This is a cavalry story that will be told by heroic horsemen in Fiddler's Green until the last lie has been heard and the final toast has been made."

He paused a couple of moments before going on, "It was a quiet fall morning in the Shenandoah Valley of Virginia in the year of our Lord, Eighteen-sixty-four. George Crook got caught sleeping at Cedar Creek by old Jubal Early and it was a black day for the Union." Placing one hand on his hip and striking a pose with his other hand that shaded his eyes, he looked off into the imaginary distance. "But, lo, off there is a puff of dust . . . by thunder, it's a horseman, and he's waving a little hat . . . it's . . . no, it can't be . . . It's *Little Phil!*" Smiling, Weir launched into "Sheridan's Ride."

> Up from the South, at break of day,
> Bringing to Winchester fresh dismay,
> The affrightened air with a shudder bore,
> Like a herald in haste to the chieftain's door,
> The terrible grumble, and rumble, and roar,
> Telling the battle was on once more,
> And Sheridan twenty miles away . . .

As Weir continued with the popular poem, Custer thought back to that day. Early had truly routed Sheridan's army, but when Little Phil, just arrived at Winchester from Washington City, heard the terrible news, he jumped on his fine horse, Rienzi, and galloped like a bat out of hell toward the battle. By sheer force of will, he turned his beaten army around, regrouped, and counterattacked late that afternoon, smashing the Rebs— one of the greatest examples in the history of warfare of a commander's will personally changing a major battle. He smiled to himself—and a young general named Custer had covered himself with more glory.

Weir grinned as he finished the last stanza:

With foam and with dust, the black charger was gray;
By the flash of his eye, and his nostril's play,
He seemed to the whole great army to say:
I've brought you Sheridan all the way
From Winchester down to save the day.

Immediately the hushed audience jumped to its feet and applauded vigorously. Of course, they all knew Thomas Buchanan Read's famous poem, just as they knew Rienzi, Sheridan's famous black horse, had been renamed Winchester. They were cavalrymen and their ladies; it was part of their heritage. Custer grinned as broadly as anyone when Weir bowed deeply in his direction and said, "Sire, had you not awaited Sir Phil and his famous charger, the day would not have been won."

Once more everyone applauded. "*Hear! Hear!*"

They all knew what Tom Weir meant. Armstrong Custer had been brilliant in the counterattack at Cedar Creek and had been one of the main factors in the resounding victory that followed Sheridan's glorious ride.

Custer raised his glass of sarsaparilla. "Well done, Tom. And now, ladies and gentlemen, I propose a toast." As glasses were raised around the room, he said, "To the glorious Seventh Cavalry, the finest cavalry regiment in the world!"

A chorus followed. "To the glorious Seventh Cavalry."

Custer smiled as he looked around. "Is there any better life?"

"*No!*" was the resounding reply.

10

That the king can do no wrong is a necessary and
fundamental principle.
—BLACKSTONE

Right after stable call the next morning, Iggy Stungewitz walked into the C Company orderly room and approached Ed Bobo. Holding out the two sheets of paper on which he'd copied in ink the carefully prepared statement of his encounter with Martin, he said, "Lieutenant Custer told me to give you this." He quickly explained, ignoring the eavesdropping company clerk.

Bobo frowned as he took the statement and glanced at it.

Looking back at Stungewitz, he said, "You think those witnesses will testify for you?"

Iggy's gaze was steady. "They saw it."

"That isn't what I asked you."

"I don't know."

"I know that McDonnell. Don't count on him. The farrier's kind of strange, I hear."

"We'll just have to see."

Ed Bobo didn't like what he had to say. "It's no good, Stungewitz. You know Martin's a first sergeant. He's got power you haven't even thought about. He can make those men wish they'd shot you. And you know most of the other senior NCOs will close ranks behind him. You'll be branded as a troublemaker. And if you ever have to leave this company, your arse could be in plenty of shit. It ain't fair, but you been around two armies. You know. That's the way it is."

Iggy stood stiffly, looking directly into Bobo's eyes. "I wish to prefer charges against First Sergeant Michael Martin of D Company, *sir!*"

"You know you don't have to "sir" me. In fact, you know so damned much about soldiering, Stungewitz, that I can't for the life of me understand why you're being so damned stubborn. Do you know where this puts *me?*"

Iggy spoke softly, "You can handle it, First Sergeant."

A slight smile touched Bobo's lips. "Yeah, and you know what—I'm kinda glad you're a stubborn son-of-a-bitch."

Captain Frederick Benteen looked at the order that gave him command of the regiment, effective October 1, when Custer was due to leave for the east. With Major Lewis Merrill and Major Joseph Tilford both on extended detached service, and Major Reno on leave in Europe, command fell to the senior captain. This didn't bother Benteen in the slightest. Rather, he wished he could actually command the regiment.

He looked out the window of his office in the headquarters of Fort Rice, which also served as his H Company orderly room. Squad drills with horses were being conducted on the parade ground. It reminded him of the war, when his seasoned troopers had performed such drills so well. Command a regiment? Huh! He thought back to October 25, 1864, when Price was falling back, trying to escape from his Missouri raid. The rebel leader had made a stand against Pleasanton's cavalry just west of the Missouri–Kansas border in a fight they called the Battle of Mine Creek. And Lieutenant Colonel Fred Benteen had led the Federal brigade that spearheaded the attack that shattered the Confederate lines.

He had commanded a *brigade*—with *three* regiments.

And here he was in temporary command of a regiment in 1875 because a lieutenant colonel five years his junior was going on leave! He shook his head. Irony. He was a brevet colonel wearing the rank of a damned captain. But he'd opted for the regular army, and that was the way things went in the soldiering business. Still—

"When's Reno due back?" Captain Tom French asked from where he was sitting, coffee mug in hand, beside Benteen's desk.

"I don't know. Sometime in November, I guess."

French grinned. "Then you've got plenty of time to make some changes."

Benteen shook his white head. "Custer would have my arse."

"Naw, he never messes with you, Fred. You've got him buffaloed."

"You never know. That son-of-a-bitch would court-martial his own brother if he thought it would get him a star again."

"That may be right."

"And now look at this!" Benteen waved a letter in the other captain's face. "The bastard wants us to emphasize *base-ball!* We're supposed to be training for a winter campaign, it's almost *October,* and *General* Custer wants our troopers to become better base-ball players! He quotes the recent results of games between the New York Mutuals and the Elizabeth, New Jersey, *Resolutes!* Who the hell cares?"

"What's his point—morale?"

"Right, and teamwork. He thinks these assorted troopers, many of whom can barely speak English, are going to throw a ball around and learn how to kill Indians!"

French shook his head. "And many of them can't even shoot. Speaking of that, what happened to his vaunted request for more training ammunition? I've got nearly a dozen recruits who haven't fired a single live round from their carbines yet."

"Nothing. I think, soon as his majesty leaves, I'll ride up to Lincoln and stir up the goddamn quartermaster."

As Tom French departed, Benteen considered what the other officer had said: *You've got him buffaloed.* He was referring to the famous or infamous—considering where one stood—Battle of the Washita in 1868. The public, fed the story of a heroic defeat of the Cheyenne by the great Indian fighter Custer, thought it was famous. Those on the inside, who knew the details, considered it infamous. Custer had launched an early morning attack on the village of peaceful Black Kettle and had been initially victorious, killing a lot of Indians. But having failed to properly reconnoiter and learn that extensive Indian forces were camped downstream, Custer refused to believe that Major Joel Elliott was in trouble there. Custer pulled the rest of the regiment out, leaving Elliott and nineteen troopers behind. They were all killed, and for the first time, doubt about Custer's leadership was voiced within the regiment. As one of the most experienced of Custer's captains, Benteen had been openly critical. He simply couldn't stand the idea of Custer preening around, so he wrote an anonymous letter to a St. Louis newspaper that charged Custer with callous abandonment. Upon reading the newspaper account, an angry Custer ordered an officers' call and announced that he would horsewhip the traitor who had written the letter. He had stepped forward, looked Custer in the eye, and claimed the authorship. Custer stared back for a moment and then turned away. From that day to the present, their relations had been strained, but Custer had never acknowledged the incident.

No, he wasn't afraid of George Armstrong Custer.

But he wouldn't give the damnned peacock a chance to get even, not ever.

In the outer office of the Fort Rice headquarters, Trumpeter John Martin didn't understand most of the conversation of the two officers that had drifted through the doorway. That was because his real name was Giovanni Martini and he was from Sola Consalina, Italy. He had been in the United States just two years, in the army fourteen months, and his English was limited. He was a good musician, having first enlisted as a drummer boy in the Italian army when he was fourteen. He had been in battle at an early age against the Austrians, and was now twenty-two years old. Today he was running errands for the H Company first sergeant. He was swarthy, with dark hair and hazel eyes, and a thick mustache.

Giovanni Martini was a good soldier, and aspired to higher rank. But mostly, he wished to show everyone, particularly these damned Irishmen and Germans, that an Italian could be just as good a trooper as anyone. He kept his uniform in top order, was erect in his carriage, and was quite precise in his bearing while in uniform.

As he stood by the window, wondering what duties the first sergeant would have for him, the trumpeter had no idea that in nine months he would perform a vital duty for George Armstrong Custer that would enshrine his name in cavalry history.

Custer had been working on an article for the New York *Herald* for the last two hours. Putting down his pen, he sat back, moved his head around in a circle to relieve the strain, and decided to go outside and get some air. With Tuck and a couple of the other hounds following, he walked around the backyard for a couple of minutes perusing the stars before settling down on the back step. The red star, Mars, caught his attention off in the moonless and light-sprinkled firmament. If ever a star was meant for George Armstrong Custer, it was Mars, named for the Roman god of war. He chuckled to himself—they really ought to name it Custer.

It was such a beautiful night, warm for this time of the year, clear, quiet—in fact so still he could hear the dogs' breathing. He felt relaxed. Everything was packed for his departure in the morning and he'd soon be back in real civilization. It seemed as though there was something special about this evening, perhaps something that wouldn't come back at any other time. No cares, no problems. No concern about success or money. He had the best regiment in the world, a command that could whip any force it would ever face . . . the elite, crack, Seventh Cavalry. It wasn't a brigade or a division, but it was his. That alone was enough to give a man pride.

He felt at peace, remembering a night like this back in the Shenandoah Valley. The poem Weir had read, "Sheridan's Ride," that was what made him think about it. Cedar Creek. Same thing. Quiet fall night, Rebs resting behind their picket lines close by. His Third Cavalry Division was nestled down, getting some needed rest. A few horses snoring. Quiet. The only sound had been a distant baying hound. . . .

He scratched Tuck's ear, smiled. He'd had command of the division for just a short time, and the men had suddenly sprouted red neckties, emulating their hard-riding young general. Quiet, like this—a still, warm night that would create fog before morning, gray mist that would spit out charging, ferocious rebel soldiers at first light. On a day that would give George Armstrong Custer one of his most glorious battle opportunities, would send him to Washington for his brevet second star, the youngest to earn them . . .

Glory.

But this was Dakota Territory and there were no Rebs out there tonight.

He chuckled. Theodore Lyman had written of him ". . . he looks like a circus rider gone mad! He wears a huzzar jacket and tight trousers of faded black velvet trimmed with tarnished gold lace . . . the General's coiffure consists of short, dry, flaxen ringlets! He has a very merry blue eye, and a devil-may-care smile."

Another chuckle. Well, Lyman, nothing's changed but the clothes.

Suddenly it was totally silent, as if all the dogs had inhaled. He closed his eyes and thought of being a cadet at West Point. Those days had never been very happy. Seemed as if he had always been involved in some kind of a confrontation or threat. Of course, he'd had a lot of fun—

The first note of the trumpet was clear, almost startling!

The soldier's hymn.

The following notes melded "Taps" together like the soldier's spiritual it was, as they drifted pervasively over the parade ground, distinct, haunting. . . .

Day . . . is done . . .
Gone . . . the sun . . .

They gave him the usual chill, the reverence—Daniel Butterfield had never guessed how much the song would mean when he wrote it. . . .

From the lake
From the hill—

He came automatically to the position of attention. He'd stood beside too many flag draped coffins, heard too many farewell funeral volleys, too many heart-rending bugles, not to be moved by the crystal notes as they hung suspended over resting horses and sleeping men and the women who loved them.

From the sky
Rest in peace . . .

It all boiled down to this, didn't it? Man decides to be a soldier or a general, it's all the same. *Day is done, Gone the sun . . .* A bugler blows the pure notes at the end, whether it's a day or a life. . . .

They said he didn't care about his soldiers, but it was a lie. He gave them meaning, a chance for pride. He loved them.

Soldier brave
God is nigh. . . .

A tear came to his eye as the final note faded away into the dark night.

11

Yellowstone Country
October 4, 1875

Red Elk was beside himself, waiting. Since the day Crooked Tree had given him the Big Twisted Flute, the old shaman had been sick and unable to teach him the magic way to play it to win over Late Star. He'd been tempted, since he was a good flute player, to disregard the old man's offer and go ahead on his own. But he didn't want to chance anything in his campaign to capture her love.

He had been gone for eight days during that period, riding on the horse raid to the Arikara village by the Long Knives' fort. He had taken seven of his young friends, including his *kola*, Black Ash, and at the risk of incurring the wrath of the village leaders, had sneaked off well before first light one morning. They had moved swiftly up the Elk River for two days and three nights, arriving near where the Elk joined the big river, which the *wasicus* called Missouri, at two hours before daybreak. After hiding and resting all day, Red Elk and one other young warrior had scouted the camp and had found the Arikara town—they lived in sod houses, not tipis—lightly guarded. Their horse herd, corralled close by, was easy pickings. Returning as the yellow moon was setting that night, Red Elk had killed the Arikara guard with his knife and scalped him. The young Hunkpapas had hurried away with the entire herd of thirty-one ponies. Since their departure was five hours before sunrise, they had a good lead on any pursuers. Certain the Long Knives would follow, Red Elk split the herd one hour south, then broke up into four groups another hour downriver. He reasoned, quite soundly for a leader of his minimal experience, that the dispersion would confuse the pursuers. At worst, only a couple of the little herds would get caught and the two warriors with them could slip away.

Apparently the chase party gave up, because the entire raiding party joined up at the designated river crossing the following day and made its way proudly back to the home village. The chiefs and the *akicita* greeted them sternly, but the success of their raid overrode their lapse of discipline. Red Elk bragged proudly of his second first coup, and of being a *blotahunka*. He kept a black pony he thought to be a warhorse to pay for his Sharps rifle, a fine white animal, and six other paints from the captured herd. After paying Crooked Tree for the flute and giving a pony to his sister and one to a recently widowed cousin, he was still well-off for a sixteen-year-old. But the ponies were far from the most important result of the raid—Red Elk was the most famous young warrior in the Hunkpapa tribe, and his praises would be sung throughout the Lakota for some time.

Grudgingly, the Shirt Wearers gave their permission for a scalp dance. After all, they had to go through the motions of disapproving an illegal raid to keep discipline, but their young warriors had done well. Gall was privately pleased with his youthful friend, and offered him the use of a special headdress of dried rooster heads sewn on a background of chicken feathers for the dance.

By the time darkness arrived that evening, a roaring bonfire was creating leaping dark shadows against the golden light it threw around the center of the village. The beat of the drums was already incessant, accompanied by both rattles and flutes, along with a shrill whistle now and then. Most of the Hunkpapas and a few members of the other two tribes had gathered to watch. Red Elk's mother, his sister, and three female cousins anchored the center of a semicircle that included the female relatives of the other seven young warriors who had accompanied him on the raid. The females wore their finest, most carefully quilled dresses. Red Elk's sister, Blue Cloud, held high the pole that bore the scalp of the Arikara horse guard whom the young leader had killed with a knife, gaining the first coup.

Red Elk, wearing Gall's chicken bonnet, had already begun to dance, mimicking the steps of a chicken now and then. His bare upper torso was painted with streaks of crimson, his favorite color of paint. The other young raiders were similarly attired with touches of their own colors of paint and headdresses representing the different animals whose steps they were imitating. All of their faces were painted black, as were those of their relatives. It was the symbol of victory.

Glancing around at the firelit onlookers, Red Elk tried to locate Late Star, but she was nowhere to be seen. He was disappointed, because he thought surely she would want to be a part of his big victory. He decided to lose himself in the dancing. When he wasn't imitating an animal, a good dancer kept his body crouched and his chest up. His knees were bent slightly and his head moved from side to side occasionally as he glanced about. And since Red Elk did nearly everything well, this was no exception. He shrugged to himself. This was his great victory. Who needed a woman on a night like this? *She should count herself fortunate to be included. Stupid girl!*

And on and on he danced in the flickering light, trying to think of words for the song he would sing later. *"Red Elk dares, with the wind. Big River camp, Arikara huts—"*

Sometime during the second hour he decided to rest for a little while and danced ou of the center into a darker shadow where he found the feast the warriors' female relatives always provided. Just as he was reaching for a piece of spicy venison, he glanced up to see Late Star standing with her father, Running Antelope. The old chief was speaking with Gall and Sitting Bull, along with the great chief's younger wife, Four

Robes. Late Star looked at him and seemed to smile for a moment, then turned her attention back to the words of Sitting Bull.

A bent figure with a drooping eye and a black face marked with streaks of yellow lightning, adjusted his cap of dried bear entrails, leered at him, and cackled. "Come to my lodge tomorrow for your Big Twisted Flute songs, and bring your new scalp. I'll give it added power."

Before Red Elk could respond, the apparition—Crooked Tree— cackled again and disappeared into the darkness on his cane.

A few minutes later, as Red Elk was eating some of the sweetened pemmican his eldest sister had provided for the feast, Late Star spoke to him from the shadow of a nearby tree, "You are a fair dancer."

He grinned. "My mother says it is so."

"Maybe some day I will dance with you."

"In the Night Dance?" It was the only dance in which the females danced with the males, so it was a stupid question and he felt silly for asking it.

She laughed. "No, at a Kit Fox dance."

That was absurd, no female participated in an *akicita* dance! "Why do you always laugh at me?" he asked testily. "Tonight I am the most cele- brated young *blotahunka* in the Lakota!"

Her eyes danced in the firelight. "Ha! You take seven other boys to get horses from old women, and you call yourself a *blotahunka?*"

That wasn't fair! "Why isn't your face painted?" he demanded.

She shrugged. "I have nothing to celebrate."

"The Lakota *people* can celebrate my great raid!"

She laughed and pulled him into the dark shadow of the tree. Leaning up, she quickly kissed him on the lips! The Lakota *never* showed any affec- tion in public. He looked at her in astonishment; it was the first time she had ever revealed any romantic interest in him. Without another word, she smiled and moved off into the dark.

The cool sun, common to the Moon of the Falling Leaves, was well past midday when Red Elk arose the next day. He had truly danced his legs off, as the saying went, not retiring until daybreak. Now, sitting on the ginger- colored bank of the brook and watching the clear, silvery crested water gurgle by, he was practicing the song Crooked Tree had given him a half hour earlier. He was quite a distance from the village, so the sound of his flute couldn't be heard as he experimented with the notes. Of course the old shaman was a Buffalo Dreamer; that was part of his power. And he had prayed to Whope, the Beautiful One, who had appeared in a dream when the music came to him. He had said so. Therefore, the music would certainly work on her.

The notes were different from anything he'd ever heard, low and somewhat monotonous, now and then rising sharply, only to softly drop to the lowest tone the fine instrument could produce. The song lasted about two minutes, ending on the softest note he could blow. He went over it and over it, for nearly two hours, until at last he thought there was nothing more to add. As the sun began to settle over the Bighorn hills, he looked at the Big Twisted Flute with pleasure. The old shaman had polished it even more during his illness, and the beautiful piece of carved cedar shone in the fall sunlight. The eye of the whittled stud horse seemed to wink at its new owner as he smiled and played one long last clear note.

She will be helpless.

It was about an hour after sunset when Red Elk arrived at Running Antelope's tipi. A glance inside confirmed that Late Star was there. The chief was away at a meeting, and the sides were still rolled up a little way with the unusually warm weather. He was glad for both counts. The noted chief was against his courting his daughter because Red Elk came from a far lesser family, and the older man wasn't yet swayed by his early war success. As the most famous orator-chief in the Hunkpapa, and one of the most respected in all of the Lakota, Running Antelope considered his family true royalty and his only daughter a princess. But he couldn't actually stop Red Elk from being a suitor. And he knew his willful daughter would probably do just as she wished. Sometimes maidens ran off with the suitor they favored—eloped—and the Shirt Wearer certainly didn't want that to happen

Red Elk knew this, of course, but he also knew if he were ever going to gain the chief's favor, he would have to play by the rules. Oh, he wanted to take Late Star into the bushes; the thought fired his blood. He thought of ravishing her so he could brag about it like a trophy to the other young warriors. It was the Way, like counting coup for a strong young warrior. And this type of thing happened. Often, in fact. The couple was usually married regardless of earlier parental objections. Girls who didn't get married after one of these sexual forays, or who ran off again, were called *witkowins*, and it was believed that they became crazy and died at an early age.

But blessed was the young man who married a chaste and well-trained young woman with all of the blessings of both families. However, none of this mattered to Red Elk; he was fiercely in love with Late Star, wanted to make her his wife, and wanted the approval of her father so he could rise to chiefdom in the tribe. Simple as that. Any young warrior who could kill a lion with a single arrow at age eleven could certainly make such a plan and accomplish its end!

But Late Star had to be cooperative. After all, she *had* kissed him at the dance, but he knew she might have been playing with him. She had this mischievous thing about her. She had teased him even when they were younger. All of this went through his head again as he crouched a few feet from the tipi, raised the flute to his lips, and softly blew some clear notes.

Moments later, Late Star's lovely head popped out of the fly. "What is that terrible noise I hear?" she asked with a mock frown. She knew Crooked Tree had carved the Big Twisted Flute for Red Elk; there were few secrets of that nature in the village. In fact, there were few secrets of any kind in the village.

"I have come to you with a special song," he replied.

She came outside and stood a few feet away, looking down at him. "And what will happen to me then? Will the music melt my heart and make me follow you, entranced, to the river bank, where you will seduce me?"

Red Elk didn't like the idea of playing up to her. And she shouldn't be making fun of the flute. It wasn't going at all as he'd pictured it. He stood up. "No," he managed, "this is a special song for you. Crooked Tree prayed to Whope, the Beautiful One, and she told him the notes for your special song herself."

Late Star was wearing a new dress she had just finished quilling. She turned around and looked over her shoulder. "But *I* am Whope, the Beautiful One," she said, smiling coquettishly.

It wasn't going at all like he had imagined it!

He pointed to a small log by the tipi. "If you will just sit *there,* I'll play the music."

"But what if I don't want to sit there? Can you get the white horse back from Crooked Tree?" She gave him her most dazzling smile.

Anger was beginning to overwhelm any feelings of desire he had. He had planned so long and hard for this special moment, and now she was ridiculing him again. Maybe this was crazy, maybe *she* was crazy! Maybe he should just walk away and go find the Sans Arcs widow and forget this stupid marriage idea! *Just take the widow out into the hills and drive her into the ground. Forget this stupid girl!*

"Can you, Red Elk? Can you get the horse back?"

He stared at her a moment through narrowed eyes, turned, and stalked off.

He'd find Black Ash and fire the Sharps.

Who needed any female?

12

The warrior, the great leader, but always the mystic.
—ROBERT ELWAYNE

While Sitting Bull was the most famous and respected *wichasha wakan,* and had been one of the greatest of the Lakota war chiefs, the name that now most inspired battle-hungry young warriors was the mystical Crazy Horse.

This great war leader was born in the Black Hills, the *Paha Sopa,* in the fall of the Year of the Big Horse Steal—or what the white man called 1841. His mother was a Brule Sioux; his father, Crazy Horse, was an Oglala medicine man and dream interpreter. But from the time he could talk, the light-skinned, curly-headed boy had only one interest: to be the greatest warrior of all the Lakota. Naturally, his name was Curly.

Like other children, he ran naked in the summer during his early years and began his warrior training as soon as he could pull a bowstring. At seven summers he was given a small brown-and-white pony. Also at this time he began his association with his *kola*, High Back Bone, whom everyone called "Hump." When he was eleven, Curly went on a horse catching jaunt and was the first member of the party to break one of the wild ponies. He sneaked off on his first war party a month after his twelfth birthday. By this time, his exceptional hunting instincts had become evident and he seldom came back from a hunt empty handed.

But Curly was different in several ways from the other young Oglala warriors as he grew into his teens. Reticent and introspective, he disdained many of the boisterous ways. As he reached manhood, Curly's appearance set him apart. He was of medium height, thin and wiry, with a narrow face, a high-beaked nose, and dark eyes that seldom looked straight at anyone. But most remarkable was his light complexion and sandy hair.

A vision he induced in his midteens deeply influenced him. A vision quest was vital to a male's life in the Sioux world. It was usually preceded by fasting and purification rites, and was brought about by remaining awake alone in a holy place, until a vision came to him. It was a man's power, it set his life course. It prescribed what path—warrior, healer, horse-catcher, even *winkte*, or homosexual, that he might pursue. Generally, though, it was the life of a warrior that was perceived in the vision.

In Curly's case, it came to him after two days of fasting—a man enveloped in mist rode a horse out of a lake. Wearing only plain leggings and a simple shirt, he had but a single feather worn first coup style in his long brown hair. A small stone was tied behind his ear. "Never wear a war bonnet," the rider instructed, "and when you go into battle, never paint your pony, just pass dust over him. And rub some of the same dirt over your own body and hair. Then you will never be killed by an enemy. Also, you must never take anything from the enemy for yourself." Suddenly, a storm broke and a little zigzag mark of red lightning appeared on the rider's cheek. Hail spots dotted his body, and all at once the storm was gone. Overhead a hawk screeched.

And the rider faded away . . .

Curly had experienced his vision, but he wasn't yet sure of it. Nevertheless, from that day on, prior to a raid, Curly followed the instructions of that mystic rider. Having counted a first coup, he wore a single hawk feather straight up in his hair in memory of the screeching bird of the vision. A stone was tied behind his ear, he sprinkled dust over his pony and himself, and he painted a zigzag red line downward from his forehead past his nose to the point of his chin. He added one effect of his own: he decided, even in cold weather, he would fight with a bare torso—and he painted white spots all over it to represent hail.

On a raid against the Arapahoes in his sixteenth summer, Curly single-handedly repeatedly charged an enemy position on high ground in the face of heavy gunfire and a barrage of arrows, earning the enduring praise of his tribesmen. At the victory dance following the war party's return to camp, Curly was pushed forward to brag about his exploits, but he refused. It set a pattern—he never joined in the universal boasting that followed a victory or act of heroism. And he didn't sit in council. He would become the quiet man of the Lakota. The day after the scalp dance, Curly's father sang a song he had written:

> My son has been against the people of unknown tongue.
> He has done a brave thing;
> For this I give him a new name, the name of his father,
> And of many fathers before him—
> I give him a great name
> I call him Crazy Horse.

Now, as Red Elk found him camped by himself above the combined Oglala and Northern Cheyenne village, the thirty-four-year-old Crazy Horse was quietly making an arrow in front of a small crevice in the rocks. A hide, such as would be part of a tipi, covered the fissure. A small fire in the center of some rocks burned almost smokelessly. Light snow, melting stubbornly in the brittle sunlight, brightened the clearing in the tall ponderosas. As the slender young man approached, the war leader barely looked up.

"Great Chief," the visitor said, "I'm Red Elk, and I've come from the winter village of Gall and Sitting Bull to speak with you."

Crazy Horse took in the youth's first coup feather, his buffalo robe decorated in crimson, and the long rifle he carried. Another glance swept over the fine pony he was leading. He nodded. He wasn't a chief, but it didn't matter. He never got excited about such things. In fact, the only time he ever got excited was in the heat of battle. He nodded and pointed to a place by the fire.

Red Elk tied his pony to a small sapling and squatted at the indicated place. "The Hunkpapa leaders send you the smoke of the pipe, Great Chief." He withdrew a small packet from his robe, an oilskin pouch holding some good tobacco Gall had provided.

Crazy Horse grunted, accepting the gift.

"I have visited your Oglala village only once, when I was a boy and my father brought me.

His name was Bad Wolf. He was killed on a Shoshone raid."

Crazy Horse nodded.

"Now I wish to learn your ways."

Crazy Horse shrugged. "They are the ways of all Lakota."

"But there is only one Crazy Horse in battle."

"It is the time of the snow. The Oglala, like the Hunkpapa, don't fight."

"I wish only to sit at your feet for a few days, Great Chief." Red Elk knew that the man across the small fire had been a Shirt Wearer at a very young age, and that his love for a woman had cost him that honorable position, and probably the title of chief. . . . He also knew that he was a mystic, and perhaps the greatest of the Lakota *blotahunkas*. He wanted dearly for Crazy Horse to let him stay; besides the honor of being near the great warrior, he would be away from his own village and the haunting eyes of Late Star.

Crazy Horse looked at the Sharps. "Can you shoot that big one?"

"Yes, Great Chief. Would you like to see?"

"Yes. Show me what you can hit."

Red Elk couldn't suppress a small smile.

Everything was going just as he wanted it.

13

Second Lieutenant Charles Varnum's sandy hair was rapidly becoming extinct, even though he was only twenty-six, and this exaggerated the top of his head, since his face narrowed down to a slender chin. A member of the West Point class of '72, Varnum had been with the regiment since his graduation and had participated in several of the Seventh's skirmishes with the Sioux. He had spent most of his service with A Company under Myles Moylan, but was now the commander of the Detachment of Indian Scouts. Currently, though, he had an additional duty: he had been appointed the investigating officer on the Martin charges.

Seated at a desk in a small office in regimental headquarters, he casually returned the salute of Farrier Vincent Charley of D Company. He pointed to a chair beside the desk, saying, "Have a seat, Charley." As the trooper obeyed, he went on, "As you know, I'm the investigating officer in the case in which Private Ignatz Stungewitz has charged First Sergeant Michael Martin with issuing an illegal order and assaulting him. Were you present in the regimental mess on kitchen duty on September twenty-sixth, this year?"

The farrier nodded his head. "*Ja*, sir, I was," he replied in his Swiss accent.

"And did you witness a disagreement between First Sergeant Martin and Private Stungewitz?"

"No, sir, I did not."

"I can put you under oath, Farrier Charley, and if you commit perjury, you'll be court-martialed."

The blacksmith twisted his hat, but thrust out his chin. "I didn't see nuthin happen between Martin and Stungewitz, sir."

"You didn't hear First Sergeant Martin order Private Stungewitz to kitchen duty?"

"No, sir."

"Did you see First Sergeant Martin attack Stungewitz physically?"

"No, sir."

Lieutenant Varnum leaned forward, frowning. "I don't know whether I believe you." He pushed a Bible forward. "Put your hand on this Bible, Charley, and raise your right hand. Do you solemnly swear that this testimony is the whole truth, so help you, God?"

Charlie obeyed, mumbling, "Yes, sir, I do." But his eyes fixed on the Bible.

"Are you a good Catholic, Charley?"

"Yes, sir, I . . . am."

"Then you know what you're doing."

"Yes, sir."

"Did you see any conflict between Martin and Stungewitz."

Charley stared straight ahead. "No, sir, I did not."

"I have one final question. Did First Sergeant Martin threaten you in any way in regard to this testimony?"

"No, sir, he did not."

Varnum nodded his head. "You're excused, Trooper."

As the farrier got to his feet, a troubled look crossed his face. He paused.

"Do you have something to add?" Varnum asked.

"Uh, no, sir."

After Charley saluted and departed, the lieutenant pursed his lips and made some notes. He knew what was going on, the whole regiment knew. The Russian trooper had erred in judgment by preferring these charges—which he was damned sure were true, and there wasn't a single thing he could do about it. The cook had stated that he saw nothing untoward in Martin's conduct that day, the other supposed witness—McDonnell—had stated that he saw nothing. Martin had naturally denied any misconduct, and the farrier, Charlie, had agreed with them. But he had thought Charlie wasn't very convincing. It was simple—the old army game, the system. Stungewitz was an unusual soldier, educated, confident, dedicated to his own sense of right. There wasn't a doubt in his mind that Martin had done just as the Jew stated, but the die was cast.

Now he hoped Stungewitz wouldn't pay too heavy a price.

☆ ☆ ☆

Geraldine Gentle's place was busy on this Saturday night, mainly because she'd decided to throw what she called a pre-Hallo'een party for her favorite customers. Tom Wier was there, more sober than usual for a Saturday night. Rita, his favorite, was watching him play poker with an arm draped over his shoulder. She was wearing a short skirt with mesh hose and a low-cut ruffled blouse—all black. Black cat whiskers were painted around her mouth, and her eyes were darkly accented in a slant, giving her a sinister look.

Geraldine was moving around the large room, smiling and playing hostess. She was dressed in red, with a large bustle over her attractive hips. Red mesh hosiery revealed her shapely legs, and a red mask surrounded her eyes. A tall, peaked witch's hat crowned her head.

Her other four girls were dressed in various witch's costumes, mixing revealing flesh with paint and satin. The poker game was full, with Tom Custer and Miles Keogh also in it. Charlie Varnum had come along at Tom's invitation and was dancing with Geraldine's newest addition, a tall, shapely redhead who called herself Santa Fe Sandy.

One other cavalryman and seven or eight civilians, the most recognizable of whom was Clement Lounsberry from the Bismarck *Tribune,* made up the rest of the party. The mayor was supposed to drop in later. The other officer was First Lieutenant Thomas McDougall, whose wife was back in Spartanburg, South Carolina, on a visit. McDougall, a slightly chubby man of medium height, had been commissioned late in the war. Appointed an infantry officer in the regular army afterward, he had received a brevet to captain for heroic action against the Indians in 1867. He had been acquitted of a charge of being drunk on duty in a general court-martial the previous March. Wearing a small brown goatee and a guard's mustache with waxed tips, he had a round face and a ready sense of humor. He commanded B Company. On this night, he was expecting to command a little blonde from Texas named Bluebell—on whom he was showering his attention.

"Goddamned cards!" the handsome Myles Keogh snapped, throwing his losing hand down and jerking up from the table. Going to the bar, he ordered a straight whiskey from Geraldine. "Goddamned cards are treating me most ugly," he told her.

"Maybe they'll change," the madam said gently.

"I'm out of money," the captain sighed, sipping the whiskey. He didn't let on to anyone that he seldom carried much money because he drank so much that he gave his pay to his orderly to ration out to him over a month's time. Now his Irish melancholy was upon him and he wanted to obliterate it. Losing in the poker game had merely enhanced it. He was out of sorts with Custer again—the general had trotted off on his trip east without giving him an answer about his own leave. Insensitive son of a bitch! Everybody thought Myles Keogh was part of the royal family—well, he bloody well *wasn't!* George Armstrong Custer could kiss his bloody arse!

"This one's on me," Geraldine said. "And if you want one of the girls tonight, you can put it on the tab as well. Your friend Molly O'Brien's gone back to Philadelphia, you know."

"I might just do that." He looked around. "Who's the redhead?"

"Santa Fe Sandy. Just came in from New Mexico. Want to meet her?"

"Does she like sentimental Irishmen?"

"I haven't asked her, but we all do."

At that moment the music stopped and Charlie Varnum went to relieve himself. As the tall redhead walked up to the bar, Keogh smiled and clicked his heels. "Brevet Lieutenant Colonel Myles Keogh, formerly of the Papal Guard and the Battle of Gettysburg, ma'am."

Santa Fe Sandy smiled. "And what a beautiful Irishman, you are, lad."

"Do I detect a bit of the blarney in your words, Miss?"

"Aye, Dublin, Colonel. But I've been out here so long I've forgotten how to speak good Irish English."

"I know what you mean," Keogh replied. He glanced down at her breasts and then back to her blue eyes. "What a handsome lass you are. Are you tied up with that boy who was dancing with you?"

"No, but you do know I'm working, don't you?"

"Of course." He turned to Geraldine, his engaging smile back. "I think I'll take you up on that tab offer, lovely lady. Give Miss Sandy a drink, please."

At that moment Varnum returned and saw what was happening. He frowned. "I thought I would buy you a drink, Sandy."

"Ah, Lieutenant," Keogh said, "I remember how it was at your age when I was outranked. But you see, it isn't really a matter of rank. Nope, the lady and I are related—that's right, we have a great-great-uncle in common back in Dublin, and we need to discuss him."

A quick look of anger flitted across Varnum's angular face, but he shrugged and moved over to watch the poker game. A couple of minutes later, Doctor Henry Porter walked in. He was wearing a black cape and had painted his eyebrows high in good villainous form. He flicked the cape around as everyone stared at his act. Pounding his fist on the bar, he snarled, "Whiskey, you slut, whiskey!"

Everyone laughed as he drained the glass Geraldine handed him.

"Doctor, you are *scary*," the madam said with a chuckle.

"I am the devil incarnate!" the red-mustached Porter replied. "Or is that *incarnal?*"

He went over to the poker table, where Tom Custer was in the process of dragging in a pot he had just won. Tweaking his mustache, Porter said, "It appears that this dog of a soldier is *cheating*, gentlemen. I say he should be *shot!*"

Tom laughed. "Go away, you quack. This is an honest man's game."

"Ha!" Porter rejoined. "Is that seat open?"

"It is, but only if you have cash money."

The doctor pulled out a roll of bills and sat down. "Deal!"

Myles Keogh shook his head sadly, taking the bottle Geraldine handed him in one hand and steering Santa Fe Sandy toward a corner table with the other. "You know," he said, "you'd think there was no tomorrow for these sinful people."

"Everyone told you," Sergeant Dan Kanipe said from where they were sitting, whittling pieces of wood on the back steps of the C Company barracks.

"I know," Iggy replied. "But it had to be done."

"At least you're lucky that Bobo dislikes Martin. Any other first sergeant would have given you the treatment simply because you went after one of their own."

Iggy nodded in agreement. "I suppose."

"But you'd better stay alert. Martin isn't going to take it lying down, you know."

Iggy narrowed his eyes. "He can't hurt me."

"He's a mean son of a bitch."

Iggy just shrugged and switched the subject. "How's your love affair?"

Kanipe frowned, turning angrily from his whittling. "It *isn't* a love affair!" As far as he knew, no one had any idea he'd met Missouri Ann in town a couple of weeks earlier—unless she'd told someone.

"What is it—are you playing Lancelot for fun?"

"I'm not playing Lancelot!"

Iggy chuckled. "Queen Guinevere Bobo thinks you are."

"Damn it, Iggy, don't even talk about it!"

"All right," the Russian replied, getting to his feet. "I know nothing about the Seventh Cavalry's romance of the century. Good night, my lovelorn sergeant."

Kanipe frowned. "And don't forget to watch your ass with Martin."

Dan Kanipe stood up as his friend disappeared inside the barracks. He glanced up at the early yellow moon and hauled out his watch. It was almost time. Good thing the moon was only a melon slice tonight. He started nonchalantly toward the married NCO quarters. Bobo had finally gone to the hog ranch tonight to have a few drinks, and she'd be waiting. His breath quickened, but the other side of him was pricked by his conscience. He inhaled deeply and blew it out. There wasn't any doubt about which side would win.

Missouri Ann stood in the dark shadow at the back of their quarters. She had pulled the drapes, but a sliver of yellow light from a kerosene lamp showed through a crack. She came into his arms as he rounded the corner of the building. "Oh, Danny, I've missed you." She kissed him robustly and hugged him tightly. "I was afraid you might not come."

She seemed lightly dressed. He loved her perfume and the warm feel of her shapely body. "What is it they say about wild horses—well, they couldn't drag me away." He glanced around to see if anyone was watching. "What about the children?"

"They're in bed."

"And you're sure Ed went across the river?"

"First Sergeant John Ryan came by to get him at six-thirty."

"I feel so—well, we shouldn't meet like this. But I want to see you so much—"

Her lips ended his words; her eager tongue wiping away the uneasiness as she melted tightly against him. After a long kiss, she murmured, "Oh, you feel so strong, so hard, Danny." She gyrated gently against his growing erection. "Come, let's go inside."

"You sure the kids are asleep?"

"They're asleep. C'mon." She pulled his hand as she went to the door.

Inside, near the cooking stove, she came into his arms again for another long kiss. Then she stepped back and unbuttoned the robe she was wearing. It slipped to the floor, revealing her naked body highlighted in the low light of the lamp. He stared. He'd never seen her nude before. Her fingers flew to the buttons on his jacket. "Hurry, darling!" she whispered.

Moments later he was on the iron bed with her, forgetting everything.

14

Washington, d.c.
November 3, 1875

Brigadier General George Crook got to his feet as Phil Sheridan approached. He had been sitting outside the president's office in the White House for seven minutes, waiting for his boss to show up. He nodded his head. "Morning, General."

Little Phil nodded back. "Mornin', George. Everybody else here?"

"I don't know. Chandler and Belknap arrived a couple of minutes ago."

They went inside, where President Ulysses S. Grant stood by the window, speaking with an aide who departed a moment later. The presidential office was a large square room on the south end of the mansion, dominated by a huge oak table in the center that served the president's cabinet meetings. Against the south wall stood a tall desk, its pigeonholes crammed with some of the huge load of letters that flooded in daily from disgruntled veterans, influence seekers, and ordinary constituents.

Two haircloth sofas and three chairs attended this desk. Framed maps hung on the walls, and over the mantle in the place of honor hung a large photograph by Matthew Brady of the great parade of the Grand Army of the Republic after the war. Standing by the oak table were the two cabinet members, Chandler and Belknap.

President Grant hurried toward the generals, smiling warmly, his hand extended. He shook Sheridan's hand, then Crook's. "It's so good to see you fellows again," he said pleasantly, handing each of them triangular cigars that were his favorite. "We'll have to have a chat later, when this important business is over."

Crook tried to remember how old Grant was. The quiet man had graduated from West Point nine years before him—in '43, so he was about fifty-three. And a bit heavier than during the war. Stocky, graying short beard, clear blue eyes, the quintessential common man. His presidency hadn't been any bed of roses, not with all those thieves circling around him like sharks. It seemed like there'd been one scandal after another in those seven years. He should have listened to Sherman and not the siren songs of the damned politicians. Washington was certainly no place for an honest man!

Secretary of War William Worth Belknap sat down at the table. He was, as usual, at odds with his former sponsor, General Cump Sherman. In fact, the commanding general was so tired of the secretary and his staff meddling in the operation of the army that he had moved his headquarters to St. Louis. And even though Sherman was Grant's longtime friend, it seemed that Belknap would keep his job. He had survived a string of articles about him being involved in trader misconduct that had recently run in the New York *Herald*, yet another obvious attempt by the Democratic press to discredit the administration.

After shaking hands, Secretary of the Interior Zachary Chandler joined him at the table.

Chandler was originally from New Hampshire, sixty two years old, and a former Michigan senator. One of the Radical Republican leaders, he had just this fall been appointed to the cabinet by Grant to replace Columbus Delano. The deposed secretary had been responsible for the widely publicized Indian agency tradership scandal that had exploded in September. Some people thought Chandler's hard-line thinking about the

Indians had been the deciding factor with the Republicans who confirmed his cabinet appointment.

At that moment, Commissioner of Indian Affairs Edward P. Smith came hurrying in, apologized to the president, and shook hands all around. Crook didn't know much about Smith.

At forty-six, George Crook was a prime example of what years in the field could do for a man. Ramrod straight and healthy, his often stern face was lighted by blue-gray eyes under dark brows. Full white sideburns blended into a strong forked beard. He used neither tobacco nor liquor, and no enlisted man had ever heard a profane or obscene word from him. Another Ohioan, he had graduated from West Point in 1852, and had been wounded by a poison Indian arrow in '57. As a Union two-star, he had served under Sheridan in the Shenandoah Valley and had commanded the Army of West Virginia at one time. In fact, the only embarrassment of his career had occurred when Confederate General Jubal Early surprised him at Cedar Creek in the Valley in '64. A quiet man of high integrity and humility, he usually rejected wearing a uniform, along with any pomp and circumstance, and even rode a mule. In the field, George Crook was the preeminent Indian fighter in the country, having recently brought the belligerent and wily Apaches in Arizona to a peaceful position. But he never hated an Indian. He always, even in his sternest moments, felt compassion for them and tried to understand them. Today, of course, he was in uniform.

President Grant called the meeting to order and everyone was seated. "As you know," he said, "We're here to talk about the Indian situation. There has been much discussion in the past few months, but few specific decisions have been made." He looked at Secretary Chandler. "Zach, can you tell me how many miners are in the Black Hills at this time?"

Chandler shrugged. "As low as eight or nine thousand, or as high as fifteen thousand, Mr. President."

"I think it's closer to the latter, maybe even more," General Sheridan interjected. "You know how they flood into a place when they smell gold. And you can't control them. Most of them aren't choirboys, you know."

Belknap nodded his head. "Far from it."

"Calling them miners is even stretching the point," Commissioner Smith added. "I suppose *prospectors* would be closer to the truth. Whatever we call them, they aren't settlers."

"Hardly," Chandler said. "We'll probably need to keep the army there just to keep them from killing each other."

"And we'll never stop that."

"The problem, as you all know," the plain-speaking president said, "is that the Black Hills are considered a sacred retreat by the Sioux. From both a legal and a moral perspective, the area belongs to them and the white man has no right to be there. Yet, we *are* there. We sent the Custer expedition in to map the area and to find a place for a fort. *We* are the trespassers, and I don't feel good about that."

"No doubt about it," Belknap said, "It's the stumbling block in trying to achieve peace in the whole northern plains region. What do you have to say, General Crook? You were up there recently for a look-see."

"It's as the president says. We haven't got any right to be in their sacred lands, but we are. As long as there's the faintest hope of finding gold up there, men will go look for it. It's like a disease. There are also settlers encroaching on the Great Sioux reservation, real settlers, going there to stay. If we make it any worse by putting soldiers there permanently, I think the Sioux will fight to the last drop of their blood."

Grant nodded his head and turned to Commissioner Smith. "How much money do you think it will take to buy them off, Ed?"

Smith shrugged. "I don't know, Mr. President. We've offered them six million for the Black Hills, or four hundred thousand a year to lease the area. But they've turned us down. I don't know what the hell to do with them."

"What you don't understand," Crook said patiently, "is the fact that Indians don't really know what money is, not large sums anyway. They don't have any idea what six million dollars is, or four hundred thousand. And they don't know what a lease is. Furthermore, their young hotheads just simply want us out of their sacred hunting ground."

"General Crook's right," Zachariah Chandler said. "I don't think we can make any kind of a deal with them."

Sheridan spoke up belligerently. "What are we going to do—cave in to them? Let 'em stop the railroad permanently and kill settlers? Hell, we haven't got nearly enough soldiers to keep people out, and you've already said we shouldn't have blue uniforms in there. Somebody's going to have to figure out if we're going to keep kissing their asses or not. I say we need to put our foot down and make sure they know it."

He got up and walked to the large wall map, pointing to western Dakota Territory. "Out here, Sitting Bull and Crazy Horse rule supreme. This is the unceded territory where the agency Indians go any time they feel like it. And you all know how big that country is."

The president frowned as he lit a cigar. "What do you recommend, Phil?"

Chandler broke in. "I say let's give them the ultimatum we've discussed, and if they don't comply, let's turn the problem over to the War Department to enforce it."

Grant looked at Crook. "What do you think, George?"

"I don't know the Sioux very well yet, but I don't think they'll come in. I know how difficult it was with the Apaches. From what I've heard about Sitting Bull from my scouts, he'll *never* come in to be an agency Indian. And he holds a lot of sway out there. I think what General Sheridan was leading up to is our only course, if we're going to stay."

"That's right—let's kick their asses, round 'em up, and make 'em stay on the agencies," Sheridan added.

Grant spoke quietly. "You want a winter campaign."

"Right. Catch 'em holed up in their lodges trying to stay warm."

The president looked around with a questioning look. Everyone present except Crook nodded his head in agreement. Grant frowned, showing his displeasure. Finally he said, "I don't like it. I've tried to keep everything peaceful, but it seems to be a lost cause. All right, Zach, take thirty days to set up the ultimatum. A month from today, you can send it out. All Indians in the unceded territory are to move onto the reservation by January thirty-first. If they fail to do so, they will be branded as hostile and the army will come after them with orders to use all means of force to make them comply. And I want it prepared in simple language they can't fail to understand."

"And what about the prospectors?" Sheridan asked.

Grant blew out a sigh. "Look the other way, I guess."

After another twenty minutes of discussion, the meeting broke up. Sheridan grinned at Crook outside the president's office. "By God, George, now it's official. We'll have a winter campaign that'll put a twist on them the likes of which they've never seen!"

George Crook nodded, but something told him it wouldn't be that easy.

15

"As I wrote in my book, *My Life on the Plains*, it is regrettable that the character of the Indian that James Fenimore Cooper describes in his interesting novels is not the true one. We must now deal with the Indian problem as it exists today. Stripped of the beautiful romance with which we have so long depicted him, and placed in his true environs, the Indian forfeits his claim to the appellation of the *noble* red man. We see him as he truly is, as he always has been, a *savage* in the true sense of the word, whose cruel and ferocious nature far exceeds that of any wild beast of the desert."

Custer sipped from the water glass on the lectern and looked around at the large crowd of writers, artists, and actors gathered in New York's popular Lotus Room. Their faces were open, expectant, as he went on, "Gentlemen, the Indian is a chameleon, if you will. He is a consummate actor who can appear in his villages—while at peace—a simpleminded son of nature, wanting nothing more than to roam and hunt, never trespassing on the rights of others.

This is simply erroneous. The Indian is usually at war and takes what he wants. Conversely, it isn't true that the Indian is merely a creature in human form, divested of most attributes of humanity whose savage customs disqualify him from the rights and privileges of life itself."

Custer looked around again, and smiled. "Gentlemen, I'm a warrior. I was born to be one as surely as Sitting Bull was born to be one. Therefore I recognize their culture. And I assure you, in closing, that they will forever be an enigma as long as they continue in their old ways.

Thank you."

Custer nodded his head in thanks as the audience broke into loud applause and several *bravos*. Immediately many of the listeners came forward to shake his hand and congratulate him on his remarks. Albert Bierstadt, the famous landscape painter, was one of the first. "Most enjoyable,

General Custer," he said, beaming. "You must come to lunch in my studio soon. There's much more I'd like to discuss."

Custer nodded. "Yes, I'd like that, sir."

His good friend, the actor Lawrence Barrett, was next. "Excellent, Armstrong! You are such a stimulating speaker. Everyone here has received a rare treat."

More of the listeners crowded around, wanting a moment of intimacy with the famous Indian fighter who was the current toast of New York. One of them was August Belmont, the owner and publisher of the New York *World*. "Splendid, General Custer, simply splendid! How would you like to dine with me next Tuesday?"

Custer smiled, shaking Belmont's hand. "Why, I'd like that very much, sir."

"Good. Shall we say twelve o'clock sharp at Delmonico's?"

"I'll be there, sir."

A writer named Archibald took advantage of the brief moment of silence to ask, "That song I've heard you like so much, "GarryOwen"—did you write it, General?"

"No, the song goes back to Ireland about a hundred years ago, when some young men rioted in Limerick. Garryowen was a suburb of that city. Soon it became the quick-step song of several Irish regiments, and the Fifth Irish Lancers adopted it as their drinking song. I heard it when I was a cadet at West Point and fell in love with it. Now it's the Seventh Cavalry's regimental song."

The writer asked a couple more questions, then stepped aside.

When the last of the audience finished congratulating him, a man in his mid thirties with salt-and-pepper brown hair stepped forward from where he'd been watching from the corner of the room. Sticking out his hand, he said, "How are you, General? It's been a long time."

Custer looked at him closely. "Do I know you?"

"Ira Vandiver, former Captain, Fifth Michigan Cavalry."

Custer nodded his head and broke into a smile. Shaking hands, he said, "Of course, you were wounded at Yellow Tavern when we got Jeb Stuart. How are you?"

"I'm fine, General. I got gut shot, and it was slow healing. By the time I was fit for duty again, Appomattox rolled around."

Custer nodded his head. "As I recall, you did plenty before that. Didn't you get a Medal of Honor for Brandy Station, and something for Cedar Creek?"

Vandiver nodded his head. "Long time ago."

"What are you doing now?"

"Newspaper reporter, New York *Times*. And I'd like to ask you some questions, if I may."

"Certainly." Custer pointed to the table. "Let's sit down right here." Looking up at a waiter, he said, "Bring us some coffee." Turning back to Vandiver, he said, "Aren't you from Michigan?"

"Yes, I grew up in Detroit—well, actually Wyandotte, slightly downriver."

"I know where it is. What can I do for you?"

Vandiver opened a notepad. "I'd like to ask you your specific opinion of the Indians, particularly the Sioux and the Cheyenne. There has been a lot of discussion about your attack on Black Kettle on the Washita when you came back after your court-martial exile. Can I be frank?"

Custer nodded his head, frowning slightly.

"As a result of that battle, you became known as the preeminent Indian fighter in America, yet there are those who wonder why you killed a chief who was one of the major peacemakers."

"I was under orders from General Sheridan: total war. And for those who question my attack on a so-called peaceful chief, let me say this—first of all, the weather was most foul, the deepest of winter, and my scouts didn't know it was Black Kettle's village that lay before us on that bitterly cold morning on the Washita River. Secondly, Black Kettle had many young hotheads in his band who wanted to fight. So it wasn't an entirely non-hostile village that I attacked."

Vandiver was one of the leading reporters in New York, noted for his incisive approach to issues. He sipped his coffee, then leaned forward a bit, looking into Custer's wary blue eyes.

"There are also those who charge you with wanton killing of women and children. What about those accusations?"

Custer's eyes turned icy. "That's pure horseshit, Vandiver! Whenever an Indian village is attacked, a number of women and children will be hurt, some of them killed. But I have *never* ordered it! If one can achieve surprise in attacking an Indian camp, panic and demoralized flight are factors. Everything is in an uproar and women and children *do* get hurt. Remember, Sheridan ordered *total war*. That means burning their villages, their food, their weapons . . . killing their horses, and taking captive their surviving family members. I *deplored* inflicting casualties on their women and children."

"In line with that, General, it has been said that you had a Cheyenne woman as a lover, one Monahsetah, and that she gave birth to your child. Is this true?"

Custer got hold of himself and smiled. "Come now, Captain, you know better than to ask such a question. I *befriended* the girl, Monahsetah. She gave birth to a child a month after we met. Do you possibly think I would have relations with a strange young Indian who was eight months pregnant?"

"But didn't she give birth to another child, one with light hair, late the next year?"

"That had nothing to do with me. Now, if you're going to print this kind of tripe, which could deeply hurt my dear wife, this interview is at an end."

Vandiver shook his head. "I can couch the wording just as you've given it to me, General. I think it would be good for you. Clear the air, so to speak."

"I'd prefer you didn't mention it."

"All right. But I have to ask you about Major Elliott."

Custer frowned again. Always Elliott. The story would never go away. After the initial attack on Black Kettle's village on the Washita, Major Elliott had hastily formed a group of volunteers, and, shouting, "*Here goes, for a brevet or a coffin!*" had led the party in rapid pursuit of some fleeing warriors. But Elliott soon ran directly into a large war party of Cheyennes and Arapahoes from large villages downstream who were rushing to help Black Kettle. Quickly surrounded, Elliott's party was annihilated. It was still one of the biggest thorns ever to stick in Custer's side. He hadn't known about the fate of those men—he had in fact been concentrating on the safety of the rest of his command as more and more warriors appeared from downstream. When he ordered the regiment to pull out, Elliott's whereabouts was still unknown. There had been no doubt in his mind that the major would show up with his little patrol.

Would the Elliott affair always haunt him?

Vandiver went on, "You were blamed by many for leaving Elliott and his men."

"I didn't know he was in trouble, and I had to disengage before a growing number of Indian reinforcements could damage my main body. I fully expected him and his patrol to come along at any time."

"An anonymous letter in a St. Louis newspaper from a member of your command accused you of callous abandonment, and reportedly created a bitter rift in the Seventh Cavalry. Supposedly, you held an officers' call and angrily threatened to horsewhip the traitorous officer who wrote the letter. I've been told directly that Captain Frederick Benteen stepped forward and claimed that he wrote the letter, daring you to follow up on your threat." Vandiver paused, then softly added. "And you turned the other cheek."

Custer nodded his head. "I should have shot him. He's always been trouble, always been defying me. I don't know why he dislikes me so."

"Can I print that?"

"Absolutely not. It's a small army, Vandiver. Officers can't be transferred in and out because of personal conflicts. And besides, whether he loves or hates me, Benteen is a dependable, experienced officer who can be counted on in battle."

Vandiver scribbled hurriedly. "What opinion can you add, General Custer, to the type of tactics a commander should use against the Indians?"

"Well, first of all, Indians don't fight like we do, with central command. Their combat is more on an individual basis. And they don't like to fight on equal or even close to equal terms. Therefore, when a superb fighting regiment, such as the Seventh, comes after them, they run. So our most important job is to block them off and hit 'em with as much surprise as possible."

"What about the Washita?"

"Their numbers were growing larger than ours, so I found it prudent in that vicious weather, after fighting a battle with little rest, to withdraw."

Vandiver nodded his head and stroked his mustache as he reflected for a few moments.

"I've heard that there will probably be a winter campaign if the Sioux leaders, such as Sitting Bull and Crazy Horse, don't come in like tame little Indians. What are your thoughts on that, General?"

"All I can say to that, sir, is that the Seventh Cavalry is ready to go into the field, and if it does, we may well end the Dakota Territory Indian problems."

"Is the regiment that good, General?"

Custer snorted and grinned. "It's the best cavalry regiment in the world."

Vandiver raised an eyebrow. "I guess that says it all. Thanks for the interview, General. I'll be circumspect about the information you've given me. One final question—there have been some rather pointed allusions to your political goals. I read one comment that the Democrats might consider you as an attractive candidate on the presidential ticket. Is that possibility on your horizon?"

Custer grinned again. "Off the record, Vandiver, all I want in this whole world is to wear stars again. On the record, all I want is to continue with a successful military career in a manner that will do the most good for my country."

Now it was time for the newspaperman to grin. "Well said, General. That comment should keep everyone happy. Thanks for the time."

Custer stuck out his hand. "Anything for an old comrade in arms."

"She certainly is no wallflower, is she?" Custer turned at the words of James Gordon Bennett, Jr. The publisher of the New York *Herald* smiled as he continued to regard Libbie, who was vivaciously responding to the attentions of a half-dozen men a few yards away.

Custer chuckled. "Hardly. That woman was born to tickle the fancy of men."

Libbie laughed aloud just as he made the comment, and all of her admirers broke out in laughter. Glancing up, she caught Custer's eye and tossed him a smile.

He winked back. He was so proud of her. And today, at the New York Historical Society meeting in the ballroom of the Hotel Brunswick, she was particularly fetching in the new navy taffeta dress she had recently finished. It seemed to set off her lovely gray eyes and give them a bluish tint. He had given her a fresh red rose to wear with it, and she had pinned it over her left breast. He chuckled again. "Yup, prettiest darned girl in town!"

Bennett offered him a cigar, which he turned down. "Do you think the Sioux will comply with the government demand to move into the agencies?" the publisher asked. "It went out a week ago."

Custer shrugged. "I doubt it, but who knows what's in their minds. From what I've heard from my scouts about Sitting Bull and Crazy Horse, they wouldn't come in even if we offered them *Washington!*"

The publisher nodded his head in agreement. "That would make a great feature, Armstrong. A view of those two chiefs from the outlook of your scouts. Why don't you write it for me? Use your usual *Nomad* pseudonym, of course."

Custer agreed. "Any other thoughts on articles, Mr. Bennett? I can use the money."

"Nothing specific. I'll publish anything you write."

"I'll get to work on it."

Following a few more minutes of conversation with the newspaperman, Custer ambled over to where his wife was still holding court. "All right, all right," he said with a mock frown, "Just what's going on here?"

Libbie batted her eyes. "Why whatever are you talking about, General Custer? I was just talking to these fine gentlemen."

He knew three of them vaguely, the others introduced themselves as he shook hands all around. Just then, Brevet Major General Rufus Ingalls caught his sleeve. "I need to talk to you, Armstrong."

Custer excused himself from Libbie's group and followed the deputy quartermaster of the army over to a corner where they could stand apart from the others. Ingalls, fifty-five and a onetime roommate of President Grant's at West Point, was the officer who had suggested to Custer in a letter a couple of months earlier that he might provide helpful information so Ben Holladay, the stagecoach magnate, might acquire sutlerships in the new forts scheduled for construction. Ingalls had been involved in Grant's ill-fated Santo Domingo plan back in 1869, and had been rumored to have acquired some ill-gotten gains there. As the best poker playing officer in the army, Ingalls had long been involved in various schemes, but had never been court-martialed for anything. Custer had no doubts about the man's honesty—Rufus Ingalls was a very moral man, according to his *own* morals. He was a most pleasant sort, always full of good cheer. It was even rumored that back at West Point he had enticed the straitlaced U. S. Grant out to the strictly forbidden Benny Haven's Tavern when they were cadets. Custer had first met him when Ingalls was McClellan's quarter-master in the Army of the Potomac.

"Armstrong," he said quietly, "do you want to make some money?"

"What do I have to steal?" Custer asked pleasantly.

"Nothing. I've just today been informed that there's going to be some rather strenuous activity in various railroad stocks. The Baltimore & Ohio, the Chesapeake & Ohio, and your own Northern Pacific are some of the companies whose stocks are going to go higher than a kite."

"Where'd you get this information, General?"

Ingalls gave him his best poker smile. "I can't divulge my source."

"Why are you sharing such valuable information with me?"

"Because I heard you can use the money. Oh, don't worry, there'll be plenty to go around. This railroad thing is going to be *very* big!"

Custer felt a rush of excitement. He'd known all along that "Custer's Luck" would take care of him along the money line. "How do I get into it?"

Ingalls handed him a calling card. "Contact Emil Justh. He's a broker on Wall Street."

"I don't have much cash."

"Your name will be sufficient."

All Custer could say was, "Hmmm."

"There's also a railroad you helped tear up during the war—the Danville and something—you might buy some of that stock." Ingalls laughed. "Wouldn't that be a twist if you made a bunch of money on an enemy railroad?"

"So what's your surprise, Nomad?"

Custer sat up on the edge of the bed, still stark naked and sweaty from their zestful lovemaking.

"Railroads. Rufus Ingalls let me in on some railroad stock information that can finally make us as rich as we want to be. He told me which ones to invest in, and how to go about it."

Libbie pulled the sheet over her and sat up against the headboard. "But we haven't got any money, sweetheart. Remember?"

"Ingalls said I could do it on the cuff."

"And you believe him?"

"Why would he lie?"

"I don't trust him."

"But why would he lie about that?"

Libbie pursed her lips, frowning. "Maybe he and that thief, Ben Holladay, want you to do something that will put you in their debt. Remember, they want your help on those sutlerships."

"I know, but they wouldn't do anything that devious. They'd just come out and offer me some money. No, I think this railroad stock thing is real. After we make a lot of money, they may think we owe them, but that doesn't mean I'm going to give them any information." He got up and walked to the window. Looking down at Fifth Avenue through the lace curtains, he nodded his head and said, "Yes, Custer's Luck is back."

The next day, Custer went down to Wall Street and found the address on the card General Ingalls had given him. Climbing the steps to a third floor office, he entered and identified himself to the receptionist. She stared at him open-mouthed for a moment before hurrying into an inner office. Moments later a thin little man with red muttonchop whiskers came out, saying, "Why, General Custer! What a fine thing. I've always admired you. Fact is, I was in your Michigan brigade, Sixth Cavalry, yessir, I was! You wouldn't believe this, sir, but I was a bugler. Still have a good lip. I play the trumpet in a pretty good brass band now. You know, one of those small bands that plays for holidays and in parades and such. Name's Justh, Emil Justh."

Custer shook his hand, and told him that Ingalls had sent him.

"Yessir, General Custer. How can I help you?"

"General Ingalls told me there were some excellent possibilities in some speculative railroad stocks. Particularly in the Virginia Central."

Emil Justh grinned broadly. "You know I helped tear up some of that track, General. You did too. In fact, you were the brigade commander when Sheridan sent us after Trevilian Station. Remember? What poetic justice, sir!"

Did he remember Trevilian? Huh! He'd gotten caught between Fitzhugh Lee's division and one of Wade Hampton's brigades. Had to circle his men just like in the old Indian fighting days. Close call. Vivid memories. He brought himself back to the present. "Yes, well, I'd like to diversify a bit too. Include a little of the B&O, and the Northern Pacific—mostly the latter. I know some of those people out in Dakota Territory."

"Yessir, General. Why don't you let me draw up a plan for you? How much would you like to invest?"

Custer stroked his bulky red mustache. "Well, Mr. Justh, the fact is, I'm a little short of cash right now. General Ingalls seemed to think I might be able to buy some of the stock on my good name, and pay later."

The broker nodded. "Yes, I believe a token sum down, say fifty dollars, would enable me to lay away quite a large amount of stock in your name. Why don't I work on it and see how much you can buy?"

"That would be first rate, Mr. Justh."

Custer simply couldn't believe it was so easy. Far better than that Colorado mine deal. He'd make a real killing on this one!

Custer could remember vividly when he met the actor Lawrence Barrett. It had been in St. Louis when he was on his way to the Plains to assume the lieutenant colonelcy of the Seventh in 1866.

He and Libbie had gone to see the play *Rosedale*, in which Barrett was the star. Impressed, he had gone backstage after the performance to meet the actor. Barrett had recognized him immediately, greeting him warmly, telling him of the admiration he held for his military exploits. He'd invited the young actor—Barrett was just two years older—back to the hotel to meet Libbie. It was the beginning of a remarkable friendship.

In fact, their friendship became so stimulating that they could spend hours together, lost in the give and take of their wide-ranging conversations. They came to love each other as no two brothers had ever loved. Apart, they wrote long letters to each other; together, they often walked down the street arm-in-arm. At one time, Libbie had said, "Autie Custer, if you weren't such a wonderful lover, I'd say there was something tainted in your relationship with that darned actor! Sometimes it doesn't *look* right!" But he'd come right back with, "If he were as pretty as you, I might marry him. But, alas, I'm stuck with the fair Standby forever and ever."

It seemed that Lawrence Barrett had been put on this earth to fill a gaping void in George Armstrong Custer's life—the theater. To some, it was inconceivable that a strong leader of men, a general who relished combat and was totally unafraid in battle, could giggle watching comedies, and sob without shame in the middle of the performance of a tragedy or a moving melodrama. And here was a man who could not only portray all of these roles so movingly, but one who would *discuss* their components and their achievement with both passion and detachment, a professional who was willing to share his innermost feelings about his craft and the works of the theater. And on *his* side, Barrett marveled at Custer's romantic role as a flamboyant army officer, and vicariously lived out his desire for the adventurous life through his friend. No wonder the two men grew to love each other—their enjoyment struck the upper limits of mutual admiration.

Lawrence Barrett grew up in Michigan, giving him another connection to Custer. In 1853, at age fifteen, he started playing small parts in a Detroit theater. He first appeared on the New York stage in 1857, as Sir Thomas Clifford in *The Hunchback,* before going on to successful performances in several of the other popular productions of the time. While appearing at the Winter Garden, he met the illustrious Edwin Booth, America's leading actor and the older brother of a fiery young thespian named John Wilkes Booth. Married in '59, Barrett served as a captain, the commander of B Company, Twenty-eighth Massachusetts during the war. Afterward, he became internationally famous as an actor and took over the management of Booth's theater in New York.

Now, as Custer watched from the wings, Barrett was into his finale. The actor was once more playing the role for which he had become most noted, Cassius in *Julius Caesar.* Custer and Libbie came often, because Custer so loved the production, and because they got in free. They were skimping by, making their limited funds stretch, while trying to appear in comfortable straits. Privately, Custer worried that people would notice how he had to wear the same suits so often. But the condition was only temporary. As soon as the railroad profits started rolling in, they'd be swimming in money.

Tonight, Libbie had stayed back in their hotel rooms because of a headache. But Custer was enjoying the performance as much as ever. He took a step forward to better hear Cassius's final words in Act V, Scene III, as Pindarus descended from the hill:

> Come down, behold no more—
> O, coward that I am, to live so long,

To see my best friend ta'en before my face!
Come hither, sirrah:
In Parthia did I take thee prisoner;
And then I swore thee, saving of thy life,
That whatsoever I did bid thee do,
Thou shouldst attempt it. Come now, keep thine oath;
Now be a freeman; and, with this good sword,
That ran through Caesar's bowels, search this bosom.
Stand not to answer; here, take thou the hilts;
And, when my face is cover'd, as 'tis now,
Guide thou the sword.—Caesar, thou art revenged,
Even with the sword that kill'd thee.

As Cassius collapsed and died, a tear slipped from Custer's eye and ran, unheeded, down his cheek. He felt nearly overcome by the sadness, watching in pain for the remaining scenes. He could watch that scene a thousand times and never become immune to its powerful tug on his emotions.

As the play came to an end, Custer watched through still-brimming eyes and applauded loudly as the actors took their bows. When the applause died, Barrett, a man of about Custer's size, strode smiling into the wings and accepted Custer's hearty handshake. "Well done, again, old sot!" Custer said enthusiastically.

Barrett heaved a sigh. "You know, Armstrong, the joy I get from playing this role never wears off. The others come and go but Cassius lives at the peak of my joy on the stage."

Custer patted his arm. "That's because you are superb in the role, probably the best ever."

Barrett shrugged. "That's high praise when you consider how many actors have performed the part."

An hour later, the actor's wife, Mary, an attractive woman in her early thirties, served them coffee and oatmeal cookies in the parlor of Barrett's apartment on Fifty-eighth Street. She told Barrett about the antics of the most trying of their three daughters earlier in the day. Custer and Libbie both liked Mary, and when Barrett didn't have to be at the theater, the four often went on excursions, visiting sights, going over to Long Island or up into the country when the weather permitted. Currently, the winter cold was penetrating, and everyone in the city was bundled up. Custer's mind wandered to the memory of the Hansom cabs he'd seen earlier that day. The white plumes of vapor from the animals' nostrils reminded him of the brutal Washita campaign—and the possibility that the regiment's horses might suffer again if Sheridan went ahead with his winter campaign. He wondered how the plans were proceeding—

"Armstrong—"

"Yes, my friend." He jerked back to the present.

"I found a poem for you today."

Custer grinned. "You're always doing something for me."

Barrett went to a small desk just off the parlor and withdrew a sheet of paper. He read it aloud in his deepest stage voice:

> The fair general bold,
> With his knights awaiting,
> Called forth his legion
> As in days of old,
> And when these brave men
> Answered the general's muster
> The world once more
> Sang the name of Custer.

Custer and Mary applauded enthusiastically. "And, pray tell, noble thespian, who wrote that?" Custer asked.

"Fellow named Elwayne," Barrett replied.

"Is that a stage name?"

"Possibly."

"For Lawrence perhaps?"

"No, the bard shall go nameless, but the fair general will gain his fame."

Custer threw his head back and laughed heartily. Where else could a man find such a bright and inventive friend? Taking the sheet of paper and folding it, he said, "Libbie will love this."

☆ ☆ ☆

The following day at noon, Barrett and Custer went to Albert Bierstadt's studio. During the short walk from the horse trolley stop, Barrett explained that the famous artist was somewhat of an enigma in the art world. "He's surrounded by controversy. The public and the newspapers love him, but the critics turn up their noses at his commercial bent."

"But isn't he America's foremost Western landscape artist?" Custer asked.

"I'm sure he is, and along with Frederick Church, probably the most celebrated artist in America. It's just that some people think he goes too far in promoting his works."

"Money is money," Custer replied. He ought to know; he'd been seeking it all his life. But those days were just about over.

Bierstadt opened the door personally. Greeting his visitors warmly, he invited them to remove their coats and offered them some hot wine. Custer glanced around at the loft studio, which had plenty of light from the large windows of the huge room's northern wall. But since it was a rather dreary, cloudy day, a number of kerosene lamps supplemented the natural light. Various paintings, most of them quite large and unfinished, added a rich warmth as they stared back from their easels or where they hung on walls like curious pets. Robust fires in the two fireplaces took most of the chill out of the room. The smell of oil paint and turpentine mixed with the pleasant odor of the burning wood, but to the impressionable Custer it was all part of the excitement.

Albert Bierstadt was born in Germany in 1830, but his family had moved to America when he was two years old. Later, he returned to Europe for schooling. Fresh from a program of study in Dusseldorf, and fascinated by the marvels of Western scenery and its Indians, Bierstadt had gone there in 1859 to sketch and study. He followed the trip with intensive work that produced a series of canvases he referred to as "grand paintings" of the Rocky Mountains that caught the public's imagination and vaulted him to fame. He made two more trips to the West, in 1863 and 1871, when he spent two years in California. Highly prolific, Bierstadt created rich canvases that won him an enthusiastic following.

A lovely young woman appeared from behind a screen that apparently disguised a galley, and served them cups of a sharp, hot, red wine from a silver tray. Custer gazed appreciatively at her as she tossed him a smile.

"My model," Bierstadt explained with a smile.

As the woman walked away, Barrett nodded. "One of the advantages of being a painter, Armstrong—particularly when an artist seldom does life painting."

They all chuckled as Bierstadt started a tour of his work. "I've published hand-colored engravings and chromolithographs of much of my work," he explained. "This gets it to the public in a much less expensive package."

"And has also made you the target of criticism, Albert."

Bierstadt shrugged. "Ah, yes, the old commercialism charge. Well, I'm not the only great painter to sell copies of his work. How many individuals can afford a twenty-five thousand dollar painting?"

The eyebrows of both of the visitors went up briefly. "You get *that* much, Albert?" Barrett asked.

"Usually," the painter replied with another shrug.

"I could run the theater for a *year* on that much," Barrett sighed.

"And I could feed my regiment for six months," Custer added. He felt comfortable with this forty-five-year-old painter—a rarity, since he was often shy with strangers, in spite of his usual flamboyance with people he knew.

"Ah, but I have expenses," Bierstadt said. He showed them reproductions of *Mount Hood, Oregon,* which he painted in 1865; *The Domes of Yosemite,* which he painted in 1867; *The Redwood Trees,* an 1865 effort; and *Sioux Village,* an 1859 painting. Custer looked at the last thoughtfully. "Were you in this village?" he asked.

"No, but I made a sketch from information I received from several Sioux. Do you see anything wrong, General? I know you've been in at least one."

Custer nodded his head. "Yes, but when one is attacking, one doesn't pay a great deal of attention. I think you've got it right essentially."

"Your approval pleases me, General."

Custer nodded his head again. And if all went well, he thought, he'd be in some more Sioux villages before this coming year was over.

The next painting was the one the artist had recently finished. It was titled *Spearing Fish by Torchlight, Lake Tahoe.* Custer and Barrett both expressed delight with the huge canvas. "You've outdone yourself here, Albert," Barrett said.

When they finished discussing the latest "grand painting," the model came in with their lunch of smoked salmon on a huge tray. Custer again admired her shapely bosom as she bent over to serve them, and made the comment, "I'm ready to begin painting lessons at once." The others laughed heartily and pitched into the food.

During his second helping of the delicious salmon, Custer said, "You know, Mr. Bierstadt, this is sort of a fateful meeting for us. As I look at your magnificent paintings of our great Rocky Mountains, I can't help but think that your work represents America's *manifest destiny* in its aesthetic, and its spiritual approach. We are somewhat akin; you paint it, I fight for it. You bring its majesty to their eyes, my Seventh Cavalry is extending the horizons of our nation's destiny."

Bierstadt smiled, pleased. "By golly, General, I think you're right! What an interesting concept. I've always said the Rockies are the new Alps. We *are*, in our different pursuits, helping to make it all available to the world." He nodded. "Yes, I fully agree. What a capital thought."

Near the end of the lively meal, Custer said, "I like your *The Last of the Buffalo*, Mr. Bierstadt. Have you ever painted any cavalrymen?"

"I've sketched a few, but never painted them."

"If all goes well, I'll be coming into some money in the near future. Why don't you think about visiting me in Dakota in the late summer, and planning a big 'grand painting' of some of my cavalrymen?"

Bierstadt sipped from the excellent wine and said, "I think that's a capital idea, General. Perhaps I could place you, on your favorite charger, in the center—with some of your best officers around you. Yes, I like that idea!"

"Done!" Custer replied enthusiastically. "I think you can count on coming out around mid-August or early September. We should be well back from our campaign then."

Libbie reread the letter she'd just finished writing to Annie Yates:

> *My Dear Annie,*
> *Your letter announcing the birth of your bouncing boy, Milner, arrived here at the hotel yesterday. Congratulations, my dear. I'm sorry the delivery was*

so difficult, but I'm glad Old Nash was on hand to help. That old Mexican laundress/midwife is such a fixture with the regiment that they ought to make her a sergeant major! We're having an Indian summer here in Manhattan, with near balmy breezes and warm sun. Of course, Old Man Winter will be right back. It's never quite as cold as those Dakota Plains though. Autie is being treated quite royally here (actually I am too.) The leading Democrats are courting us as if we were politicians (Heaven forbid!). I think Democrats are handsomer on the whole than Republicans, at least more romantic. In fact, I'm enjoying myself immensely. Autie has been steered (I hope that's the right word) to a promising stock investment, and soon we hope to have a barrel of money!

Oh, Annie, I wish you were here as well. We could have a delightful time in the afternoons, shopping and taking in the sights and events. The newspapers are full of things to do. We mostly read the Herald because that's where Autie sends many of his articles. I don't want to "name-drop," but its publisher, James Gordon Bennett, Jr., took us out to dinner the other night at Delmonico's—a lovely restaurant.

I read a beautiful poem in the Times newspaper yesterday. It's titled "Lavender" and it is almost as if it were written for army wives, because it's about the death of loved ones. I want to share some of it with you, dear Annie. It says, after a couple of opening stanzas:

We gather what is left . . .
The books they loved, the songs they sang,
The little flute whose music rang
So cheerily of old:
The pictures we have watched them paint,
The last plucked flower, with odor faint,
That fell from fingers cold.

We smooth and fold with reverent care
The robes they, living, used to wear;
And painful pulses stir,
As o'er the relics of our dead,
With bitter rain of tears, we spread
Pale purple lavender. . . .

And then it goes on, for several more verses, Annie, so sad and beautiful. I cried when I first read it. It doesn't have an author. It must have been written by a widow in the big war. I hope it doesn't ever pertain to us. But how could it? Aren't we the merry wives of the Seventh?

Get strong, my dear friend, so your handsome husband can take you back east on a long vacation next year. Autie said for sure he could let the commander of the proud Band Box Troop get away after the coming campaign. All my love,
Libbie

Libbie sealed the envelope, put a stamp on it, and pinned on her hat. She and Mary Barrett were off to Governor's Island by ferryboat shortly. One place they were going to see was the set of old army quarters where General—then Captain—Robert E. Lee lived all those years while he was constructing harbor defenses for New York before the Mexican War. She'd heard that he'd fallen in love with his wife's young niece while residing there, and that their love had lasted as long as he was alive. Markie, her name was. How spicy. *Imagine* that fine old gentleman! But then, she'd always thought he was the most romantic general in the war—next to her Autie and Phil Sheridan, of course.

The Custers' absorbed New York. With the fervor of two enthusiasts visiting from the wilderness they tasted many other sights. These included the still unfinished St. Patrick's Cathedral, which had been under construction for seventeen years, and the Central Park Zoo, which had opened its doors in 1872. Libbie most enjoyed going to Bloomingdale's, the fashionable store at Third Avenue and Fifty-sixth Street. Well north of the popular shopping district on Broadway between Twenty-third Street and Union Square, the four-year-old store was the most popular in the city. Custer liked to browse in Brentano's Literary Emporium. Located on Union Square at Sixteenth Street, the former newsstand was the favorite bookseller in town. Another new bookstore that had opened three years earlier, a wonderland to both Libbie and Autie, was Barnes & Noble. On that day while buying a special edition of Burns for his brother Tom, he ran into the great actor Edwin Booth.

"Aren't you General Custer?" Booth asked in his marvelously deep voice.

"Yes, sir," Custer replied, delighted to meet such a theater luminary. The fact that the actor was the older brother of the man who killed Abraham Lincoln was far overshadowed by his wide fame. They chatted briefly, Booth recommended a new book, and they parted as quickly as they'd met. Custer was most pleased that America's leading thespian had recognized him!

Of course, both Custers enjoyed visits to the Metropolitan Museum of Art on Fifth Avenue between Eightieth and Eighty-first Streets. Opened in 1871, the red brick, neo-gothic edifice held not only a fine collection but interesting exhibitions. On one of their visits, Custer tried his hand at sketching a wonderful painting of Washington crossing the Delaware.

But Custer had other things on his mind.

As the month of December flew by, Custer became more and more enamored of his railroad stock enterprise. He spent several hours a day reading the various newspapers and sitting in his stockbroker's office. The buying and selling of the varied stocks by the middle of January had been frenzied. All told, the transactions with Emil Justh totaled $189,983!

And then the bubble broke. Railroad stocks dropped in value like girls of the evening with the pox. One day, behind the closed door to his private office, Justh said, "General, as sad as this makes me, I must put an end to your investing at this firm."

Custer stared at the small thin man with the red muttonchop sideburns. "You must be jesting, sir. What's wrong?"

"The railroads haven't been doing as well as we anticipated. To continue as you've been investing would be sheer folly, sir—both for you and for me. I'm close to being in financial difficulty as it stands right now."

Custer still couldn't believe what he was hearing.

Justh handed a sheet of paper across his desk. "I've worked it down as liberally as possible and the very best I can do is this."

Custer stared at the paper and the numbers blurred, then shouted back. He owed $8,578!

All of that money he was going to make! The long-awaited escape from money worries! No! It couldn't be gone. Why only yesterday he had considered buying a house, just to reside in during his New York visits. Libbie, my God, Libbie was never supposed to make her own clothes again. . . .

He continued to stare at the blinking numbers.

$8,578!

He didn't have eight *hundred* and seventy-eight dollars!

"Sir," he said quietly, "I can't possibly pay this at this time. I told you I was short of cash when we went into this business."

"I know, but you went too far. Had the stocks increased as everyone thought, you would have been a rich man." Justh shrugged, "It didn't work out."

"I can't pay you, Justh."

"I've anticipated that problem, General. If you can find a good co-signer, someone with enough money to cover the sum, perhaps we can work it out."

"But there isn't anyone I can ask."

The broker shook his head. "You know many rich men."

Back at the hotel, Libbie listened white-faced as he told her about their predicament. When he finished and slumped down in a straight chair, she gathered herself, went to him and put her arm around his shoulder. "It's all right, Darling," she said softly, kissing the top of his head. "I *enjoy* making my own dresses. That way, no one else will have anything like them."

He looked up and found a brief smile. His wonderful Libbie.

"Besides, you know what a trendsetter I am, what with all of my military touches."

"We won't even be able to afford thread."

"Oh, I have *plenty* of thread."

A tear slipped down his cheek. "It seems as if every time I turn around, I fail you."

She brushed the tear away. "No you don't, General Custer. You've brought this little Michigan girl more joy and more fame than she could ever dream of. Do you know that I am one of the most famous and envied women in America? That's right. There are over a million women in this country who wish they were in my shoes, so what's a little old eight thousand dollars? We'll find it. Custer's Luck, remember?"

He pulled her to his lap and took her in his arms, holding her tight for a moment. Then he sighed and put her down. "Yes, Custer's Luck. I hope it hasn't deserted me."

16

Sitting Bull and Gall had their Hunkpapa winter camp on the Yellowstone at the mouth of the Powder River in a small valley where they had once before weathered the cold for those months when most animals hibernate in one way or another. The valley had steep sides that could imprison but also shelter them to some extent from the icy blasts of wind that could descend on that country like the fierce breath of the Arctic. And since enemy tribes spent the winter months in the same manner, little danger was expected from that quarter. Long Hair's assault against the Cheyenne on the Washita indicated that the Long Knives *could* attack in the snow, but that had been many winters ago. Besides, there was no indication of anger or war from them, so defeating the cold was the major campaign of the season. At the present, however, a mild period was giving the inhabitants of the village a respite. The few inches of snow had been whittled down to traces that haunted trees, bushes, and the back side of anything else that provided shade against the long, bright rays of the sun. The ground was wet, but that was a small price to pay.

Red Elk had stayed with Crazy Horse and his Oglalas for nearly two moons, and now, in the Tree Popping Moon (so named because the severe cold sometimes caused trees to burst with loud cracks), he was growing bored and impatient. With everyone holed up like timid rabbits, he couldn't raid, could barely even hunt—although today he was returning with a fox that had grown too bold. Of course, the big bullet from the Sharps had blown most of one whole shoulder away. He should've gotten closer and used an arrow, but he wanted to shoot *something* with his wonderful gun.

He'd learned much from hunting with Crazy Horse, and the great warrior had even spoken of fighting a few times. Mostly, in camp, the war leader just kept his thoughts to himself. In fact, he was the quietest man Red Elk had ever met. He had fired the Sharps, and had grunted satisfaction with it. But he preferred the power of close-in fighting with the great coup tools, the battle-ax and the lance. He wanted to *feel* his victories. Red Elk felt the same way, but he didn't want to wait years to acquire great recognition. He wanted it *now*, and he was sure the Sharps could give him fame quickly.

But until winter passed he had to bide his time, and he intensely disliked doing so.

The other problem in his life was still Late Star.

He simply couldn't get that witch out of his head. He had shown *her*, though. He had ignored her completely since his return to the village, had absolutely let her know that he wasn't to be trifled with like some little boy. But, just as he had grown two fingers taller since summer, she had grown more beautiful. On the couple of occasions when they had met more or less accidentally, her dark eyes had danced and she had flashed him smiles that revealed her bright teeth. He thought she had the whitest teeth he'd ever seen.

The one thing that troubled him the most and which he could barely put aside, was that she was being courted by several young men. None of them were his equal and he didn't know why she accepted their attentions. Surely, she'd never marry one of them. One the other hand, one never knew. . . .

It had happened to Crazy Horse.

An Oglala warrior had told him the story. . . .

At the age of some twenty-one summers, Crazy Horse had fallen in love with an Oglala girl named Black Buffalo Woman, a beautiful niece of the great Chief Red Cloud. And even though Crazy Horse was one of the Oglala's most important war leaders, he was still of a lesser family and had to take his turn in the line of suitors. Then in the summer of the Year of Few Trees, Crazy Horse had joined a huge war party under Red Cloud to go after the Crows. The mission lasted two weeks. When he returned a *winkte*—a homosexual—named Woman's Dress rode out to whisper to him that Black Buffalo Woman had married a "good family" warrior named No Water. Crazy Horse was dumbfounded, then stricken, but there was nothing he could do about it.

Time passed and Black Buffalo Woman had three children by No Water. During that period Crazy Horse became the youngest Shirt Wearer in the history of his tribe. As a ruling executive, a Shirt Wearer was responsible for deciding matters of tribal concern, such as providing good campgrounds and successful hunting. They were the supreme counselors whose primary obligation was the welfare of the people. At their investure, they were presented with a shirt fringed with hairlocks, the colors generally based on those of the supernatural Controllers, the Sky, the Rock, the Sun, and the Earth—blue, yellow, red, and green. The Shirt Wearers were sometimes referred to as the owners of the tribe. There were four of them in the Oglala. For the son of a shaman, even with the great war achievements of the young Crazy Horse, it was extremely rare to attain this position.

But in spite of his exalted place in the tribe, Crazy Horse still longed for Black Buffalo Woman. They spoke often and were seen together, and the gossips' tongues wagged. Since divorce was so easy—a woman could go away with another man, or she could toss her husband's belongings out of her tipi—everyone expected something to happen. It was also custom that if a Lakota woman left her husband for another man, the husband would accept some ponies from the new husband, and prove himself a strong man by shrugging off his loss as something below his dignity to challenge. But No Water was a jealous man. And a Shirt Wearer shouldered a heavy responsibility to maintain peace within the tribe, to not create trouble.

Nevertheless, Black Buffalo Woman and the light-haired Crazy Horse finally eloped in the fall of the year of Buffalo Ceremony Failed, or the white man's year of 1871. When No Water finally found them in the tipi of a friend of Crazy Horse's, he fired a pistol at the famed war leader, hitting him a glancing shot in the left jaw, which left a nasty scar. This caused trouble in the tribe and Crazy Horse was forced to give up his position as a Shirt Wearer. Eventually, Black Buffalo Woman went back to No Water and a few months later gave birth to a light-haired, light-skinned daughter.

The man's story ended with the statement, "And so Crazy Horse finally married an older woman of twenty-eight summers named Black Shawl, who presented him a daughter a year later. But all of the Lakota know that he will never lose his love for Black Buffalo Woman."

Red Elk had heard bits of the story before—every Lakota had. And now he faced part of the same dilemma. Regardless of what he told himself, he couldn't shake off the fact that he loved Late Star. He simply couldn't get her out of his head! And, even if she was treating him badly, he knew deep down that he still wanted her for his wife. But it was just like what happened to Crazy Horse—he had to court her, along with all the other suitors, because she came from an important family and he didn't. Or he could continue to ignore her and hope she would see what an important war leader he'd soon become.

She did have *eyes*, didn't she?

He was taking advantage of the warm spell to brush the long winter coat of his warhorse Lightning when she spoke from close behind him. "What does a pretty horse do that an ugly horse can't?"

He turned his head, continuing to brush. "A horse knows."

"What do you mean?"

"A horse knows when he looks good, and that pride makes him fight better."

She shook her head. "I don't think so."

He shrugged. "Why do we always paint them and tie things to their tail and mane before going into battle? You think you know so much, why has the custom gone on since the beginning?"

"To please the warriors."

"No, it's medicine. It gives the horse powerful medicine that joins the warrior's medicine to make him invincible. But how can you understand that? You're just a girl."

She laughed, showing those lovely teeth. "No, I'm just a *woman!* Or has your little bit of success as a warrior made you blind?"

"My *little* bit of success?" he sputtered. "I am the best warrior of my age in all of the Lakota!"

"Oh!" She laughed again and turned away. He watched her walk. She wasn't wearing a robe on this warm day, and her dress seemed to fit tightly, accentuating her shapely buttocks. In spite of his resentment, he thought about how much he would like to stroke them—under a robe . . . bare.

The witch!

☆ ☆ ☆

Red Cloud, the powerful Oglala chief, and Spotted Tail, the polished leader of the Brules, had spent five years slowly picking the government's pocket as Grant's minions tried to set up a lasting peace and get the respective bands of these two powerful leaders away from the unceded territory and onto the reservation where they would be harmless. Now, having won various concessions, their followers were residing on agencies named for the two chiefs. The sites were close to each other on the upper reaches of the White River in the northwestern corner of Nebraska and well away from the territory where the non-agency bands roamed. Runners from the Red Cloud Agency had been dispatched in early December to deliver the government's message to all of the roamer band chiefs, including the Cheyenne, who were camping with the Sioux. It was the ultimatum in which the roamers were to report to the agencies by January 31 or suffer the consequences that President Grant had approved back in early November. And it was a difficult task, because the agency messengers had to first *find* the roamer bands of all seven tribes of the Lakota.

The courier who reached the valley where Sitting Bull's Hunkpapas were settled down for the winter was named Little Cat. He was an Oglala of thirty summers who had once joined Gall on a raid under Red Cloud when he was a young warrior. Gall brought him to Sitting Bull's tipi the day the cold weather moved back into their valley on the Yellowstone.

Sitting cross-legged around the fire inside the tipi, the three men, accompanied by Running Antelope and another Big Belly, listened as the Red Cloud man delivered his message: "All bands of Sioux and other non-agency Indians must report to their respective or nearest agency headquarters by the end of the Tree Popping Moon or they will be considered hostile and the Long Knives will come after them. They call it 'turning it over to the War Department.'"

Gall laughed aloud. "Is that all?"

Little Cat shrugged. "That is what they told me. There was more white man's talk, but I decided not to bother with it."

Running Antelope shook his head. "All talk. Nothing new."

The other Big Belly agreed. Sitting Bull cleared his throat and after a few moments said, "I don't know what the White Father means. So, Little

Cat, you go back to those agency loafers and those white chiefs and you tell them this—once before I said, 'Look at me—see if I am poor, or my people. You are fools to make yourselves slaves to a piece of fat bacon, some hard-tack, and a little sugar and coffee.' Nothing has changed. Here, we can hunt any place and when we wish. My people are free. And here we stay."

Gall nodded in agreement. "It's the same as always. They talk, they do nothing. There is no war for us except with the Crows."

"But, Great Chief," Little Cat replied, "I may not get back to the agency before they send the Long Knives."

Sitting Bull shook his head. "They won't send the Long Knives that soon."

"No," Gall added, "I hear from *Lin-cun* that Long Hair is far away in the big village with the tall tipis, and his Long Knives drink and fight among themselves. They have no interest in the Lakota or our friends."

After more discussion and the smoking of Sitting Bull's polished pipe, Little Cat said, "I was told specifically to find Crazy Horse and the rest of the Oglala. Do you know where they are camped?"

Gall looked at Sitting Bull. "Red Elk knows."

"Good," the chief replied. "Send him as guide."

Little Cat grunted thanks.

Red Elk stomped his feet in the cold air outside Running Antelope's tipi. A young warrior by the name of Dog Bull was paying a visit to Late Star, and he had to wait his turn. The moon had been up for nearly two hours and the air was getting brittle. He could see his angry breath in the silver light, and all it did was make him more impatient. He ought to take Dog Bull up on the ridge and shake his teeth out. *The intruder!*

Finally, the tipi flap lifted and the young warrior came out. He gave Red Elk a cool look and moved off. And even though Late Star knew he was there, Red Elk had to keep waiting. He was just about to depart when the flap lifted and she stepped out into the moonlight. She smiled as she pointed to the extra buffalo robe he had brought along. "Do you wish to come inside?"

In courting, since the participants were never supposed to be alone together, they normally sat under a robe in front of the girl's tipi to talk. When it was too cold to do so, they sat inside and covered themselves. "No," he replied, "I'm not a *boy*. But I wish to show my respect to you and your father, so I brought the robe. It's large and warm. May we sit here on this by your tipi entrance? I don't intend to stay long."

She smiled again. "Yes, I believe so, if you do not attack me."

"What if I do?" He smiled back, enjoying the banter.

"Then I'll cry out and my father will come out and kill you."

"Ha! He wouldn't kill me."

They both sat cross-legged on part of his robe as he covered them with the rest. Except for a bit of moonlight that crept in from one side, it was quite dark under the robe. He could smell her scent as he touched her, and it excited him.

"So what is it you wish to say to me?" she asked. "Are you really courting me?"

He had been rehearsing his speech all day. "Yes, I'm courting you. I don't know why, because you are a very difficult girl, but for some strange reason, I think I want you to be my wife."

She pursed her lips. "I see. But you know that courting means you are supposed to entertain me, and tell me things about yourself."

"I haven't got time for that. I leave at daybreak with Little Cat to take him to Crazy Horse."

"What has that to do with me?"

"If you loved me, it would make you proud that I am entrusted with such an important mission."

"And what makes you think I love you?"

"You kissed me last summer."

She giggled. "Oh, *that*. It was a nice night, and I liked the way you danced. It was a reward."

"A reward?"

"Yes, for being a good dancer."

"What about my successful raid—being a war leader?"

She paused. "Oh, that too, I guess."

He shook his head. A bit of light from the moonlight revealed her white teeth as she spoke. He took her hand in his. "So, now I've told you I wish for you to be my wife."

"So?"

"So, what do you say?"

She leaned over and kissed him on the nose, then quickly pushed the robe away from her head. As he, too, came out from under it, she said, "I think the next time you come courting, you should tell me about what you will do for me, about your ponies, and about what you will pay my father."

"Well, I can do that right now."

"No, that isn't courting. Next time."

He frowned. "But I have to go away, and besides—"

She interrupted. "The *next* time, my impatient one. And that will be one of many visits under the robe." She smiled and moved to the tipi flap. Lifting it, she looked back. "Have a good trip, impatient one."

Before he could say anything else, she had ducked inside and dropped the flap.

He stared angrily. *Impatient one! I'll show her—I'll never bring a robe to her tipi again, never!* And if she didn't like it, he'd take another girl for his wife!

Crazy Horse and the thirty-six Oglala lodges with him were camped in another valley some forty miles away, near where the Tongue hit the Yellowstone. Adjoining his camp were eighty-three lodges of Northern Cheyenne. This particular winter, quite a few of the Oglala had joined their relatives at the Red Cloud Agency, including No Water and Black Buffalo Woman.

No Water's brother, a Shirt Wearer named Black Twin, had remained friendly with Crazy Horse following the shooting and had remained with the war leader. The band was known as "Crazy Horse People" by the other Oglalas. Effectively, the nearby Cheyennes, under Chief Old Bear, were under his control as well. Warrior strength was estimated roughly at two fighting men per lodge, so the combined village had about two hundred forty of them. But, just as it was in the Hunkpapa camp, winter survival was nearly all that was going on when Little Cat arrived with Red Elk.

Crazy Horse, Black Twin, Old Bear, and He Dog met in the central council tent to hear him out shortly after the courier's arrival. Red Elk, even though he had no leadership role, was invited to sit in as a

Hunkpapa emissary. Old Bear insisted that they smoke the pipe first, and he pulled out his Cheyenne pipe. Black Twin unwrapped his ornate replica of the Sacred Calf Pipe and they were both lit and passed around the small group. It was the only time in nearly two years that Crazy Horse had agreed to sit in council. He smoked and listened quietly while Little Cat delivered the Great White Father's edict. When he was finished, the war leader asked, "What is meant by 'the matter will be turned over to the War Department?'"

"The Long Knives," Little Cat replied.

"And they will fight us?"

"That's what I was told."

Crazy Horse grunted. "It's the *Paha Sopa*."

"What do you mean?" Black Twin asked.

"The Whites want the *Paha Sopa*, and because the Big Bellies can't agree on what to demand from them in return, the Whites are doing this."

"Sitting Bull says the Long Knives aren't going to fight. Long Hair is away," Little Cat said.

"There are others," Crazy Horse said, "up north, and Three Stars is down south."

Three Stars was Brigadier General George Crook. "I think the Long Knives will come. I'll keep my wolves awake."

The wolves were his scouts.

"I agree with Sitting Bull," Old Bear said. "There will be no war with the Long Knives."

Crazy Horse just looked at the Cheyenne and said nothing.

Little Cat shrugged. He was doing his job; if these leaders didn't want to comply, it wasn't his business. "What shall I tell the Whites when I return?"

Crazy Horse's eyes narrowed as he replied coldly, "Tell them Crazy Horse will *never* bring his people into their stinking agencies to live like slaves."

17

Major Marcus Albert Reno had returned from his extended European leave in late November. Already a bit overweight, he had added a few pounds by eating too many rich foods and drinking a great deal of wine in both Paris and Berlin. He had felt he had a license to have a good time, since he had departed for the continent on the first anniversary of his wife's death. Mary Hannah Ross had been her maiden name. They had been married in Harrisburg in the fall following the Battle of Gettysburg. Hannah had come from one of the socially prominent and well-to-do Harrisburg families, and they had been blessed with a mostly pleasant marriage. Their now eleven-year-old son, Robert, had been conceived practically at the altar.

Mary Hannah's death had been difficult for him to accept. He had been in the field, and was denied leave to go to her funeral—an omission that didn't sit well with her non-military family. They had been married eleven years—not always the best of times, but she had been a good woman who had accepted his problems. Now he knew how much she meant to him. After the funeral, he'd decided his son, Robert, would be better off with his wife's relatives, thinking a woman's influence was necessary for a growing boy.

He glanced down at the boyish scrawl on the letter he'd just received from him. His son wrote about heavy snow back in Pennsylvania, and a good time for sledding. He'd given the boy a nice new sled for Christmas, but there hadn't been any snow while he was there. He had taken Robert along on the trip to Europe, even though it meant pulling the boy out of school. He'd felt that education derived from travel was more valuable. He sighed as he thought about his son; they'd had a warm enough day to go fishing on the Susquehanna before he left, but that was the only time they'd had to themselves.

Marc Reno shook his head as he reread Robert's words. He'd bring the boy back one of these days. In the meantime, it was pleasant being in command of the regiment in Custer's absence. So far, nothing of significance had gone wrong. But the extra ammunition had never arrived, so there had been very little firing of individual weapons. He didn't like that. New recruits—and the Seventh Cavalry had its share of them—should learn how to shoot.

He pulled out his pocket watch and looked at it. Two minutes after ten, time for his mid-morning sip. He reached into the lower right hand drawer of his desk and pulled out a flask. Tilting it back, he took a good hard swig and recapped it as the fiery bourbon flooded down into his stomach. He had just put it back in the drawer when the regimental sergeant major William Sharrow stepped into his office. "Newspaperman named Vandiver here to see you, sir."

"What paper's he from?"

"New York *Times*."

Strange, Reno thought. "Well, bring him in."

Ira Vandiver introduced himself as Reno stood, shook his hand, and pointed to a chair. "How may I help you, sir?" the major asked.

"I've been sent out here to do a story about the situation with the recalcitrant Sioux and how it affects our military. I interviewed your boss, General Custer, in New York a while back. Now I'd like to get a little local information."

"Bring us some coffee," Reno called out to the clerk in the outer office. "Very well, Mr. Vandiver, ask away." Some of Custer's love for the press had brushed off on the executive officer.

Vandiver pulled out his notebook and a pencil. "I did some research on you, Major. Counting the war and Indian action, you've been in fifteen battles or engagements and have received four brevets for gallantry. Is it true that you are a brevet general, sir?"

"Yes. Got promoted at the end of the war."

"But you don't go by the title 'general.'"

Reno smiled. "Sometimes, but I don't push it. There are so many brevets in this command that if every one of them were addressed that way, you'd never know anyone's rank. You may have met Lieutenant Cooke, our adjutant. *He's* a brevet lieutenant colonel."

"I didn't hear anyone referring to General Custer by his real rank."

"That's a different matter. He *lives* that role, and it's his prerogative."

"About President Grant's ultimatum to the roamers, the hostiles, to come into the reservation—I just left the Red Cloud Agency and was told that most of them aren't coming in. Particularly Sitting Bull and Crazy Horse. Does this mean war? Does it mean the Seventh Cavalry will start a campaign?"

Reno rubbed the little goatee that formed a small dark triangle under his lower lip. "I don't know for sure, but I imagine we'll be going into the field one of these days soon. If I did know, Mr. Vandiver, it would be improper to tell you."

"I realize that, sir. I was a cavalry officer myself." He gave a synopsis of his wartime service.

Reno nodded. "I commanded a regiment in Wesley Merritt's First Cavalry Division late in the war, and once we had to bail Custer's Third Cavalry Division out of a hole his brashness got them into."

"I understand there was some rivalry between Custer and Merritt."

"It was only natural. They were both young, and both got promoted straight from captain to brigadier at the same time. That was when Pleasanton wanted some young command blood to get the Union cavalry off its ass. It worked too. Those young hotshots did quite a job."

Vandiver scribbled. "They took a lot of casualties."

"Custer, in particular."

Vandiver looked up, detecting rancor. "Why was that?"

"He was aggressive, had a gift for spotting enemy weaknesses and knew how to charge right in and exploit them. Yet this cost a lot of casualties. His brigade had the highest casualty rate in the war."

"How about now? Has he changed?"

"I can't say. The regiment hasn't had much *real* action, at least not in a military sense, since the Washita, and even that was really just a raid on an unsuspecting village."

"Yes, and that was seven years ago. In other words, he hasn't been tested, is that right?"

Reno shrugged. He had to watch himself, couldn't let his true feelings about Custer be known to a reporter—much as he'd like to. "I'd just say he hasn't had to meet an organized enemy of any strength lately. But I don't want you to print these comments, Mr. Vandiver. I'd sound disloyal."

The journalist nodded his head. "I won't quote you."

"That's enough about General Custer."

"Of course. How do you feel about the roamers—do you think Crazy Horse and Sitting Bull will be worthy enemies, if you have to fight them?"

This was better; easy ground. No way to get misquoted and get in trouble. "They are strong leaders of a warrior nation. But if we go after them in full strength, we can't lose. The general must have told you, a handful of troopers can lick a whole bunch of Indians. Everyone knows that."

"Why is that?"

"Because the Indian doesn't fight like we do. Tell you what, why don't I send you over to talk to our scouts. Lonesome Charley Reynolds just got back, and Mitch Boyer speaks English and can interpret for Bloody Knife, if he's around."

"Bloody Knife?"

"Custer's favorite scout. Half Sioux. Hates them, particularly one of their best chiefs—Gall."

Vandiver grinned. "Good! I'd also like to interview some of your other officers, if you have no objection. Tom Custer, for instance."

"I have no objection, as long as you remember that I want nothing printed that would be inflammatory or critical to the regiment or its members. I want your word, as a former cavalry officer, on that."

"I'll be discreet, General Reno. Thanks."

Reno got to his feet, extending his hand. "My pleasure."

As the journalist departed, escorted by Sergeant Major Sharrow, Lieutenant Cooke, the adjutant, walked into Reno's office. "What was that all about, Major?"

"He's putting information together for some kind of a series on the Seventh and the Sioux."

The Canadian with the huge stand of whiskers scowled. He had caught snatches of the end of the conversation when he walked into the outer office. "Why were you discussing the general to that reporter?" he asked somewhat coldly.

Reno didn't particularly like Cooke because he was part of the royal family, or at least a retainer. And he bordered on being impertinent, if not insubordinate. "I gave him little that isn't general knowledge. Besides, Cooke, I don't particularly like your tone."

The Canadian caught himself, flushed momentarily, and replied, "Sorry, sir, but you never know when some shifty reporter is out to besmirch our commander."

Reno nodded his head. He didn't want to struggle with the adjutant, but he was undermined enough around the regiment without taking that kind of guff. "Right. Now I'd like to have you compile a summary of the court-martials in the command for the last year."

"Yes, *sir*," Cooke replied stiffly and strode out of the office.

Lonesome Charlie Reynolds was another of the enigmas in the Seventh Cavalry. Thirty-three years old, shy, stoop-shouldered, with a soft voice, he lived alone without even a dog for company. He didn't smoke, chew, drink, or curse—a distinct oddity on the frontier. His speech revealed education and his early years in Kentucky. To some, his sad gray eyes and reluctance to speak of his past hinted at some tragedy. Like most cavalrymen, he was around five-foot-seven.

Actually, Charlie had served three years in the Union Army during the war, where he had made his superb hunting instincts and sharpshooting ability pay off in later years. He began scouting for the army in the early '70's, and served with Custer on the famed Black Hills expedition in '74. He had spent the early part of the winter scouting for the Indian agent at Fort Berthold. Captain Nowlan, the quartermaster, had just hired him back as a scout for the coming campaign at a hundred dollars a month.

Reynolds was watching the game in progress inside the scouts' common room. They were hard at Shooting Dice with a Basket since payday money was still around. Both Bloody Knife and Boyer were in the game, and the latter was winning.

Ira Vandiver walked up, asked for Reynolds, and introduced himself. "I've spoken to Lieutenant Varnum and he said it was all right for us to talk, Mr. Reynolds."

They decided to go outside, since it was a clear day and the wan sun was doing its best to bring the temperature up to bearable. As they strolled toward the stables, Vandiver said, "I hear you've been scouting Sitting Bull's Sioux out of Fort Berthold."

"Yes, the Hunkpapa," Lonesome Charlie replied.

"Did you come in contact with them?"

"Only a couple of hunting bands. The kind that gets bored with being holed up and goes out looking for small game . . . or something to steal."

"Did you get close to them?"

Reynolds chuckled. "I'm here."

Vandiver smiled. "Right. Dumb question. What do you think Sitting Bull's going to do about the ultimatum?"

"He's already done it. That's my guess. Laughed at it."

"What'll he do if the army goes after him?"

"Hard to tell. He's like a god to them, you know. But I think we have to worry more about Crazy Horse."

Vandiver was writing hurriedly on his small note pad. "Why is that?" "Because he's a fighter, and he's younger. From everything I've heard, he's aptly named."

"Meaning?"

"Meaning no one knows what's in that odd mind of his."

"Do you know Bloody Knife, the half-Sioux scout?"

"He's the general's favorite."

"I hear he and the Sioux war chief, Gall, are enemies."

"He hates Gall, and I understand the feeling's mutual. Story is that one time when Gall and some of his people camped near Fort Berthold, Bloody Knife recognized him. He then led a platoon of soldiers to the camp, and when Gall stepped out of his tipi, they attacked him. Gall was shot and knocked to the snowy ground. Then a soldier ran up and ran a bayonet through his huge chest, pinning him to the ground. Another soldier stabbed the chief in the neck. As blood spurted from Gall's wounds, the lieutenant in command said he was dying. But Bloody Knife wasn't satisfied. He placed his gun against Gall's bloody head, but just a split second before he fired, the lieutenant knocked the gun aside and the round tore into the ground, inches from the prostrate chief's head.

Bloody Knife was upset, but he went on back to the fort with the sol-diers. Supposedly, he stewed all night and went back to Gall's camp at first light the next morning to scalp the corpse and get first coup. But the camp site was vacant. Bloody Knife figured that the camp had pulled up stakes and hauled him back to the main Hunkpapa tribe. Gall apparently recovered completely, and the story is, he's got a special bullet he's saving for Bloody Knife." Lonesome Charlie shrugged. "Of course, Bloody Knife has a special bullet for Gall as well."

Vandiver shook his head. "Quite a story. Do you think they'll run into each other if there's a campaign?"

"There's a good chance."

The newspaperman changed the subject. "What do you think of this regiment—is it as good as Custer thinks it is?"

"Can't say, Mr. Vandiver. I just got back to it. I 'spose it can fight well enough."

They arrived at the stables and went inside, where several of the troopers were working with the horses. "One more question, Mr. Reynolds. Is there much strife in the regiment?"

Reynolds raised his eyebrows and shrugged. "All regiments got strife."

In C Company's orderly room, First Sergeant Ed Bobo escorted Ira Vandiver into the commander's office, where the journalist introduced himself to Captain Tom Custer. The general's brother had been promoted back in early December, along with B Company's Tom McDougall. "Do I call you Colonel, or Captain Custer?" Vandiver asked.

Tom Custer smiled. "'Captain' will do. Hell, I'm just getting used to *that* rank again." His smile broadened into a grin. "If there are any women involved, just call me Tom and call me soon."

"All right, Captain, I'm trying to get a good round profile on your brother. I don't know much about his youth. Were there incidents or inclinations then or at West Point that might point to his brilliant future as a military leader?"

Tom frowned. "Hmmm. Of course, I'm younger, but my older sister told me some things. He wore a soldier suit when he was a little boy, and he liked to play war. But he wasn't fixated on it all those years. We all read Sir Walter Scott's books. I guess at West Point he always just scraped through. Everybody knows he graduated at the bottom of his class, and almost didn't graduate because he slugged a sergeant and got court-martialed. But he almost always won in any game he played."

"Perhaps to him war was by extension the 'greatest game'—I believe someone once called it. The two of you have served together a long time, haven't you?"

"Since the last year of the war."

"You were awarded the Medal of Honor *twice*, I understand."

"Uh huh. I captured some flags." Tom's smile was almost bashful. "I was young and didn't know any better."

"I heard you were fearless and didn't give a damn."

The smile again. "We Custers have this dumb streak in us that makes us think we're indestructible. Autie's the same way—the general."

Vandiver pursed his lips. "Tell me about that. How do you feel when the lead's flying, when all hell's breaking loose and men are dying everywhere?"

Tom frowned, thinking. "Well, I guess it goes back to the game idea. You're all excited, but not crazy. With Autie and me, we're gonna win 'king of the hill'—remember that one? Get those other fellows, get their *flag*. Except it's noisy, with all the shooting going on, maybe some artillery, horses and men screaming, shouting. Dust and smoke. Hell, Vandiver, you said you were a captain, you know."

The journalist shook his head. "But I'm mortal. *I was afraid.*"

"But not a coward."

"I don't think so. But you and the general, you thrive on it."

Tom Custer raised an eyebrow. "Like I said, we're either dumber than the next fellow, or we just like it more."

"Is it a chase for glory?"

"I don't know. Maybe a little bit. Maybe the Sir Walter Scott stuff rubbed off on us. Yes, I'd say some of that hero and glory thing is involved."

"Maybe a little more so on the general's part?"

"Possibly. He's sure had a lot of the glory."

"Far more than most."

Tom stroked his mustache as a contemplative expression touched his eyes. "Tell you what you can print, Vandiver. There's no better battle commander in the U.S. Army, or maybe in any other army, than George Armstrong Custer. Not only is he experienced, he's *talented*. It's instinct, sir, instinct. A commander can have just so much information about the enemy, just so many troops and supplies, just so much of the good ground—the rest is what he does with it. All those apologists for the rebels during the war, hell, they like to say that Grant had all the good numbers—you know, the most troops and the most guns and powder and all that. Well, I'll tell you right now, if Grant hadn't a had the *talent* to use it, all that wouldn't of done him any good. It sure as hell didn't do McClellan and some of the others much good."

Tom's blue eyes narrowed as he looked out the window and paused for a moment before continuing. "Autie can look at an enemy formation or position and instinctively know where to hit it. And that kind of thing isn't in any book at West Point or anywhere else. That's why he's the best."

"Being as close to him as you are, do you ever question his decisions?"

Tom grinned. "Yeah, twice I've told him he's taking the wrong hounds hunting."

"I'll be heading back to Bismarck in the morning, Colonel."

Captain Benteen eyed his visitor. "Well, that hotel in town isn't much. We'll put you up here." Turning to his first sergeant, he said, "Fix Mr. Vandiver up at the visiting officers' quarters for the night. Returning his gaze to his visitor, Benteen said, "Fort Rice isn't Fort Lincoln, but you'll be comfortable enough." He reached into a box of triangular cigars that he kept on his desk for visitors, and handed one to Vandiver. "This is the same brand as General Grant smokes. He gave me one, once, and I kept it until I got caught in a rain storm, and then I smoked it, half-soggy and all. Been smoking them ever since. Now, just what do you want to talk about?"

Vandiver struck a match to the cigar and got it going as Benteen puffed on his ultra long-stemmed pipe. "I'm trying to get a good picture of Lieutenant Colonel—or General—Custer, and I heard that you can be quite outspoken in that area."

Benteen snorted. "That's an understatement. What do you want to know about Custer?"

In fact, Vandiver had heard that the white-haired, owl-eyed Benteen *hated* his commanding officer. He'd also heard that the commander of Company H and of Fort Rice could be mean-spirited, crotchety, and vindictive. But he could also fight. "I want to know what you think of him."

"He's a selfish, arrogant, glory-hunting, self-seeking ass, that's what I think, but you can't print that. What you can print is that I think he gives more thought to what will benefit George Armstrong Custer than he does to the welfare of his subordinates."

Vandiver scribbled in his notebook. "Even that's pretty serious, Colonel."

"This is serious business, not a Shakespeare play!"

"I was at Yellow Tavern and some other places with him. I think when the chips are down, he's pretty good."

"Oh, he's supposed to have good instincts—intuition, they call it. But I'm talking about taking too many chances. That's where I don't trust him."

"Tell me about the regiment. Will it fight?"

"Of course it'll fight. How well, I don't know. I see only the troopers in my own command, and you know we get a pretty big turnover due to enlistments expiring. You were in the war, you say. You know how it is— we never know how good they're going to be until it happens. We've got mostly good, experienced officers, and some of our sergeants know how to fight. I guess the rest is up to God."

Vandiver liked that quote. "What about the Sioux leaders? Crazy Horse, is he as good as they say?"

"Don't know. I do think that bunk about one trooper being worth twelve braves is bullshit. The Lakota didn't push these other tribes around for no reason. And they's got guts. I've already seen that."

They chatted on for another twenty minutes before Vandiver asked, "What about the drinking? I've heard it's pretty heavy in the Seventh."

Benteen shrugged. "No more, no less than other regiments, I'd say. Boredom promotes it. I drink my share."

"Me too. In fact, Colonel, I'd offer you a drink right now if it weren't duty hours."

Benteen smiled. "Offer away. I'm the boss around here."

Vandiver pulled a leatherbound flask of bourbon from his coat pocket as the captain withdrew two water glasses from his desk. Pouring a liberal measure into each one, and lifting one, the journalist said, "GarryOwen!"

"GarryOwen!" Benteen replied, clinking their glasses together and taking a big sip. "If you know the regimental toast, you *have* been doing your homework."

Savoring the harsh flavor of the whiskey, Vandiver smiled. "Once a cavalryman, always a cavalryman."

Mark Kellogg handed Vandiver's credentials back to him and invited him into the editor's office of the Bismarck *Tribune*. "Mr. Lounsberry, the editor, isn't here, but I'll try to answer your questions." Kellogg was the forty-two-year-old assistant editor of the newspaper. Rather handsome in a craggy way, he had combined a career in newspaper work with telegraphy.

"Good. First of all, is this paper part of James Gordon Bennet's empire—you know, the New York *Herald* and company?"

"In a way, but not exclusively. It's just a working arrangement."

"Then you can cooperate with me?"

"Maybe. What do you need?"

Vandiver explained that he was doing background work on the likely forthcoming campaign against the roamer Indians. "I don't know if the *Times* will ever do much with it, but who knows, I may write something someday."

"Are you going along when the regiment goes into the field?" Kellogg asked.

"Oh, no. I'm going back to New York tomorrow. Soon as I wrap this up and put it away, I'm off to Berlin to do an in-depth piece on how well the Kaiser is handling Bismarck, or vice versa."

Kellogg chuckled. "I wish I could get such juicy assignments. However, I *am* slated to go with Custer when they pull out."

"That's exactly why I'm here. Would you be willing to share your releases with the *Times*?

My editor is willing to pay rather handsomely—in newspaper fashion, that is—for whatever you're willing to give him of an exclusive nature."

Kellogg frowned. "I wish I could, but I don't think Lounsberry will go along with it—not if he keeps anything going with the *Herald*."

"I understand. But what about when you get back, would you send me a summary of the whole campaign?"

"Perhaps. Depends on how much you're willing to pay, or if I might decide to write a book about the expedition myself. I've already had a query about the same thing from some dime novelist named Frederick Whittaker."

Vandiver brought out his flask. "Well, let's have a drink anyway. We can see how the land lies when the troopers pull out."

18

It would perhaps be pleasant to be alternately victim and executioner.
—Charles Baudelaire

At the main post, the problems of the regiment were simmering under a deep blanket of cold snow that was slowly gaining a crust of ice created by periods of bright sunshine. It was simple chemistry. And simple northern Dakota winter. Down in the leeward side of the Black Hills, abnormally balmy weather was often the norm, but the northern plains would try a polar bear's patience at times. Temperatures during the bleak days had to struggle to climb above ten degrees Fahrenheit, and at night it plummeted as much as thirty degrees. Supposedly, it had once gotten down to seventy below. The current weather had lasted for nine days, and almost everyone at the post was cranky. Around the stable even the most placid of the horses had to be respected, or a sudden kick or nip might result.

And that's where Private Iggy Stungewitz spent much of his leisure time. He was quite comfortable in the bitter cold, having been raised in the frigid winters of Russia, and he could prop himself up on a bale of hay with a good book and lose himself in it. Or he could work on his plan. He had just begun the first stage to get Martin. Having patiently waited until well after his charges had been dropped so he could catch the first sergeant off-guard, he had made his first thrust—the letters. The first one had been mailed in Bismarck days earlier. The only problem with his plan was that he couldn't see Martin's face when he opened them.

The letter arrived at the D Company orderly room from the regimental mail room with the rest of the mail at shortly after three o'clock. Martin opened it a few minutes later, glancing at the crudely written yellow foolscap note attached to a longhand copy. It read:

Deer furst Sergent Martin: I found this copy of a leter to the generl and thought you ought to know bowt it, becuz it's a bad thing and you should be reddy.

—Your obdt svt, a friend

The letter itself stated:

Dear General Custer,

I believe you should know some facts about one of your first sergeants, Michael Martin of Company D. He is a brutal bully who lies, beats his subordinates, and will kill them, given the opportunity. He is not the kind of man who should be in any position of authority. He should be court-martialed and not only reduced to private, but imprisoned.

I know this is not the normal way to present a wrong, but I have to be careful, and since you are on leave, this is the only way I can give you this information. But I have him dead to rights on something criminal. When you return to the post I'll provide the details. . .

Your Obediant Servant,

Ja—

A true copy.

The signature was torn off.

Sitting at his desk, Martin let out a roar and turned to the company clerk. "Where in the bloody hell did you get this damned thing?"

The clerk replied, "The mail clerk, First Sergeant."

Martin stared at the offensive piece of paper. The author of this garbage had to be someone close to him. Why would the son of a bitch's name be torn off? He looked closely. Whose name started with *Ja*? Had to be James somebody! He turned back to the clerk. "Get me the name of every member of this company whose name starts with *James*, and be smart about it! Oh, and he has to be able to write."

"That'll leave out a couple I know of," the clerk replied.

Minutes later Martin glared at the names on the sheet of paper. The first was Sergeant James Flanagan. No, couldn't be him—Flanagan owed him his stripes, and his fellow Irishman could barely write. Private James Harris—crossed out because he was illiterate; Private James Hurd likewise. Couldn't be Jimmy Wynn, the fat old tailor. He could barely write, let alone put anything like this letter on paper. So that left Alberts, Private Alberts.

"Could it stand for Jacob?" the clerk asked.

Martin nodded his head. "How many of them we got?"

"Just one—Hetler."

"Get him and Alberts in here!" Martin scowled at the letter, reading it again. *Who in the hell would be out to get me, if it wasn't someone in my company?*

Stungewitz!

But his first name was some kind of Jew shit—Ignatz! Not even close.

Who were his other enemies? Bobo didn't like him. That C Company sergeant of his, the one who was mooning over his wife, Kanipe. No, he couldn't pull off anything like this. And even if it was them, they didn't have anything on him. A couple of others. But the writing smacked of it coming from an officer. *Shit!*

A few minutes later the two privates walked into the orderly room. He handed each a sheet of paper and a pencil. "Here," he snapped, "write out 'I believe you should know some facts.'"

They both looked at him in alarm.

"Just do it!" he barked.

Shortly he looked at Hetler's sample. Not even close. Alberts handed him a similar result, laboriously scribbled, with "facts" misspelled.

"Okay, get outta here," Martin growled.

"What do you want to do now?" the clerk asked softly.

"Nothing!" Martin shouted, kicking over a chair.

Martin drank half a bottle of whiskey that night and still couldn't sleep. The letter was burned into his memory and every time he rolled over it came back to him. Two days later the second letter arrived. It was slightly different, mailed by some supposedly well-meaning person from Bismarck, but its content was similar. This one was addressed to General Terry in St. Paul.

Again the signature was partly torn off, leaving only most of the letter "J."

He checked the first names of all the officers at Fort Abraham Lincoln, including those in the infantry command. There was only one whose name started with "Ja"—First Lieutenant James Calhoun—Custer's brother-in-law. And he wouldn't write that kind of letter to his own kin. He even had First Sergeant Butler, his drinking friend over in Calhoun's Company L, give him a copy of the lieutenant's handwriting, and there was no similarity.

That night, Martin drank nearly a whole bottle.

It was the beginning of many nights of troubled sleep.

The cold weather put a severe damper on Danny Kanipe's love affair. It was so cold outside that hanging up anything wet on a clothesline quickly produced a garment stiff enough to use as a toboggan for snow sliding. He'd slipped into the laundry a couple of times during the last week, but all of the laundresses had been there, scrubbing away and ironing. Missouri Ann couldn't figure out a good enough reason to go to town, and they certainly couldn't go out somewhere in a buggy again, even if she did. Danny wanted to figure out a way to use a hotel room, but that was way too risky.

To get his mind off his desire to see her, he was spending Sunday afternoon in his room in the barracks, reading the latest book his friend Iggy had recommended, Scott's *Lady of the Lake*. He didn't understand everything in the long poem, but there were places that made him think of Missouri Ann. Sometimes he memorized parts that he thought she'd enjoy. And she did, in their stolen moments. She'd laugh or even let a tear slip, and often she'd clap her hands when he finished. But those moments were so few. Still, he felt she was there, sharing the book with him, and that gave him pleasure. He was now working on stanza XVII, in which the hunter first encounters the Lady of the Lake. He closed his eyes and recited,

> And ne'er did Grecian chisel trace
> A nymph, a Naiad, or a Grace,
> Of finer form, or lovelier face!
> What though the sun, with ardent frown,

Had slightly tinged her cheek with brown,
The sportive toil, which, short and light,
Served too in hastier swell to show
Short glimpses of a breast of snow:
. . . A foot more light, a step more true,
Ne'er from the heath-flower . . . dash'd the dew . . .

No, that wasn't right. After "snow," it went, "What though no . . . rule—"

"That's really pretty, Kanipe."

He looked up, startled, at Ed Bobo's words. "Uh, yes, well I'm just trying to memorize some . . . that is, I like Sir Walter Scott, and I think this passage is kinda pretty, that's all."

The first sergeant nodded his head. "I don't read much, myself. Just orders and manuals and such. Haven't read a book in five, six year I 'spect." He blew out a deep breath and stamped his feet. "Colder'n a glacier out there. You got any whiskey?"

Dan still hadn't gotten control of himself. "Uh, yeah, I've got some cheap whiskey in my trunk." He went to the locker and took out the bottle he'd been saving. "Gotta hide it or Finckle will get into it," he added. Sergeant George Finckle, a thirty-one-year-old Berliner, shared the room with him, but he was in town on a pass. He handed the bottle to Bobo. "Help yourself."

The first sergeant took a healthy swig and handed the bottle back. Going to the potbellied stove, he picked up a poker and stirred the fire around.

Dan watched him, knowing he had something on his mind. He also knew what it was . . . *finally!* He could almost hear the man's breathing. He held his own breath for a moment, then slowly let it out as he watched Bobo turn back with the inevitable words. . . .

"There's something I gotta say, Kanipe. I don't want to because then our friendship won't ever be the same, but I have to." His hazel eyes were steady under his frown. "I'll get right to the point—there's talk that you're sweet on my wife. Now, I know she's a pretty lady, and they's probably a number of youngsters around here'd like to have her and all. But I hear it's gone further than that with you."

Dan tried to keep his voice steady. He had to bluff this out, *had* to. "Where have you been hearing this stuff?" he heard himself saying. "That bastard Martin likes to spreads rumors."

Bobo's voice was low. "It ain't just him."

"Who else then? This is crazy."

"One of the laundresses, don't make no difference who."

"It's a lie."

Bobo blew out a deep breath. "Well, be that as it may, I can't have talk. And I don't want trouble with you, but . . . damn it, Kanipe, I've seen you look at her. I know damn well you like her, but I don't want to have to—"

Dan stared into his eyes as Bobo paused and put his final words together, "I don't want to have to *kill* you, and that's just what I'll have to do if I ever catch you fuckin' around with her. Do you understand that?"

Dan nodded, hoping his voice would stay steady and his expression wouldn't betray him.

"I understand, Ed. You haven't got anything to worry about."

Bobo held his eyes for a moment, then pulled his gloves back on. "All right. It's been said. Now you can go back to your book learnin'." He walked out.

Dan closed his eyes for a moment and then glanced at *The Lady of the Lake*. The book seemed to glare back at him.

He had never felt lower in his entire life.

19

Chicago

February 6, 1876

Lieutenant General Philip Sheridan called his aide, Lieutenant Colonel Sandy Forsyth, into his office. "I want to get a letter out to Crook and Terry."

"Yes, sir," Forsyth replied, opening his note pad.

Sheridan sometimes liked to dictate orders on his feet. He put his hands behind his back and walked to the window. Looking down at the cold breath of two heavy-coated dray horses clip-clopping by as they pulled a brewery wagon on the cobblestone street below, he began, "This is an informal note to inform you that the long-awaited campaign against the hostile Indians is now a fact. I am developing a plan that will put a squeeze on them from which they won't be able to escape. It'll take place generally in Yellowstone country, but will not be limited to a particular area. The mission is to find the hostiles, block their escape, fight them as necessary, disarm them, and bring the survivors into the appropriate reservation agencies."

Sheridan took a few steps, returning to his desk. Picking up a Gatling shell that he used for a paperweight, he went on, "However, I'm hoping to catch them in their winter lairs. General Crook is to probe north from his base next month, endeavoring to locate and attack the enemy wherever he finds them. General Terry is to do the same from his location. Specific orders for all commands will follow."

The lieutenant general turned to Forsyth. "Attach an order requiring each command to provide an up-to-date strength and status of training summary. I want to know how effective they are."

As Forsyth scribbled, he replied, "Yes, sir. I'll try to get this through by wire today, and I'll back it up by courier."

The black Irishman nodded his head. "Good. By God, Sandy, we're going to get those bastards this time."

New York
February 10, 1876

Custer had arrived at the Justh offices ten minutes before his appointment. He didn't want to appear eager, but he absolutely could not afford to be late. This might be his only opportunity to raise those funds. God, $8,578! Where could he *possibly* find that kind of money? He should never have listened to Rufe Ingalls to start with, and now here he was, having the man help bail him out. *Can't miss on railroad stock!*

He glanced at his watch. Ben Holladay was twenty-two minutes late. Could something have happened to him? Was he backing out? He felt a stab of something akin to fear. No, it was futility. What would he do if Holladay backed out? The man really didn't owe him anything. Oh, he knew Holladay probably still wanted some inside information now and then to assist him in his Indian agency decisions. But that wasn't anything big.

Ingalls had arranged it. It had been necessary to make a fast train trip down to Washington, where he'd met with the quartermaster and Holladay. They'd gotten together at Holladay's pretentious home on the occasion of a dinner party, replete with politicians. The man was a king in his own right—not only in stagecoaches, but in railroads and steamships. So what if his reputation was clouded by duplicity and machination? Wasn't that part of business? Look at Jay Gould and all the chicanery he'd pulled, cornering the gold market and throwing the country into a massive panic—wasn't *he* still around?

He looked at his watch again—where *was* the man?

As if in answer, the door to the outer office opened. It was Holladay. The stagecoach magnate removed his hat and gloves as he smiled and said, "Good afternoon, General Custer. Got held up at my hotel. Everything all set?"

Emil Justh came to his office doorway. "Yes, sir. Come right on in, if you will, gentlemen, and we'll get to it at once."

After the handshakes, the muttonchopped broker handed Custer and Holladay copies of the note to read. "The wording is standard, Gentlemen. General Custer is signing a six-months' promissory note effective today to Justh & Company for the full sum, at seven percent interest, and you, Mr. Holladay, will cosign and be liable for the entire amount, should the general forfeit."

Holladay gave the note a quick glance. "Looks fine to me."

Custer knew every word of it. "Yes, it's okay."

Justh pointed to a table that held pens and ink. "If you will, gentlemen. General Custer first. Sign all six copies."

The other two men chatted as Custer pulled up a chair and dipped the pen. It was an awful lot of money to be owing on a lieutenant colonel's pay, all right. But if it had worked out, he'd be spilling this kind of money! That was the gamble he took. He started signing. Something had to turn up. Custer's Luck would take care of that. New success and glory on the coming campaign . . . with enough of that, a new book could make him rich. Something would surely come along—

"There," he said, finishing the last signature.

Except for the slight scratching noise of the pen, it was completely silent in the room as Holladay signed the copies of the note. When he finished, he smiled. "All right, General, now let's go get a drink."

Custer shook his hand again. "I'll have a sarsaparilla."

Any way he looked at it, he was some nine thousand dollars in debt. He didn't like being beholden to Ben Holladay, and he was certain the conniver would want something in return, but he'd handle that problem when he got to it.

The dinner was held the next night at the Belmont mansion. August Belmont, the wealthy owner of the New York *World*, had decided to throw a farewell soiree for the Custers before they headed back to Fort Lincoln the next morning. The cream of the New York Democrats were on hand at the newspaperman's lovely home, where a white-gloved waiter served fine champagne the moment their winter wraps were removed. James Gordon Bennett, Jr., of the *Herald*, was there, as was Horatio Seymour, the former governor of New York who had been the party's presidential candidate against Grant in 1868. Also present was Montgomery Blair, the sixty-two-year-old West Pointer who had been postmaster general under Lincoln, but had returned to the Democratic party. Bejeweled ladies abounded. Since he knew everyone would be in evening dress, and because he also knew he would be the star attraction, Custer wore the dress uniform he'd brought along on the trip. Libbie was sparkling in a dark-blue silk brocaded dress with military epaulets and a fake multicolored medal that caught many a lady's alert eye. But Libbie seldom went anywhere without being noticed. As she had told her Autie, she was one of the most envied women in America—and not just because she was his wife. At thirty-three, Elizabeth Custer was a decidedly beautiful woman who was sure of herself.

Custer had long made known his sympathy with the Democratic party. He believed the South had been treated unfairly during Reconstruction and other postwar policies, and he had old friends in the South, such as classmate Tom Rosser, a Confederate general who had survived the war and was in the railroad business.

The reception had lasted an hour, the six-course dinner, accompanied by a string quartet playing soft music, another two hours. Befitting Mr. and Mrs. Belmont, the champagne was superb, and the food—with a main course of broiled lobster—excellent. When dinner was finally finished, the men retired to the library where Napoleon brandy and

Havana's best were served. Belmont, Bennett, Blair, and Seymour wound up in a corner of the richly appointed room with Custer and talked about the most recent peccadilloes of the Republican administration. Through the thickening cigar smoke, Montgomery Blair finally said, "General Custer, I've heard that you have some strong thoughts about Secretary of War Belknap. Would you share those with us?"

Custer toyed with the coffee cup he was holding. "First of all, gentlemen, you must realize that the man is my boss, at least I *think* so."

Everyone chuckled. They all knew about Sherman's feud with the secretary of war regarding who would run the army—the general in chief, or the general staff and the secretary. The outspoken four-star Sherman had told his former friend Belknap specifically which part of his royal ass the secretary could kiss.

Bennett said, "I heard from my reporter out in Bismarck that you wouldn't even receive the secretary when he visited."

Custer shrugged lightly. "I received him, just not right away."

"And why was that?"

"I believed him to be less than honorable in some of his sutler dealings."

"Such as?" Seymour asked.

"I'm not at liberty to discuss them," Custer replied.

"What about Orvil Grant's part in those sordid affairs?" August Belmont asked.

Custer blew out a deep breath before replying, "I've been led to believe that the president's brother is into improper selling of sutlerships right up to his neck."

All four of the other men looked at each other smugly.

"Can you be quoted on that, General?" the publisher of the *World* asked.

"Absolutely not, sir," Custer replied. "I'd have to look for another job."

Everyone chuckled as Bennett said, "I'd make you editor of my new newspaper out on the Yellowstone."

Custer grinned. "After our next campaign, sir, I intend to *own* the Yellowstone."

☆ ☆ ☆

Arriving at their boardinghouse a half hour later, the Custers were met by a man waiting in the lobby. "Excuse me, sir," he said, nodding in greeting to Libbie, "but my name is Ambrose and I'm from the Redpath Lyceum Bureau, the booking agency for lecture tours. We were told that you were leaving the city tomorrow, and we have a proposition we would very much like to present to you."

Custer glanced at Libbie in surprise and replied, "There's a little coffee shop over at the Hotel Brunswick that's open. Why don't we go over there and talk."

Ambrose readily agreed and a few minutes later they were seated at a corner table with coffee on the way. "Now," Custer said, "What kind of a proposition is it that brings you out so late on a cold February night?"

Ambrose had a drooping blond mustache and bushy eyebrows to match. His smile was broad. "Sir, the Redpath Lyceum Bureau would like to extend an invitation to you to lecture for us on a tour that would last from four to five months. We've been told that you might be able to secure leave later in the year for an extended period and be available for such a tour."

"About what would you want me to speak?"

"Your adventures, General—in the war and on the plains against the Indians."

Libbie smiled as Custer's eyes lit up. He said, "And should I decide to do this, what kind of money are we talking about, Mr. Ambrose?"

"I've been authorized to offer you two hundred dollars per night, for five nights per week."

Custer tried to keep a poker face. *Eight hundred to a thousand dollars per week for nine to thirteen weeks!* "Well," he said, keeping his voice calm, "I think we might be able to arrange something." His eyes glowed as he once more looked at the smiling Libbie. "Tell me more about it."

They talked on for another twenty minutes as their coffee cooled, and finally Ambrose excused himself, shook hands, and departed. The moment he was out the door, Custer jumped to his feet, grabbed Libbie, swept her up in his arms, and swung her round and round to the astonishment of the rest of the people in the coffee shop. *"Custer's Luck! Custer's Luck!"* he shouted, then, putting the breathless Libbie back on her feet, he bowed low to the watchers and escorted his lady from the room.

As the door closed, a small round of applause followed them.

St. Paul, Minnesota

February 15, 1876

Brigadier General Alfred Howe Terry stood by the large map of Dakota Territory and the Yellowstone country that hung in his large office at Headquarters, Department of Dakota, in Fort Snelling. Terry, the forty-nine-year-old Connecticut lawyer who became a Regular Army general because of his superb record as a Volunteer corps commander in the Civil War was the outsider who kept a star on his shoulder while so many other wartime generals scrambled for whatever rank they could get. A wealthy bachelor, he spoke several languages, loved art and literature, and enjoyed wide respect in the army. He was soft-spoken and generous, a six-footer who wore a dark beard and had been the target of more than one husband-seeking woman.

"It's official," Terry said. "Sheridan's orders came in yesterday, so I'm pleased to see you here, Armstrong. As you know, I've been commanding down in the Department of the South, and I haven't been in the field against the Indians."

Custer kept a relaxed expression, although he wasn't pleased that so little had been done in planning the forthcoming campaign. He and Libbie had arrived in St. Paul by train late the night before, and he was ready to turn back into a one hundred percent fighting leader. Play in New York was enjoyable, but this was war. And that's what he did best. Besides, so much that was personal was riding on this campaign. "That's all right, General, I know what I'm doing out there, so you can count on the Seventh Cavalry."

Terry nodded. "We thought the hostiles were wintering on the Little Missouri, but a week ago I learned that most of them—Sitting Bull and Crazy Horse—are farther west in Yellowstone country."

Custer nodded.

Terry went into Sheridan's general plan. "The possibility of doing anything before April is out. And we're not working in concert with Crook, who will move up from Fetterman whenever he's ready. Colonel Gibbon, commanding what we'll call the 'Montana column,' composed of several companies from the Seventh Infantry and some troops from the Second Cavalry, will move east from Fort Ellis. They'll patrol the north side of the

Yellowstone, blocking it. I've named our column, which will depart from Fort Lincoln, the 'Dakota column.' That movement and plan of operation is what we need to discuss."

Now Custer frowned at the map. "Who's to be in command?" he asked. "You are," Terry replied. "I'll provide infantry to set up a base camp and guard supply trains, so the Seventh will be free to probe as you see fit. I'll also see what other support I can give you."

Custer felt the excitement. *Just as he wanted it—his own campaign!*

They talked on, discussing possibilities and going over the hostile area. It was strange that the country for four hundred miles east of the Pacific Ocean was settled and generally pacified, but that so much vast territory east of that and west of Minnesota was unsettled and capable of holding thousands of hostile Indians! But, Custer had to admit, it was a huge area out there, larger than all of France. "Can you depart Fort Lincoln on April sixth?" Terry asked.

"Definitely," Custer replied. "Sooner, if you wish." He'd be ready to ride as soon as he got back.

20

You can do anything with bayonets except sit on them.
—Count de Cavour

Fort Fetterman, Wyoming Territory
March 1, 1876

Brigadier General George Crook sat on his favorite mule, Apache, just outside the main gate of the little post where his army had staged for the last few weeks. Actually, the term "army" wasn't accurate; it was an "expedition." It consisted of two companies of the Fourth Infantry, five troops of the Second Cavalry, and five troops of the Third Cavalry—the famous Brave Rifles of Chapultapec fame. His trains were extensive, with eighty wagons loaded to their limit and some five hundred mules, including the pack animals. There was also a herd of nearly fifty beeves to be butchered as needed on the forthcoming forty-day campaign. Counting the civilians to operate the trains, and scouts, his force numbered almost nine hundred.

Crook felt a little like Grant must have felt when the Army of the Potomac headed south in May of 1864—he was the senior officer and the boss, but he'd given actual command to another officer. In fact, Colonel Joseph J. Reynolds had been a classmate of Ulysses S. Grant at West Point, actually graduating higher in standing, and had been a major general and corps commander during the war. He was now the colonel of the Brave Rifles. Unproved gossip had it that Reynolds had let his fingers get sticky down in Texas, where he had been on detached service from the regiment, and his heroic reputation from the war had been tarnished. Crook was giving the older man a chance to silence the whispers.

A heavy storm had blanketed the area with snow the night before, and now the bright sun in the clear sky cast off brilliant reflections as the heavily outfitted column moved out to cross the North Platte River. It would then head northwest up the old Bozeman Trail and skirt the Bighorn Mountains. It was quite cold, but Crook was on record with his dictum—"The worse it gets, the better; always hunt Indians in bad weather."

It was doubtful that his muffled soldiers agreed with him as the procession of horsemen, marching infantry, and laboring trains trudged across the frozen river. Sitting astride their horses and watching the column pull out with the general were Colonel Reynolds, and the adjutant and brilliant chronicler, First Lieutenant John Bourke, as well as the colonel's trumpeter. Also observing the departure from a nearby vantage point was a scout who, although new and unproven to the command, would play a major part in the campaign. His name was Frank Grouard.

It seemed that Grouard enjoyed keeping the facts of his life slightly fogged. But what most people believed was that he was the son of a Mormon missionary named Benjamin Grouard and a Polynesian by the name of Nahina, the daughter of a high chief of the Paumoto Islands. Elder Grouard had married the princess and in 1850 a dark-skinned boy had been born. Around 1852, the little boy was somehow adopted by another Mormon family, who returned to California. When Frank was eight years old, the family moved to Utah, and at the age of fifteen the adventuresome young man ran away to become a teamster in Montana.

Probably as a prisoner, young Frank wound up in the Hunkpapa camp of Sitting Bull a few years later. Weighing in at well over two hundred pounds, the burly Mormon was saved from death when Sitting Bull overrode the suggestions of Gall and No Neck to do away with him. The great chief went even further, adopting the half-breed as his brother. He named him Standing Bear, but everyone called him "Grabber," the means by which a bear on his hind legs grappled with an enemy. Grabber Grouard quickly made friends with his captors, including Sitting Bull's sister, and learned the Lakota Way and language. In return, he provided information about the white man's world, and Sitting Bull grew fond of him.

In the spring of 1873, Grouard told Sitting Bull he was going on a horse-stealing raid, but visited the Fort Peck trading post instead. The chief found out and was furious. Under threat of death, the Mormon finally deserted the Hunkpapas and joined the Oglala. There, as a capable warrior and advisor on the white man, he became quite close to Crazy Horse. But finally, Grabber longed for his old life, and in the spring of 1875 he left the Lakotas and went to work for the government.

Colonel Reynolds was used to using his brevet rank, and had—until the recent problems in Texas—enjoyed a comfortable life in the army. Except for about four years when he had been out of the army as a college professor and grocer in the late '50s, he had served his country well. He was a Kentuckian who had never wavered in deciding which side he'd fight for when the war broke out. But, although the Brave Rifles had a reputation of distinction, he had little personal experience fighting Indians. Worse, he was suffering from some arthritis at the age of fifty-four, which wasn't helped by the severe cold. Nevertheless, he was duly appreciative of the opportunity George Crook was affording him on this expedition. It was a reprieve. He didn't know how he'd ever be able to repay the man.

As the last squad of cavalry cleared the departure point, Crook said, "I think we've got a fine force here, gentlemen. Would you like to go up and ride at the head of the column, General Reynolds?"

The former artilleryman smiled and nodded his head as he urged his horse forward. "Yes, sir!"

Crook followed a minute later, taking up a position directly behind the Infantry. He was pleased. The storm was behind them, the command was well-equipped and well-stocked with rations and forage, and he was sure he would have no trouble accomplishing the mission.

☆ ☆ ☆

The next evening in Washington, D. C., an event took place that would reach far into Dakota Territory, the lives of the Seventh Cavalry, and those of the Lakota nation. As the setting sun was turning the capital sky purple, Secretary of War William Worth Belknap was shown into President Grant's study in the White House. Tears filled his eyes, and his usually eloquent speech faltered as the fleshy two-hundred pounder began his confession to the trusting man he faced. "Sir, as you know, it costs a lot of money to entertain at cabinet level in Washington . . ."

The trice-married Princeton lawyer turned Civil War general and cabinet officer told the president that it was his marriages that had, in fact, brought him to this sad point. His voice broke as a tear ran down his cheek. "As you know, my second wife was Carrie Tomlinson, a fine woman who died six years ago from consumption. Without my knowledge, Carrie had worked out a scheme whereby a New York friend, one Caleb Marsh, entered into a contract with the holder of the Fort Sill trading post in Indian territory."

Belknap stopped and brushed his eyes with a handkerchief "The Indian trading posts are supposedly quite profitable for their operators."

"Yes," Grant murmured, "the Democrats and their press are busy pointing that out."

"As I said," Belknap went on, steadying himself, "I didn't know about those arrangements. She just suggested to me that the holder of the contract, a John Evans, be permitted to continue in that capacity—which, of course, I agreed to. But I later learned that Carrie was to receive some six thousand dollars per year from Marsh, who was being paid by Evans. She received only one payment, because she passed away a month after our poor little boy was born. Her sister, Amanda, took the child to care for, and shortly after, Caleb Marsh came to her and told her that the payments would continue with the child as beneficiary. As you know, Mr. President, I was terribly shaken by Carrie's death, and then a few months later our fine little son died. . . ."

Once more Belknap paused, blotting his eyes and collecting himself. "When Amanda went to Europe, the payments came to me. I don't know what possessed me, sir, but as I said, it costs a lot of money to entertain in this town, and, well, you know I married Amanda in seventy-two."

Grant knew very well. The beautiful and curvaceous Amanda, or "Puss" as her friends called her, had become an intimate of his wife, Julia.

They shared several activities such as luncheons and charities. To make what he was hearing even more implausible, the Belknaps attended the same Bible class with the Bristows. Secretary of the Treasury Benjamin Bristow, as the self-appointed reformer of the conservative Republicans, considered himself the watchdog in the Cabinet. It sounded like a plot from the worst dime novel.

No, it was more like an Edgar Allan Poe story.

"And Amanda is an expensive woman. You know what I mean."

"Yes," the president replied. Amanda always dressed exquisitely. "All told," he asked, "how much money did you realize from this trading post arrangement?"

The reply was a whisper. "A little over twenty thousand dollars."

"Does the opposition know this?"

"I believe so."

Grant frowned. The whole doggone story would hit the front pages everywhere, billed as another crooked Grant scheme! *When was it going to end?* This man had been his secretary of war for nearly seven years! Was no one honorable anymore?

"Here is my letter of resignation," Belknap blurted, handing over a sheet of bond paper.

Grant scanned the single line: "I, William Worth Belknap, resign as Secretary of War, effective this date, March 2nd Inst., 1876.

The president nodded. By resigning, Belknap couldn't be impeached. He dropped the note on his desk, and dipped his pen. As he wrote, he said, "Perhaps I shouldn't accept this, let the wolves have you instead. This is a terrible thing you've done. But you've served your country well in other respects." Signing his short acceptance, he looked up sadly, and held it out. This man, his friend and brother general, had committed a criminal act. And, incredibly, two of the accomplices had been his wives.

The next night at shortly before one A.M. in Lakota country, Joseph Reynolds jerked up from his sleep. The roar of pounding hooves would awaken anyone. "What is that?" he shouted to the sentry outside his tent as he reached for his pants.

"I don't know, sir!"

"Well, find out!"

The private was back by the time Reynolds had his boots and fur coat on. "It's the cattle, colonel! Some damned Injuns stampeded 'em!"

Reynolds rushed out into the sub-zero weather, slamming on his fur hat. The sound of the fleeing beeves was fading in the distance. "Sergeant of the Guard!" he shouted as he began to run toward the area where the herd had been kept.

A figure appeared. "Yes, sir! Sergeant O'Malley, sir!

"What's going on, Sergeant?"

"Our sentries were probably hunkered down in their blankets trying to stay warm, sir. Who would think some stinkin' Injuns would sneak up on a night like this?"

"How many cattle did they run off?"

"All of 'em, I guess, sir."

At that moment, Lieutenant Bourke ran up. "Do you want to go after them, Colonel?"

"No," Reynolds replied. "That'd be useless in the dark. But I want cavalry ready to ride after them at daybreak."

Another figure appeared beside them. It was General Crook, wanting to know what was happening. Reynolds explained. Crook gave him a searching look and went back to his tent.

It was as if the cattle herd had disappeared. The detachment of scouts and cavalry that tracked it the following morning returned, stating that the missing herd had gotten too far ahead. Reynolds ordered another company of cavalry to go after the missing beeves. But at nightfall, they rode back into the evening camp to report that the cattle had evidently been disbanded and had disappeared.

"*Disappeared?*" Reynolds asked incredulously as the lieutenant stood uneasily in front of him and shifted his weight from one foot to another. "How can over forty head of cattle *disappear?*"

"Sir," the cavalry officer replied, "I can't answer that. They're just gone."

Grouard, one of the scouts who had gone along in the search, backed up the officer. "Maybe they scattered them, or drove them fast toward Fetterman," he said.

Reynolds shook his head grimly and glanced at the listening Crook. "That cuts us down considerably on our rations."

Crook frowned. "Yes, down to one-third bacon for the next thirty-eight days. General Reynolds, I strongly suggest that you increase our security at night." The older officer nodded his head. "I'll see to it personally."

As Reynolds walked away, Crook made the decision. Before anything more went wrong, he'd damn well better keep a closer eye on Reynolds.

They never did find out what happened to the cattle. A private who considered himself a wag suggested that all the Indians from miles around had gotten together for the biggest beefsteak fest ever, but when Crook heard the story, he wasn't amused. Three days later the expedition reached a good place to camp near the ruins of old Fort Reno on the Powder River. The campsite was most welcome because the column had trudged through a nasty snowstorm to get there. That evening Crook sent out a party of six scouts under Grouard to look for any sign of the Sioux or Cheyenne. Finding hostiles didn't prove to be a problem though—a number of brazen Indians came in close and fired shots into the well-lit camp later that night. There was only one serious casualty, but Crook was concerned that the enemy should be so bold. It simply wasn't normal for them to get that close to such a huge military force. He asked his chief of scouts, Major Thaddeus Stanton, about it.

Stanton shrugged. "Only thing I can figure, General, is they got away with our cattle right off. That made 'em cheeky, probably made 'em think their medicine was pretty strong. Another thing is this firing into our campfires and lanterns is pretty safe for them. Best thing we can do is shoot back at their rifle flashes, and you can't hit a damn thing doing that—which they know."

"You got any recommendations?"

"Just that I think we'd better extend our security, and maybe our thinking."

Crook agreed.

The next day the column continued north in a sudden burst of warm and pleasant weather, and made twenty-seven miles to Crazy Woman's Fork. Indian sign was everywhere—distant smoke signals, the flash of hand mirrors. The troops were acting a little spooked, and Crook was displeased that his every movement seemed to be observed by the hostiles. On the sixth, prior to holding an officers' call, he spoke privately with Reynolds. "Joe, I have to change things a little. I'm going to take a more active role in command. You'll be more my deputy from here on in. However, if we get a chance for any kind of an engagement, you'll command the troops. All right?"

Reynolds nodded his head. "Yes, sir." It wasn't his fault that the damned cattle had been run off, and that the Indians shadowing the column were so damned arrogant. God, he couldn't lose this command opportunity. But neither could he argue with Crook.

At the officers' call, Crook announced, "Tomorrow night under the cover of darkness, we'll take the ten cavalry troops and depart on an offensive to search for and locate the hostiles. We'll march until just before daybreak, and should be able to shake these Indian spies that have been haunting us. The cavalry will travel light, meaning they will take only the clothes on their backs, two blankets or one buffalo robe, one shelter cloth per two men, and minimum cooking utensils.

He glanced around at the cavalry officers. "Each trooper will take one hundred rounds of ammunition. A like amount will be carried by the pack train, as well as fifteen days' rations. The pack animals will also carry one-sixth forage of grain for the cavalry horses for the same fifteen days. That's as much as those mules can carry.

"The morning after we depart, the wagon train will head back to our former campsite at Fort Reno, accompanied by the two infantry companies. They'll make as big a show out of it as possible, so maybe the Indians will think it's our whole column."

Crook paused again before continuing, "Gentlemen, our scouts are going to *find* those Indians, and we are going to *defeat* them."

21

Who squired the glacier woman down the sky?
—HART CRANE

FARGO, DAKOTA TERRITORY
MARCH 7, 1876
If it had been anyone besides Custer, the Northern Pacific Railroad would not have considered even going to as much trouble. There had

been a closure of the rails to Bismarck for nearly two weeks due to heavy snow, but Custer had used his influence with the district superintendent to get the tracks cleared and him back to his command. Since the railroad executives considered Custer the company's special friend, and perhaps because they felt he might be able to render future assistance to them that would be above and beyond the call of duty, they decided to make up the special train.

With the severe weather, it was the only logical way the colonel and his lady could make it across that winter-locked two hundred miles. The special train consisted of two snow plows, three locomotives, a special car for the Custers, four other coaches, and eight freight cars. In one of the freight cars, three Gatlings were secured; one of the coaches held the crews for these guns—men from the Twentieth Infantry Regiment.

The Gatling gun, the forerunner of the machine gun that was developed during the Civil War, fired 350 rounds of ammunition per minute, a very high rate of fire. It had twelve revolving barrels that were turned by a hand crank, drawing rifle shells from a hopper. The gun was a mixed blessing—at relatively short range it could be deadly, but it tended to jam when overheated and was fouled easily by debris from black powder cartridges. The gun was usually drawn by condemned cavalry mounts. Senior artillery officers in the army complained that the Gatlings should be manned by trained artillerymen, and drawn by first-class horses. But their arguments had nothing to do with these particular guns.

Custer had no idea at the time that these very guns would play an important negative role in his future.

The Custer car was plush, one of the company's special cars that were reserved for important persons. It had sleeping berths, a toilet, a wood-burning stove, and a small galley, and was decorated in red velvet. A Negro attendant who could cook was assigned to the car. With steam climbing like pillars of snow-white cloud into the frigid blue sky, the three big engines readied themselves for their assault on the albino wilderness ahead of them. Finally, at 10:07 A.M. their engineers released the brakes and slowly headed west.

That had been the day before, on the sixth.

Now, at 9:30 the next morning, heavy snow had been falling since daybreak. A fierce wind, howling like a pack of mourning wolves, made even the well-insulated executive car a chilly place to be. Libbie, wrapped in her heavy fur coat, stood by the stove looking out the window as she felt the train jerk to a halt. "What now?" she asked Custer, who was sitting at a table on the other side of the stove.

Custer put down his pencil. He'd been working on another article for *Galaxy* magazine. "I don't know, but I'll find out."

He jammed his fur hat on his head and buttoned his overcoat. Closing the door quickly as he left the car, he squinted through the blowing snow and went into the next car, the one that housed the infantry soldiers. Some of them had spilled outside, but a couple more came to attention, including their commanding officer. "Stand easy," Custer said. "Why are we stopping?"

"A drift, I think, sir."

Custer went out through the front of the car and stepped down to the first step. The lieutenant was right. Up ahead the engines were pouring out black smoke and steam as they churned mightily, but the train merely jerked as if it were held by a giant hand. The same happened in reverse. Drifted snow was up over the wheels of the car. He climbed over the back of the next car, a tender, and made his way to the rear of the nearest engine. The fireman was busy stoking big shovelfuls of coal into the bed of the boiler, where hot, black, smoke-laced flames licked outward. The engineer had his head poked out the window into the driving snow, swearing angrily. The noise was deafening as the huge engine's wheels spun in the heavy snow.

Custer tapped him on the elbow and leaned into his ear. "How bad is it?"

The red-faced engineer shouted back, "Don't know, but we can't move one way or the other!"

Custer moved around the busy fireman and went back to the opening between the tender and the first car. It was a white-out. He couldn't see over a dozen feet.

It was stark winter everywhere on the northern plains. At Sitting Bull's Hunkpapa winter village the snow was as deep as the knee. Paths beaten between the tipis and the horse corral provided the only means of getting around. There wasn't too much socializing in this kind of weather, although it was said that Lakota women would find a way to gossip if the snow was over a horse's head. Red Elk didn't let the weather keep him inside, though. Birds had to eat and fly, so he would be out there to greet them with the smallest-headed arrows in his collection. On this overcast afternoon, when one's breath made a cloud the color of the snow itself, he had five relatively fat partridges in the buffalo-skin pouch draped over his shoulder. Cleaned, they would be tasty in a good soup. Nearing Running Antelope's tipi, he got an idea. He called out to Late Star, and shortly she stuck her head out of the front flap. "How, Red Elk. What do you want?" she said, stepping out into the cold.

He unslung his shoulder pouch and reached inside. Withdrawing two of the partridges, he held them out. "Please give these to your father, the great chief, as a token of my respect."

She accepted the dead birds and looked up into his eyes for a moment. "I thank you for my father," she finally said. "In fact, I've been thinking about you. Would you like to come and court me tonight, Red Elk?"

Would he? He kept his reserve. "It's too cold for me to wait in line."

A smile touched her lovely mouth. "There won't be a line tonight."

"You're sure."

"I'm certain."

The tall son of Bald Wolf nodded his head, taking his time. "Then I'll be here."

He started to turn away, but she caught his arm. "And I thank you for the partridges."

He looked for mischief in her eyes, but found none. Reaching into the pouch again and withdrawing a particularly large bird, he said, "This one is especially for the great chief's pretty daughter."

Late Star smiled broadly and bowed her head a bit. "The chief's daughter thanks you, tall warrior. Bring your best robe tonight."

Before he could say more, she had ducked inside.

Red Elk finished dressing in his finest doeskin shirt. He was wearing his best breechclout over his newest trousers and the finely quilled knee-high moccasins that his favorite cousin had made for him. After attaching his best pair of white-shelled earrings, he combed perfumed grease into his hair and bound it back tightly before attaching the erect eagle feather that denoted his first coup at the back of his head. Looking into the piece of white man's "seeing glass," he pronounced himself fit and reached for his beautifully tanned robe. Lone Star would see him at his finest tonight, he thought to himself with an approving nod.

Even though the weather was frigid, it was the Moon When the Grain Comes Up and the days were getting longer. Therefore when Red Elk came calling, Running Antelope was at the social lodge for the evening and Late Star was alone in the tipi with her aunt Crystal Pool. The older woman smiled when her niece invited the visitor inside, a rarity, because chaperones were always stern. He took it as a good sign. The aunt mentioned the cold, then retired to the back of the large tipi and began to quill by the light of the small fire burning in the middle of the room.

"We don't have to put your robe over our heads," Late Star said. "My aunt doesn't hear well, so if we speak quietly, she won't know what we're saying. Besides, she likes you."

Red Elk nodded his head. He didn't want that silly robe over his head anyway.

They sat and talked about little things for more than twenty minutes before she asked him to tell her about Crazy Horse's love for Black Buffalo Woman.

"I don't know much," he replied, "except it is said he still loves the woman. One would never know with him. He says nothing about himself. I did hear gossip that he is a good husband, but would run away with her again."

Late Star looked wistfully into the fire. "It sounds so sad, yet beautiful." All at once she turned to Red Elk and asked, "Do you think you could love me like that?"

He blinked. What an abrupt question. He looked into the fire, then at the aunt, and finally into her waiting, open eyes. "Yes. I feel strongly about everything I do." He made a fist and held it to his heart. "I want to have a great love with a beautiful woman and have sons who will be chiefs."

"But if that woman married another, would you give up everything and run away with her, as Crazy Horse did?"

"Perhaps—if she loved me enough. But I want a woman who believes in me, one who will climb the high mountain with me as I become a great leader. I want one with the strength to love me as I can love her."

Late Star's dark eyes sparkled. "And if I told you I can be that woman?"

He crossed his arms and frowned. She was finally being nice to him without ridiculing him. Could he trust her? Her eyes told him yes. "I would be honored," he said softly. I would ask you to be my wife and promise you the stars and all their friends in the great sky."

She reached out and touched his hand. "What a beautiful thing to say."

He could hear his own breathing as she stared back into the fire, saying nothing. Finally she looked up. "I will honestly think about it, my handsome Red Elk. By the first day of the Moon of the Birth of Calves I will give you my answer."

"And how many times will you go under the blanket with other young men?"

The twinkle came back to her eye. "Who knows? My decision wouldn't be right, if I weren't sure, now would it?" She chuckled, then looked around at her aunt. Seeing the older woman engrossed in her quillwork, she leaned up and kissed him on the cheek, then said, "Now you must go."

He nodded and smiled briefly before getting to his feet and stepping out into the cold night air. After a moment, he ducked back inside and said, "Go under the blanket all you wish, you won't find another like me."

With his heart singing, Red Elk walked over to the Kit Fox tipi and went inside. Several members of the society were there, including Chief Gall, who was making a rare visit. He sat down cross-legged as an older member said to the great war leader, "Tell us, my brother, about the bad one known as Bloody Knife."

Gall stared into the fire for several moments before replying, "Everyone knows that he was the son of an Arikara women who spent his early years with us, but was never really a Lakota. And you all know that he left us with his mother, and that he hated me. Later, in a raid that had nothing to do with him, I killed his brother. Then, at the bad time when I went to the agency with my family, he saw me and brought the Long Knives to kill me. They shot me and stuck those long knives on their guns into me many times and held me to the ground. As blood poured from me, I saw Bloody Knife raise his gun to my head. His eyes were wild with hate. But just then the young war leader of the Long Knives knocked his gun away, and they all left me for dead. I should have died, but my family carried me away on a travois and an old woman shaman, a friend of my mother's who was living with us, gave me her special potions and said many magic sayings over me. In two months every wound was healed and all of my strength came back.

"What charms did she use, Great Chief?" Red Elk asked eagerly.

"Two dried leopard's balls," Gall replied. "Twisted in the scrotum. She rubbed them on my wounds several times a day, and then made me suck them for several minutes."

Everyone shook their heads in wonder, particularly Red Elk. "What kind of a leopard?" he asked softly.

Gall looked back into the fire. "She said it was the large black one."

The younger warriors all looked at Gall in awe. One asked, "What did the old shaman ask in payment?"

"That I kill another of the great black leopards, and bring her the balls while they were still warm."

"And did you?"

Gall looked up from the fire. "Of course."

"And what about Bloody Knife?" Red Elk asked.

"In my last dream of him, I saw him dead in some kind of a green and noisy forest, with blood streaming from his mouth. I hope it was my battle-ax that killed him."

"I heard from an Oglala that Three Stars is coming with many Long Knives," Red Elk said.

"Yes," Gall replied. "I heard it. But he won't find us. His scouts are stupid and we are too far from him."

"I want to shoot him with my Sharps."

Gall snorted. "Go shoot a Crow when Wi melts the snow."

Late in the afternoon on March 12, Custer made up his mind. The train was still stuck tightly in the huge drift that had ensnared it six days earlier. The temperature was continuing to hover well below zero, and all of the wood fuel was gone. Coal from one of the tenders was keeping the car as warm as could be expected, but even that was being used on a limited basis. Fortunately there had been a large number of army rations on board the train, so hunger wasn't a factor. "I'm going to wait until morning," he said, impatiently, "and then I'm going to strike out for Bismarck."

He'd been threatening to do it for two days, but Libbie had talked him out of it. "I hate to think of you out there in this terrible weather," she replied from where she was bundled up in a buffalo robe on the seat by the stove. "It must be thirty below out there, Autie, and you don't even have—"

"*Halloo the train!*" The words were faint but distinct from outside. Everyone looked out the windows as the porter shouted, "Look, a sleigh!"

Sure enough, a large sleigh drawn by four mules, with two fur-clad figures, had pulled up just outside the luxury car. As it drew closer, Custer said, "By gad, it's Tom!"

Libbie ran to the window. He was right—Tom Custer was standing in the front by the driver, waving his arms and shouting, *"Halloo, the train!"* Suddenly he saw her at the window and waved excitedly.

In moments, everyone in the cars was crowding outside.

"That trapper, Bedford, who came by the train a few days ago, came to the post and told us you were here," Tom said. He pummeled Custer as he went on, "Now I frankly don't give a damn about him freezing out here until summer, but when that old trapper told me the 'old lady' was out here, I just hurried into town and rented this here winter hackney, and here I am!" He climbed down from the sleigh. "'Course, I could sure use a belt of good whiskey and some sleep before we head back in the morning."

"I've got some brandy!" the conductor said.

The sergeant from the Twentieth Infantry said, "And I'll take care of this here mule skinner."

"What's for dinner?" Tom asked with a wide smile as he climbed up into the entry to the luxury car and stomped the snow off his boots.

"Hardtack under glass," Libbie laughed, giving him a big kiss.

Custer pounded him on the back. "I sure never thought I'd be this glad to see you, little brother. Was it bad getting through?"

"Only for about the last eight or ten miles," Tom replied. "After that, there isn't quite as much snow. If it doesn't snow again, we should make good time going back."

"How's everything at the post?" Custer asked. "Everybody ready to go after Sitting Bull?"

"Rarin', to go, big brother."

"Good. We'll be riding out in about three weeks."

The trip back to Bismarck was cold, but uneventful. The mules were unusually hardy in the snow and having an easier time than on the outbound trip because, except for where the wind had blown drifting snow over the trail, the route had been broken. When the sleigh pulled up to the main gate of Fort Abraham Lincoln just as the sun was going down the next night, Custer returned the sentry's salute and smiled. "By glory," he said emphatically, "it's good to be back!"

Mary Adams and Private John Burkman kept had the quarters warm and spotless. The third Custer brother, Boston, was back, signed on as a quartermaster guide at one hundred dollars per month for the forthcoming campaign. Nine years younger than his elder brother, Boston had similar blond curls and enjoyed his position in the fun-loving royal family. He was waiting at the Custer house, as was their eighteen-year-old nephew, Autie Reed, who was visiting from Monroe. Actually, young Reed's name was Harry Armstrong, but he was called Autie for obvious reasons. A mass of eager dogdom also greeted them as twenty or more hounds barked, wagged their tails, jumped all over each other, and tried to get in a lick. Maggie Calhoun, all weepy-eyed, was there, and Annie Yates had a glass of hot spicy wine ready for Libbie. As soon as warm greetings and hugs were finished, and the dogs settled down a bit, Mary Adams said, "Now, you'all just get those heavy clothes off and get yourselves out there to the dining room. I know you ain't had no good home cookin' in a long time, and you must be starvin' to death."

Custer grinned. "I could eat a whole bear, Mary. What've you got on the fire?"

"A pot roast, and some dumplins; that'll put somethin' on those skinny ribs of yours, General. And all kinds of other things you like, glazed artichokes, sweet potatoes and honey. Three kinds a pies. I been cookin' since Captain Tom left to go get you in that stranded train, that's what."

Later, as Custer and Libbie dropped wearily into their warm bed, he said, "You know, darling, I can't ever remember it being so good to be back. This is our home, truly. When I heard that first bugle call, it just warmed my heart."

Libbie moved close, into his arms. "That's because you're a soldier, sweetheart. Through and through."

"I know, but it's more than that, and I can't explain it."

"I can. We *belong* here. Everywhere else we're just the Custers.

"You think that's it?"

"Oh, we're the *famous* Custers, but it's as if we're circus people passing through."

"Except with the Barretts."

"No, they're like family.'

Custer stared at the high ceiling of the dimly lit bedroom. "I don't think there's anything in the whole world like returning to a place where you're the commanding officer. You know everything out there, everything around you, is yours. You're the king, and all of those officers and soldiers out there will go through fire for you. Do you know that right now there aren't two safer people in the whole world? Look at the way we were greeted. All those officers and wives who dropped by to say hello tonight. Isn't that the most warming thing in the world?"

She snuggled in closer. "Sure is."

He went on, "Oh, I don't mean we'll be here forever, but wherever we go, it'll be about the same thing."

"I know," Libbie said wistfully. "The army's good for us."

"There's something I haven't told you, and now's as good a time as any. Back there in New York, Bennett and a couple of the others sounded me out one night about my interest in being president of the United States."

Her eyes widened as she looked at him. *"Really?"*

"They said I might have enough charisma, enough popularity, to make it."

"Why didn't you tell me?"

"Because I know they're just kind of desperate, sort of looking at all possibilities. They'd drop me like a hot potato the moment they saw I couldn't make it. And I didn't want that for you, darling. Or me. Get all excited about it, lose all sight of everything we know and like. And I've got enough enemies in the army as it is."

"The White House," she whispered.

"I know, it was alluring to me too. But this is what our life is, *right here* in a commander's house, hearing bugle calls, and having soldiers around us." He looked into her eyes. "The only thing I want in life is to get solvent and get my general's stars back. I want you to be the general's lady again, and not the *brevet* general's lady. We've got maybe fifty years ahead of us, and why not keep on hearing bugle calls and enjoying the kind of thing we've got right now?"

Libbie felt her eyes brimming as she kissed his cheek. "I agree, but Pennsylvania Avenue would have been kind of nice . . . you know . . . for *a while.*"

He frowned. "Do you really want that? I mean really?"

She smiled. "No, not really. I was just, well, it is a pretty house."

He shook his head. "I never should have told you."

"I'd have killed you if you hadn't."

"Anyway, Mrs. Custer, we've got a campaign to get ready for, and I'm going to kick the buffalo out of those hostiles, and then they'll *have* to promote me."

He felt her hand move down his abdomen as she kissed his cheek. "If you aren't too tired, would you like to make love to an almost first lady?"

He chuckled. "Will I ever hear the end of that?"

Her tongue flicked into his ear. "Only if you keep making love to me regularly."

Over in the sergeant's quarters, Missouri Ann Bobo put aside her knitting as her husband came out of the bedroom in his long underwear. "Aren't you *ever* coming to bed?" he asked somewhat testily.

She was in her flannel nightgown and robe, since she always undressed and cleaned up in the kitchen after putting the children to bed. She'd brushed her dark tresses and left them loose; they reached nearly to her waist. Sighing, she turned the kerosene lamp down low and followed him into the small bedroom. She was tired after a long day at the tub, scrubbing clothes and hanging them out in the cold wind. And she wasn't particularly interested in performing any further wifely duties on this cold March night. Oh, sometimes making love with him wasn't a duty. Sometimes, in fact, Ed stimulated her mightily. But since Danny Kanipe had come into her life, it was seldom. Oh, she still *liked* it with Ed; it was just that she wanted to pick the time. Particularly when she *needed* it. And she certainly didn't need it tonight.

She hadn't even seen Danny in a couple of days. He'd told her about his confrontation with Ed a while back, and he'd quit coming by the laundry room except when he absolutely *had* to get some clothes washed. With the bad weather, it hadn't made much difference. She couldn't get away to go to town, and there wasn't any other place where they could be alone.

Ed was in bed. "What are you fooling around for?" he asked impatiently.

She finished loosening her robe and hung it over the chair. "I ain't fooling around."

They had one of those warmer stones under the covers at the foot of the bed, so it would at least be cozy once she climbed in. She turned the bedside lamp off.

"Dammit, will you get in bed?" her husband demanded.

"I'm coming, I'm coming," she replied, getting in beside him. He smelled of tobacco, which was all right with her. And he'd washed good.

He rolled over on top of her, naked, and kissed her. Groping with her nightgown, he grumbled, "You don't need that damned thing on."

She could tell him she wasn't interested, but that would just hurt his feelings, maybe make him mad, so she just sighed and hiked the gown up over her hips. It was kind of hard to do, with the flannel on the flannel sheets. But she managed. She always managed, that's what life was about. That's how she'd wound up as a laundress with the regiment.

Iggy Stungewitz was enjoying his revenge on First Sergeant Martin. He had sent two more pieces of mail similar to the first and second, and he knew it was highly troubling to the less than literate Irishman because the company clerk in Martin's company had leaked the story to the company clerk in C Company, who had told him about it. He'd kept a straight face as the clerk said, "I guess that Irish bastard really has someone out to get him."

"Sounds like it," Iggy said.

He went to Danny Kanipe's room that evening to share the news. Kanipe was the only one in whom he had confided. The sergeant guffawed when he finished. "I wish I could see the son of a bitch's face when he sees those tidbits," he said. "You going to send him any more?"

"No. He'll wise up when nothing happens. It's worth it to know I've destroyed his peace of mind for these weeks."

"It was brilliant, Iggy. What's next?"

"You know Brennan. Well, his brother back in Dublin works for the post office. He's getting me an envelope postmarked in Dublin that's addressed to Martin, and a letterhead from a local law firm. I'm going to tell him he has inherited a great sum of money back there."

Kanipe laughed again. "That ought to keep him occupied. Then what?"

Iggy chuckled. "He'll never get an answer from Dublin."

Kanipe shook his head. "No matter how many times he writes. That'll absolutely make him crazy! I don't know if I can keep this secret."

"You can. I keep your lovelorn secret."

Kanipe sobered, nodding his head. Sometimes, like tonight, he couldn't even think about Missouri Ann without it hurting. She was right over there in Quarters No. 8 in bed with her husband, and he simply couldn't get the picture out of his head of her rutting with him.

Maybe when this campaign was over he'd transfer out.

If he could.

But he knew he'd never be able to get away from her.

Two days after Custer's return to Fort Lincoln on March 13, a telegram arrived from Washington. It was from Congressman Heister Clymer and it summoned Custer to the capital to testify before the House Committee on Expenditures in the War Department, of which Clymer was the chairman. The committee was specifically investigating former Secretary of War Belknap's activities in regard to post traderships, even though the secretary had resigned.

Unstated was the fact that it was an opposition party investigation aimed at embarrassing the president and his administration. But anyone who had read a recent newspaper knew that. And Custer had also gotten a wire from Belmont in New York stating that he had recommended the general for testimony because it was a good chance to go after Grant.

But Custer had too much to do to go to Washington. He wired Clymer, asking to be excused on grounds that his presence was vitally needed with his command.

A prompt reply stated that he would depart forthwith.

22

Frank Grouard, the part Polynesian scout, had located Crazy Horse's village on Powder River. He believed some of the ponies belonged to He Dog, Crazy Horse's closest friend. Generally the two Oglala were never very far apart, so he assumed that the powerful Sioux leader was in the village. "What a catch!" he told Crook. It would be second only to catching Sitting Bull napping. He had no way of knowing that He Dog was peacefully on his way to check into an agency with a large contingent of Northern Cheyenne under Old Bear, along with some Miniconjous. General Crook wasted no time in setting up the attack on March 16. After careful consideration, he decided to give Colonel Reynolds his big opportunity. "You'll have command, Joe," he quietly told the Kentuckian before dictating the orders to Lieutenant Bourke.

The strike force would have three of the two-company battalions, giving him fifteen officers and 359 men, not counting Major Stanton and half of the available scouts. Ammunition and hardtack was all the troops would carry. Crook would meet Reynolds after the attack farther up the Powder.

Reynolds marched out at five P.M., his troopers grousing about the night march, but excited about the forthcoming action. Shortly after dusk, the sky grew dark and snow flurries made tracking on the scouts' back trail very difficult. But Grouard uncannily managed to stick to the route to the village. Unfortunately, when the sky cleared around midnight, the temperature nose-dived to well below zero. Frostbite and actual death by the merciless cold became a danger as the column halted on a high ridge above the Powder at four A.M. Unable to light fires and in danger of slipping into fatal drowsiness, the troops had to keep moving around in the brittle air. Shortly over two hours later, Grouard reported back that the village of about one hundred hostile lodges lay sleeping in the river bed a thousand feet below.

The descent would be difficult owing to the rough terrain, but the troopers were ready to do anything but continue to freeze on that hilltop. One battalion was to attack, another was to block, and the third was to follow the attacking force inside the village. In the attacking battalion, Colonel Reynolds directed Captain Egan's company to use its pistols as it spearheaded the assault. The other company was to cut out the pony herd and drive it upstream.

It was bitterly cold as the sky began to light up.

Since the terrain was even rougher than anticipated, it was nine o'clock before the attacking battalion under the command of Captain Noyes was in position. The blocking battalion never did reach its position on the other bluffs overlooking the village, and the support battalion was at the command of Reynolds, who was beginning to show signs of hesitancy.

But surprisingly, the unsuspecting Indians, who hadn't even posted guards, were still wrapped up in their blankets inside the tipis and unaware of the approaching Long Knives. With Lieutenant Bourke at his side, Captain Egan ordered the charge and his forty-seven revolver-shooting, shouting troopers burst into the surprised village. Firing wildly, the company roared through the throng of tightly sealed lodges. Naked Indians burst in terror from the tipis as flaps flew open and women and children screamed. But the two-hundred-and-some warriors were well trained to meet just such an assault; they grabbed their rifles and quickly herded the women and children into the nearby brush. In short order they had rallied to return heavy fire. As the other company herded the Indian ponies upstream, Egan dismounted his troopers and shouted, "Go to your carbines!"

But now, instead of the blocking troopers controlling the opposite heights, the hostiles were pouring lead into the attack force. Even with the belated arrival of the rest of the command, the fierce warriors held the upper hand from their cover. Reynolds decided that he could do nothing but suffer heavy casualties, so he told his adjutant, "Get the horses down from the hill and send word to the battalion commanders to burn everything and prepare to pull out."

A short time later, the colonel saw that troopers were delaying as they looked for meat and robes to take with them in the clinging cold. He roared his displeasure, but time was flying as tipis went up in flames and the hostiles continued to sting the troopers with their rifle fire. The disorganized withdrawal from the smoking village began at 1:30 P.M. In the next few hours the disgruntled column made a hard march twenty miles up the Powder to arrive at the predetermined rendezvous point.

But Crook wasn't there!

The cold, weary, and hungry troops had marched some fifty-five miles in frigid weather in thirty-six hours when they settled into their blankets. And everyone was pointing fingers. To cap off the mismanagement, no guards were posted on the Indian pony herd, and as the camp stirred itself awake the next morning, a handful of audacious warriors triumphantly made off with more than five hundred of the captured ponies, leaving only two hundred to show for the raid. To make matters worse, Reynolds vetoed requests to go after the recaptured ponies.

When Crook rode in at noon with the rest of the command and some fifty of the Indian ponies his troopers had caught, he was at first pleased with the results of the attack. But upon listening to the vitriolic complaints of officers and soldiers alike, he slowly became more and more disenchanted. Calling Lieutenant Bourke, whose judgment he trusted implicitly, aside, he asked, "What's your assessment, John?"

Bourke was never bashful around the general. He replied, "It was just plain bad, General. Colonel Reynolds was indecisive. He lost control, and it was a damned shame. Sir, we caught them flat-footed! All sewed up like rats in their tipis! The decision to attack with pistols was wrong. I don't think our noble pistoleers hit much of anything. Then Captain Moore was negligent. His blocking battalion never got into position. The colonel's command was terrible, as well. Then we burned perfectly good food in that camp, food that we direly needed. And then, to cap it all off, Reynolds let them get their ponies back. And as you've heard, everyone from the lowest trooper on up is mad and disgusted. Our morale is shot, and I'm as disgusted as everyone else." He paused a moment before adding softly, "And its just a shame, General. Those are brave boys we've got, and they suffered terribly just to get to that village."

Crook listened grimly and finally nodded his head as he made the unwanted decision. "Very well, it sounds like we've been bungled right out of our big victory. Go ahead and pass the word to butcher some of those Indian ponies to eat. Give the rest to the scouts, and let's head back to old Fort Reno, where we'll join the infantry and our wagon train, and then go on back to Fetterman."

Bourke nodded. "Yes, sir. I'm sorry, but it was just plain bad." Crook frowned and turned away. Not only had his winter campaign failed—not a pleasant fact to report to Sheridan—but he knew what he had to do when he got back to Fort Fetterman. And it wouldn't be pleasant.

23

As Custer tucked the manuscript of the article he was writing for *Galaxy* in his valise, Libbie wrapped her arms around from the rear. Hugging him tightly for a moment before she released him, she said, "Do us both a favor, darling—keep your big mouth shut in Washington."

He turned. "Why, whatever in the world do you mean, Mrs. Custer?"

Her voice became serious as she looked into his eyes. "I mean it, Autie. That whole thing back there is political, and they're using you."

"Don't worry. I'll be circumspect."

"I hope so."

Tom Custer walked into the study. "C'mon, big brother. We'll have to hurry to catch that stage in Bismarck, the way it is."

"They'll wait," Custer replied, taking Libbie in his arms. Smiling down at her, he said, "Now you keep this doggone regiment in good shape, and I'll be back before you know it."

She leaned up and kissed his lips. "Yes, General."

It was March 21, and the April 6 departure date for the campaign was looming. But that wasn't what was worrying Libbie.

Back on the Yellowstone, Crazy Horse listened impassively as He Dog, his old friend and the Oglala leader from the village that Reynolds had attacked on the Powder River, finished relating his tale of the battle. He Dog's eyes were shining. "We chased them away, old friend. They must have had two or three times as many Long Knives as we had warriors, but we *beat* them! And then, I took only fifteen warriors to get the ponies. We stole them right out from under their white eyes!"

A brief smile touched Crazy Horse's lips as he nodded his head in satisfaction. "You did well, He Dog. How many men did we lose?"

"Two Oglala killed, four wounded. The others lost about ten."

"And the Long Knives?"

"More."

"And what about the rest of the village?"

"They were taken in by other villages."

Crazy Horse nodded his head again. "It's good medicine. And now we know for certain the Long Knives are coming to war with us. We must get ready."

It was only because he had spent so much time with Crazy Horse that Red Elk was permitted to sit in on the council three days later. The light-haired war chief had ridden into Sitting Bull's Hunkpapa village sixty miles down the Powder from the burned camp that morning. He Dog was the only one accompanying him. Running Antelope, Gall, and the other members of the *naca ominicia* were gathered around a fire in the Red Council Lodge. At the center sat the quiet Sitting Bull. The outside weather had finally relented and the warm air was rapidly melting the snow that had plagued the villagers for weeks. But weather was the last thing on the minds of these tribal leaders.

When He Dog finished his account of the Reynolds battle, Gall leaned forward and asked, "How many Long Knives did Three Stars have with him?" Since they knew it was Crook's column, they assumed he had been in command at the Powder.

"Many, maybe four hundred or more," He Dog replied.

This statement was followed by excited comments from several of the chiefs. When Sitting Bull raised his hand, the big tipi grew quiet. Seated behind Gall, Red Elk leaned forward to hear the great man's words.

"What do you say, Crazy Horse?"

The Oglala stared into the fire for a few moments before replying, "It's war."

"Do you think it's big war?'

"It's big war."

"What should we do?"

"Fight." It was a typical Crazy Horse answer.

After a few moments of silence, Sitting Bull looked around the circle of faces and said, "We must gather our warriors. Bring the small villages to me to center our strength. And as the grazing grass grows green, and the buffalo grows fat, the summer roamers from the agencies will join us. And we'll get ready to fight. But we should not look for fights until we are strong enough. Wakantanka will watch over us and give us guidance."

Crazy Horse showed his disagreement.

"I see Crazy Horse differs," Sitting Bull said.

The Oglala replied quietly, "No, I will bend to the great chief's decision. We should not look for war with the Long Knives until we are ready. If they come again, it's a different matter."

Sitting Bull went on, and as he did so, Red Elk glanced across the diminishing fire to Crazy Horse. The Oglala war chief's stolid face couldn't mask the fight in his eyes, and the young warrior was certain he knew what was going on in his head. "Wait" didn't totally mean wait—no, it meant get prepared to attack! The medicine from the village battle was there—plenty of it! The greatest fighting medicine ever! Red Elk thought he even saw the flicker of a smile touch Crazy Horse's lips.

I must go with him!

The council finished with the pipe and the speeches and broke up two hours later. As Crazy Horse walked outside into the gathering dusk, Red Elk caught up with him. "Great Chief," the young war leader said, "Let me go with you. I saw in your eyes that you won't wait to make war on the Long Knives, and I want to fight with you. I still have my big gun, you know, and I—"

"Come with me," Crazy Horse said abruptly.

"When do you leave?"

"At dawn."

"I'll be ready."

The Oglala turned and walked toward the remaining light. The tall son of Bald Wolf smiled; he'd always insist that a glow surrounded the great war chief, a glow that could come only from Wakantanka.

Yes, he'd be ready.

Late Star met him at a thickly wooded glen she had discovered halfway up the valley walls and some six hundred yards from the camp. The limbs of the trees hung heavy with thick snow, and the large fallen ponderosa in the glen's small clearing bespoke the visit of a relatively recent lightning bolt. She had cleared off a place to sit on the pine by the time Red Elk arrived. The sun, already behind the ridge, was falling rapidly toward the horizon, so the light in the glen had a shadowy quality.

The windless air was so cold that a snapping twig could sound like a rifle shot.

Foregoing custom, they had met here, out of sight, twice before. Now, bundled in their heavy robes, they sat together holding hands. These two were beyond custom. Without pretense or teasing, they were growing comfortable with each other. Their passions flamed when they were alone together, but there was an unspoken pact between them that was easy to keep in this weather: their lovemaking would be confined to the private holding of hands or merely touching. How it would work when warm air arrived was another matter, a triviality that didn't trouble them. They knew if they were caught, the worst would be thought of them, and a blight would be placed on their heads. But again, they knew by now that they loved each other, and that was all they cared about. "What is it you have to tell me?" Late Star asked.

Red Elk's eyes shone as he replied, "I'm going with Crazy Horse in the morning."

"Why?"

"Because he'll fight the Long Knives first."

"But I heard the *nacas* had decided to wait."

Red Elk shook his head. "Not Crazy Horse. I saw it in his eyes."

"But why do you have to go?"

"It's my way. If I'm to be a great chief, I must be in every fight."

She scowled. "But you are a Hunkpapa, they'll fight as well."

Red Elk smiled. "Not like Crazy Horse."

"What makes you so sure about this?"

"I know. Remember, I stayed with him. He's special, perhaps the most spiritual, most inspired war leader in the years of the Lakota."

"Even more so than Gall, or Sitting Bull?"

"Yes."

She gripped his hand tighter under the robe. "Promise me one thing. Make sure the man who will be my husband in two months returns safely."

He gripped her arm and pulled her close. His eyes were intent as they bored into hers. "I promise," he said softly.

24

No man has yet lived long enough in this world to doubt
the infallibility of his own judgment.
—Josh Billings

Custer boarded a horse-drawn trolley in front of the White House, having walked there from the War Department. The car was quite crowded, so he hung on to the strap as he looked out the window toward the canal and the string of boarding houses that faced Pennsylvania Avenue. Or at least he tried to see out the window, because the huge feather on a young woman's hat kept blocking his view.

The woman wearing the hat noticed him moving his head to see around it. Smiling pertly, she said, "Sorry, Colonel, I'm afraid it isn't a very good trolley hat."

He shook his head, returned her smile. "No, 'fraid not."

Her eyes returned to his, lingered. She was quite lovely, nice teeth, apparently buxom. The invitation was there, a gold wedding band on her finger probably meant that she would make it a short fling. A few years earlier, he might have followed it up—

"Have I seen your picture in the newspaper?" she asked.

He grinned. "Possibly. Name's Custer."

Her eyes widened, "You're *General Custer?*"

"'Fraid so."

"Well, I declare. I've read so much about you, General."

He always liked being recognized, and particularly by a beautiful woman. He smiled as she went on for a minute before saying, "And I've read your book!"

That pleased him immensely.

The discussion about his book got them past Four-and-a-half Street, and she said, "Oh, I missed my stop. Oh, General Custer, I wish we could talk more." The invitation in her eyes was now naked.

He smiled. "Perhaps we can." She lingered a moment, then started to move away. He touched his hat brim. "Pleasure, ma'am."

His attention drifted to the outside once more. It was warm for the fourth of April, and muggy. Clouds that would grow into giant thunderheads were building up in Maryland and across the river in Virginia. Today's *Star* was predicting a high temperature of eighty-six degrees and had recommended that no one go out that evening without an umbrella. But the ladies liked carrying their parasols whether it was going to rain or not, and it seemed to him they'd developed a special language with them. Like the Southern women had with fans. Ah, Washington, he thought, remembering his brief visits during the war when generals were a nickel a dozen and so were the women.

The women of Washington were a special breed, many of them strong and beautiful, capable of spending fortunes on appearance and status in the swirling, unceasing social life of the nation's capital. This early warm spell that would bring out the cherry blossoms had also brought out the bright spring bonnets from William's exclusive shop farther up Pennsylvania Avenue. Status was further marked by superbly liveried gigs, surreys, coaches, and other types of carriages wherever the swarming competitors went. Party invitation lists were major productions. But, of course, the Washington women weren't alone in their aggressive nature; their men could be as predatory as any animals in the country.

And speaking of competitors, the Democratic congress was making life difficult for the Republican administration. The Belknap scandal had given the Democrats the perfect tool, and they were riding it to the hilt. And it didn't bother Custer a single bit. Ever since he'd known about politics, he'd thought as a Democrat. His family had voted that way, and that was how he grew up. And obviously it hadn't affected the way he fought in the war. But he'd just left Sherman, and the general in chief had admonished him to tread lightly with regard to politics. Sherman was caught in a hard spot. He disliked Belknap intensely, and *hated* politicians, but he was an old friend of the president.

The first hearing at which Custer had appeared on March 29 had gone smoothly enough. He'd told them what they wanted to hear, and what he actually believed to be true about Belknap and the crooked trader situation. And the results had been inflammatory. But his stay apart from the hearings was what had been most enjoyable. He utterly disregarded his wife's and Sherman's admonitions.

As in New York, the leading Democrats were quite taken with him. He got along famously with Congressman Heister Clymer, the chairman of the investigating committee, and had gone to dinner with him three times. He'd also had lunch with and had been to a couple of dinner parties with Representative Henry Banning, the chairman of the Committee on Military Affairs that was taking a hard look at the army and was purportedly close to making drastic reductions. He'd appeared before Bang's committee and had given testimony that he thought would stay their sword. At least he hoped so. The army simply couldn't take any more cuts.

And how would *anyone* get promoted to general if everyone was thinking reduction?

The trolley stopped just down the hill from the Capitol, across from the botanical gardens. Having some time to kill before going to the hearings, he stepped down into the middle of Pennsylvania Avenue. He picked his way through the slow-moving traffic on broken cobblestones, avoiding the mud, to get to the brick promenade on the north side of the broad thoroughfare. He spied an oyster bar with a bright-yellow awning. Any place with all that cavalry yellow had to have good food, he thought. Ordering a dozen on the half-shell and a glass of tea, he quickly began to put them away.

"Ain't I seen you somewhere before?" the young man at the counter asked.

It must be his day to be recognized. "Possibly. I'm General Custer," he replied.

The young man laughed. "Uh huh, and I'm General Grant."

Custer laughed with him and turned his attention back to the oysters. He also thought about other things he was doing in the capital. He'd seen nothing wrong with staying at Ben Holladay's house during his time in town. After all, the stagecoach magnate had rescued him on the New York stock deal by cosigning the note. And he did have a beautiful home where Custer could stay for nothing. By the time these hearings were over, which he hoped would be soon, he'd be in so solid that the Democrats would have no choice but to nominate him for promotion when he returned victorious from his upcoming campaign. Of course, the Dakota column would never leave on April 6 now, but it could depart as soon as he got back.

He finished the last oyster and headed for the Capitol.

"Tell us again, General Custer, the information about the machinations in the post traderships in your area of knowledge," Congressman Clymer directed from his chairman's seat in the middle of the long committee table.

It grew totally quiet as the large audience strained to hear every word.

Custer shifted his weight in the witness chair and said, "It was common knowledge among the senior troop commanders that Secretary Belknap had his fingers in the post traderships somewhere. I showed him only cold courtesy when he visited Fort Lincoln, and I had to force myself to do that." He went on to describe the secretary's visit in detail, then explained how the traderships graft worked. "The appointment goes to a middle man, who usually pays a bribe to get it. He then farms out the actual operation to someone local, usually the incumbent trader . . . who in turn pays a yearly kickback to the middle man, who has to split his cut with an influence peddler or the secretary. In the case of the Fort Sill tradership, I understand the money went to the secretary's wife."

Custer cleared his throat and continued, "In the case of the Fort Lincoln trader, he pays about twelve thousand a year to stay in business."

"What do you know about Orvil Grant in this type of manipulation?" Clymer asked.

"I've heard that Mr. Grant was quite active peddling his influence up and down the whole line of army posts out there, particularly on the upper Missouri," Custer replied. "It was said that some money in his palm would do wonders in getting a tradership."

The hearing room buzzed noisily as the spectators broke out in comment. Clymer banged his gavel for silence. When the room was once again quiet, he asked, "Do you know of any army officers who were involved in these crooked dealings?"

Custer nodded. "I testified before the Banning committee that Major Lewis Merrill, formerly of my own Seventh Cavalry, was involved in some swindles while part of the regiment was stationed in South Carolina a few years ago. But I don't think that has any bearing on this investigation." Forgetting completely Libbie's warning to keep his mouth shut, he then launched into a long discourse about political intervention and lack of integrity on the part of the politicians as they interfered with army activities.

After a couple more questions about Belknap and Orvil Grant, he was excused as a witness, but was told that he might be recalled. Once more the expedition against the Sioux would be held up while he awaited congressional orders.

The following day, the Republican newspapers screamed *"HEARSAY!"*—in huge headlines. *"CUSTER VILIFIES SECRETARY AND ORVIL GRANT WITH HEARSAY!* AN ANGRY PRESIDENT U. S. GRANT REMAINS SILENT AS ENEMIES STRIVE TO BLACKBALL ADMINISTRATION!" *"CUSTER COMMITS PERJURY! CUSTER DISPARAGES FELLOW OFFICERS."* And more. The Democratic papers, on the other side of the coin, made him out a hero and lavished space on his testimony.

Custer hung around the capital for the next two weeks, going to more social events with prominent Democrats as the House of Representatives finally indicted William Belknap for trial before the U.S. Senate. Since none of the charges involved Custer's testimony, he was freed to return to his command. He left Washington on April 20 and went to Philadelphia to visit the Centennial Exposition, then went on by train to New York the next day to meet with his publishers at *Galaxy*, and with the Redpath Lyceum Agency people to discuss how a successful military campaign would bear on his forthcoming lecture series in the fall.

Even his mentor, Sheridan, wondered why he was dallying while the Dakota Column awaited. And the dallying cost Custer. Before he could finally head west, he was ordered to return to Washington, which he did on April 27. Many believed the order came from Grant himself.

Following a full cabinet meeting on April 28, President Grant held another meeting. This one included General Sherman and the new secretary of war, Alphonso Taft. Sherman was lounging in a chair in front of Grant's desk as Taft walked in. The redheaded general was relatively pleased with the selection of the new secretary, who had assured him that more control of the army would be returned to the office of the general in chief. The president offered Taft a cigar as he pointed to the chair next to Sherman.

As was his custom, Ulysses S. Grant quickly got to the heart of the matter. "As you know, gentlemen, my administration has been badly bloodied by this post-trader affair. My family as well—not that I'm condoning in any way what my pip-squeak young brother may have done. But that's another matter. What has my ire up is the doggone way Custer has gone about this thing. Doesn't he remember that he's an army officer?"

Sherman shrugged as he lit a fresh cigar. "I guess he thinks he's doing his duty."

Grant seldom showed emotion or anger, but he was also no actor. He growled, "If he had information that was detrimental to the army, he should have made it known to his superiors—not wait until the Democrats pulled off their big witch hunt."

Sherman raised an eyebrow. "His superiors—like who, Belknap?"

"He could've gone to his old boss, Sheridan. Or you, Cump. He knows you'd have done something—probably come to me with it."

"Maybe he wasn't sure about that."

Grant shook his head. "That won't sell, Cump. I'm not only a full general, but as president of the United States, I'm his commander in chief. As far as I know, he didn't go to anyone except the Democrats."

"What are you going to do about the campaign against the Sioux?" Secretary Taft asked. "Isn't Custer supposed to command Terry's part of it?"

Grant shook his head again. "Not now. If he can't be trusted in a matter such as this, I don't see how he can be trusted to command in a major campaign."

Sherman showed his surprise. "You're actually removing him from command of the Seventh Cavalry? Isn't that a little below you, Sam?"

"Perhaps, but I consider it a matter of discipline." Grant got up from his desk and walked to the window. Finally, turning, he said, "Oh, I know, I'm damned if I do and damned if I don't. The whole country's going to say I did this out of malice because he defamed my brother. But I won't look the other way over his lack of loyalty. That's the core of this thing—loyalty. Custer drew the line in the sand, not the army." He glanced from one to the other and went on, "Cump, notify General Terry that he's to be personally in field command on the campaign—and let Sheridan know what's going on."

Sherman looked at Taft and shrugged. He knew from long experience that when Sam Grant spoke like this, he'd given the matter extensive thought. He also knew the man seldom backed down on anything.

☆ ☆ ☆

"He can't do that to me!" Custer said, his face turning white after Sherman told him of Grant's decision the next day. "He can't remove me from command over honest testimony before a government investigative committee!"

Sherman watched Custer jump up from the chair in front of his desk and stare at him.

The cavalryman's voice dropped to nearly a whisper, "He just can't do it."

"He *has* done it," Sherman replied. "What you've apparently forgotten, Armstrong, is that you have attacked your commander."

"It was the truth!" Custer's eyes were wild as he began to pace in front of the general in chief's desk. "I told the truth on that stand!"

Sherman waited a moment before he said, "As you believe it from others. It was unverified hearsay. But that's not the point. What's at stake here with the president is a matter of loyalty and judgment, both of which he finds lacking in your recent conduct."

Custer stopped, staring at the general. "He's just getting even because his own brother is implicated!"

"No, Sam Grant doesn't get even. He just can't endorse you at this point. You have, by playing the political game, placed yourself as an unfaithful adversary giving comfort to his enemies. And . . ."

"Oh, that's bullshit, General!"

The redhead's brown eyes hardened. "Be careful, Armstrong. I may be your only high-placed friend in this matter."

Custer nodded, closing his eyes momentarily. "Forgive me, sir. It's just that I *can't* be stripped of that command. The Seventh Cavalry's *mine!* We're ready to win the Indian war.

"You should have thought of that before your indiscreet behavior."

"I was *ordered* here, sir, and I was under oath on that witness stand!"

"That's true, but you should have given us the gist of your testimony *before* you testified. That would have taken the sting out of it."

Custer dramatically threw his hands up in the air. "How could I have known what they were going to ask me?"

Sherman banged his fist on the desk! "Goddamn it, Custer, *you* quit the bullshit! You knew damned well the nature of what you were going to say. And you didn't give a single goddamn. You were on center stage, where you like to be, enjoying the attention. The only reason I'm even trying to help you is because I know you can fight, and I think you ought to take the Seventh on that campaign. Now, if you want to stand *any* chance of getting that command back, you'd better go see Grant and beg his forgiveness before you leave. At least try to square things with him."

Custer swallowed hard. No one had talked to him like this since he was a cadet—discounting that scene with Benteen years ago. "Yes, sir," he replied softly.

Rufus Ingalls shook his head. "He won't see you, Armstrong."

It was Monday, the first of May, and Custer had just cooled his heels for five hours trying to see the president. Then he had run into Ingalls in the hallway and had gotten him to intercede.

He said, "But why not, Rufe? Doesn't he feel any guilt about treating me this way?"

Ingalls shook his head. "Armstrong, you amaze me sometimes. Don't *you* feel any guilt about attacking your commander in chief? And I don't want to hear any of that duty bullshit. Your first duty was to the army, and you damned well know it."

Custer's voice was low as he said, "What am I going to do?"

"Go back to your house and sit tight."

"I'll go see Sherman again."

"He's in New York."

Custer shook his head. He was stymied in every direction. The Senate had no further need for him, and Sherman had, in effect, dismissed him. Maybe Sheridan, or Terry might help him. . . .

Lieutenant General Philip Sheridan was home with a light touch of the flu when Custer arrived at his headquarters in Chicago on the morning of May 3. Sandy Forsyth, his aide, brought papers into his bedroom for signature and said, "Custer wants to see you, General. It's about his being relieved by the president."

Little Phil was particularly crotchety when he was sick, and he'd never been known to fight the party line. Sam Grant had given him his first major command in the war, and had saved his ass when he'd been insubordinate with Meade in the Army of the Potomac. Besides that, the president and he were friends. Yet he had liked his blond cavalryman for a long time. He scowled as he said, "Why can't that goddamned Custer keep his mouth shut?"

Sandy Forsyth had been with Sheridan since the war, in fact had been along on Little Phil's famous Winchester ride. "It's far too late for that, General."

Sheridan scowled. "I know, I know. Well, I don't know how Terry's going to get along without him, but I'm not going to go up against Sam Grant on this damned thing. Damn fool, why couldn't he at least have told me before spouting off in Washington!"

"What should I tell him, sir?"

Sheridan snorted. "Tell him the truth. I'm sick! And send him on to St. Paul, where Terry can figure out what to do with him."

Brigadier General Alfred Howe Terry listened compassionately, as was his wont, while Custer told him about his troubles in Washington. It was the sixth of May and Custer had arrived in St. Paul the night before by train from Chicago.

In summary, Custer said, "I don't know why everyone has it in for me."

The handsome forty-eight-year-old Terry responded quietly, "I don't think that's the case, Armstrong. Your actions, regardless of your intent, have been perceived as disloyal. And from what I know of the president, that's a strong black mark against you. As a result, he probably has doubts about your judgment."

Custer clenched both fists. "Giving testimony and fighting at the head of my regiment are two different matters! No one, General, *no one* leads better than I do in battle."

Terry watched him quietly. He couldn't dispute the statement. And he needed Custer in command of the Seventh Cavalry. He'd never fought the Indians himself, not actually in the field. And he didn't think Marcus Reno had the requisites to pursue an energetic campaign. What he saw next astounded him.

George Armstrong Custer, the most fearless cavalry leader alive, had dropped to one knee in front of his desk. With tears causing his eyes to brim, Custer said, "Sir, I'll do *anything* for a chance to prove my loyalty. Get my command back for me and I'll deliver Sitting Bull's and Crazy

Horse's heads on a *platter!* I'm so profoundly sorry that I used bad judgment, sir. Please help me."

Terry pointed to the chair beside his desk. "Come, come, Armstrong, you don't have to beg, Sit here and let's figure out what to do." He reached for a pencil. "Tell you what. Let's see if this old lawyer can figure out how to plead a case. Of course, you'll have to eat crow with the president."

"If it'll get my command back, I'll eat *vulture!*" Custer replied.

Terry smiled. "Oh, it won't be *that* bad."

As Custer quietly watched, the general scribbled a few lines, changed a word here and there, and then called in his aide. "Take this down," he instructed, "and send this by telegram through channels to President Grant."

Custer broke in. "I might add, sir, that I'll gladly do precisely as you desire if you get my command back."

Terry just nodded as he turned his attention back to the aide and began to dictate:

"I regret, Mr. President, that I used poor judgment in repeating hearsay information in the recent Clymer hearings. I should have brought these reports to my superiors so they could have been forwarded to you. I assure you that I will do so in the future, and will exercise the utmost of prudence in all political matters. I wish to apologize for any injury my ill-considered action may have caused. I humbly request that you restore me to field command the Seventh Cavalry. I appeal to you as a soldier to spare me the humiliation of seeing my regiment march to meet the enemy, and I not share its dangers."

Terry winked at Custer. "No officer of General Grant's caliber will be able to withstand that last statement." Turning back to the aide, the general went on, "Sign that Lieutenant Colonel George Armstrong Custer, and add this endorsement from me: 'Mr. President. In no way am I questioning your judgment in the Custer matter. The officer was undoubtedly indiscreet. However, I recommend you favorably consider his request. Lieutenant Colonel Custer's services would be very valuable with his regiment.'" General Terry turned to Custer. "I think Sheridan will add his favorable two cents, and we'll just have to wait and see. As soon as we get an answer, I'll contact you at your quarters."

Custer smiled and tossed off a salute. "Yes, sir!"

General Cump Sherman personally brought the telegram to President Grant the next morning. As Grant quietly read the message and its endorsements, the general in chief chuckled. "Little Phil has become quite the politician."

The president looked up over his small reading glasses. "How's that?"

"Did you notice all of those negatives in his endorsement—how he regretted that Custer had shown less ambition to stay at Fort Lincoln and get ready for the expedition than he now does to go along with it. And how he hopes this time, if you grant Custer clemency, that you might *restrain* him in the future. Pretty good, huh, Sam?"

Grant shook his head. "Doesn't help me any. I told you Custer put me on the spot. You've seen the doggone papers. 'Vengeance,' they're calling it. Well, I'll tell you right now that I could square my shoulders and let them fire away 'till doomsday. And personally, I could let Custer rot. But it's more than that, Sherman. If this campaign fails and Custer isn't in on it, the opposition press will hang me from the tallest cottonwood. Arrogant, and at times as boorish as he may be, he's a fighter. And his regiment needs him. That's one thing we soldiers know, the importance of a man's regiment. It's one thing to command a brigade, a division, a corps—even an army—but a man's regiment is always his family. I can't let the Seventh Cavalry go without him."

"Shall I send the telegram?"

"Yes, but Custer is only to command the Seventh Cavalry. Order Terry to take command of his entire force in the field."

"Yes, sir, anything else?" Sherman asked.

Grant sighed, stroked his gray beard. "No, I guess not. You know, Sherman, when there are so many things wrong with a military operation in its infancy, it usually has troubles. I have a strange feeling that I'm doing something wrong."

The commanding general shook his head. "I don't think you have any choice, Sam."

Grant spoke softly, "I hope you're right."

☆ ☆ ☆

The telegram arrived at Terry's headquarters in St. Paul the following afternoon, May 8. After reading it, the general sent a runner to Custer's nearby hotel to fetch him. A few minutes later, the breathless cavalryman rushed in, tossed off a salute, and took the proffered message.

Custer's eyes lit up as he read it. Grinning, he looked up at the general and exclaimed, "By glory, now we'll get after 'em! Grant knows he needs me out there."

Terry smiled. "Yes, I felt sure he'd relent."

Custer was so elated that he tossed his hat in the air and caught it. "I'll be on the next train. And—oh, are there any changes in the basic plan?"

"No. The supporting companies of troops and the supply train will be assembling at Fort Lincoln in the next few days. Reno should have the Seventh ready, as well. I'll be along in a couple of days and the column will depart on the fifteenth."

"We'll be ready, sir!"

"Oh, and Armstrong—"

"Yes, sir?"

"Stay out of the newspapers."

"Yes, sir!" Custer stopped at the door and turned. "General, I want to thank you again and tell you how much I appreciate what you've done for me."

Terry nodded. "See you in a few days."

Custer hurried out through the headquarters and down the street. He hadn't gone a block before he ran into Captain William Ludlow, Terry's chief engineer. Ludlow had known Custer for a long time, having been with him at West Point and having gone along on the Black Hills expedition in 1874. The ebullient Custer told him the good news of his reinstatement.

"Well, that's just fine, General," Ludlow replied. "I'm certain you'll more than justify the decision."

"Of course," Custer added, "I'll cut loose the first chance I get and swing clear of Terry."

George Armstrong Custer had no idea that his words—blurted out in a show of ingratitude and further impropriety—would live into posterity.

25

It had been raining for several days, a cold drenching type of rain that soaked everything and left the Missouri River Flats, two miles south of Fort Lincoln a muddy bog. There, stretched out, in a veritable sea of canvas, the Seventh Cavalry was gathered in myriad tents with the rest of the Dakota Column. The expedition had been scheduled to depart for the Yellowstone the day before, but the fifty heavy supply wagons had been unable to move. It was the first time all twelve companies of the regiment had ever been assembled together, and, in spite of the sogginess, there was a certain air of camaraderie and purpose. Just the prospect of forthcoming action was enough to lighten the spirits of the regiment as a whole, and a kind of muted energy permeated the Flats. Here and there a mule brayed, a dog barked, and a horse neighed. To liven things up, Custer had ordered the regimental band to set up under a large tent and give a one-hour concert just before the noon meal. Not too many troopers came out from cover to listen, but the music could be heard all over the drenched camp, and that was all that was important.

Custer, wearing a slicker and a dripping broad-brimmed hat, was accompanied by his Dundrearied adjutant, Lieutenant William Cooke, Sergeant-Major Sharrow, and several of the hounds as he made the rounds, asking about the welfare of a soldier here and there, greeting an NCO he remembered, returning salutes, checking equipment, patting a horse's rump now and then. It was one of those things a smart, competent commander did to show the men that he cared and was personally excited about the pending departure.

"Hey, General, where're we goin' after them damned redskins?" a private shouted from where he was feeding his horse at the I Company stable.

Custer laughed aloud. "Soon's it quits raining, trooper."

"We're gonna give 'em hell, ain't we?"

Custer grinned. That's what he wanted to hear. "You *bet!*" he shouted back. He splashed through a big puddle to the headquarters tent of Company A and returned Captain Myles Moylan's salute. "Afternoon, Myles. How're things?"

"Fine, just fine, General. Want some coffee? Cook just brought over some fresh."

"No, thanks. Got to move on. You all ready to roll?"

"Yes, sir. We gonna leave tomorrow?"

"Yup. Rain's about played out."

Moylan saluted as Custer and his entourage moved on. Stopping at C Company's headquarters tent, he returned Ed Bobo's salute as the first sergeant jumped to his feet. "Stand easy, First Sergeant," Custer said. "Is the captain around?"

"No, sir, Captain Custer's gone over to see his brother in the trains area. I can send a runner over for him."

"No, that's all right. I'm going over there later. Are your men comfortable?"

"Just fine, General."

Custer nodded, and ducked out of the tent. As he and his group passed D Company, First Sergeant Michael Martin was opening yet another note from his unknown tormentor. He hated to even open them because they were always annoying and made him feel such futility, but there was no way he could ignore them. This was the first one in nearly a month and it read: "The time has come for us to meet, you cowardly bastard. Be at the F Company stable at Fort Lincoln at seven P.M. on the sixteenth. Come alone, or you'll never see my face." It wasn't even signed, but Martin knew. He made a fist and slammed it into his palm. "I'll see your face, all right, you bloody arsehole," he said through his gritted teeth.

The company clerk looked up from where he was working on the field filing cabinet. "Did you say something, First Sergeant?"

"No," Martin replied, "I was just talking to myself."

Custer glanced at H Company as he strode by. Fred Benteen looked up from inside the tent where he sat reading on a folding stool. Neither officer changed expression as their eyes locked momentarily. Custer turned away and saw a handful of officers under the fly of the L Company mess tent and approached them. Captain Tom Weir, Captain Myles Keogh, and Captain George Yates were all drinking coffee with the company commander, Lieutenant Jimmi Calhoun. "This private stock?" Custer asked.

They all saluted. "No, sir," Calhoun replied. "There's enough here for three more, but those mutts of yours don't get any."

Everyone chuckled as the mess sergeant hurried up with two cups of steaming coffee. A cook brought another. "What are you gentlemen plotting?" Custer asked, after thanking the mess sergeant.

"How to stay out of the mud and fight a gentleman's war," Myles Keogh replied, exaggerating his Irish accent.

"Actually," Tom Weir said, "we're discussing the possibility of joining the navy."

Custer laughed. "Come now, we haven't had that much rain."

Following his cup of coffee and more banter, the regimental commander moved on. Rain or no rain, it was a great day!

Later that afternoon, Custer held an officers' call in the regimental headquarters tent. All thirty-two officers attended, plus Dr. Henry Porter, who had accepted a three month contract as Acting Assistant Surgeon. After covering the general mission of the Dakota column, Custer said, "The proud Seventh Cavalry will spearhead the column. As of this morning, we have seven hundred eighteen enlisted men present for duty, which is about seventy percent of the expedition. For command purposes, I'm dividing the regiment into two wings, each with two battalions of three companies each. The right wing will be commanded by Major Reno, and the left by the senior captain, Benteen." He looked down into Benteen's cool pale eyes for a moment as the captain finished lighting his long-stemmed pipe and blew out a cloud of smoke.

"Gentlemen, as you know, we have a veteran regiment. Seventy-five percent of our men have over a year's service, some go on up to twenty years. Only ten percent have less than a year. The men's average age is twenty-seven, many years older than the average soldier in the last war. Every trooper has a good horse and is otherwise well-equipped. I've spoken with several in the last couple of days, and morale is high."

He grinned. "They're spoiling for a fight, and so am I. As you can see, the weather's changed, so we'll pull out tomorrow morning. But first we'll put on a little show on the way out—a parade for the families. Lieutenant Cooke will issue a parade order to coincide with the march order."

Custer paused, looking around the assembled faces for a couple of moments, and said, "All right, gentlemen, if you have any questions, direct them to Major Reno or Lieutenant Cooke. Thank you." As he headed for the tent entrance, all of the officers came to attention.

Private Iggy Stungewitz was busy cleaning his long-barreled .45 revolver in his C Company squad tent. He had cleaned it thoroughly the night before, but he didn't want to take any chances of it rusting in the moist air. He looked up from his bedroll as Private Lucien Burnham, the lawyer, walked up. "You're going to wear that out," Burnham said.

"Hardly," Iggy replied. "I think we might have some hard fighting before this campaign is over, and I don't want my weapons to fail me at any time."

Burnham sat down on a box. "You're the most perfect trooper I've ever met. You should be a sergeant."

Iggy shrugged. "No chance after my trouble with Martin. Not even Bobo will recommend me for promotion."

Burnham was the other person who knew about his campaign to get even with the D Company first sergeant. He looked around to see if anyone was listening before he lowered his voice and asked, "What's next with that son of a bitch?"

"I'm going to settle with him tonight."

Burnham looked as if he was going to wring his hands. "Oh, God, what are you going to do?"

Iggy didn't even look up. "I'm going to get even."

Burnham's eyes grew wide. "You aren't going to kill him, are you?"

"I don't know."

Burnham reached out and touched his arm. "Don't let anything happen to you. I don't think I could stand it."

Iggy looked up into his friend's troubled eyes. He'd known for some time about the lawyer's unspoken feeling for him. It made him uncomfortable, but being a Russian, he was more understanding about it than others might be. There had been quite a bit of that sort of thing in the Czar's cavalry. "I'll be fine," he replied.

"I, I've never told you this, but I—"

"Don't," Iggy broke in. "It can never be more than friendship with me."

Burnham looked away, "I know."

Bloody Knife had experienced his old dream again the night before. In it, he rammed a sharp-pointed lance right through Gall's arrogant face. Right through his nose, shattering his face and skull, making splintered white bone show and blood spurt everywhere. Then he had grabbed the bulging, staring eyeballs and ripped them out and eaten them. He had this dream every few moons and it always gave him great pleasure. He didn't know why it had just recurred, but he assumed it was because of the campaign. There wasn't a doubt in his mind that he would meet Gall on this Sioux hunt. It was a certainty. And this time Gall would die, if not by a lance, then by a bullet, or a knife—at the hand of Bloody Knife, the Arikira Sioux who had been treated like a *snake* instead of a brother! If he didn't have a lance, he would jam his big knife straight into Gall's ugly face, and then he would cut off his tongue and eat his eyes.

And then he would scalp him and forever wear his enemy's hair on his belt.

He leaned down and checked his pony's left front shoe. Actually, he was a dun horse the army had provided him. A good one—Custer had seen to that. A man couldn't be Long Hair's favorite scout without having a good horse. The shoe was all right, and would last until they returned to *Lin-cun.*

"Bloody Knife!" Bob-Tailed Bull called out in Ree from a few paces away. Varnum wants you."

"Why?"

"I don't know."

"You're the corporal, you should."

Bloody Knife!" Bob-Tailed Bull laughed. "You're always complaining. You could be lead scout if you didn't take the 'Grand Bounce' so much."

Second Lieutenant Charlie Varnum was waiting by the Scout Detachment tent. Mitch Boyer was with him. Varnum could Indian sign, but when Boyer was around he didn't bother. Boyer was suffering from a bad cold and was wearing his trademark black-and-white calfskin vest. He translated as the officer said, "Bloody Knife, the general wants you in his party, where he can have you handy at all times. If he sends you out to do any scouting, I want you to check out and back in with me."

Bloody Knife grunted in agreement. No need to tell him. It wasn't the first time he'd be on an expedition with Long Hair.

Varnum added, "This will be a big hunt of perhaps several moons."

Bloody Knife nodded, signing back, "We'll find Sitting Bull close to the Yellowstone."

"How do you know?"

"I know. I dreamed the buffalo were there and south of there."

"It's a good guess," Boyer added.

Varnum nodded his head. "There's going to be a parade just before we leave. We'll join the column and ride along at its tail."

Bloody Knife nodded his head. Gall would also be close to the Yellowstone.

Missouri Ann Bobo took down some long underwear she had been drying by the potbellied stove in the laundry. "Damn rain," she muttered as she folded it and put it in a basket. Ever since Custer had returned and everyone had known when the regiment was pulling out, she had been trying to figure a way to see Danny. With everyone assembling down on the Flats, he had been busy and right under Ed's nose. So he couldn't get into town. And there was no way she could've met him anyway. She could just see herself saying, "I have to go to town shopping," when the rain was coming down in sheets. Ed would *never* have bought that.

God, she ached to have Danny close . . . inside her. She could just feel him right now. Not having him was really bad for her. Oh, how had she ever gotten into this mess?

She folded some more underwear. Nothing dried properly when you couldn't hang it out on the line. She wouldn't have much to do for a while, what with the regiment gone. She was the only laundress working right now, and that was only because she was doing some of the kids' stuff. Damn! There had to be some way she could see Danny before he left!

At that moment the door opened slowly.

"Annie?" Dan Kanipe said as he stuck his head inside.

She dropped the laundry and ran to the door. "C'mon in. I'm alone," she said excitedly. She didn't even notice that his slicker was dry as she flew into his arms and kissed him. "Oh, sweetheart," she murmured, "I was so afraid I wouldn't get to see you before you left." She kissed him again.

"Captain Custer sent me in to get a couple of things from the orderly room," he replied.

"Take that darned slicker off so I can hold you," she said.

He looked around. "What if someone comes in?"

"Don't worry about it. Everyone's doing something else."

He put his hat on a bench and tossed the slicker down beside it. She came back into his arms, holding him tightly. "Oh, darling, I've missed you so," she said reaching up to his lips.

"I know. I can hardly sleep, knowing you're so close," he said softly.

Their kiss was long, growing in intensity as she pushed up against him. Her hands slid down to his buttocks and found his suspenders. Pulling them down, she drew his shirt out of his pants and stroked his bare back. Slowly she began undulating against him. Breaking the kiss, she said, "Oh, honey, I want you so much!"

"You're the one with all the darned clothes on," he replied, putting both hands under her buttocks and holding her up tighter.

She pulled him over to the heavy clothes-folding table and hiked her long skirt and petticoat up above her hips. "Oh, sweetheart, hurry!"

In moments, she was matching his every thrust. She'd managed to get her blouse loose so she could feel his bare chest against her breast. There wasn't time to suck even one of her nipples—he would, he would. She'd told him how much she liked that. As she drove up against him, she wrapped her legs even more tightly around him and let the words and sounds go unrestrained. She *loved* him like this, so wild and forbidden!

She had just let out a shriek of passion when she opened her eyes and saw Mary Hohmeyer standing in the doorway *watching!*

"Mary!" she exclaimed, freezing.

Seeing the look in her eyes, Dan jerked his head around and saw the woman. She was First Sergeant Fred Hohmeyer's wife! The E Company first sergeant. *Oh, shit!* He pulled back, sliding off the table and jerking his pants up.

Missouri Ann got her skirts down and swung her legs to the floor, as Mary Hohmeyer, hand at her mouth and shock still in her eyes, started to back out the door. "No, *wait!*" Ann exclaimed. "Wait, Mary. Let me talk to you!"

Mary Hohmeyer, a stocky blonde woman in her mid-thirties, was a humorless mother of four from Wurtemburg, Germany. She had been a laundress in the regiment for nearly ten years, and had been married to the German first sergeant for several of them. Ann got along with her, but there was no love lost between them. The German woman was too bossy and unbending for her tastes. She still hadn't said a word.

"Mary, I want to ask a favor of you," Missouri Ann said anxiously, trying to sound calm as she took the laundress's arm. "Please forget you saw us like this. Please. I'll make it up to you, I swear I will. Just keep this to yourself and I'll work it out, honest."

Mary Hohmeyer glanced from her to the silent and frowning Dan, who was buttoning his shirt. Looking back into Ann's deep concern, she said in her thick accent, "I'll think about it. But you know what you do is bad, makes laundresses look bad. I don't like it one bit!"

"Mary, please. I'll explain later. You know the regiment's leaving. Keep this quiet until they're gone and I swear to God I'll make it up to you."

The German's eyes narrowed as she looked from Ann to Dan again. "I don't know. I'll think about it." Before anything more could be said, she gathered up her skirt and hurried away.

"Damn," Danny said, blowing out a deep breath.

"Double damn!" Missouri Ann sighed.

"Think she'll keep quiet?"

Ann shook her head. "I doubt it. She doesn't particularly like me. All we can do is hope she doesn't say anything until the regiment gets outta here, then maybe I can bribe her. I've got a few dollars saved."

"I can give you a few dollars."

Ann leaned her head against his chest and held him. "I think she's going to tell someone. I just hope it doesn't get to Ed."

Dan shook his head. There were a dozen ways Bobo could find out.

Damn!

"Private Stungewitz want's to talk to you."

First Sergeant Ed Bobo looked up from the company punishment sheet he was working on and replied, "Send him in."

Moments later Iggy stood in front of Bobo's field desk and said, "Request permission for a three-hour pass to go to Fort Lincoln tonight, First Sergeant."

Bobo frowned. "You know all the lower ranks are restricted to the Flats, Stungewitz."

"Yes, but this is a special occasion, and I give you my word that I'll be back on time."

"Why should I make an exception?"

"Have I ever failed you on anything?"

"No, you're the best trooper in the company."

"All I want is three hours."

"What can be so all-fired important at the fort?"

Iggy's gaze was steady as he looked into Bobo's eyes. "I have some unfinished business that you don't want to know about."

"Huh. Now what the hell could that be?" Bobo frowned, then a slow smile touched his lips. "I heard that Martin's been getting some funny mail lately. Does this have anything to do with that?"

"I wouldn't know what you're talking about."

"The hell you wouldn't. What're you going to do to that bastard?"

Iggy snapped to attention, staring straight ahead. "Private Stungewitz requests permission to go on a three-hour pass tonight."

Ed Bobo nodded his head. "All right, trooper, you can have it."

Libbie served the tea herself. She liked using the silver service and her best china when she had guests. Today it was an informal get-together with her closest friends, sort of a last minute thing before the troops left. She'd have all the officers' wives in for something sometime after the regiment departed, maybe on the first day of summer or the Fourth of July. Something like that. She smiled as she filled Annie Yates's cup, and turned to Maggie Calhoun, Autie's sister. Fresh Smith's wife, Nettie, was also there.

"Annie," she said, "You look so good today. I declare, I think you're going to live."

Everyone laughed as Annie replied, "If I do, it won't be because that little tyke cares. He burns up more of my energy than I used climbing mountains."

Maggie shook her head. "Listening to your travails, Annie, makes me wonder if I *ever* want to have children."

"I feel the same way," Nettie Smith chimed in as she plopped a second lump of sugar in her tea.

"Isn't it strange that three out of four of us are childless?" Libbie returned.

"And when *I* have one of the little blighters, I suffer for all three of you," Annie said with feigned disgust.

"Is it true that Mary is going along to cook for the general?" Nettie asked.

"Yes," Libbie replied as she sat at the large dining room table. "That's why she isn't serving the tea. She's getting everything ready for the expedition."

"Gosh," Annie said, "Imagine being the only woman to accompany a campaign that will surely make history. You know, I'd cook for the General's whole staff if they'd let *me* go along. And I know for a fact that I can shoot better than a whole bunch of his troopers."

Again everyone laughed. "You're just the queen of the tomboys, Annie-girl," Libbie said.

Maggie added, "And I'll bet you *can* outshoot a bunch of those boys. Autie thinks everyone's a dead-eye, but I know for a fact that some of those new troopers haven't ever fired a hundred rounds of *anything*. George told me. Even the recruits in his famous Band Box Troop barely know which end of a rifle is which."

Libbie didn't like to hear it. As far as she was concerned, Autie's troopers were the best soldiers in any regiment in the world. She switched the subject. "I asked him if he's going to have the band go into battle with him—you know, have them play music that will charm those Indians to death. Like those fellows in India with the snakes."

Another round of chuckles followed, after which Annie sobered and quietly asked, "What do you really think about this expedition, Libbie? I mean, you hear things we don't. How dangerous is it?"

The others watched her eyes as Libbie pushed aside the desire to share the nagging little fear that had been picking away at her. "I don't think it's much different than other campaigns. You know, the biggest problem is finding the hostiles and cornering them. That's Autie's biggest concern, *catching* them."

The women looked quietly at one another. They'd all heard the same thing from their husbands a dozen times. Maggie Calhoun was the first to smile. "And if they don't catch them, there won't be many brevets handed out."

They all agreed and went on to some gossip. Annie said, "I hear that so-called officers' sporting house in town will just about have to close up while our wicked Tom is away." Libbie laughed. "Yes, him and Keogh and Weir, and even our favorite surgeon, Henry Porter. Rumor is, they all keep that place going."

Maggie frowned. "Yes, well, we'll have to get busy and get those fellows married off when they get back. They're just having too much fun!"

Annie chuckled. "Let's make that our mission this summer—write letters to all of the pretty, eligible young women we know, and invite them out here this fall. We'll *smother* those damned professional bachelors with gorgeous women!"

"Hear, hear!" Nettie Smith said.

"Great idea," Libbie said. "We'll have the finest ball the peacetime army has ever thrown." She laughed. "They won't have a chance!"

Just then the doorbell rang, It was the new twist type that Libbie had John Burkman install while Custer was in Washington, and which served to open a chorus of barks from the hounds who were hanging around the house. Opening the door, she saw Sergeant Jeremiah Finley, the provost sergeant who doubled as a tailor and sometime bartender at the Bower Hog Ranch, standing on the porch. A yellowish buckskin outfit was hanging over his arm. "Afternoon ma'am," he said. "I finished the general's suit, and thought I'd bring it along so he'd have it for the campaign, if he wished."

"Come in, Sergeant," she replied. "I'm afraid I'm entertaining, but I can take the uniform."

Entering, he handed the suit to her. It was the softest of skin, light-cream in color, with plenty of long fringe. She stroked it. "It's so nice, Sergeant Finley. You do such good work."

Pleased, Finley replied, "Thank you, ma'am. I understand you're no slouch with a needle yourself."

She smiled. "I do what I can. I'll give this to the general when he comes in later. I'm sure he'll absolutely love it. And I imagine he'll settle with you later."

"Yes, ma'am, that's fine. I'll be amblin' along."

As Finley walked off the veranda, Libbie closed the door and hung the new suit over a hook on the coat tree. Walking back to the dining room, she took her seat and said, "Now, where were we in the plot to end the wild freedom of those randy bachelors?"

When Custer arrived home a little after five, he immediately tried on the suit. His angular figure never changed much with his energetic daily life, so the fit was just right. Libbie sat on the bed as he paraded past her and turned around. "Pretty nice, huh?"

She stood, coming close and stroking his back. "It's nice material."

"He's a fine tailor. Did this for me for four dollars. Imagine what it would have cost me in New York."

She nodded her head. "Uh huh, another of those nice little things about being a commanding officer."

He started taking off the jacket. "Now I want a haircut."

"A what?"

"You heard me. I want you to trim off these famous locks of mine."

"But, Autie, how will anyone know you?"

"I've decided to change my image, become the dutiful subordinate and all."

She broke out laughing. "You, change your image? Autie Custer, you couldn't change your image for a million dollars!"

"Go get your barbering kit."

A few minutes later, she was lopping off big lengths of yellow-gold curls. "How much did you say?" she asked.

He was sitting under an old sheet, holding a mirror. "Clear up to the tops of the ears, but you can leave a little bit on the back of my neck."

"Why is it I suddenly feel like Delilah?" she asked, meaning for it to sound funny. But suddenly it wasn't. The comparison, in fact, stuck her like a knife. She tried to push the thought away.

He squeezed her knee. "Samson's still got his strength."

"Ouch!" she said, drawing back. "I *do* feel like Delilah, Autie. Robbing you of your power."

He laughed. "Nobody can take my power, sweetheart, not even the queen of the Philistines. And I'll tell you what—just as soon as we get in bed tonight, I'll prove it!"

She smiled and kissed him on the cheek as she snipped off the final lock of hair. "I'll hold you to that, brave cavalier."

But the frightening allusion didn't leave her.

Iggy Stungewitz arrived at the F Company stables at 6:40 P.M. Checking to make sure he was alone, he removed a small oilskin package from the inside of his jacket. He hadn't seen its contents since he was in Russia. He thought back to that time as he untied the string; it seemed a century away. Inside were two white cotton garments. He stripped off his clothes and stepped into the white trousers. Quickly he slipped on the wide-sleeved jacket and knotted the black belt that completed his *judo-gi*. Holding his arms out in front and dropping into a squat, he wiggled his fingers to loosen up. Then he eased into the *Randori*, the free-style warm-up exercises.

After ten minutes of strenuous movement, he stopped to wait for his visitor.

When First Sergeant Michael Martin left his quarters at five minutes to seven and headed for the F Company stables, a number of children were playing baseball on the parade ground, but the main post was practically deserted. The infantry, up on the hill, was remaining at Fort Lincoln to protect its inhabitants, but no sign of fife other than wisps of gray smoke from a few chimneys evinced its presence. A number of clouds were moving through the clearing sky and the temperature had risen considerably since the morning's dreary start. The sun, a large and dark-orange ball, was settling toward the horizon as it shot its long rays through the early evening air. Except for the shouts of the baseball players and the barks of a few dogs who were trying to get in the game, the post was quiet. Entering the stable area, Martin stopped, pulled the .45 service revolver out of his belt, and rechecked it. On safe, it had a round in the chamber. He stuck it back in his belt and moved on past his own stables to E Company's area, where he stopped and looked around.

A few horses with assorted infirmities had been left behind. Over in F Company's stable, a black gelding looked at him and wandered over to the fence. The light in the shade of the long shed was beginning to diminish. Except for the soft whinny of another horse, there was little sound. He stepped warily toward the neighboring stable, looking around for the first sign of his tormentor. The voice startled him.

"Over here, Martin," Iggy said quietly. He was standing in the shadow, leaning on a pitchfork.

Martin's eyes narrowed, "I shouda bloody well known it was you, Jew-boy. Who'd you get to write all those stupid letters?"

"Did they give you a little concern, Martin?"

Martin edged closer. "Who wrote them? And what are you doing in those bloody pajamas?"

Iggy's reply was a brief smile.

"What are you doing away from the Flats, Jew-boy. You deserting"'"

"No, Bobo gave me a pass."

"I don't believe it. All troopers are restricted. I oughta just shoot you and say you were trying to steal a horse to take the Grand Bounce."

Iggy shook his head. "No, you can't do that, Martin. You're a sadistic prick, and you want my blood in your hands. You want to hurt me and taste it."

When they were about eight feet apart, Martin stopped. "You're right, arsehole, I'm gonna break your goddamn neck!"

Suddenly Iggy raised the pitchfork and jammed it into the ground in front of Martin's feet. While the surprised Martin jumped back, Iggy moved slowly forward, hands raised. Martin let out a roar and lunged toward him. His roundhouse right caught nothing but air as Iggy slipped backward and dropped into a classic *jujitsu* crouch. He held his open hands in front of his chest as Martin missed with a wild left, then lunged at him with another overhand right. Iggy caught Martin's wrist, twisted sharply, and slammed him viciously to the ground. After a flashing judo chop to the sergeant's neck, Iggy was on his feet like a cat, resuming the defensive position.

Martin climbed angrily to his feet. Wiping his mouth and glaring, he shouted, "I'll kill you, you stinking Jew bastard!" He jerked the revolver from his belt, but just as he brought it up to fire, Iggy's right foot knocked it spinning several feet away. With a furious grunt, Martin dove at Iggy with his head down, only to find himself flying to the ground from a perfect *tsurikomi goshi*—Iggy's powerful lifting hip throw. Once more, the knifelike hand chopped painfully into his neck. But there was no follow-up, as the white pajamas backed away once more. Martin roared to his feet, and in a glare of red moved slowly toward Iggy, stalking, shuffling with both hands out, reaching. He'd crush him. "You don't even know how to fight like a man, you Jew garbage," he snarled.

Iggy edged slowly toward him, eyes narrowed, loose, ready to end it. It was perfect—the Irishman's fingers were coming at his throat, finding his jacket, the other arm looping. . . .

In a blur, he drove up hard with his shoulders and hooked Martin's arm, pivoted counterclockwise, and threw him over his shoulder. The burly Martin crashed to the ground on his back, screaming in pain and rage. Before he could move, Iggy pounced on him, applying a paralyzing *nami juji jime*—a stifling cross-choke on his throat. Increasing the pressure, he stared coldly into Martin's bulging eyes until he saw the quit in them. The sergeant's struggle ended abruptly as he fought for air. Just as his eyes began to flutter, Iggy loosened his grip and growled, "You aren't worth the firing squad, but if you ever trouble me again, I'll kill you in an instant."

He got to his feet as Martin continued to gasp, and found the Irishman's revolver. Emptying the bullets from it, he tossed it at the first sergeant's feet and walked away.

Geraldine Gentle's place was decorated with red, white, and blue bunting, and a replica of the regimental flag hung over the mahogany back bar. She had also hired a piano player to join her regular guitarist. Her new addition, Santa Fe Sandy, the redhead, had gotten over her summer flu, so all of her girls were present. Geraldine had also procured some cheap but tasty champagne, so it was a delightful party. As soon as Tom Custer sent word from the cavalry camp in the Flats that they wouldn't be moving out until the morning of the seventeenth, she'd gone to work on the event. She still had a number of civilians as customers, but it was Tom and his friends from Fort Lincoln who were her mainstays. The least she could do was throw them a farewell party. Then she could close the place for a few weeks and take a well-earned vacation. Not too long, because she didn't want somebody else coming into town and opening up.

It would also be a good way to keep from missing Tom Custer.

As usual, he had been in the poker game since arriving a little after seven with the other regulars—Myles Keogh, Tom Weir, Bill Cooke. A couple of the younger lieutenants had come along as well—Charlie Varnum, Ben Hodgson, and Jimmy Sturgis. And the older one, the Italian named De Rudio. The mayor had been there for a while, as had Clement Lounsberry, the local newspaper editor, and some merchants. The house doctor, Henry Porter, had arrived a bit late, accompanied by Mark Kellogg, the reporter for the Bismarck *Tribune* who was going along on the campaign as a special correspondent.

It had been a lively party, all right, with lots of dancing and singing—just the kind of affair a bunch of hard-drinking, devil-may-care, young cavalry officers ought to have before going out to fight hostile Indians.

Now, with a couple of the lieutenants pretty drunk and trying to dance with Santa Fe Sandy and one of the other girls, Tom Weir was upstairs in a room with his regular, Rita. He reached for a bottle of Geraldine's champagne on the night stand and poured its remains into a water glass. Taking a big drink of it, he handed it to Rita, who was lying on the rumpled double bed. She was still wearing her black garter belt and black mesh hose because Tom preferred her like that. Otherwise she was naked, as was Weir. That is, except for her heavy makeup.

"Why are you so morbid tonight, Tom? You haven't made me laugh like you usually do."

`He frowned. "Not much to be funny about."

"Oh, the going off and all?"

"No, I don't think it's that. I don't mind being in the field. I guess I just had a bad dream last night and it's still bothering me."

"About those dead little Indian children again?"

"Uh huh."

"Think something like that will happen this time?"

"Maybe."

"Well, perhaps we ought to go down and dance a little, then we can come back up."

Weir finished the glass of champagne and reached for his underwear. "No, I think I'll get on back. If I'm gonna feel this way, I might better be alone. You know how I get." He had hit her once, back at Christmastime when he was feeling blue. Besides, Libbie was on his mind and he couldn't shake her. He wouldn't be seeing his Libbie for weeks now, and that void would be hard to accept.

His beautiful Libbie.

Captain Miles Keogh had decided to wear his papal medals that night, but they didn't matter because his uniform was draped over a bed post. Two bedrooms down from where Tom Weir was getting dressed, the handsome Keogh had just finished an energetic session with Molly O'Brien, the supposed Dubliner. Her disheveled auburn tresses tumbled down as she stroked the back of his neck and hummed an Irish tune. He sipped some champagne. "You know," he said reflectively, "There was a physician way back in 190 A.D. named Claudius Galen who said, 'Every animal is sad after coitus except the human female and the rooster.'"

"Does that mean you're sad, or are you a rooster?" She smiled. "You're certainly not a female."

"No, I'm sad."

"Why, because you won't be seeing me for a while?"

"Maybe. Or maybe because I think things are going to change after this campaign. And change always makes me sad."

"Ah, you beautiful Irishman," Molly said, kissing his cheek. "There is no greater loveliness in any man as there is in a melancholy Irishman. It's a special mark of the breed, Miles Keogh, a blessing from God Himself."

Keogh smiled. "And all the blarney in Dublin wasn't handed out to the men, Molly O'Brien."

"Come," she said, pulling him to her shoulder. "Let me hold your pretty head and comfort you."

"You know," he said, "I've never told you, but I inherited this lovely Georgian mansion back in Connemara. It's called 'Clifden Castle.'"

Molly's blue eyes widened. "A *castle?* What in bloody 'ell are you doing *here*, Myles Walter Keogh?"

"I guess I like being a cavalry officer too much."

"Then toss your sword away and go home for good, lad. I'll come and be the mistress of your gorgeous castle."

He shook his head and looked away vacantly. "No, someday I want to command a regiment. And maybe win the American Medal of Honor. Perhaps when that's all over and I have white hair and weary bones, that's when I'll hang my saber on the wall of my castle."

"Will you remember me?"

He grinned. "And then I'll sing a song to the redheads of the world, and to all the joy they bring the melancholy men they touch with their merriment and wisdom. I'll ride out among my tall trees, with my loyal hounds, and I'll take off my floppy old cavalry hat, turn to the setting red sun, and in reverence to them I'll lift my voice to the heavens in their praise." A tear slipped down Molly's cheek as she kissed him again.

The musicians were playing quietly and several of the visitors had departed when the poker game broke up and Tom Custer came up to the bar. "I s'pose I could handle a little bourbon," he said with a smile.

Geraldine put her hand on his. "I guess I can see to that. How'd you do in the poker game?"

"I won a little over nineteen dollars."

"Pretty good. You like the party?"

"Honey, you did yourself proud."

Geraldine smiled, then sobered. "Do you have any idea how long you'll be in the field, Tommy?"

"Nope. Could be 'til fall. If we get lucky and catch the hostiles early, we could be back by early August."

Her smile was soft, not the type one would expect from a frontier madam. "I'll miss you."

He patted her hand. "And I'll miss you, sweetheart."

"There aren't any good sporting houses out there, are there?"

"Nope."

"I hear those Indian girls will roll over in a minute."

Tom shrugged. "I s'pose some do."

"I also heard you and the general had a beautiful Cheyenne squaw a while back. This fella told me the two of you took turns, and she had a baby."

Tom shrugged again. "You know how stories go. You hear a thousand of 'em."

"What time do you have to be back at camp?"

"Pretty soon. Every officer's got to be at reveille in the morning, and it's almost eight miles down there, not counting the ferry." He hauled out his pocket watch. "I imagine Keogh will be heading back soon. Where's Doc Porter?"

"Upstairs with Santa Fe Sandy."

Tom leaned over and looked into her eyes. "Why don't you just let this bar tend itself for a little while, honey?"

Geraldine smiled as she jumped down off her stool. "I was about to say the same thing."

They ride in ranks of two,
a double nocturne in serge.
The sky, so they fancy,
is a showcase of spurs . . .
—FEDERICO GARCÍA LORCA

Chilly fog covered the Flats as the Dakota Column fell out for reveille the next morning and staccato reports from the company commanders to the officer of the day shattered the early stillness. *"A Company all present and accounted for, sir!", "B Company all present and accounted for, sir!", "C Company all . . ."*

When the report was complete, the men turned quickly to the business at hand: clean up, finish last-minute packing, eat breakfast, tend to the horses, and get ready to move out. As the formation broke up, Captain Tom Weir stopped his first sergeant. "Something wrong, Sergeant?"

Michael Martin had dark bruises on his throat, couldn't speak above a whisper, and his back was so sore he could hardly walk, but he had managed to make reveille. "My horse threw me last night," he rasped.

Weir, who had his own health problems in the form of a distressing hangover, said, "Better see the doc."

Martin nodded and painfully touched the brim of his hat in a salute.

Custer had ridden down from the post at four A.M. with Lieutenant Cooke and his orderly, John Burkman, and had stood reveille with his regiment. His cook, Mary Adams, would join the column with the headquarters kitchen wagon when the column passed through the fort. Custer was all smiles as he again mixed into the bustle—*this* was what it was all about. This was why a man sought military command. These men were *his,* as was every element of this proud regiment. And they were going off to find *action!* As he watched the men hurrying around, heard the familiar noises of a camp breaking up, he thought back to the war. How many mornings, warm, bitterly cold, raining or snowing, often sunny, sometimes foggy like this morning, had he experienced the same thrill of forthcoming action? It never failed to excite him. Perhaps this one even more so. He had the whole regiment, they hadn't been on campaign in a long time, and a great adventure awaited him out there.

At five minutes after eight, the first elements of the column started up the road to the fort. Custer, astride his fastest horse, Vic, sat watching with his headquarters detachment until the last of the regiment had cleared the encampment, then he trotted ahead. He was wearing his new buckskin suit, the usual bright-crimson scarf, and a wide-brimmed white hat. The muffled sound of hooves striking the sodden road filled the air.

Fifteen minutes later, Custer reined in at the main gate to Fort Abraham Lincoln. Maggie Calhoun and Libbie sat on their saddled horses, waiting to join the column. It had taken some persuasion, but Libbie had finally talked her husband into allowing them to ride along the first day, spend the first night in camp, and return with the paymaster the following day. Custer had decided to hold up on paying the troops in camp because broke soldiers seldom went on the Grand Bounce and only so much whiskey could be purchased on the cuff. "You ready, ladies?" Custer asked, saluting them.

Both Maggie and Libbie were wearing dresses with military accents that Libbie had designed. And each had on a pert, brimmed hat that added to the effect. Libbie tossed off her version of a hand salute, saying smartly, "Yes, m'lord, the female scout detachment is formed!"

Custer chuckled and turned to General Terry. "You ready, sir?"

The pleasant Terry nodded. "I am, sir. Let's commence."

"All right, Mr. Cooke," Custer said to his adjutant, "Let's head for Sioux country."

With the ladies riding just behind Custer, the headquarters complement rode over to the head of the waiting column, the trumpeter blew the command, and the procession began to make its way through the post. As soon as the first contingent rode in, the regimental band, sitting on white horses, zestfully played "GarryOwen." Other airs followed as the long column clip-clopped by the assorted family members who were lined up in front of their quarters. The Indian scouts' wives wailed as their men rode impassively by; nothing had changed about their way of sending their men off to battle. As Company C reached Suds Row, Missouri Ann Bobo saw Dan Kanipe first and quietly put her hand over her heart as he looked over and nodded his head slightly. Riding at the rear of the company, the traditional trail position for a first sergeant, Ed Bobo touched his hat brim in salute as Missouri Ann waved at him and pointed him out to their kids, who were waiting restlessly at her side. God, she hoped both of her men would be all right. Both of her men—sounded kinda crazy. She caught one more glimpse of Danny Kanipe's head, and suddenly she felt a stab of fear. *What if something happened to him?* As the next company passed, she looked up into the tight-lipped glare of Mary Hohmeyer, the icy German laundress. *That* problem was still hanging fire.

The column continued on, its bright national colors and swallow-tailed guidons hanging nearly limp in the still-gray mist, past the officers' quarters. By now, several of the young boys were running alongside, laughing, shouting, playing soldier. A handful of Custer hounds, joined by some of the other post dogs, barked and joined in the festivities. Some civilians from town, including the mayor and the newspaper publisher Clement Lounsberry, had braved the cool early morning mist to see the regiment off. Annie Yates, holding her baby son in her arms, waved exuberantly as the Band Box troop passed. If it hadn't been for her baby, she'd be right up there with Libbie and Maggie. *Damn!* Her George Wilhelmus Mancius Yates looked so handsome on his prancing horse. Her three-year-old son, George, tugged at her skirt. "Mommy, when will Daddy be back?"

She patted his head. "Oh, maybe in three months." She looked back at her departing husband, "But I sure hope it's sooner."

The sky was brightening, as it usually does when the sun is busy dissipating morning fog. Up at the head of the column, Libbie felt the drama of the moment as the column worked its way up the slope to the infantry post on the upper trace. The lively strains of "The Girl I Left Behind Me" reached through the thinning mist as she looked back. At that moment, the rays of the sun burst through and part of the lower panorama broke out in brilliant repose. Bright reflections from a couple of French horns flashed back, and the vivid colors of the guidons suddenly found life. Momentarily, a glow seemed to envelop it all. She heaved a deep sigh. "Look!" she exclaimed to Maggie, "It's like a mirage down there. It's as if the regiment is marching across the heavens to meet it's glorious destiny!"

Maggie agreed. "How symbolic! She looked back, trying to find Jimmi, riding at the front of L Company.

When the entire column reached the upper-bench land, it flared out into its prescribed marching order. The ponderous supply train was the heart, with two companies of the Seventeenth Infantry and one of the Sixth Infantry marching close to it. The companies of the two wings were divided into the front, rear, and on both sides for maximum security. General Terry didn't believe there was much chance of being attacked, but he didn't want to take any chances. The beeves that rambled on one side, and the remuda of mules and spare horses that moseyed along on the other side, offered a tempting prize to any meandering Indians who might sneak in given an opportunity. Lumbering along behind was the four-gun Gatling battery, while Lieutenant Charlie Varnum's thirty-nine scouts now roamed well to the front. The formidable force was heading due west toward its rendezvous with the two chartered steamboats, the *Far West* and the *Josephine*, at Stanley's old stockade on the Yellowstone. Three companies of the Sixth Infantry had set up a supply base there. Their first destination was some 250 miles away.

And since it was also a delayed payday, just about everyone was in high spirits. Even the sutler and his wagons were trailing along, ready after the expedition made camp to capitalize on the fresh greenbacks the paymaster would parcel out. And everyone knew there was *some* whiskey in those wagons.

The column halted and made camp on the north bank of the Heart River late that afternoon. As soon as the site was organized, the paymaster went to work. Lines at the sutler's wagons quickly formed, and in the tent area the card games began. Private John Burkman had set up the Custer tent and Libbie had helped Mary Adams organize the mess for dinner. She wanted it to be a gay affair, with Maggie and the rest of the royal family invited for a last supper. But the moment that phrase slipped out, she regretted it. It wasn't going to be a "last supper," just a parting dinner preceding a campaign . . . preceding a short separation.

That was all, Libbie told herself as she tasted the roast turkey. The Samson and Delilah parallel had pestered her off and on throughout the day, but each time it had reared its nasty head, she had pushed it away. Silly thought! She wanted this night to be very special. The sky had cleared, so it promised an evening under the stars—romantic. And Autie would be in a frisky mood; hitting the campaign trail would do that for him.

She looked out from the tent fly. The camp was bustling—suppertime for the troops. She wondered if any of them would take the Grand Bounce tonight. It was doubtful. Autie had mentioned having a strong guard on the horses, and it was a pretty long walk back to Bismarck. She sighed. Entertaining in the field—she'd done it before, a few years earlier. But that was different. Tonight, General Terry would be at table, Jimmi Calhoun and Maggie, and the boys—Tom, Boston, and young Autie. That was as many as she could handle in the field, unless she wanted to serve picnic style, and there was no way she'd do that on a night like this.

She turned to John Burkman, who was unpacking the candles. "John, do you have time to find just a handful of wildflowers? I like to have some on the table."

He nodded his head. "Yes, ma'am, Miz Custer. I'll go look right now."

She watched as the orderly walked away. It would be lonely back at the fort without all of them. Suddenly the sadness hit her and her eyes brimmed. No, she couldn't have any of *that*. . . . Besides, it wouldn't be long before she'd be a general's wife again.

Later, while Libbie was pretending she was entertaining in a grand hall in one of the great palaces of Europe, and trying to fight off the ants and flies that enjoy attending feasts in the open spaces, Major Marcus Reno was finishing his evening meal with Captain Myles Moylan, Doctor Henry Porter, and Second Lieutenant Ben Hodgson over in A Company's mess tent. Reno poured some brandy from his flask into his coffee and offered it to the others. Moylan made a liberal addition to his coffee, as did the good doctor. Hodgson, who was Reno's adjutant, declined.

Second Lieutenant Benjamin Hodgson, a native of Philadelphia, would be twenty-eight years old in six days. He'd graduated from West Point in the class of '70 and had gone directly to the Seventh Cavalry. In the subsequent five years, he'd been moved around considerably, and had been stationed down in Shreveport, Louisiana, ever since returning with the Black Hills expedition in '74. He'd just returned to Fort Lincoln two months earlier, and had been assigned to McDougall's B Company.

The ruddy complexioned Myles Moylan was born in Galway, Ireland, but grew up in Massachusetts. He had been in the army since he enlisted in 1857, nineteen years come June 8. A first sergeant when Custer graduated from West Point, some of his Civil War fighting was in Grant's command at Forts Henry and Donelson, and later at Shiloh and Corinth. He saw a lot of action with the Fifth Cavalry as a second lieutenant in the Gettysburg campaign, but got into trouble and was kicked out of the army for being AWOL in Washington in the fall of '63. But that couldn't keep the dark-haired Irishman out of the fight. He enlisted as Private Charles Thomas, and within a month was a first lieutenant. In late '64 he was promoted to captain. His brevet as major, USV, was effective the day Lee surrendered at Appomattox. After the war, he again enlisted as a private, but was soon the sergeant major of the Seventh Cavalry. Three months later, Custer got him a commission as a first lieutenant and promoted him to captain in the spring of '72 when a vacancy occurred in the regiment. Along with Benteen, he was a highly experienced company commander.

It had been a long day for all of them, particularly for Dr. Porter, who had spent more time at Geraldine Gentle's than he had sleeping. They talked casually about the day's ride, and the weather, which had turned out quite pleasant. "I 'spect you'll be seeing a few sick lads in the mornin'," Moylan said to Porter.

"Don't worry, Captain, I'll have them in the saddle quickly."

Talk turned to the Gettysburg campaign. "What was it like," Lieutenant Hodgson asked, "after the battle of Brandy Station? Everyone says that was when the Federal cavalry finally earned its spurs."

Moylan smiled. "We were like frisky colts. We didn't actually *beat* old Jeb that day, but he sure as hell got a fight and he didn't beat *us!* Gave us spirit we'd never had before. In the scraps at Aldie and Middleburg—those places on the way toward Gettysburg, there was no holding us."

Reno nodded his head. "I was up at Carlisle in Pennsylvania, about to get married when all that was going on, but I heard about those young colts, heard that Pleasanton had hung stars on officers young enough to be drummer boys, and that there was going to be hell to pay the next time Jeb ran into our cavalry."

"And sure enough," Moylan chuckled, "That new brigadier, George Armstrong Custer, sure did rough up Stuart and his rebel cavalry at Gettysburg. That was when those Michigan horsemen and their flamboyant blond-haired general first began to make history. I was a lieutenant then, one year older than that young fire-eater."

Hodgson offered his thought, "I guess he could fight from here to Sunday, couldn't he?"

"I heard he had casualties from here to Sunday, as well," Dr. Porter added.

Moylan nodded. "Those things go hand in hand."

"What do you think's going to happen out there, sir?" Hodgson asked Reno.

"Don't know," the major replied, fighting his pipe. "We might not even corner old Sitting Bull and his friends." "My guess is," Moylan added, "that the general won't stop until he corners *some* of those hostiles. Then we just may have all the fighting we want."

"I certainly hope so," the lieutenant said. "It's hard for us younger officers to find any distinction, just sitting around in peacetime."

"Ah, the siren song of glory," Porter said, raising his coffee cup. "I took an oath to old Hippocrates to patch people up, and you folks want to tear 'em apart."

Moylan smiled, adding a touch of brogue to his broad Massachusetts accent, "Sure and why didn't you stay back in Bismarck, abirthin' babies, if this maiming bothers you, Doc?"

Porter grinned back. "Doctors need adventure too, you know. Besides, *somebody's* got to treat the clap out here."

They all laughed.

Libbie watched her naked husband dry himself with a towel as she sat propped up on a pillow on her cot. She barely heard the strains of a harmonica someone was playing somewhere in the big camp. A few minutes earlier, they had broken one of the legs on the other cot and it had fallen to the ground in the middle of their lovemaking. They laughed as Autie had said, "Now, that's what's called a *smashing* climax!"

He turned, saw her soft expression. "What?" he asked.

"I was just thinking about how much I love you."

He hung the towel over a folding chair. "Good. Keep thinking about that all the time I'm gone, my pretty one. And tell me about it in your letters."

He sat, still naked beside the cot, taking her hand. "I'll write as often as I can, most days, I'm sure."

"Me too." She smiled, touching his cheek with her other hand. "I may bore you with all that household chatter."

"It won't bore me. I'll be able to feel you that way."

"Autie?"

"Yes, honey."

"You will be careful, won't you?"

"Of course."

"I mean it," she said softly. "I know how you are."

He smiled into her eyes, now dark in the light of the kerosene lantern. "I'm indestructible. You know that, darling."

She swung her legs over the side of the cot and got to her feet. Pulling him up to her bare skin, she said, "Hold me close."

He took her in his arms and held her tightly as she turned her cheek to his chest. After a moment, she said, "I can't get that Samson thought out of my mind."

He chuckled. "It doesn't matter how long my danged hair is, sweetheart, so forget that silliness." He gently turned her face to his and kissed her.

☆ ☆ ☆

Camp broke early the next morning, as it always does on the trail. There were the usual payday hangovers, but not one soldier had taken the Bounce. At seven-fifteen, the detail that was returning to Fort Lincoln was assembled. It included the two ladies mounted on their horses, the paymaster and his guard, and a mounted infantry escort that would remain back at the post.

Jimmi Calhoun sat on his horse beside Maggie and took her hand. He'd said his good-byes to her in the tent a half hour earlier. Libbie looked up as Custer finally rode up from where he'd been checking on the formation of the column. He reined in and tossed her a broad smile. "Well, Standby," he said, "You ready to go back and run things at Lincoln?"

She touched her little hat brim in a mock salute. "I am, sir."

"Good. Then you're relieved from duty here." He leaned over and kissed her hard on the mouth, then smiled again. "Carry on!"

She smiled bravely, fighting the tears. "Yes, sir." Wheeling her horse, she rode away to the waiting small Lincoln contingent. Reaching it, she finally turned back and waved.

Custer removed his big, broad-brimmed white hat and bowed slightly from the saddle, then jammed it back on his head and galloped off toward the head of his waiting column.

Watching, Libbie Custer couldn't control the tears that suddenly flooded her cheeks.

27

In attaching ourselves to the Hunkpapas we other tribes were not moved by a desire to fight. They had not invited us. They simply welcomed us. We supposed that the combined camps would frighten off the soldiers.
—WOODEN LEG
    Northern Cheyenne chief

The remarkable medicine of the repulse of Three Stars on the Powder River in March had blown around agency campfires like a ghost in the wind. It was now obvious that the Great White Father's threat had been sincere; he was going to make big war. On whom exactly was a matter of uncertainty because it was easy for the Long Knives to find the agency Indians. To them, an Indian was an Indian, if they were on the warpath. The hostiles in the unceded territory were united under Sitting Bull, and that was where the Lakota strength lay. Besides, it was hunting time for those on the agencies, the part of the year when the buffalo were fat and the Lakota could enjoy life as in the old days. And for the young men, the allure of war sounded its siren song. By May, hundreds of agency Indians were headed for the great adventure and the spiritual appeal of Sitting Bull in Yellowstone country—more than at any other time.

Crazy Horse had kept his word with Sitting Bull. They would wait until the Long Knives came again. If this happened, there would be no holding back. The medicine of Powder River was too strong. The strength of the rapidly growing village of Sitting Bull and his Hunkpapas had never been so great. It all made a fighting man's blood tingle! As the remarkable war leader that he was, Crazy Horse roamed the territory, making notes about how he would attack if Three Stars came this way or if he came another. By the Moon of the Birth of Calves, the greatest tactical general the Lakota had ever known had at least a half-dozen logical war plans.

Red Elk had been with him every step of the way, asking questions, learning as much as the reticent Crazy Horse would divulge about his particular specialty, the tactical ploy of showing retreat and decoying an enemy into a clever ambush. That was how he'd set up the so-called Fetterman massacre on the Bozeman Trail a decade earlier.

And now the Long Knives *had* come, but not from the south, as they had expected. Up on the north bank of the Yellowstone, a strong force that was part of Colonel John Gibbon's command had arrived and settled in. Crazy Horse's "wolves" had discovered them. On May 2, a raiding band in which Red Elk participated, but had no command function, stole all of the ponies belonging to Gibbon's Crow scouts. Red Elk heard a rear guard "wolf" report that the Crows set up a weeping wail so tragic they sounded like a huge band of crying children. The story provided the biggest laugh of the year as it was passed around Lakota land. There was one more minor attack on those Long Knives, but both Sitting Bull and Crazy Horse knew that wasn't where the danger lay. The Great White Father would send far more.

Now, some four hundred fifty lodges filled Sitting Bull's encampment with well over three thousand Sioux and Cheyennes. When Red Elk returned to the Hunkpapa encampment, more than eight hundred warriors were available and itching to fight. And more agency Sioux were arriving daily. But he had something else on his mind.

Reaching the village, Red Elk quickly bathed in the nearby stream, put on fresh clothing, and took his Big Twisted Flute from its wrappings. During his long ride with Crazy Horse, he had composed a new love song, one he was sure would greatly please Late Star. Now, in the falling dusk, he sat near Running Antelope's tipi and began to softly play the notes of love.

In moments the flap flew open and Late Star hurried out. "Oh, *Red Elk!*" she exclaimed. "What a wonderful surprise!" Oblivious to her aunt and anyone else who might be looking, she sat on the ground beside him and touched his arm. Greatly pleased by his means of announcing his return, she asked, "Where did the new song come from?"

When he finished the final note, he replied, "I created it for you, my love. It's one of my wedding gifts to you."

She touched his cheek. "And when will you be giving these wedding gifts to me?"

"Soon. At the upcoming sun dance, when we'll be married."

Her white teeth flashed. "I'm all ready. My father isn't full of joy, but he knows I'd run away with you if he didn't approve. My aunt and I have been quilling and sewing."

"Have you made beautiful things?"

"Yes, surprises you'll like."

"Such as?"

She laughed, touched his cheek again. "When we marry, you'll see."

It was the most energetic and enjoyable spring Sitting Bull could remember. The impending danger of the Long Knives added a certain spice to daily life, the pulling together of the tribes, the added numbers of summer roamers from the agencies who were on their way and continuing to arrive, and the large numbers of fat buffalo that were available—all portended a very good summer. But it was more than that; never before in his life had he felt so strong spiritually. It seemed that Wakantanka was touching him constantly and had placed the other gods in close proximity. From the time he arose in the morning until he at last drifted into slumber late at night, he felt a certain special power, a warmth, a pervasive strength that seemed to surround him in subtle ways. His powers of prophecy and mysticism were at a peak he'd never before experienced, and he knew, most importantly, that he could fulfill his commitment to the welfare of his tribe.

His huge lodge was full. His mother presided over the two young daughters he'd fathered with the wife he'd tossed out, Snow-on-Her. The additional residents were his son by his dead wife, Red Woman, his sister Good Feather, two stepsons, his two wives, their brother, and the squalling twin sons Four Robes had given birth to three weeks earlier.

His sphere of influence was full as well. All elements of the Lakota, as well as the Cheyenne's, seemed to sense his special powers, and were seeking his benevolence. He felt his responsibility, and was utterly confident in being able to meet it. On May 21, while his large village sat by the Rosebud River, several miles from its mouth, he felt a compulsion to climb a nearby butte by himself. Reaching the top, he looked around in the late spring warmth, and sat on a large rock. "Great Wakantanka," he began, "offer me guidance. Is there more I can do than wait for our enemies to descend? Should I, instead, send my people after them?"

When there was no answer readily apparent, Sitting Bull prayed more, and meditated. In a few minutes he lapsed into sleep. A dream soon descended upon him—a dream so vivid that when it passed, he sat upright and looked at the sky. *Where was the cloud?*

He went back to the village and immediately summoned the elders and other leaders. He centered his attention on Gall, who sat directly across the fire from him. "This morning," Sitting Bull began, "I spoke on the hill with the Great Mystery, and he gave me a wonderful dream. In it, I saw a huge dust storm swirling toward me from the east. And from the west, heading directly for this massive cloud of dust, was a white cloud that looked like an Indian village. As the dust storm charged nearer, I could see behind it many ranks of blue-coated soldiers, grimly readying their weapons for battle. All at once, the storm smashed into the cloud and a monstrous sky battle erupted. Thunder and lightning, rain and hail filled the sky. And when the great crashing was over, the storm had been crushed and the dust fell to the wet ground. The white village cloud then drifted quietly on to the east and disappeared over a hill."

Sitting Bull looked around into the quiet, still faces. "And that, great chiefs, was Wakantanka's prophecy. The Long Knife soldiers will come from the east, but we will defeat them and have a great victory."

Energetic nodding of heads and comments of approval followed.

Gall, who was in charge of the scouts, announced, "Great Chief, I will instruct the wolves to be particularly alert for an army coming from the east."

After the horse raid on Gibbon's Crow scouts, Red Elk's pony herd stood at six, plus his warhorse Lightning. He would give three horses to Running Antelope as Late Star's wedding gift, and give one to her. He had made a swap of a good pinto and the Big Twisted Flute for a magnificent white pony, emblazoned only by a few tan markings on its back and lower legs, and a star shape on its forehead. It was a large two-year-old mare, with plenty of spirit. He called her Starlight. Since he had made the swap with a Cheyenne a couple of days earlier the pony had been quartered by his *kola* so Late Star wouldn't know. Now his *kola*, Black Ash, watched as Red Elk brushed Starlight's bright coat. "She's a beauty," he said. "I sure wouldn't give such a horse to a woman."

Red Elk removed a snag from her mane. "You would if you could catch a woman like Late Star."

"Ha, I can catch any woman!"

Red Elk chuckled. "I saw that old crone Oglala you're sweet on. She hasn't even got *teeth* anymore."

"She's got just one missing and she has only twenty-six summers. Besides, I only see her for the blanket."

"Ha! You'd marry her the moment she agreed."

"At least she's easy, not pushy like Late Star."

"They're going to cut off her nose if you don't marry her. Or old Three Leg will shoot you. You think he's blind?"

Black Ash was proud of his adultery with the Oglala, his coup with a woman. "Three Leg is too lazy; he'd just walk away."

Red Elk chuckled again. "Then you could marry your toothless beauty."

At that moment, Gall walked up. "How! Nice horse."

"The idiot's giving her to his bride," Black Ash said, shaking his head.

Gall shrugged. "She's probably worth it. Are you coming to the Midnight Society meeting tonight, Red Elk?"

"Yes, Uncle." He had been inducted in the exclusive society that included Sitting Buffalo just three months earlier, and was proud of being its youngest member.

"Good. We are going to discuss battle plans for the *akacita*, and I want you as a potential *blotahunka,* or as my own assistant."

"Yes, Uncle."

"Can you shoot that big gun yet?"

"Very well, Uncle. I can hit that white cow skull three out of four times at six hundred paces."

Gall grunted his satisfaction and walked on.

A few days later, after the *akacita* had moved the village a few miles down the Rosebud to the mouth of Greenleaf Creek, Sitting Bull called his adopted son, Jumping Bull, his nephew White Bull, and Gall to his tipi. The chief was attired plainly, with no adornments. He wasn't even wearing his single first-coup feather. He held his famous pipe in its ceremonial sage wrapping as he said, "Wakantana has summoned me again to the hills to pray. I want you, my sons, to join me."

The hilltop was not far away, and the small party reached its crest within fifteen minutes. Sitting Bull wasted no time in unwrapping his pipe and lighting it, but the smoking, as it was handed from one to another, was the usual protracted ceremony. As the sun began to settle, orange near the horizon of hills, the chief arose, held the pipe high to the west and intoned, "Wakantanka, save me and all my wild game animals. Have them close enough so my people will have food this winter, and the good men on earth will have more power so their tribes get along better and be of good nature so all the Sioux nations will have peace. If you will do this for me, I will sun dance two days and two nights and will give you a whole buffalo."

He handed the pipe ceremoniously to Gall and wiped his face with sage.

He had made his pledge.

The next day the growing village would move farther down the Rosebud.

28

Brigadier General George Crook assumed command of the "Bighorn and Yellowstone Expedition," as the body of newsmen who were covering the campaign dubbed it. Over a thousand men strong, and outfitted for weeks in the field, the force that had gathered at Fort Fetterman in late May was a powerful one. Major Alexander Chambers, who had been a classmate of Crook's at West Point, commanded the five companies of infantry, while Major Alexander Evans commanded ten companies of the Third Cavalry, the "Brave Rifles." Captain Henry Noyes, who had not exactly covered himself with fame at the Powder River fiasco, commanded five companies of the Second Cavalry, while Lieutenant Colonel William Royal, the handsome Virginian, was the overall cavalry commander. Nine hundred of the men were fighting soldiers.

Crook wasn't happy about not having any scouts. He had even gone to the Red Cloud Agency and had conferred with the famous old chief himself. But the former fighting leader of the Oglalas treated the general with disdain, saying, "The Gray Fox must understand that the Sioux are brave and ready to fight for their country. Every lodge will send its young men, and they will all fight the Great Father's dogs to the death."

Crook didn't get a single scout.

He heard the Dakota column had departed Fort Abraham Lincoln on the seventeenth, and on the twenty-ninth, his long column had pulled out and headed up the old Bozeman Trail. That had been five days earlier. Now, having sent Frank Grouard and two of his other permanent scouts off to the distant Crow agency up in Montana to enlist the services of the Sioux adversaries, Crook had the column headed from the ruins of old Fort Reno toward Goose Creek. Even though spring was in evidence, the weather had turned cold and overcoats had been donned. Crook, with his beard braided and taped back, in his usual casual clothes, also wore an enlisted man's overcoat.

Now, as the column trudged north on June 3, the snowcapped Bighorn Mountains loomed to its left. Dust permeated everything behind the lead elements of the snaking stretch of men, horses, and wagons. "Ifn it ain't snow or rain and mud," groused one older private, "it's the goddamn dust. I'd be a first sergeant today, ifn I didn't have to ride at the rear of my company. That's why they die of consumption."

Lieutenant John Bourke, as usual, made copious notes as the command continued on.

The following day, the fourth of the Moon of the Ripe Juneberries, was the first day of Sitting Bull's promised sun dance. This event was the most important ceremony in the spiritual life of the Sioux, and more than any other symbolized for them their intrinsic relationship to the supernatural. It was a communion between the people and the universe. A person's role in the Sun Dance could be for his own good, it could be a repayment, it could be for someone else—for sparing the life of a sick child—or it could be for the good of all. Many who danced for personal favor from the gods did so to seek a vision or to become a shaman by acquiring supernatural power for themselves. In Sitting Bull's case, this Sun Dance was a payment for his requests on the hill to Wakantanka.

Normally the Sun Dance, the *wiwanyag wachipi*, was a twelve day event, but with so many lodges and grazing ponies present, the village would have to move on in four. Therefore it would be necessary to compress the schedule. It was solely a Hunkpapa affair, with the Lakotas' tipis pitched on the east side of the Rosebud. The Cheyennes were located on the west side on some higher ground, along with some of the other tribes. Sitting Bull and those other men who were to participate went inside hastily constructed sweat lodges to purify themselves. Crooked Tree had been selected as the Mentor, the shaman in charge of the entire event.

The man who was chosen by the shamans as the symbolic Hunter readily found a forked rustling leaf tree, a cottonwood, suitable for use as the sacred Sun Dance pole, and the virtuous woman chosen to fell it was Late Star's longtime friend Blue Feather. Her assistants, other honored chaste young women, helped her "find" the red-marked tree and quickly "captured" it, tying it with thongs. Red Elk was the messenger chosen to run back to camp to report the capture, and the rejoicing tribesmen paraded back to the tree. Red Elk, Black Ash, and two other warriors were then selected to strike the tree and "count coup" to subdue its *nagila*, its spiritlike essence. This done, the children lined up and were awarded gifts.

Then Crooked Tree, the Mentor, silenced everyone by raising his arms high and intoning, "Kill the tree!"

Immediately, each of Blue Feather's honored women assistants took turns chopping the trunk. When it was nearly ready to fall, the ax was handed to Blue Feather, and in a few well-placed chops, the large cottonwood came crashing down amid songs, shouts of joy, and happy singing. Then the peeling began; the bark was removed up to the fork as women gathered twigs to ward off *Anog-ite*, the supernatural who tempted women.

When the tree was finally carried into the center of the Dance Lodge area, its north side was painted blue, its west side red, its south side yellow, and its east side green. It was now time to scourge the bad gods. *Gnaske*, the Crazy Buffalo, was the patron of wrongdoing who might bring paralysis or insanity; *Iya*, a monster who ate men and animals, was the master of spite and malice whose foul breath brought disease. Black rawhide effigies of these two evil gods, with exaggerated genitalia, were attached to the fork of the tree, and immediately the people began to jeer and banter about things implicitly sexual in a manner taboo in everyday life. Other attachments at the top of the pole were an arrow for buffalo killing, a picket pin for tying a captured horse, a cherry stick containing tobacco, and the Mentor's banner of red buffalo skin.

Late Star and Red Elk, standing together during the castigation of *Iya* and *Gnaske*, each shouted an obscenity, he declaring that both gods fornicated like sick puppies, she saying, "A female *snake* wouldn't want your organ!" And everyone laughed.

It was finally time for the pole to be raised. The hooting at the evil gods came to an end as warriors fired arrows into the effigies, which fell to the ground and were soundly trampled by those closest to the pole. Once the pole was securely erect, rawhide ropes were attached. From these, some of the dancers would be suspended when the ceremony began. The sacred drum that would be played continuously throughout the dance was positioned at the Dance Lodge. As darkness fell, it was time for the shamans to consecrate the dance area. The people retired to their tipis to wait and pray until morning.

But Red Elk was far too excited to keep his mind on prayer. All he could think about was sharing his blanket with Late Star. He'd groomed her white pony one more time before nightfall, and the new buckskin shirt his aunt had made for him was ready. The fringed, knee-length moccasins were also new. A couple of hours before dawn he gave up and went for a walk. Naturally, he went by the Sun Dance pole, stopping to watch the single shaman on duty as he prayed. Red Elk prayed quietly as well, "Oh, Great Mystery, help me to be a good husband to my beautiful Late Star. Give me patience and gentleness for her, and understanding. I know wives can have their difficult times, but a good husband should be able to overlook them. So please help me, Wakantanka, and next year I will dance at the Sun Dance for you."

He ambled on, drawn irresistibly to Running Antelope's tipi. But while still some thirty yards away, he saw movement in the fading moonlight. His hand went to the knife at his waist as he edged closer. A new tipi had been pitched right beside Running Antelope's! It looked almost white. A figure was bending over, tapping a stake. He moved closer. *It was Late Star!* He stopped, drawing in his breath. Since both his own mother and father were dead, as was her mother, they had decided to live with her father. And Late Star had arranged for a borrowed tipi from one of her friends—something to use for their honeymoon until the village made its next move after the Sun Dance.

But this was no borrowed, second-hand tipi!

He started to walk up and ask her what was happening but something stopped him, and he quietly withdrew several paces to watch what she was doing. A short time later she went into her father's tipi. He returned to the dance pole area and sat beneath a cottonwood tree, doomed to another three hours before he could get ready for his marriage to the most beautiful girl in all of Lakota land.

As the sun's first long rays pierced the morning shade, Sitting Bull gravely came out of the sweat lodge, barefooted and attired only in a breechclout. His hair hung loose, with no feathers, and he wore no paint. White Bull and Jumping Bull flanked him as he walked slowly and majestically to the tall dance pole. The dancers were there waiting, as were many of the people. He quietly extracted his pipe from its wrapping and performed the pipe ceremony while his adopted son and his nephew hung a fine buffalo robe on the pole and placed two more by the base of the pole. These were gifts to Wakantanka; the whole buffalo carcass the chief had promised to the Great Mystery would be offered later. The smoking finished, Sitting Bull sat with his back against the pole and his legs straightened out to his front.

While White Bull sat on his right, Jumping Bull held a sharp awl high and intoned, "Great Mystery, guide my hand."

Moments later, he broke the skin and inserted the tiny point into Sitting Bull's left arm just above the wrist. Removing a tiny piece of flesh, he held it aloft to Wakantanka for a few moments before returning to his chore. Sitting Bull sat impassive as his stepson worked upward, gouging a total of fifty bits of tissue from his arm. His blood flowed freely down his arm and dripped to the ground. Jumping Bull moved swiftly to the chief's right arm and repeated the process. In the thirty minutes it took to complete the rite, Sitting Bull cried out only once, and that was when he beseeched Wakantanka to accept his sacrifice, "Oh, Great Mystery, take my body and use it to feed my people for all time and to keep them safe."

With blood still dripping from his arms, he arose and began to dance. At other Sun Dances, he had danced suspended, attached to the pole, but today he followed only the first form of the dance. He would continue to fast and keep his eyes fixed on the sun, the warming, brightening, ever powerful sun. . . .

Late Star had begun fixing her hair just after returning from her early morning river bath. Any bathing privacy, with so many added people in the vicinity of the main Hunkpapa village, was difficult to find. But she'd managed to find a secluded spot near an overhanging willow tree, and had dried herself before the sun came up. The small White Eye "seeing glass" was a great asset in the chore of placing her hair jewelry after the braiding. She told herself she shouldn't be so excited, but, after all, this was the biggest day of her life. She looked around the inside of the tipi with pride. Their life would be so rich together. . . .

Sitting Bull had been dancing for over an hour when Red Elk finished the final grooming of Starlight, the white pony. He'd ridden the animal a full day before buying her and considered her nearly as fine a pony as his warhorse. He wondered if the two animals would mate, and what kind of a colt might result. He'd have to talk to Crooked Tree about it; the old shaman had potions for such things. Now, with Wi, the sun, rapidly climbing through the sky, it was time. He climbed onto her bare back and began to pick his way out of the huge corral of nearly ten thousand horses. Looking around, he thought of the gossip that another four or five hundred lodges might bring to the village in the next few weeks. Where would they ever find the grass to feed their ponies?

Once clear of the corral, Red Elk rode on to the Hunkpapa tipis. Nearing the one that housed Running Antelope's family, he pulled up in surprise. The tipi next to the chief's, the one he'd glimpsed in the near darkness that morning, was a new, nearly white tipi! Late Star stepped out of its entrance and said brightly, "Welcome to your new home, Great Warrior."

"Where did you get it?" he asked, jumping down from the pony.

"I made it," she replied, flashing her lovely smile. "Mostly when you were gone running around with Crazy Horse. My aunt helped, and Little Grass Woman sewed the smoke flaps." Everyone knew that smoke flaps not sewn by Little Grass Woman would be improperly done, and would create a smoky tipi. She pointed with pride at the tipi's quills—short strips of rawhide wrapped with brightly colored porcupine quills to which were attached feathers and horsetails. Two rows of them hung down the front. "And here—" she added proudly as she pointed to some figures, "are the stories of your great feats, which I've painted. Your first first coup, your next first coup, and your war leader exploit."

Usually the man of the family painted these war accomplishments, but Late Star was such a better artist that he didn't mind her usurping his privilege. The art was excellent and pleased him considerably. He followed her inside, where his eyes drifted to the pile of new buffalo robes that would be their bed. As she pointed out the dew cloth and other features of the well-designed and sewn tent, his eyes kept returning to the bed skins. "This is a fifteen-skin tipi," she said. "Of course, it's large for just two people . . . but—" She took his hand and smiled. "Perhaps there will be more."

The thought of little children playing on the floor of skins quickly took him back to the bed, and he felt aroused. When she finished pointing out the different features inside the tipi, he finally said, "And I have something for *you*."

He took her hand and led her the few paces to the white pony. "This is Starlight," he said proudly. "She's yours."

Her eyes widened. "She's beautiful!" she exclaimed, softly touching the animal's velvety nose. "Oh, Red Elk, we're going to have such a good life together!"

As Late Star and her aunt began putting out the different dishes for the wedding feast, Sitting Bull and the other dancers continued in their ritual. The great shaman kept his gaze centered on the sun, as he had throughout the long morning. As it reached its zenith shortly after midday, he suddenly stopped, shook his large body for a few moments, and continued to stare at the bright orb. Onlookers rushed to him, certain that he had experienced something weighty and insightful. They took his arms and lowered him gently to the ground. His eyes closed as a shaman asked, "What are you seeing, great chief?"

Sitting Bull didn't respond. Beads of sweat stood out on his forehead and he moaned. A woman came and sprinkled water on him.

The word spread and within minutes a throng of people, local Hunkpapas and others from the assorted tribes, had ringed the pole, stretching, peeking, trying to see the great man or hear whatever he might have to say.

Finally his eyelids fluttered, then opened. His voice was low, hoarse, as he said, "I saw the vision."

Everyone waited, straining to hear his words.

He paused for several moments, then went on, "A voice told me to watch an image just below the bright sun. It was a white buffalo. And then I saw that the voice came from the white buffalo as it told me the soldiers were coming. I looked hard and there, numerous as grasshoppers, were the soldiers. They were Long Knives in their blue clothes, and they were riding their horses toward a Lakota village below. As they came on, I saw that they were upside down, both soldiers and horses. Their feet were in the sky and their heads were to the earth with their hats falling off."

Sitting Bull paused, as his voice cracked, then continued, "There were some of our people below, and they, too, were upside down. And then the buffalo voice spoke again and said, 'These soldiers do not possess ears. They will die, but you are not supposed to take their spoils.'"

The crowd began to whisper, then the volume of its voices grew. *The soldiers* were *coming!* And they would attack the village! Some of the people would be killed, but the vision clearly promised that the soldiers would be vanquished. It was great medicine. The people would be victorious! It was the final and most powerful part of the vision about the soldiers. It was known that the Long Knives were coming from the north and the south. They had seen them on the Yellowstone, and Three Stars' column had been shadowed since leaving Fort Fetterman. Then Sitting Bull's earlier vision showed them coming from the east. Now *this!* Upside down, no ears, hats falling off—defeated!

The word spread as more people arrived.

It was powerful medicine!

It was a great day for a marriage. Everyone was caught up in the fervor of Sitting Bull's vision, the weather was beautiful, the Sun Dance added a spiritual power, and the new husband and wife were beautiful young people who would one day mean much to the Hunkpapas. Red Elk danced for a time, then came back to the beautiful tipi to accept the warm wishes of the people who stopped by to partake of the feast. Gall came and handed him a box of one hundred bullets for the Sharps.

"Where did you get these, Uncle?" he asked.

"A golden eagle gave them to me," Gall replied. "You will need them soon."

Red Elk beamed. They were a wonderful gift from the great war leader. His giving meant that he accepted Red Elk's judgment in warfare, a cherished compliment from such a man.

Gall went on, "Enjoy your marriage blanket because we may leave soon to fight."

Red Elk looked at him with sudden sharp interest. "Fight? Where?"

"Our scouts report that Three Stars is coming with many Long Knives."

"When do we leave?"

Gall smiled. "Not for three days or more. Go to your blanket."

☆ ☆ ☆

The incessant beat of the drums, muffled, but permeating the air, overrode all other noises as the slightly distant celebration of the Sun Dance continued. But inside the fresh white tipi, the occupants barely heard it. Late Star had closed the flap tightly to shut out the last long rays of the rusting sun. The glow of light inside the structure was slightly luminous, as if it were intensified by the newly cured skins. The buffalo robes on the floor that comprised the bed were also soft and fresh, more of Late Star's diligence in readying the tipi for its young love. She had carefully placed Red Elk's possessions and his huge rifle in a specific place on the side. Her belongings were also carefully stored. She had even found some wildflowers to provide a sweet scent inside. And she had promised herself that she wouldn't tease her new husband in any way. She felt the excitement as he came inside and smiled at her. They had waited so long. She knew he was experienced, but she had listened carefully to the instructions of the older women. She knew she would be competent, and more. She loved her young warrior fervently and wanted him to be inside her, *thrusting*, as the women called it.

He came to her and kissed her softly on the cheek.

He fumbled with his clothes as he watched her slowly draw her lovely pale buckskin dress with its ornate quill work up over her bare legs to her hips. He had never seen her bare legs before and was pleased at how long and shapely they were. In a moment she had pulled the dress over her head, and turned to him from where she stood, smiling and naked. He stared for a moment at her full breasts with their rosy aureoles and perfectly erect nipples. A sigh escaped his lips as she held out her arms and came to him. He fumbled with his belt, but she helped him undo it, continuing to smile into his eyes. And when his trousers fell to his ankles, she looked at his long, muscular body taut with desire. She found his erect penis and gently stroked it for a moment before she kissed his mouth and pulled him down to the bed of skins. Gyrating gently against him as her desire grew, she gradually drew him closer to her. He tried to be gentle, but all at once she placed her hands on his buttocks and pushed upward, pulling him strongly inside.

"Aaahheeeee!" Her little scream escaped as he drove fully inside her. The soft inside of her thighs against his hips when she began to rock against his thrusts excited him even more. He felt stone hard, like a spear reaching

inside her. She overwhelmed him with her moist warmth and words of love as he lost control and burst.

29

"I was hoping Mrs. Custer might have stowed away on your boat," Custer said with a quick smile.

Captain Grant Marsh, skipper of the *Far West,* shook his head. "Matter of fact, she tried to talk me into it, but I just couldn't let her, General. Don't have any accommodations fit for her. And I didn't know when I could get her back to Fort Lincoln. We could be out here 'til fall, you know."

"She's pretty hardy."

The veteran captain shrugged. "Sorry."

"I see you had room for the sutler."

"Yes, General Terry's orders."

Sutler John Smith, no particular friend of Custer's, had assembled enough wooden planks with his barrels of cheap whiskey to open an outdoor saloon and temporary store. Terry had also okayed the sale of whiskey for one day, along with the other stores Smith had loaded on the riverboat. The new depot was a makeshift canvas supply point on the southeast side of the confluence of the Yellowstone and the Powder Rivers. Terry had just moved his base there to be closer to what he was sure would be the area of action against the hostiles.

Custer looked at the line of enlisted men queued up at the makeshift store. Wasn't anything he could do about the whiskey, and except for the possibility of a few fights, there wasn't really any trouble for the men to get into. He'd go back to his tent and start working on that new article for the New York *World.* He'd just completed the *Galaxy* magazine feature and had sent it with the courier to Fort Lincoln. He was getting paid well for these journalistic efforts, and it kept his oar in the water back east. With the victory that lay ahead of him against the Sioux, a Democratic victory in the forthcoming election could certainly ensure that star.

He just wished Terry would get his mind made up and let him get on with it!

He touched the brim of his slouch hat in salute and nodded his head. "Thanks for your consideration, Captain. I'll see you at dinner."

Sergeant Danny Kanipe stood in the sutler's line next to Iggy Stungewitz. Iggy quietly withdrew a letter from his coat and handed it to Kanipe.

"I figured it was from her when I heard your name at mail call," Danny said.

They had agreed that she would send her letters to Stungewitz. Iggy nodded, looking around. "Bobo's not here. Go ahead."

The troopers on either side of them were from other companies, so Danny eagerly looked at the envelope. Missouri Ann had a slightly slanted, but very legible hand. He tore the envelope open and withdrew the inside page. He quickly scanned the words, then read it again more slowly . . .

> *Ft. Lincoln*
> *May 28th Inst.*
>
> *My Dearest Danny,*
> *I miss you so, dear one. I know I'm taking a chance writing to you like this, but I simply must share my thoughts with you. The dreadful lady who caught us in the laundry room, Mary Hohmeyer, has threatened to tell on us. She's a nasty German religious type. I offered to give her the twelve dollars I had saved up, just so it wouldn't cause any more trouble between you and Ed, but she just sniffed and stomped away. So I don't know what she'll do. I just know I love you, so take good care of yourself and come back to my welcome arms as soon as you can.*
> *Your loving Missouri Ann*

Kanipe jumped as Ed Bobo strode up and said, "Get me a gallon of the sutler's best whiskey, Kanipe. Here's the money."

Danny quickly folded the letter and stuffed it into his pocket as the first sergeant handed him a dollar. He was so flustered he dropped the coin and had to lean down to pick it up. *Did he see her handwriting?*

☆ ☆ ☆

Captain Frederick Benteen came out of his tent and beckoned to his first sergeant, Joseph McCurry, "Here, First Sergeant, send someone over to the sutler and get me a couple gallons of his rot gut whiskey." He handed over two one-dollar coins and looked up as Captain Tom Weir sauntered up. Weir pulled out a five-dollar bill and said, "Long as you're at it, McCurry, have somebody get me three gallons and take it over to my tent."

"Yes, sir," the former coachmaker replied, taking the money.

"Got any fresh coffee?" Weir asked.

"We'll see," Fred Benteen replied, striking a match and puffing on his pipe.

They walked to the mess tent and went inside, where Benteen told the cook to bring them some coffee. Sitting down at the officers' table, Weir asked, "What do you think Terry's going to do?"

"I heard he's sending Reno on a scout up the Powder."

"Taking troops?"

"Battalion size."

Weir sipped his coffee with a slight tremor. The shake in his hands had become more pronounced lately. Happened mostly when he hadn't had any alcohol for several hours. He pulled out a flask and poured a liberal jolt of whiskey into the cup, then offered the flask to Benteen, who poured some into his cup. "Think he'll find anything?" Weir asked.

"Hard to tell. Charley Reynolds told me he thinks Sitting Bull and company are farther west and south. Up around the Tongue or the Rosebud, maybe near the Bighorn Mountains."

"What about Gibbon's scouts, have they seen anything?"

"Nothing recent or specific."

John Gibbon's Montana column was mostly off to the west a ways, up the Yellowstone, but their colonel had come downriver to meet with Terry on the Far West. "I heard Terry isn't too pleased with Gibbon," Weir observed. "Been draggin' his feet."

Benteen shrugged again and ran a hand through his white hair. "I don't know. They don't invite me into their private councils, particularly our fair-haired prima donna."

"Think you'll ever quit disliking him?"

"Huh, maybe the day the sun rises in the west."

"He's got remarkable vitality. Runs me into the ground."

"But what does he accomplish? Shoots some game, writes all those letters. I heard he's spilling his guts to those eastern newspapers. No, you can have Custer. If I had any choice, I'd be transferred in a minute."

Weir poured some more whiskey in his coffee. "He'll fight."

"No question. But we all know how to do that."

"What do you think about Reno?"

"He did a pretty good job in the war. There just seems to be an aura of bad luck hanging around his neck."

Weir grinned. "Well, I'll put my chips on Custer any day."

Benteen shook his head. "You're just an inveterate hero worshiper."

30

At the forks of Goose Creek
June 14, 1876

"I don't believe this, John. What if I simply must get a message to General Terry?"

Lieutenant John Bourke shook his head in reply to his boss's question. "General, the only alternative is to send couriers out to scour the territory looking for him. And that could take weeks."

Brigadier General George Crook stared at the sheet of paper that stated:

> Means of communication with General Terry; Cmdg, Dakota and Montana columns: Crook to send courier to Ft. Fetterman, Wyoming. From there, the message to be relayed by telegraph to Crook hq. at Omaha. From there by telegraph to Sheridan's hq. in Chicago. Thence to Terry's dept. hq. in St. Paul, and on by telegraph to Ft. Lincoln at Bismarck. At this point the message to be placed aboard one of the riverboats and taken on to Terrys advance supply depot on the Yellowstone. The final leg by courier to Terry in the field. Elapsed time—about two weeks.

Crook shook his head. "That's not a very good way to run a war. I—" He looked up as a horse and rider trotted up to his command tent.

Scout Frank Grouard, the tall and swarthy onetime Mormon who was Sitting Bull's adopted brother, jumped out of the saddle and touched his hat brim in salute. "We got 'em, General. They're almost here, a hundred and seventy-six of them."

Crook blew out a sigh of relief. He'd been worrying about the arrival of his Crow allies for several days and had sent several emissaries out to find them. "Good work, Grouard," he said. "What chiefs are leading them?"

"Old Crow, Good Heart, and Medicine Crow."

"Are they dependable?"

"I think so, and they all hate the Sioux."

"Speaking of our friends, the Sioux, you got any good guesses about their location?"

"I think they're on the Rosebud, General."

"Why do you say that?"

"Sign. I think there are a lot of them."

"With their Cheyenne friends?"

"Yes, sir."

Crook pursed his lips. "How far?"

"I'd say maybe fifty, sixty miles, maybe less."

Just then a shout went up as the first of the large contingent of Crows rode proudly into the sprawling camp. Old Crow, seeing the flags in front of the headquarters tent, rode his paint up and with a grunt, nodded his head to Crook, and then to Grouard. Turning back to his warriors he raised a rifle streaming with banners and ordered them to dismount. As the Crows settled into the middle of the camp, another greeting erupted on the south side of the bivouac. Eighty-six Shoshone warriors, or Snakes as they were also called, galloped into camp and assembled before Crook.

The general had his Indian allies, but he had no way of knowing how much these enemies of the Sioux would mean to him in the near future.

Although Red Elk was enjoying his marriage bed with Late Star, he was equally drawn by the excitement of an impending fight with the Long Knives. When he heard that a Cheyenne war leader named Little Hawk was going to take a hunting party out to shoot buffalo, he hurried over and asked if he could go along.

Little Hawk eyed the big rifle. "You aren't going to use that on buffalo, are you?"

"No," Red Elk replied, "but maybe on Long Knives."

Little Hawk shrugged. "Come along, if you wish."

Now, on the sixteenth day of the Moon of Ripe Juneberries, the hunting party spotted a huge herd of buffalo quietly grazing on an open plain. Little Hawk gave the signal to advance slowly. When they were about a mile away, they ran into another hunting party, also Cheyennes. They were from Magpie Eagle's band that was camped not far away on Trail Creek. After a short parley, Big Wolf, the leader of the other band, agreed to move off to the west side of the herd.

At that moment, Red Elk spotted two of Crook's scouts off to the southeast of the herd. They were with a strong party of Crows. *"Look!"* Red Elk shouted, jamming his rifle in the air toward the hated Crows.

Little Hawk's eyes narrowed. "Too many," he said. "It's best to go back and tell the chiefs."

At this point, Plenty Coups, the Crow war leader riding beside Frank Grouard as the Crow scouting party approached the herd, stood tall in his saddle, grabbed his crotch, and shouted, *"Daughters of Cheyenne Pigs! Come fight!"*

Red Elk's eyes narrowed as he raised his big Sharps, but Little Hawk pushed the barrel down. "No! Don't let them know anything. We go back to Crazy Horse!"

Red Elk scowled. "I'm Sioux! No one, let alone a lowly Crow, calls me a pig!"

"Do as I say!" Little Hawk snapped. "You'll get your fight!"

As Grouard and the Crows urged their ponies toward them, the two parties of Cheyennes split and galloped off toward their respective camps.

But Red Elk rode only until he found an arroyo that gave him enough cover to split away to the south. He would find Three Stars, not run away with his tail between his legs!

Galloping into Sitting Bull's main village that now consisted of over six thousand people, Little Hawk jumped off his horse at the Oglala camp. Men and women, children and old ones, hurried away from whatever they were doing to hear the news. Dogs barked loudly as the remaining Cheyennes dismounted. Gall hurried over from the Hunkpapa camp as someone went to fetch Crazy Horse.

When the former Shirt Wearer arrived, Little Hawk told him what had occurred at the buffalo herd. "I recognized the Grabber," the Cheyenne added.

Crazy Horse's eyes narrowed. It was confirmed that Grouard was still scouting for Three Stars. "Do you know where they are?" he asked.

"Southeast. Red Elk went to look for them."

Crazy Horse's bright eyes narrowed. He looked at Gall with a touch of a smile. "Do your Hunkapaps want to fight, my brother?"

Gall, too, smiled. "We'll follow the lead of the great Crazy Horse, my brother!"

The Oglala nodded his head and gave the order to prepare for battle.

Frank Grouard and the Crows had quickly given up chasing the Cheyennes, wisely not wishing to run into an ambush. Returning to the army camp at a little after seven, the Grabber stopped momentarily to watch the show that was the center of attention in the broad valley where Crook was bivouacked. For some part of a square mile, mules were kicking, bucking, and tossing would-be riders every which way. The general had decided he didn't want his infantry wearing itself out from walking into battle, so he had ordered the foot soldiers to get acquainted with mules from the supply train. The skittish infantrymen, many of whom had never been on a horse or any other four-legged creature, were far from being in control of the contrary mounts. The mules, in turn, had decided they were against the whole idea. And while this sideshow was gong on, the watching cavalrymen were beside themselves laughing and jeering at the mishaps of the poor neophyte riders. The Indians and the teamsters also joined in the uproarious funmaking.

Grouard found Crook in his tent, writing a report. He tossed off a sloppy scout-type salute and said, "No doubt about it, General. They were the Cheyennes who are running with Crazy Horse. Plenty Coups recognized Little Hawk, a Cheyenne war leader. They have probably reported our presence back to Sitting Bull by now."

"Why didn't you have someone follow them to find out where the big village is located?" Crook asked quietly.

Grouard bit a piece of tobacco off a plug. "General, we're smack dab in the middle of a whole lot of hostile Sioux, and them Injun scouts ain't too interested in traipsin' very far off."

Crook nodded his head, turning to Lieutenant Bourke. "Let's stop the rodeo and make plans to move north."

Red Elk had followed Grouard and Little Coups to Crook's camp. After spending several minutes observing the mule show from a tree he had climbed well above the river bed, he nodded in satisfaction and scurried down to his horse. Mounting, he eased the pony away from the encampment and within a couple of minutes broke into a fast trot into the long slanting rays of the sun. He was filled with excitement. Three Stars had many Long Knives, but the Lakota and their friends had Sitting Bull's power! He would cover himself with battle honors before the sun set on another day. He knew his people would be coming down Corral Creek to meet the Rosebud. He would have no trouble finding them.

This was the great prophecy of Sitting Bull. It had all started in the Moon When the Grain Comes Up, when Three Stars' Long Knives had attacked the village in the cold on the Powder River. It was then, when the warriors stole back their ponies, that the Long Knives became nothing as warriors—nothing but to be laughed at, and jeered. Worse than Crows.

Crazy Horse would have a great army on the morrow. Every warrior, Sioux and Cheyenne, wanted a part in it. There would be hundreds, the most ever. And they would spill the blood of the Long Knives.

It was a great time!

In the center of the Hunkpapa camp on Reno Creek, Sitting Bull drank the potion that the medicine man Crooked Tree had prepared for him and handed the leather cup to his younger wife. The Hunkpapa chief was greatly weakened by his arduous Sun Dance rituals, but he sat rigidly cross-legged as he watched impassively while Crazy Horse and Gall, along with the Cheyenne chief, Spotted Wolf, sat before him in his tipi.

☆ 263 ★

Crazy Horse spoke softly, his eyes glowing, "It is just as you have foreseen, Great Chief. Three Stars comes to our rifles and arrows. He will not expect us to flash down on him like the mountain wind. We will pick the place wisely and strike him when he is unaware." Crazy Horse's eyes narrowed as he jammed his big knife into the ground in front of his feet. "And we will *kill* him!"

Gall and Spotted Wolf echoed their approval.

Sitting Bull nodded his head, looking from one to the other. "I'm too weak to go with you."

Gall spoke up. "We will carry your lance, Father."

"We will destroy them!" Spotted Wolf added. "Crazy Horse is right!"

Sitting Bull again looked into the eyes of each of the fighting leaders and was reassured by what he saw. He nodded his head again and grunted in agreement. "You lead them, Crazy Horse, and lead them well."

The Oglala nodded his head as he got to his feet. "I will, Great Chief."

It was after the moon climbed above the horizon, huge and yellow in its early phase, that Crazy Horse finished applying the white spots to his bare torso. His light hair was braided tight, and the lightning was painted jaggedly on his left cheek, covering most of the scar. His wife, Black Shawl, returned to the tipi with their daughter, They-Are-Not-Afraid-of-Her, just as he gathered up his materials to go paint his warhorse.

"How many Long Knives ride with Three Stars?" Black Shawl asked quietly.

Crazy Horse shrugged. "It doesn't matter."

His wife looked at him with a touch of fear. "It always matters."

"We have the greatest medicine ever."

"Will it stop a bullet?"

"No bullet can stop me. You know that."

His daughter looked up. "What stops you, Father?"

He smiled, touching a dab of white paint on her turned up nose. "Only a pretty little girl."

She smiled back, touching her nose.

"Will you come back to the tipi before you leave?" Black Shawl asked.

He took her hand and held it a moment. "No."

"Then I'll see you as you leave."

He nodded and ducked out through the flap.

Crazy Horse knew the moonlight afforded any watchful eye an opportunity to see them, but it was the only way he could have a minute with her. On the small knoll above the small, separate corral where he and his Oglala warriors kept their ponies, there was a small grove of cottonwoods that stood like tall sentries, creating just enough shadow to conceal the lovely Black Buffalo Woman. As he stepped into their darkness, he immediately detected her scent. She reached out, took his hand as he dropped his war kit to the ground. Her words were whispered, "I've missed you."

He took her in his arms and held her tightly. "And I've missed you, my pretty one."

"You leave soon to fight Three Stars?"

"Yes, tonight."

She hugged him tightly. "I love you."

"You're still my woman."

"Yes, I will always be your woman."

Two Oglala warriors stopped near the Cottonwoods on their way to the corral. The two lovers held their breaths as the two young men spoke of the coming fight. Finally the warriors moved on. Black Buffalo Woman's eyes were wide as she brought Crazy Horse's cheek against hers and once more squeezed him tightly. "Bring my great *blotahunka* back to me, Great Wolf," she whispered, closing her eyes tight. "I pray to you."

He pulled out of her embrace. "I will always come back," he said gruffly.

She watched, eyes moist, as the man she would never stop loving strode down to decorate his warhorse.

Red Elk had waited at the confluence of the Corral and the Rosebud since shortly after midnight. Now, a little over an hour later, he watched the lead elements of Crazy Horse's force ride silently down the west bank of the Rosebud. Two scouts came first, then five more, then, in a few minutes, the head of a large body of warriors. He knew Crazy Horse would be there. Pulling out of the clump of bushes where he'd been waiting, he rode up to the lead group and identified himself. Immediately, Crazy Horse called out to him.

Riding up to the Oglala leader, he said, "I've been to Three Stars' camp and counted his soldiers, Great *Blotahunka.*"

Gall and two of the Cheyenne leaders were with Crazy Horse, as well as other Sioux war leaders and chiefs. Red Elk reined in beside Crazy Horse's war pony as the Oglala said, "Tell me."

Red Elk quickly described what he'd seen, including the mule fiasco.

"How many soldiers?" Crazy Horse asked.

"Over ten hundred."

Crazy Horse nodded, the remaining moonlight making his eyes glitter. "Three Stars knows we are up here. He'll move early." He called out to his lead scouts. As they hurried up, he turned to Red Elk. "Tell them exactly where the camp is."

Red Elk described the location, then turned to Crazy Horse. "Do you want me to lead them back?"

"Yes. And return to me as soon as Three Stars begins to move."

Red Elk nodded in agreement and rode off with the scouts.

Brigadier General George Crook was definitely not pleased with his scouts. They had been too skittish to go out during the night. Now, at 3:15 A.M., as the gray light of dawn began to tighten the eastern horizon, he spoke to Frank Grouard outside his tent as an orderly brought a cup of steaming coffee. "Get those scouts out there, Grouard. I know it's dangerous, but everything's dangerous from here on. Find those Sioux for me, and there's a bonus in it for you."

Grouard had a way of saluting that reminded anyone who had been around the navy of an old tar. He made a fist of his right hand, with the forefinger slightly bent as it protruded. Now he touched it to the brim of his hat. "I'll get the Crows out there, General. And don't worry, we'll find the Sioux."

Still in just his long underwear, Crook finished his coffee and turned back in for another hour's sleep. He guessed he'd need it before the day was over.

The column pulled out right on schedule at six A.M. down the south fork of the Rosebud. Counting eithty-five miners and packers, and nearly 170 Crows and Shoshones, Crook had some 1,325 men in his command as he followed the river in its northerly flow. The little stream, quite narrow and slow moving in many places, was a blaze of color on this June morning. Rain showers had freshened the whole area the night before. The valley was a virtual sea of blue wildflowers dotting the verdant grass and shrubbery, while the stream banks themselves were covered by a profusion of wild roses in various stages of bloom.

After all, it *was* the Rosebud.

Riding at the head of the column, Crook turned to his aide, Lieutenant Bourke, and said, "I want to take an early break so the horses don't get too tired. They had a long haul yesterday."

Bourke nodded. "Yes, sir." He pulled out his watch. "It's nearly eight o'clock."

Crook nodded. "This valley looks as good as any."

Bourke wheeled his horse. "I'll pass the word."

Within minutes the various elements of the huge column fell out of the line of march.

Fires were quickly started to heat coffee, and the horses were unsaddled so they could graze and rest. Many of the men did what soldiers had done for centuries—they relieved themselves, plopped down for a cat nap on their saddles or bedrolls, and a couple even wrote a note to a loved one. It was just another of those rests on the way to a war that might or might not happen.

It was then that some of them heard the distant shots.

First Sergeant William Kirkwood in Captain Noyes's I Company of the Second Cavalry shrugged and said, "Those damned scouts must be shooting buffalo again."

The troopers nearest him closed their eyes again and drifted back to sleep.

But the shots started getting louder.

☆ ☆ ☆

The shots came from Red Elk and the main group of scouts when Grouard and his Crow scouts ran into them several miles north of Crook's temporary camp. Knowing the Crows would run into their larger body of warriors, Red Elk and the scouts had decided to distract them. And before anyone could stop him, Red Elk let out a war whoop and charged straight at the enemy horsemen. When he was a hundred yards from them, he began shouting Lakota obscenities. The other scouts fired to cover him as he pulled up and shouted, "Today you die, Crow dogs!" Then he wheeled his pony and returned to the group of scouts.

The Crows with Grouard had seen all they wished to see. There wasn't a doubt in their minds that the entire Sioux nation was about to clamber out of every ounce of concealment around them. Kicking their ponies in the flanks, they galloped away from the disgusted Grabber. He raised his rifle to shoot at Red Elk, but the young warrior was already too much of a moving target.

Farther back, sitting on their war ponies along a small ridge, Crazy Horse and Gall watched the engagement between the two groups of scouts unfold below them. He turned to the scout who had just returned from Crook's camp. "Tell me quickly about their position," he snapped.

The scout quickly described the relaxed layout of the army position.

Crazy Horse grunted and urged his pony forward.

Gall and the scout followed him down the ridge to where the other leaders, Lakota and Cheyenne, waited eagerly. Crazy Horse raised his rifle and shouted in Lakota, "We have them! Ride hard behind me. My scout, Red Elk, will lead us right into them before they know we are there!"

General Crook had decided to sit in on a few hands of Whist, the popular card game, when a commotion was heard off to the north of the camp. Suddenly a Shoshone scout named Limpy came roaring down from the ridge, nearly losing his seat on his pony. *"Lakota Lakota!"* he shouted at the top of his lungs.

The Whist game broke up immediately as shouts of "Injuns!" reverberated through camp. Officers and sergeants shouted orders. Soldiers awoke abruptly and ran toward their mounts. "Bring that scout to me!" Crook told Bourke. At that moment Frank Grouard also galloped into camp.

But it was almost too late. Large numbers of Sioux and Cheyenne warriors were appearing on both sides of the valley and at the north end.

Without waiting for orders from the general, Major Randall, the chief of scouts threw up a skirmish line of Indian allies on the nearest ridge to the north. Pickets, already geared to fight, joined the steadfast Crows and Shoshones as the first wave of Crazy Horse's warriors crashed into the camp from the north.

It would prove to be the difference between a rout and a battle.

Randall's allies stood fast amid the piercing war whoops of the attackers. Rifles cracked everywhere. Crazy Horse himself rode to within 450 yards of the ring of fire, but didn't tempt fate when he correctly read the effectiveness of the skirmish line. Red Elk dismounted behind him and brought his big rifle up. With satisfaction, he saw his first round hit home as a Crow defender jerked up and slumped.

In the meantime, General Crook had mounted his big black horse and had quickly formulated a battle plan. As Lieutenant Colonel William Royal, the tall Virginian, organized the cavalry, Crook gave orders to take the high ground to the north. But his gaze swept around. "I think we're up against at least a thousand of those hostiles!" he shouted to Royal. "We'll have to take *all* of the high ground if we're going to win this thing!"

He rode over to speak to Captain Noyes as his battalion of Second Cavalry formed up. Then it was on to where the infantry was beginning to take shape under Major Chambers, his old classmate at West Point. He observed that the Crows and Shoshones were still valiantly holding their own against the brunt of the hostile attack, and made a mental note about their steadfastness. Shots continued to ring out in all quadrants. The firing was now a staccato crackling in the high air.

He couldn't shake a dark feeling. It had been back in October of 1864, the nineteenth to be exact, when Jubal Early and his Confederate army had crashed in on him at Cedar Creek in Virginia. Oh, Sheridan had turned the battle around later in the day, after his famous ride, but one fact was certain—Old Jube had stolen a march on him, and George Crook had been caught with his pants down!

And it had just happened again.

By Indians!

What a nagging thing to remember.

But that was history—he had a command to save. Where in the devil had all these hostiles come from?

To the soldier fighting in his first action, the attacking hostiles could seem fearsome. Many wore half masks of the heads of beasts, nearly all of their faces and parts of their bodies were painted devilishly. Many others wore the eagle feather war bonnet that trailed through the air behind its bearer like a fluttering snake. Their horses were painted all the colors of the rainbow in dizzying designs. And war whoops mixed with other screams of war lashed out over everyone.

Now the clear air was rapidly filling with dark smoke.

Captain Noyes, apparently making up for his deficiencies at Powder River with Old Joe Reynolds, aggressively led his dismounted cavalry, in conjunction with Chambers's infantry, to vital high ground to the north. Crook's force was rallying, but Crazy Horse was a superb general in his own right, directing one slashing attack after another into the recovering troops.

Captain Anson Mills, an experienced cavalry officer, began what would be a full day of cavalry glory—on both sides. The hostiles were so adept at riding with one arm around the neck and one leg hooked over the back of their horses, that they could ride full-tilt and still fire a weapon or fling a lance without exposing themselves to the soldiers' fire. As Mills would later state, his troopers were up against the "best goddamned cavalry soldiers in the world!"

As the battle ricocheted on, one side would attack and the other would counterattack. Then the reverse would happen. Just as it appeared the tide would turn, it would go the other way. Two hours passed, three, four—and still the fight raged on. Smoke and dust hung like a dirty brown and black cloud over the valley, filling the hot noisy sky with the acrid smells of war. Red Elk had been patiently waiting his chance to do something special, but Crazy Horse had ordered him to remain close. Finally, with the sun just past midday, he edged away from the command point and began working his way down a narrow arroyo toward a position where some cavalrymen were holding a small knoll. He held his pony's nose, keeping the animal quiet as he crept into the cover of some bushes slightly east of the little hill. They were large enough to hide him from the eyes of anyone looking down from above, but he was in danger of being spotted from other directions. Apparently everyone was occupied, because no one challenged him.

As near as he could tell, there were seven troopers holding the position, which was about forty paces from his bushes. And they all seemed to be intent on something to the south. They were firing their carbines quite furiously in that direction. There was plenty of noise, and this bit of high ground had its share of smoke. His eyes narrowed. It was time. Stuffing his big Sharps into its buffalo skin scabbard, he checked the Colt six-shot revolver he'd recently acquired. Removing its safety, he climbed into the saddle and urged the horse up the incline. He'd have to ride fast!

Ten paces blew by in a few lunging strides, then twenty more, and suddenly he was over the crest and into the small defensive perimeter. He blasted away with the big pistol, hitting one startled trooper. He swung the Colt at another and fired. *There! That was what he wanted!* Leaning down, he grabbed the brim of the big Long Knife's hat, tore it from his head, and with a wild war whoop urged his pony over the edge of the position into a wide open gallop back toward the Sioux position.

What a first coup!

As Red Elk reined into the nearby Hunkpapa position, Gall shook his head and grinned. And a dozen warriors who had seen his feat let out war whoops. He smiled and looked at the hat. It was made of straw, with a wide brim, slightly stained around the sweat band area, and a bit tattered. On its front, the former owner had pinned the crossed sabers of the cavalry insignia.

Red Elk grinned. At campfires in generations ahead, storytellers would recount the day the fearless Red Elk rode into many Long Knives and stole the hat—a first coup to top all first coups on the Day When They Beat Three Stars.

At shortly after two in the afternoon, Crazy Horse held a council of war on a ridge west of the huge battlefield. Red Elk stood off to the side as the Oglala spoke to his war leaders. Pleasure showed in the great *blotahunka's* expression as he said, "It is time. We have fought a great victory. Never before have this number of our people fought that many Long Knives. We are still *here!* We leave of our own will, and we will take our dead and wounded along with us." He grinned, which was uncharacteristic for Crazy Horse. "This is the greatest victory in a long time for the Lakota and the Cheyenne!"

He raised his rifle and emitted a piercing war whoop!

All of the others did the same.

And then they turned to go back to their commands and ordered them to withdraw.

Red Elk had never felt more fulfilled.

When it was certain that the attacking hostiles had indeed broken off the engagement, Crook was faced with a major option. It was extremely tempting to follow them to their village. A major pursuit could still save this day and give him a resounding victory. But as Captain Anson Mills came back from a fruitless scout for the village, the general decided to put his expedition back together and lick his wounds. It was a good thing. Crazy Horse, in his tradition of sucking enemies into traps, had laid another ambush for the Long Knives. But when they didn't follow, the brilliant Oglala finally ordered his exultant warriors, except for a few watchful scouts, back to the huge Sitting Bull encampment. All of the dead who could be found, and the more than sixty wounded, were brought along. At shortly after six o'clock the *blotahunka* called a halt to bury the thirty-eight dead warriors. One more, a Black-Little-Bird, was believed dead but hadn't been found.

As the sun went down once more on the sober army encampment, John Bourke came to the general's tent where he found Crook finishing a conversation with Frank Grouard. "I have the casualty list, sir," Bourke said as the scout departed.

Crook looked up from his camp stool. "How bad is it?"

"It's remarkably low," the lieutenant replied. "Ten men, including one Indian scout, killed; twenty-one soldiers wounded."

Crook quietly nodded his head. "Yes, I would have expected far more. How many of the Crows and Shoshone?"

"I don't have that figure, sir, but I think about fifteen dead and maybe some thirty wounded. They made a remarkable stand as skirmishers at the start of the fight."

"Yes, they did, and I want to tell their leaders how much I appreciate it."

Bourke waited, then finally asked, "What are you going to do next, General?"

Crook tugged at his heavy beard. "I want to go after them so badly I can taste it, but Grouard thinks it could be bad news. The hostiles have a huge force and they're fired up. Besides, we shot up a lot of ammunition today . . . considering how few hostiles we must have hit. So I guess we might as well pack up and go back to Goose Creek where we can refit and take care of our wounded." He frowned.

"I'll issue the orders."

"Yes, and John, also thank the commands for a job well done. I consider today's battle a hard-fought victory. We fought on rough ground selected by a well-armed enemy, not to our advantage. We recovered from a surprise attack, the enemy withdrew, and we held the ground at the end of the fight. Yes, offer them my rousing congratulations and tell the commanders to get all recommendations for awards of valor in as soon as possible."

Bourke touched his hat brim in a salute, but stopped as he started to depart. "What about Sheridan and Terry, sir. Should we send them anything?"

"No hurry," Crook replied. "They won't get it for weeks anyway. As soon as the commanders get their formal reports in, I'll consolidate them and get it all off to Sheridan."

It was well after dark when Red Elk rode into the big village with Crazy Horse and a large segment of the warriors. Hundreds of women and children, and most of the older people, joined a still weak Sitting Bull in greeting them. The tall son of Bald Wolf proudly wore his new straw hat as he searched for his bride. Affixed to the back off the crown, first coup style, Red Elk's eagle feather stood straight up. He knew his feat on the cavalry knob would be told as soon as someone had a chance. But the giant celebration would have to wait. War whoops were prohibited; only the bark of a dog here and there joined the incessant beating of the drums.

The nearly forty dead warriors could not be disgraced by holding a victory feast in the same village where they had proudly trod so recently. It was a time, first, for wailing. Sitting Bull had decreed that the massive village would move in the morning, and when it reached its new location, the festivities could begin.

Red Elk felt a tug at his right foot. Looking down, he saw Late Star's beaming, fiery face. "What are you doing with that silly hat?" she asked with a smile.

He smiled back, "A Long Knife gave it to me."

"Will you tell me about it?" she asked as she walked slowly along, hanging on to his moccasin.

He grinned. "Only two hundred times."

She said, "I'm so happy for you, and proud!"

He sobered, "But we must also mourn. Black Ash was killed."

Late Star frowned and squeezed her husband's foot. She knew how much he loved his *kola*. It was worse than losing a brother.

He swung down from the pony and put his arm around her waist. "But it was the greatest Lakota victory since before the rocks were hard."

31

It was warm in the cabin of the *Far West*. A high pressure system had moved into the area near the junction of the Yellowstone and Rosebud Rivers, and the wind was but a light breath in the clear, sunny sky. Custer stood, hatless, to the side as General Terry began his briefing. The brigadier's map was spread out on the table in the middle of the cabin and was the object of everyone's attention.

The other two officers in attendance were Colonel Gibbon and Major James Brisbin. The major, Gibbon's second in command, had been rather undistinguished in his postwar service in the cavalry. He had risen to the rank of brigadier general during the war and now commanded the four companies of horses from the Second Cavalry. He was just a year older than Custer. The forty-nine-year-old John Gibbon, on the other hand, had been described by Theodore Lyman—from his oft-quoted descriptions of Civil War officers—as "steel-cold, the most American of Americans, with his sharp nose and up-and-down manner of telling the truth, no matter whom it hurts." Like Custer, Gibbon had a brilliant Civil War record and had been a two-star general. His postwar Indian fighting experience, as colonel of the Seventh Infantry, was more extensive than Custer's. Whatever his opinion of Custer may have been, his approach to what Terry wanted done was strictly business.

Terry spoke up. "I'm very displeased with Major Reno for going too far on his scout. He has undoubtedly alarmed the hostiles about our intentions, and it could well be that Sitting Bull will scatter his people before we can find him. Both General Custer and myself have repri-manded Reno for insubordination."

Terry used a Crow arrow as a pointer, marking their position on the map and moving its tip up the Rosebud to the Little Bighorn River. "Gentlemen, I think Sitting Bull is up here somewhere. As near as I can guess, he has some four hundred lodges in his village, meaning somewhere around twenty-eight hundred people and some eight hundred warriors. Of course, if any summer roamers have joined him, there could be more. "General," he said to Custer, "I want you to take the entire Seventh Cavalry up the Rosebud, and then down the Little Bighorn, if necessary, to see if you can find him."

Turning to the commander of the Montana column, he said, "General Gibbon, I want you to move your column up the Big Horn to the confluence of the Little Bighorn River, where you will set up a blocking position. If General Custer manages to flush the hostiles in your direction, we'll have them bottled up."

Alfred Terry paused, looking at each of his subordinates. "The four-gun Gatling battery is here. It's yours for the asking, General Custer."

Custer shook his head. "I don't want those guns, sir. They'll cut down on my mobility."

"That's a lot of firepower, Custer," Gibbon said.

"Nope, I pass. You can have them."

Terry nodded. "The four companies of Second Cavalry are also yours, General Custer."

Custer pursed his lips. There wasn't a pack of Indians in the world that his Seventh Cavalry couldn't handle. Besides, this was strictly a Seventh Cavalry party and he didn't want to share any of the glory with any other unit. "No, sir," he replied. "My troopers will fight better with our regimental integrity. Besides, General Gibbon may need those boys from the Second to pursue the hostiles if they get away from us. No, I think you can better use them in the other column."

John Gibbon looked into Custer's eyes for a moment, then shrugged.

"As you wish," Terry replied.

My Dear Libbie,

At last I've been cut loose to go after Sitting Bull & Co. Terry has given me the whole Seventh and free rein to scout for fifteen days if necessary. I'll be traveling light, with only pack mules and no wagons. Gibbon gave me six Crow scouts who know the area to supplement my own scouts. Terry's written orders to me are quite discretionary. He stated that it is impossible for him to give me any definite instructions . . . that he places too much confidence in my zeal, energy and ability to impose on me precise orders which might hamper my action. So you see, my Darling Standby, the glory is to be all mine, if I can bring the enemy to a fight. I hope only that the hostiles don't run before I can hit them. And I hope we catch them soon. Wouldn't it be glorious news for the Democratic convention? Young Autie is going along, but I'm leaving Mary here on the FAR WEST. If all goes well, my love, I'll be heading back to you in the next two or three weeks, loaded with Custer's Luck.

Your Devoted Nomad, Autie

Custer sealed the envelope and walked outside his tent, where he handed it to his orderly. "Get this over to the mail clerk on the boat, Trooper."

The orderly took the letter, saluted, and hurried away.

Captain Tom Custer sauntered up, tossing off a casual salute and dropping on a camp stool beside the tent. "Mornin', Autie. Any hot new news?"

Just that Mitch Boyer talked to those Crows Gibbon gave us, and he's pretty sure Sitting Bull's on the Little Bighorn.

"We still going up the Rosebud?"

"Yup. They could've cut back."

Tom wiped the back of his neck with a red bandanna. "They can do anything, damned Sioux. We gonna pitch right into them if we run into them?"

"Absolutely. If they'll fight."

Tom Custer got to his feet and removed the new slouch hat he'd purchased just before leaving Fort Lincoln. "I could use another medal of honor, big brother. I don't know of any cavalry officer's got *three*."

Custer grinned. "Reckless as you are, that shouldn't be a problem."

Tom grinned back. "Look who's talking."

☆ ☆ ☆

Iggy Stungewitz passed the colonel's orderly as he left the post office on the boat. He had just mailed Danny Kanipe's letter to Missouri Ann, as well as a letter of his own that he'd written to his mother back in Russia. As he turned and headed for C Company's area, a strong hand grabbed him by the arm. He turned and looked into Martin's black expression. His voice was low as he said, "Take your hand off me, First Sergeant."

Martin glared into his eyes, then smiled icily before releasing his grip. "I just wanted to get your attention, you Jew prick."

Iggy stood loose on the balls of his feet, ready for anything the bullish Irishman might want to try.

"Listen closely," Martin said, "There may be some good fightin' out there when we find those yellow belly Sioux, and when it happens, sure and you'd better keep your bloody eyes open, *Jewboy*, because I've got a bullet right here in my belt with your name on it."

Iggy looked straight into the hate, a faint smile touching his lips as he patted the revolver on his own hip. "You'd better sneak up on me."

Martin nodded his head emphatically. "That's just what I'm gonna do, Jewboy."

The regimental band had remained back at Terry's base camp as part of its security force, so the only music available was from the various trumpeters. At twelve o'clock sharp, they massed and blew "GarryOwen" to start the column forward. General Terry, Gibbon, and Custer stood on a makeshift reviewing stand as Lieutenant Charlie Varnum and his scouts led the column out of the camp. The headquarters detachment, led by Lieutenant Cooke and bearing the bright command flags was next to pass in review. The rest of the regiment followed. Many smiles were in evidence, marking the high spirits of the men. They knew. They knew they'd been selected to go find Sitting Bull, they knew it was because they were a good outfit. They knew their colonel was a fighting son of a bitch, and they were raring to get at it.

Over a month in the field had tanned the troopers and hardened them. Their uniforms were mixed with individual articles of civilian clothing, with the predominant issue items being the sky-blue trousers tucked in cavalry boots. Most shirts were blue or gray, the suspenders various colors.

A number of troopers sported the traditional red kerchief that dated back in Custer's commands to his first brigade during the war. Headgear varied widely, but civilian straw hats to ward off some of the sun's heat were popular. Most of them were styled somewhat similar to the issue slouch hat. Many troopers had stuffed into their pants cushions to ease the discomfort of the coming long hours in the hard McClellan saddle.

The troopers were armed with long-barreled Colt revolvers and the Springfield single-shot carbine. Aside from what ammunition they carried in their cartridge belts, the remainder of the hundred rounds of carbine shells and the twenty-four pistol rounds they'd been issued were in their saddle bags. The rest of the regiment's load of ammunition was aboard the unruly pack mules that were accustomed to hauling wagons, not having strange weights stuck on their backs.

Custer, of course, was attired and armed differently. He was wearing the new, soft buff, buckskin jacket that Sergeant Jeremiah Finley had made for him. The white, broad-brimmed hat had been cleaned by his striker, John Burkman, just two days earlier, but there was still a stain around the sweat band.

Custer had decided against wearing the ivory-handled Smith & Wesson revolvers that he usually wore for show. No, he wanted the best firepower he could get in a handgun, so he opted for the .45 Webley. It was the latest thing, a snub-nosed Bulldog Royal Irish Constabulary revolver with a ring in the butt for a lanyard. Custer had fired it enough to get thoroughly familiar with its double-action, and since it didn't have to be "thumb-cocked" like the army issue revolver, he could fire it as fast as he could pull the trigger. Since his favorite hunting weapon was the .44 Remington sporting model, and he had special brass cartridges for it, that was his rifle of choice for the expedition. These cartridges were the Remington .44–90–550 Specials and were chambered specifically for the Remington Creedmore matches. Since Custer had written to Remington Arms, praising his rifle for its accuracy, the company had gladly provided him with these special rounds. He had plenty of ammunition for both firearms.

John Burkman, Old Nutriment, naturally took care of Custer's horses and dogs, in addition to pulling his share of headquarters guard dry. The colonel took turns riding Vic and Dandy, as both of the fine horses were in excellent condition. The only two hounds Custer had allowed to come this far were Bleuch and Tuck, his favorites, and they seemed to sense the excitement of the chase.

A few of the other officers also wore buckskin jackets, but if it got warm, these would come off in a hurry. Captain Tom Weir had enough whiskey in his saddlebags to last more than the two weeks they might be on scout—if he rationed himself. Others, who had a daily need for spirits, had also stocked up from the sutler's barrels before leaving, and that included several other officers and sergeants.

As it moved smartly up the west bank of the Rosebud, the regiment totaled thirty-one officers and 566 enlisted men. There were twenty-five Ree scouts—Arikaras, four Sioux scouts from the non-related Dakotas, and the six Crows from the Montana column. Hired on as quartermaster employees were five scouts, two interpreters, and six mule packers. Autie Reed, Custer's nephew, and the reporter from the Bismarck *Tribune*, Mark Kellogg, brought the total strength of the column to 647—actually 646 initially because Bloody Knife had gotten drunk early in the morning and didn't catch up with the regiment until it bivouacked that evening. Since he was Custer's pet, he got away with it.

The regiment's sabers had been left back on the Yellowstone. When chasing Indians who had to be caught to get a fight out of them, the weapon was obviously useless, and Custer had decided that was one way to lighten the troopers' heavy load.

Twelve companies of cavalry were jangling their dusty way toward what they hoped would be new glory and fame.

Custer's mind was busy and his spirits sky-high as his strong regiment moved along, twelve miles the first day, thirty-three the second, although he was again convinced that the hostiles would somehow escape him. On the twenty-fourth, he planned to make nearly another thirty miles. Now Lakota and Cheyenne sign was everywhere. Recent trails and old campfires were becoming commonplace. Soon after the column moved out early on the twenty-fourth, Mitch Boyer and Bloody Knife, along with three Ree scouts, ran into a large campsite, one that could have held as many as four hundred lodges. The cropped grass extending far from the edges of the campground indicated that a large herd of ponies had grazed there for an extended period. Most important, a Sun Dance lodge still stood and from its pole hung a white man's scalp! Other sign around the site spooked the Rees. Mitch Boyer tried to tell them the place had been just another camp, but they couldn't wait to get away from it.

However, no one had any idea of the powerful medicine that had been developed on that sacred ground. No one would guess that the greatest Sun Dance in the history of the Lakota had taken place there just a short time before, or that the most inspired leader they had ever known had envisioned blue-clad soldiers falling upside down among his people.

But somehow, the Rees felt something. They hurried back to Custer with the news. Later when Custer and the column stopped for an extended break at the site, a scout who had been with Gibbons identified the light-haired scalp as belonging to a Private Stoker, one of three men killed outside of the Montana column's camp in late May.

Custer knew he was getting warm.

At shortly after two P.M. the scouts encountered a wide trail heading to the right, west-northwest across the Rosebud. It was a profusion of tracks, many crossing others, some fresher than others. It was about a mile wide in places, with old sign, and some horse manure that was only two days old. When Custer reached it, he gathered his scouts and asked them what they thought. Boyer summarized their opinions, "Well, General, seems we agree that a big village broke up and moved off thataway to the north. That's most of the older tracks. Them new ones are probably from summer roamers acomin' from the reservations. There just may be a whole hell of a lot of hostiles out there, and we don't think they're too far away!"

Custer nodded his head. "Good. We'll follow this big trail." He turned to Charley Varnum. "In the meantime, I want the scouts in their saddles as long as they can stay there. Have them swap out their ponies with fresher army mounts if necessary, but I want to know where that village is!"

Custer could feel the excitement. He wasn't just getting warmer anymore. This was going to be a big one, bigger than any victory he had imagined. There might be as many as a *thousand* warriors out there! It wouldn't be a victory like the Washita that his jealous detractors would criticize. It would be one heard round the world! Now if they would only fight. . . .

At 7:45 P.M., having covered over twenty-seven miles, Custer called a halt to the day's march. The troops quickly took care of their horses, ate, and got ready for a good night's rest.

Custer waited impatiently as the sun began to settle and retire to the west.

32

The river was called the Little Bighorn by the whites to distinguish it from the other stream known as the Bighorn. Both were named for the nearby Bighorn Mountains from which their waters emanated. Now in late June, these waters were still cold, filling the river beds with swift flowing spring runoff from the hills. The valley of the meandering Little Bighorn was plush and green, bordered by grassy hills and populated by stalwart thickets of shady cottonwood trees as the stream flowed generally from the southeast to the northwest. On its east side, several abrupt bluffs, broken by rough arroyos, rose sharply to as high as three hundred feet.

The Indians called the stream the Greasy Grass.

On this night of June 24, nearly one thousand lodges of Sioux, Cheyennes, and a few other assorted tribes who had decided to cast their lot with the fame of Sitting Bull, filled the valley. The summer roamers had ridden in almost constantly since the great Hunkpapa had moved his already large village to the Greasy Grass the day after the battle with Three Stars. Word of his visions, and the story of the remarkable fight with the Long Knives on the Rosebud a week earlier, had spread like wildfire, and it seemed that every lodge of reservation Sioux and their allies that could move had headed for the huge encampment.

It was without a doubt the largest collection of Indians to gather in one location, in one encampment, since the Grand Teton council in 1857. No one knew for sure, but it was estimated by Gall, when he spoke with Sitting Bull earlier on this warm early summer night, that probably seven thousand of their people were assembled in the valley.

And the newcomers had joined quite a celebration. From the moment the tipi poles were in place after the arrival of Sitting Bull's people on the Greasy Grass, the commemoration was on. Everyone danced and stuffed himself with good food night and day, and many of the reveling warriors from the Rosebud battle had been at it for six days. Only the hunters and the cooks who prepared the game had to interrupt their fun to keep the festivities going. Now the huge village was recovering like a mammoth bear that had gorged himself, danced for a week, and was trying to shake off the effects of a drinking bout.

The huge encampment was anchored by the Hunkpapa circle, or village, on the upper, or southeast end. As was the custom to retain tribal integrity, the other five circles stretched up the valley—the Miniconjous, Oglalas, Sans Arcs, Blackfeet Lakota, Brules, and Two Kettles. One hundred twenty Cheyenne lodges constituted the rest of the main body. A small number of Santee Sioux, Yanktonnais, and a few Arapahoe lodges completed the enormous body of tipis.

The village stretched along the rapidly flowing Greasy Grass for three miles from the first Hunkpapa lodge pole. The pony herd on a mesa above the western side of the valley was also mammoth—over twenty thousand head. In fact, the grazing needs of this huge number of horses, combined with human needs for food and firewood, had dictated that Sitting Bull move on from this pastoral setting. Only the report of nearby game had kept them there this long. And still the newcomers were arriving.

Gall had not fought in the battle against Three Stars. He had been overcome by a blinding headache the morning before and had been forced to stay in his tipi, his head wrapped in a poultice of mashed antelope bone and the grease of an old black bear. The medicine had worked; his headache was gone by the time the village had relocated on the Greasy Grass. He had participated in the long celebration because most of the warriors from the Midnight Strong Heart Society and the Kit Foxes had played major roles in the battle, and because of his status as one of the most important war leaders of the Lakota. But he was disappointed that he had missed the great fight.

Now as he sat in front of his tipi in the Hunkpapa circle in the fading gray light of evening, he was replacing a thong on his battle axe. The leather had grown worn over the last year, and since it was his favorite weapon, he wanted it to be in top condition. He had already cleaned his Henry rifle and lubricated it with a light oil that had been boiled out of some goose meat. Much to his dismay, most of the warriors never cleaned their firearms. But when Frank Grouard had been with the tribe, the half-breed had told him about the value of such care.

"Are you getting ready for another raid?" his wife, Night Shawl, asked.

"No," he replied. "But Sitting Bull's prophecy of soldiers falling on the village hasn't been fulfilled yet. So Three Stars may still be coming after us."

"But I thought you said he took his Long Knives back to Goose Creek."

"He did, but the prophecy won't lie."

Night Shawl was in her thirty-first summer. She was tall, like her husband, and more buxom than most Lakota women. The rest of her body was sturdy as well. Gall's other wife, Beads Fast, had died of a strange malady of the lungs early in the Moon of the Birth of Calves. But Night Shawl easily managed the care of their three daughters and Little Hawk, their son. Gall was still sad about losing Beads Fast, because she had been his first love. But the merry Night Shawl was one of the most beautiful women in the tribe, and she not only entertained him with her wit, but she kept his blanket interesting at night.

In the past year, his son had grown a great deal. He smiled as the boy ran past with two of his *kolas*. His little friends weren't really *kolas* yet, but Little Hawk liked to call them that. His daughters were all away from the tipi with their own friends. Blue Sky was nine years old, Catch-a-Robe was eight, and Hurry Water was five. He felt a tug of pleasure when he thought of them as he finished lacquering the leather thong where it wrapped around the wooden handle. What beauties they were! They'd bring him many fine ponies when it came time for their marriages, and the best of the young Lakotas as sons-in-law. He would be rich all his life.

He swung the battle axe, liking its familiar feel. Several enemy heads had felt this particular axe's crushing blow. He hoped there would be many more. He was perhaps the most noted of the Lakotas in its use.

Night Shawl moved her thigh against his shoulder, saying softly, "I finished with the menses."

He looked up, felt a stirring, and smiled. "Good. No raids are planned."

Their exchange was complete. A warrior didn't have intercourse for four days before a raid; it diminished his strength to fight.

She rubbed against him again and smiled back.

They would make love that night.

Late Star finished quilling a new moccasin as the light faded too much to see well enough for her precision work. She sighed, glad that the long celebration was over. She was extremely proud of her famous young husband and of his most recent accomplishment against Three Stars, but life had been hectic since even before their marriage. First the sun dance, then the wedding, then the big battle, the long celebration after the move to the Greasy Grass, and all of these summer roamers continuing to flood into the huge village. She knew many of the newcomers, because her father, Running Antelope, had taken his people back to the reservation off and on. She smiled, remembering the remarkable occasion when she had eaten in Long Hair's enormous tipi. He had seemed such a strong man, for some reason reminding her a bit of Crazy Horse. And the long yellow hair that curled without braiding it, it had been so different. It had been a great experience for a Lakota girl. She wondered if she'd ever see Long Hair again.

At that moment she felt a pair of arms come round her, and her husband's body fit itself into her back. She laughed as he said, "And now I will take my beauty in my tipi."

"And what makes you think your beauty wishes to be taken in your tipi?"

Red Elk squeezed her, then turned her around. "Because she dreams night and day of him taking her."

She pulled back. "Ha!"

"She dreams of his hard body and can't sleep because of it."

"Ha!" she laughed again, her lovely dark eyes dancing. "Last night I dreamed of Long Hair."

He frowned. "That isn't humorous."

She shrugged. "I thought you should know."

"He's an old man."

She laughed again. "Not on the blanket."

He shook his head. "Some day you'll have his scalp. I promise."

For sev'n long years, I've courted Nancy.
Hi oh! the rolling river.
For sev'n long years I've courted Nancy.
Ha! Ha!
—Ninth Cavalry March Song
    arranged by F. C. Mayer

"The Crows have brought us vital intelligence," Custer said, looking around at the faces in the yellow lantern light. The last glimmer of the day was failing to black and the regiment was settled in for a good night's sleep. But it would be a short one. His senior scouts were assembled in front of his tent, squatting before him. Lieutenant Varnum, Lonesome Charlie Reynolds, Bloody Knife, and Mitch Boyer listened attentively. Custer went on, "Boyer has just reported that they found enough sign to prove the large village has not broken up. This places the Sioux over that low mountain divide to the west, on the *lower* Little Bighorn, an easy day's ride from here. If this is the case, I'll get the regiment back in the saddle at midnight and we'll ride the six miles to be near the summit. We'll rest all day, then ride the rest of the way tomorrow night and hit them at dawn on the twenty-sixth."

He looked around, then settled his gaze on his chief of scouts. "Varnum, I want you to take some assorted scouts, both Crows and Rees, go back up into the Wolf Mountains, and get me further information." He looked at Reynolds. "Oh, and you go along with them, Charlie."

Varnum asked, "Anything in particular you're looking for, General?"

"Yes, *any* new intelligence about them, but mainly pinpoint their new location."

Everyone got up; Varnum saluted, and the little briefing broke up. Custer turned to Lieutenant Cooke. "Set up a company commanders' call in fifteen minutes."

☆ ☆ ☆

Captain George Yates rode quietly at the head of his Band Box Troop. Like his men, he was sleepy and would have enjoyed remaining in his blanket for the rest of the night instead of making this post-midnight move. But the general could smell Sioux, and that was all that mattered. He thought of Annie's last letter and could feel it in his breast pocket. It, too, had come with the *Far West* and had brought her merry good wishes. Ah, Annie, he thought, what a remarkable person you are. Had you been born a male, you surely would be one of the best officers in the United States Army. At least in the cavalry. How I ache for your bright laugh, for your beautiful voice in song, for the beauty in your expression as you play your violin.

He shook his head as he rolled his shoulders to shake off the tired feeling.

Everyone liked Libbie, and Libbie was an exceptional woman . . . but there simply was no woman anywhere with the talents of his Annie. If there was ever a contest, his Annie would be voted the very best wife. There just couldn't be a better woman married to a soldier. And she deserved to be better off than a captain's wife. . . .

If everything went right, and they could catch up with the hostiles, there might be new fame for him. He was already a brevet lieutenant colonel, perhaps this campaign would set up a real promotion in the not too distant future. And he was only thirty-three—there was plenty of time for him to make colonel. Maybe even before he was fifty. It happened now and then in the peacetime army. And then perhaps a star . . .

She deserved it, she was born to be a general's wife. . . .

For sev'n long years I've courted Annie, Hi ho!

Thirty yards back down the column, Private Lucien Burnham rode half asleep in his saddle. His horse, Blackstone, was also partially asleep as it followed along in the faint light of the stars. Suddenly the animal stepped into a hole and stumbled. Burnham was nearly thrown from the saddle as the bay's head jerked down. He snapped alert and said, "Okay, fella, just a little hole or something." Patting the animal's neck reassuringly, he looked around. It was just a short night move. Soon as they got near the top of the summit up ahead, they'd pull into a bivouac and get plenty of rest. The captain had told them so.

He thought about Iggy. If they indeed rested on the morrow, he'd have time to get in a talk with his friend. The possibility warmed him and he felt a quick flash of arousal. Maybe someday the Russian would see how wonderful things between them could really be.

It hadn't been easy, giving up his genteel life among educated people. The law was a challenging field, and the world of chamber music, the opera, and people who were well-versed in literary pursuits had been a most enjoyable part of his existence. It all seemed so far away now. He'd had to leave it, that unfortunate exposure with the philosophy professor had been too much scandal for a small university town. And he *could* have gotten a commission in the army, but then he'd have been far too visible for his liking. No, it was much more enjoyable being almost buried as a private . . . that was a good term, or immersed in the enlisted broadcloth of the regiment. Surrounded by men, mostly young men. As long as he was discreet, serving in a frontier cavalry regiment had many possibilities.

But then Iggy had come into his life—bright, educated, literate Iggy. And what a soldier, what a man! A beautiful black-haired man who could be a *colonel!* That was an interesting thought: Iggy could be a colonel back in Washington, and he could be his *aide*, his man for all things—legal counsel, writer, researcher. *Captain* Lucien Burnham. All things . . .

Further forward, riding at the head of E Company, First Lieutenant Algernon "Fresh" Smith was drowsily leading his company along behind Tom Weir's D Company. Just ahead of him, bringing up the rear of Weir's command, the bulky body of First Sergeant Martin bobbed in the dim light.

He'd heard quite a few rumors about that Irish non-com and guessed they were probably true. Many of the current crop of first sergeants had a bit of a mean streak in them, but that was probably why they could do the job. The regular army had a lot of misfits in it, and they needed to be controlled by men who understood what was needed.

He didn't condone any mistreatment in his own company, and kept an eye on his own first sergeant, Fred Hohmeyer. The German and his wife, Mary, seemed pretty straitlaced, so he didn't think he had too much to worry about there. He didn't care much for the German laundress, but she helped his wife, Nettie, now and then.

He wondered all at once if some glory might strike him in this upcoming fracas. His old brevet for major was a nice thing to have, and he was often addressed by that rank, but it would be good to get a real promotion and the added pay.

It was getting a bit chilly, he thought, pulling up his jacket collar. These June nights could do that in this country. He'd be glad to get the campaign over and be back in his warm bed at Fort Lincoln. Ah, Nettie, my dear, I wonder what you and the other ladies are doing to pass the time. You and the rest of Libbie's clique always seem to dream up something interesting. . . .

First Lieutenant Charles De Rudio trotted his horse up to the head of A Company's column and greeted Myles Moylan, his burly captain. "Decided I needed to wake up, Myles, so I came up to chat." The accent of his youth in Italy still marked his speech. Two months short of his forty-fourth birthday, he was not only the oldest lieutenant in the regiment, he was the oldest officer! Perhaps because George Armstrong Custer had risen so quickly, or because he didn't care for the general's flamboyant ways, DeRudio disliked his regimental commander. But he couldn't say anything derogatory to Myles Moylan—the captain owed his rank to Custer.

DeRudio relit his cold pipe. "What do you think about Custer's plan?" he asked.

Myles Moylan shrugged. "I suppose he knows what he's doin'. He usually does." The Irishman wasn't noted for his garrulousness.

DeRudio unconsciously twisted the waxed tip of his mustache. "I know one thing. A trooper needs to get more rest than what these lads are getting."

"I've seen 'em fight with less rest than this. The general ain't overextended us yet."

"How many Redskins you think we're going to run into when we finally find this damned village?"

Moylan shifted his weight in the saddle. "I don't know. I heard Charley Reynolds say there might be thousands of them down there on the other side of those hills."

"That many?"

Moylan shrugged again. "What's the difference? We're gonna fight 'em anyway."

Captain Myles Keogh was restless as he led I Company along behind Tom Custer's C Company. He had C's first sergeant, Ed Bobo, in sight a few yards ahead. He thought of the old saying about first sergeants dying from all that dust they swallowed from bringing up the rear. But no one ever said anything about all of the rest of the men in a long column. Dust didn't pick and choose who it got to. What about the *next* to last man in a column? Or the trooper in front of *him?* There had to be some kind of Irish saying or song about the men in life who were second worse off. But tonight's march wasn't very dusty at this point—the trail was rocky enough to keep it to a minimum. That was often the value of riding through mountains.

Although Custer had ordered all command for the march be directly with the company commanders, he'd stated that he would revert to battalion control when it came time to fight. And he was a battalion commander. The line of march tonight had his companies in that configuration. Tom, with C, was in front of him; Jimmi Calhoun, with L, was behind him. To break the monotony, Keogh decided to pull out and watch the rest of his company ride by. "Take over the lead," he said to First Lieutenant Jim Porter, his second in command.

Porter touched his hat brim in salute. "Yessir."

He found a small flat area and dismounted. A pinch of tobacco was in order. He pulled out his pouch, took a medium-sized amount, and stuck it in his mouth. Tasted good—biting, fresh. In no time, he had a good chaw going. And by then the tail end of his company approached. His first sergeant, Frank Varden, saluted as he rode by. They didn't have anything to talk about. But First Lieutenant Jimmi Calhoun did. As L Company approached, Jimmi swung over beside Keogh's horse and dismounted.

"Brrrr," he said, rubbing his hands together. "I get cold sitting immobile in the saddle for so long. You got anything to drink on you, Myles?"

"In my saddlebag," Keogh replied. He went to his horse and pulled out a bottle, removed the cork, and handed it to Custer's brother-in-law.

Calhoun took a good swig and handed it back. "Thanks, old man."

Keogh removed his wad of tobacco and tipped the bottle back. Wiping his mouth, he said, "Not bad-tasting stuff. How're your troopers holding up, Jimmi?"

"All right. Got a couple of horses a little lame."

The Irishman nodded. "We all do."

"Think the general's right about finding the Sioux tomorrow?"

"Yes. Sign is everywhere, and I think we've got pretty good scouts."

"Yeah, and I hear old Bloody Knife's got a personal score to settle, so he'll find them for damned sure."

Keogh put the tobacco back in his mouth. "I 'spose there'll be enough bloody fighting to suit all of us."

Farrier Vincent Charley chewed on the cold two cent stogie he'd had in his mouth ever since the column had pulled out. He was riding in the rear, close to First Sergeant Martin. Martin had been pretty good to him since that mess hall fracas with that stupid Russian Jew. At least he hadn't bothered him. It paid to know on which side one's bread was buttered. *Ja*, that was for damned sure. But he'd almost done the wrong thing and bucked the system. Huh, and a Swiss ought to know better.

Ah, the thought of his homeland was warming.

Riding up this Montana Territory hill was a far cry from his boyhood home near Lucerne, for Gott-damned sure. Sometimes he wished he was back there. But life wasn't too bad here. Here he was twenty-eight years old and he was a good farrier in a good regiment. At least the general told them it was a good regiment. He didn't know about that for sure. He knew one thing—many of the troopers didn't shoot too good. Wasn't their fault; they hadn't done too much practice. Him and Finley could hit most anything, but they'd been shooting all their life. Farmers did that.

Gott-damn that thing with Martin and the Russian!

That damned Jew! Why had he done it? Why couldn't he have just let it go? First sergeants could be mean. Any soldier who'd been around a few paydays knew that.

Still . . .

He'd lied.

Vincent Charley lied; he sold one of his few possessions, his integrity, for safety. The Jew had enough guts to buck that damned Martin, but he hadn't been able to do it.

And he lied on a Bible—him, supposedly a good Catholic.

Well, maybe I can do something in this coming fight with the damned Injuns to make up for it. . . .

Major Marcus Reno had dozed for about a mile. Riding with Captain Tom French's M Company, he had his acting adjutant on his right side as the regiment moved along in a column of twos. That is, Ben Hodgson would be his acting adjutant whenever Custer made any kind of a split in the command. And that would probably happen when they surrounded the village. Being the executive officer automatically gave him the other command.

He pulled out his flask and had a little nip. Making a little shudder, he thought it was too bad there wasn't some hot, bracing coffee with which to chase it. He stood up in his stirrups to give his arse a break. Looking over at Hodgson, he said, "You awake, Ben?"

The acting adjutant replied drowsily, "Yes, sir."

Hodgson was Reno's right arm. In fact, he and the lonely Reno had become friends in the time the regiment had been in the field. It was a rather rare combination because of the rank and age difference, but Hodgson highly respected Marcus Reno for his wartime record, and Reno was just simply happy for the companionship.

All three doctors were riding together up in the headquarters contingent. They'd been running a joint dispensary for the regiment, so they stayed together in the column. First Lieutenant George Lord, being a medical officer on active duty, was the senior. After graduating from Chicago Medical School in 1871, Doctor Lord had served several contracts with the army. A serious man who wore eyeglasses and wasn't much of an athlete, the Massachusetts native had been born illegitimately and raised by a Bowdoin College professor. He was now thirty years old. He had been attached to the regiment from the Sixth Infantry shortly before the Seventh's departure up the Rosebud. He was performing the duty of regimental surgeon, but was carried on the rolls as assistant surgeon.

Doctor James DeWolf, who had also signed on recently, was a graduate of Harvard Medical School, but had failed the examination for assistant surgeon in the army in 1875. Later that year, he entered service on a contract as an acting assistant surgeon. He had served nearly eight years as an enlisted hospital steward before becoming a physician. He was thirty-three years old.

Doctor Henry Rinaldo Porter, the twenty-eight-year-old resident physician of Geraldine Gentle's sporting house in Bismarck, had entered into a three-month army contract just three days before the regiment pulled out of Fort Lincoln in May. Now as he rode, half asleep, George Lord brought him out of his drowsy reverie. "You've been in a few fights with the Apaches, Henry. What's it like when you aren't shooting a rifle?"

Porter shifted his weight to get more comfortable in the saddle. "What do you mean?"

"Well, you know, all hell's breaking loose around you, and you aren't actually fighting."

At that moment, Jim DeWolf edged his horse in on the other side of Henry. "Yeah, I want to know too, Henry. I've was in plenty of battles during the war as an artillery man, but never as a doctor."

George Lord added, "I heard General Crook himself commended you for heroism against the Apaches."

Henry Porter tugged at his big red mustache and sighed. "All I can remember is bright sunshine and rifle fire, and those hostiles on painted ponies. And all I can tell you is, you do what comes naturally. If soldiers are getting hurt, you treat them as well as you can with what you've got."

Lord asked, "You ever shoot an Apache?"

"No, I was too busy."

Lord was persistent. "Would you shoot some of these Sioux if you had a chance?"

Henry pursed his lips as he mulled the question over. "If it were a matter of saving my life, I suppose so."

They rode along in silence for a couple of minutes before Lord said, "By God, if I thought it meant my life, I'd grab a rifle and start shooting it in a split-second."

Sergeant Jeremiah Finley had a headache. He was troubled with them now when he didn't get enough sleep, and he hadn't adjusted to sleeping on the ground in his bedroll on this campaign. He spoke to his horse, "Just a little longer, old boy, and both of us can get a little rest."

He wondered if Custer really knew where the damned Sioux were this time. Those hostiles were so unreliable. One thing Finley was sure about—when this campaign was all over and they started taking the general's picture, it would be his needlework they'd be showing for posterity. He'd get some of the pictures and send them back to his mother in Tipperary, bless her saintly old Celtic soul. Let's see, she was—he was thirty-five and she'd been thirty-two when he was born, so she'd be sixty-seven now. He hadn't seen her in over eighteen years—not since he'd killed that Protestant in Belfast. He'd stowed away on a freighter to Canada and had enlisted in the Seventeenth Royal Canadian Regiment the moment he stepped foot in their country. As with the American army, a name didn't mean anything to them.

He'd deserted to join up in the War Between the States in '61 and had served four years, some of the time as a sharpshooter. He chuckled as he remembered that old Civil War sharpshooter joke he liked to tell. . . .

"Seems a Johnny Reb picket and a Billy Yank picket were passing the time of night when the Union soldier asked, 'I say, can you boys shoot very good?

'Wall, I reckon we can,' the Reb replied. 'Down in Carolina we can knock a bumblebee off 'n a thistle-blow at three hundred yards.'

The Yankee laughed. 'That ain't nothin' to the way we shoot up in old Vermont. Why, I belonged to a military company up there, with a hundred men in it, and we went out and practiced every week. The cap'n he'd draw us up in single file and set a cider barrel arollin' down a hill. Each man took a shot at the bunghole as it turned up. Afterwards, the barrel was examined, and if any shot missed the bunghole, that man was kicked out of the company. I belonged to the company ten years, and there hain't been nary a shooter kicked out yet!'"

Finley chuckled again. He loved the joke.

His wife got tired of it, but he didn't care—his Canadian Ellen. She was saving their money, all right. Between his pay, what he earned as a bartender at the hog ranch and with his sewing, and her earnings as a laundress, she was putting a few dollars a month into a house fund. She had a house all picked out in Bismarck, and wanted him to get out of the army and open a tailor shop.

"How're you doing, Sergeant Finley?"

He was jolted to hear Captain Tom Custer's voice as the officer rode up beside him. "Just fine, sir, I was doin' a little reminiscin'."

"That's a good way to pass the time when we're moving."

They rode quietly for a couple of minutes, the silence of the Montana night broken only by the creaking of leather, the horses' breathing, and the noise of their hooves dully clip-clopping on the hard ground. Finally Finley asked, "Think we'll find them Injuns today, Cap'n?"

"Most likely."

"Think there'll be some fightin'?"

"I hope so. We haven't been in a good scrap in quite a spell."

"Yeah, I'd like to get a few of them in my sights."

Tom Custer nodded, urging his horse forward. "See you at the new bivouac, Sergeant."

Finley touched his hat brim. He liked being with the Custers; they were both bodacious fighters.

34

CROW'S NEST, 4:50 A.M., JUNE 25, INST.

To Gen'l Custer
Sir:
Soon after the sun arose, the scouts saw the smoke of the Lakota village. It is in the Little Big Horn valley. They said it was huge, and tried to show me a huge pony herd, but I couldn't see it. They told me to look for something like worms, but I still couldn't see it. You know how these Indians can see what we can't. They said there were thousands of Indian ponies. We also saw two Sioux spies nearby, and they probably saw the smoke from your campfires, which we can see clearly from here.
C. A. Varnum
Chief of Scouts

Custer frowned as he reread Varnum's message. The Crow's Nest was an excellent observation point on top of the Wolf Mountains divide. The surrounding country for miles around was visible from there, including the valley of the Little Big Horn, some twenty miles away. Spotting the village was good news; the fact that his presence might have been detected was bad news. He handed the note to his brother Tom, who was standing off to the side with Cooke, Bloody Knife, and the interpreter Fred Girard. Turning to Red Star, the scout who had ridden the eight miles to deliver Varnum's note, Custer knelt on one knee and signed, "Did you see the Lakotas?"

"Yes," Red Star signed back. "I saw the smoke and horses. And Charlie Reynolds look through glass and see them."

"Are there many?"

"The village is big."

Bloody Knife spoke to the scout in Ree, then turned to Custer and told him, "We will find enough Sioux to keep us fighting for two or three days."

Custer laughed. "We'll get through them in one day, my friend!"

Turning to Cooke, he said, "I'm going up to the Crow's Nest to see for myself. Have the regiment ready to ride as soon as I get back or you hear from me."

A few minutes later, Old Nutriment had his horse Dandy saddled and waiting. Custer sprang into the saddle, signaled to Bloody Knife and the scouts, and cantered out of camp.

It was twelve minutes after nine when Custer and his party climbed the short distance from where they hid their horses to the Crow's Nest. Varnum and the other scouts were waiting. The lieutenant quickly took him to the point from which they had been observing the valley of the Little Bighorn. "Since it's past the morning cooking period, smoke from the village fires has diminished," Lonesome Charley Reynolds said quietly. "Also, probably due to the difference in the suns rays, the general visibility has declined." He handed Custer his field glasses and pointed toward the valley. "There's movement of some kind, General. Look for a dark mass clouded by some dust."

Custer used his own glasses and strained to see what Reynolds was describing. At first he didn't see anything, then finally he nodded his head. "I see something like a cloud of dust."

Varnum spoke up. "The Indian scouts swear they've seen both a large village and a huge pony herd in that valley. And you know how well they can see."

Bloody Knife had been talking to the Crow scouts as Girard listened. Now they turned to Custer. "Four Lakota scouts have seen your camp smoke," the interpreter said.

"From where?"

"They were spotted nearby, but they got away."

Custer shook his head, holding back his displeasure. Hostiles *here?* Discovered. No, couldn't be. He shook his head. "No, I looked back at the bivouac several times on the way up here, and I don't think they saw anything."

"They insist the Sioux saw you," Girard said.

"Well, I don't believe so. I'm going to stick to my plan of waiting until dark to move the regiment into position. Then we'll attack at first light tomorrow."

Girard translated to the scouts, who reacted heatedly to his decision. The interpreter said, "General, they don't think you should go through with it. That village could be huge."

Custer ignored the comment. "Let's get on back to the regiment."

He mounted Dandy and led the observation party back down the slope at a canter.

It was a short ride. The head of the column was waiting just a mile away. And as the party trotted up to the headquarters detachment, Lieutenant Cooke reported that two Sioux had been seen within 150 yards of the column, and that they had fled before anyone could catch them.

Custer frowned as he climbed down from his horse. "You're sure they saw us?"

Cooke nodded his head. "The scout was positive. Is the village on the Little Bighorn, as Varnum reported?"

Custer nodded. "They're down there all right."

At that moment, Tom Custer hurried up. "Autie!" he said excitedly, "We been spotted for sure. F Company just had a run-in with some hostiles! Some of their packers had lost a load of hardtack, and when we stopped, George Yates sent a squad back to find it. They ran smack dab into a handful of Sioux breaking into the boxes. After exchanging shots, the Injuns scattered and got away!"

"Darn!" Custer snapped. "It's for sure they know we're here now! Won't be any time until some of them get to that village and tell Sitting Bull we're sitting here." He paced, hands behind his back, struggling with the decision. His troopers and animals weren't very well rested, but a fifteen mile ride wouldn't hurt them too much. . . . As soon as the word of his presence reached the hostiles, they'd start moving. And Gibbon wouldn't have his command in a blocking position until the next day. By then the enemy would be gone! No, if he were going to have any chance of hitting them, it had to be today! "Cooke!" he barked, "I want an officers' call right away!"

Custer looked around at the intent faces. The officers sitting around on the ground in front of him showed their desire to fight. He'd told them about the information from the Crow's Nest, and how the regiment's presence had been detected. He had explained that there was no choice but to attack the hostile village in broad daylight after an immediate approach through open country.

There wasn't a single demure reply.

"All right," Custer said, "you company commanders assign one NCO and six privates to the company pack mules to make sure your troopers are properly supplied with ammunition. I'll assign the order of march based on when the companies are ready."

"My company is always ready," Captain Benteen announced.

"All right, you take the advance," Custer replied.

It was 11:45 P.M.

At 12:07 A.M., Custer halted the column just a short way over the crest of the divide. He had, at this point, thirty-one officers, 566 enlisted men, and fifty others. Dismounting, he told Sergeant-Major Sparrow to get the B Company and pack train commanders in for an immediate briefing. Benteen and Reno were within earshot and walked over to where Custer spoke to Old Nutriment. "All right, John," he said, "I want you to saddle Vic for me. Dandy here's had a busy morning."

Burkman nodded his head. "Right, General. I'll have him here in a couple a minutes." As the orderly scurried away, Custer turned to Benteen. "Captain, I'm afraid there may be some outlying villages to the southwest of the valley. I want you to form a battalion out of your H Company, along with D and K, and go off on a scout along those bluffs you see to the west. See what you can find out, then hurry back to the main column."

Benteen nodded and touched his hatbrim in a salute, then hurried away.

Custer turned to Reno. "General Reno, form your battalion with A, G, and M Companies. I'm keeping C, E, F, I, and L with me. I'm giving you Varnum and the scouts as well. I want those Rees to go straight for the pony herd when we get there. When we get closer in, I'll figure out how we're going to deploy."

Reno nodded, "Yes, sir."

At that moment, Captain McDougall hurried up with First Lieutenant Edward Mathey, the pack train commander. Mathey was a thirty-eight-year-old Frenchman from Indiana who had not only risen to the rank of major during the war, but had temporarily commanded his infantry regiment during two important battles near the end of the struggle. He'd been in Captain French's M Company before the campaign. McDougall's B Company was the pack train's escort. Custer pointed toward the valley and addressed both, "That's where they are, gentlemen. We'll be moving briskly, so don't let the support column fall very far behind."

Both officers saluted and Custer mounted up as Burkman handed him Vic's reins.

One of the most memorable events in American history was about to unfold.

35

*Far better it is to dare mighty things . . . than to take rank
with those poor spirits who neither enjoy much nor suffer
much, because they live in the gray twilight that knows not
victory nor defeat.*
—Teddy Roosevelt

Unbelievably, none of the Sioux hunters who had encountered the cavalry, including those who had been chased off from the lost hardtack, had reported back to the village. Therefore, the largest independent cavalry force ever to seek out hostile Indians in America was now moving at the trot down the long slope from the divide of the Wolf Mountains, *undetected,* toward the largest gathering of such people in history.

Now and then Custer slowed the pace so as to not get too far ahead of Benteen, but the column was still eating up the miles at a steady rate. It was difficult for him to be patient. As he rode along, a sense of urgency grew in him. What might be his greatest victory could lie ahead. If the village was as big as the trail indicated, and his scout's warnings carried any credence, it could indeed hold a very big number of hostiles. Well, the more the merrier. He could *feel* the tingle of excitement. *C'mon, Benteen!* If this fight were to come off his way, he'd be feted like a triumphant Caesar returning to Rome. He thought of the great words *veni, vidi, vici—I came, I saw, I conquered,* and it seemed a certainty that they were meant for George Armstrong Custer.

Yes, the multitudes would strew garlands of roses in his path as he rode down Pennsylvania Avenue. . . .

In the huge Indian village, life in its tribal circles languidly trickled through this hot twenty-fifth day of June. Women performed their everyday tasks, some picking berries with their daughters, while many of the children played or splashed in the cool water of the Greasy Grass. Dogs barked occasionally and now and then the cry of a circling hawk could be heard over the mammoth pony herd on the bench to the west of the camp. It was there that a few of the men worked with their animals. But most of the men drowsed in their tipis, still recovering from the long celebration of the Three Stars victory. The village wasn't totally asleep, however, because there were some who remembered Sitting Bull's dream of soldiers falling upside down on them. These warriors had their horses tethered at their lodges. The men of the *akicitas* who were on duty also had their ponies at hand for any police work that might be required. Overall, though, the massive Lakota and Cheyenne city was wafting its way through a lethargic Juneberry afternoon.

Sitting Bull was one of those taking a nap, since he hadn't totally recovered from the ordeal of his Sun Dance ritual. His wife, Four Robes, was quietly tending to their infant twins in the sunshine outside of their large tipi.

Red Elk had taken only a short midday nap. He was one of those who had his war pony tethered at his white tipi. He was busy braiding the animal's tail, wanting to be ready for what he was sure would be a fulfill-ment of his great chief's vision, possibly in the next few days. He had traded for more shells for the big Sharps rifle with a reservation Mini-conjou who had just arrived in a small group two days earlier. He now had enough rounds for nearly any kind of a battle.

A large hunting party had gone off to the northeast looking for a reported herd of antelope that morning. He had almost gone with them, but something had told him his place was here at the village. He had dreamed about Sitting Bull's vision the night before, and that may have been it.

Late Star was up on the bluffs with a handful of other young wives, looking for Juneberries. She walked to the edge, sighed, and sat down for a moment to look down at the village. Some of the tipis were mixed in amongst the green-leafed cottonwoods that stood tall beside the mean-dering river, but most of them were out in the open valley, filling it. The grass was still green, giving the Greasy Grass lowland a most pleasant look. She wished they could stay longer, but there were too many mouths to feed and they would be moving on in another day or two. She smiled to herself. Life could be so pleasant for the Lakotas in a summer rich with food and fair weather. The good fortune of the victory over Three Stars had already made this a summer few would forget. And she, personally, would always treasure it because it was the summer of her marriage to Red Elk. She smiled. Yes, it was a fine time. She looked down to the river again and spotted her tipi. It was easy to detect because of its light color. And she could see her proud husband with his war pony. Yes, a rich, good summer.

It was so good to be Lakota.

Near the head of the Hunkpapa circle down in the camp, Night Shawl worked on her quilling in front of her tipi. Her husband, Gall, was snoring inside, and she thought she might playfully go in and shout that the Long Knives were coming. But he might react too vigorously, so she decided not to do it. Besides, there was a lot of snoring going on in the various tipis. It seemed that only the women and children of the Hunkpapas were awake this fine afternoon.

She wiped some light sweat from the back of her neck and her brow. It was a little too warm in the sun. She was doing an antelope design in blue beads on a fine piece of exceptionally soft hide that would eventually become a jacket. A woman had to work hard these days to beat these talented young quillers like Late Star. "All right, girls, let me see what you've done."

Her three daughters held out their basic quilling projects. Her middle daughter, Catch-a-Robe, was the best quiller, but Hurry Water, even at five, showed signs of becoming quite good.

She looked at the handiwork of each, nodding in approval at each. "Very good!" she exclaimed. "All of you will be better than I."

Blue Sky, the eldest, giggled and said, "Father sounds like a sick horse." The other girls also giggled.

Night Shawl smiled. "I know. Maybe we ought to tickle his feet."

Hurry Water grinned. "I want to do it!"

"All right," Night Shawl replied, "But you have to be careful. He might swing his battle-ax at you."

The girls all giggled again as they quietly entered the tipi.

Night Shawl sighed. Life was so good. Being a Lakota was the Great Mystery's finest gift. And being Gall's wife was not only a pleasure, but an honor.

36

Pity the warrior who is content to crawl about in the beggardom of rules.
—KARL VON CLAUSEWITZ

The Little Bighorn River varied in size and depth; in places it was as wide as eighty feet, in others it narrowed to some forty feet. It ranged in depth from six inches at a couple of the fords to around ten feet in other spots, contingent upon the amount of mountain runoff that fed it. The speed of its current and its width were also dependent on the runoff. Its color could vary with its speed, going from a deep green to a more muddy chocolate brown following a heavy rain. It wasn't navigable except by small craft in certain parts, including canoes, and the Greasy Grass wasn't part of canoe culture. The tribes who now and then stopped there were strictly nomadic and their stay was always short. In the area where the village was located, the river ran generally north–south, with a couple of sharp hooks and meandering bends, over five hundred yards long to the south of the Hunkpapa circle. Approximately three miles south of the village the river was joined by a smaller, nearly dry stream, later known as Reno Creek, that ran in from the east. The high ridge on the east side of the valley blocked any view of the village from an eastern approach.

And the Seventh Cavalry was moving rapidly in from the east at a fast pace.

Twice, Custer had sent messengers to Benteen to extend his scout. Now he wanted his recalcitrant but able captain and his battalion back with the main body. The pack train had also fallen well behind, which worried Custer. At two o'clock, approaching a point where the two forks of Reno Creek joined, the excited scouts reported a lone tipi ahead. Custer pulled Reno back to his side of the fork as they stopped at the tipi. Inside were the remains of a dead Lakota warrior. The Rees got even more excited about the coming fight. As Reno led his battalion across the little stream, Custer turned to Lonesome Charley Reynolds. "What does this mean?" he asked.

Reynolds shrugged. "A big village camped here for some time. Its inhabitants apparently honored this dead warrior for some heroic deed by leaving him here."

Just then interpreter Fred Girard waved his broad-brimmed hat and shouted down from a nearby bluff, "General, here are your goddamned Indians, running like devils!"

Custer urged Vic up the face of the bluff and joined Girard. Sure enough, he could see pony herds and what looked like tiny Indian figures milling around in the distance. All of the conjecture was over. The hostiles were there! And they were fixing to flee! He look back to his rear. No sign of Benteen or the pack train. But it didn't matter, he had to pitch into those Sioux as soon as he could get there!

"Major Reno!" he barked, *"Move your battalion and the scouts into the lead and step up the pace!"*

Reno nodded and swung around to shout the order. In less than a minute, his column quickly headed downstream.

Up on the bluff above the village, Late Star looked up from where she was talking to her friend Blue Feather and two other women when she heard a tiny rumbling sound to the southeast. Glancing in that direction, she saw a small cloud of dust. In front of it was a flash of bright red and some tiny reflections the sun was casting off metal! She squinted, focusing on the movement. *Horses! And riders in blue! Long Knives are coming!*

She shouted, *"Look!"* and pointed.

The other women screamed and dropped the berries they picked.

Late Star didn't waste a moment. She scrambled down the hillside shouting, *"Long Knives! Long Knives! Many! Many!"*

Several women looked up in alarm and shrieked the news.

Red Elk, recognizing his wife's voice, hurried to meet her as she nearly fell the last few feet down the escarpment. *"Where?"* he shouted.

"There!" she replied haltingly, nearly out of breath, and pointing southeast. "Many! Coming fast!"

He stared for a second where she pointed, then whirled back to her. "Go to the tipi and get my revolver and some shells. Then run over to the Miniconjou camp to your friend. Wait there!"

He spun back toward his tipi. *Had to get his war paint on!* This was it—Three Stars was back, just as Sitting Bull had prophesied! He let out a *whoop* of warning, which was nearly drowned in the rising number of shouts that began to fill the air.

Warriors began spilling out of their tipis as shouting women started rounding up their children. The alarm continued to spread. Dogs barked excitedly, sensing the urgency. Everyone knew what to do. It was what every village, every tribe, every small party practiced . . . women and children scatter to safety, out of direct harm's way—in this case, into the hills to the west.

The men splashed paint on their faces and some on their bare torsos. Those who had their ponies handy, including the *akicitas*, mounted as soon as they were prepared. Others raced up the hill toward the herd. Still others ran toward the edge of the Hunkpapa circle; it was the outer edge in the direction of Three Stars!

Word of the intruders flashed through the huge camp. Over in the Oglala village, between the Cheyennes and the Sans Arcs, Crazy Horse hurriedly applied the lightning blaze to his left cheek and dabbed the white hail spots on his torso. His first coup-feather was in place, standing straight up behind his head. He stuck the small stone under his arm and fastened it, then removed his sack of fighting dust from his war bag. Sprinkling it over his head, he hurried to his tethered war pony and sprinkled more dust over its neck. The animal tossed his head and whinnied. The war chief grabbed his weapons and sprang onto the back of his pony. He had to get his followers ready!

Gall also put his paint on quickly and had his weapons in hand. His favorite battle-ax hung from his belt and his scarlet robe was draped over his arm. He nodded to his wife as she ran to find their son, Little Hawk. "Don't wait too long!" he warned. "The boy will be with his *kolas* if you don't find him." He looked at his wide-eyed daughters and nodded reassuringly. "Don't worry. The Long Knives can't harm us!"

As Gall ran to get his horse from the remuda, Sitting Bull stood outside of his tipi and watched the pandemonium around him. Red Elk hurried up to tell him what Late Star had seen, then rushed back toward the south side of the village. On another day, Sitting Bull reflected, at an earlier time, he too would be hurried, dabbing paint on his face and rushing off to lead his warriors into battle. But now it was different. The women and children were his responsibility more than glory in battle.

His nephew One Bull trotted up with three horses, including the big black stallion that was his uncle's favorite. Hurriedly, they helped the women onto the other two horses. As she mounted, Four Robes didn't even notice that she had only one of her twins.

Throughout the circles of the Sans Arcs, the Black Kettles, the Blackfeet, the Miniconjous, the Oglalas, and the Cheyennes on the far end, the escape plan for the women and children went rapidly into effect down through the three miles of the huge encampment.

The shouts and noise of people rushing about, of dogs barking their concern, and of pounding hooves filled the air as the huge village rushed into its defense plan.

The trotting cavalry column had reached just minutes earlier the point where Reno Creek fed into the Little Bighorn. Custer, now stripped down to his dark-blue shirt and suspenders, was certain the activity ahead of him in the village meant that the Sioux were indeed fleeing. He didn't know how long they had been aware of his presence, but he knew it had been for at least many minutes. Once more he looked up toward the back trail. Still no Benteen or McDougall! He shouted to the adjutant, *"Cooke!* Hurry over to Reno and order him to move forward at as rapid a gait as prudent, and to charge afterward. *Tell him the whole command will support him!"*

"Yessir!" Lieutenant Cooke replied and spurred his big mount forward to relay the orders to Major Reno.

Two minutes later, after hearing Cooke's verbal orders, Reno led his command, splashing across a shallow ford to the west bank of the Little Bighorn. At this moment, Bloody Knife hurried back with two other scouts from the advanced position where he had finally seen the actual village as it prepared to fight. Signing to Girard, he hurriedly relayed the information.

"Lieutenant!" Girard hollered to Cooke, who was about to hurry back to Custer. "The scouts saw the village. It's huge, and those hostiles ain't fleeing anywhere! Fact is, they're gettin' ready to attack us!"

The Canadian took one long look at the village, searched Bloody Knife's face for a moment, then turned his horse to get back to Custer with the news.

Once all of his troopers were across the river, Reno called a halt. The Rees with him were impatient, and after all, Custer had ordered that they go after the pony herd. He looked down the valley toward the village, and raised his field glasses. It was exactly as Bloody Knife had reported, a whole lot of hostiles were getting ready to fight him. He turned to his adjutant Ben Hodgson. "Send two troopers back with a message to General Custer. Tell him the hostiles are definitely not in flight, but are preparing to fight us."

The lieutenant nodded. "Yes, sir!" and spun away on his mount.

Reno went back to what he could see of the village. This wasn't going to be easy. He signaled for the three company commanders to join him. Captain Myles Moylan, Captain Tom French, and Lieutenant Donald McIntosh trotted up quickly. Pointing to the village, the major said, "Looks like we're going to have a pretty stiff job up there." His horse swung around, as if anticipating what was ahead. Reno brought him under control and continued. "I make it two miles to those first tipis. Get ready and we'll go straight at them."

Lieutenant Varnum and his assistant, Second Lieutenant Luther Hare, listened in, as did the remaining regular scouts and the doctors.

Moments later, with some of the Indian scouts heading toward the hostiles' ponies that were grazing by the river, and the rest on his flank, Major Reno raised his pistol and shouted, *"Forward, hoooo!"* The trumpeter at his side echoed his command by blowing *Charge!*

Aside from his civilians and Indians, he had 129 men behind him as his small battalion broke into a gallop and thundered down the valley.

It was 2:57 P.M.

☆ ☆ ☆

Bloody Knife had never known a moment of greater passion. This was what his whole life had been about. Somewhere a short distance ahead of him lay his destiny. Nothing in his life had ever been as important. He would avenge all of the hurt, all of the shame these terrible people and that vicious Gall had visited on his head and his name. His heart was pounding and he felt as if he'd explode! It seemed as if every beat of his horse's hooves said, "Kill Gall, kill Gall, kill Gall. . . ."

As the flying command rapidly closed on the village, Marcus Reno stared straight ahead at the hostile Indians swarming to his front. He had never seen so many warriors massed before! He turned once to see if he could spot Custer and his force anywhere. *Cooke had said the general would support me.* But he was nowhere in sight. Another look at the quickly approaching village told him the charge was madness. Custer didn't have the slightest damned idea of what was there. *To continue is pure suicide! There is simply no sense in leading these brave men to a gallant but futile death!*

He turned to the trumpeter and gave him the signal to blow *Halt*.

As the trumpeter complied, Reno hauled in on his reins and quickly dismounted. As near as he could tell, he was about four hundred yards from the first tipis. He ordered the command to dismount and fight as skirmishers, which the trumpeter sounded. The guidon bearers from the three companies jammed their flag staffs into the ground as troopers hurriedly jumped off their mounts. Immediately every fourth trooper withdrew to hold horses, bringing his fighting strength to ninety-five sober-faced men kneeling to shoot at a growing mob of howling hostiles.

Meanwhile, Custer had decided to turn *right* and up the ridge to proceed downstream, with the bluffs on the east side of the river covering him from the valley. Since he had the largest segment of the regiment, he wanted to keep his troops out of sight as much as possible. He continued trotting along on the east side of the river, hoping Reno's attack wouldn't spook the rest of the camp. Reaching a place that afforded a climb to a high point above, he called a halt and followed Mitch Boyer and a couple of the Ree scouts up the steep incline to a clear position that afforded a good view of the valley below. Boyer turned his head as he pointed downstream. "Looky here, General! Ever see this many damn tipis?"

Custer stared. The floor of the valley was filled with lodges for as far as he could see. "My God," he sighed. *I've never seen so many tipis!*

"I reckon they's over a thousand of them," the scout offered.

"At least."

Custer heard "Skirmishers" being blown below and looked across the river where he saw Reno dismounting with his tiny battalion. Seeing the number of Indians forming to meet the charging Reno, he shook his head. The major had no idea what he was running into. . . .

Custer looked back. *Still no Benteen!*

He wheeled Vic and hurried down the incline to the waiting command. "Get me a reliable NCO to take a message back to the pack train," he barked at Tom. Moments later, his brother returned with Sergeant Dan Kanipe from C Company. As the South Carolinian saluted, Custer said, "Ride back and find Captain McDougall. Tell him to bring the pack train directly across to high ground. If packs get loose, don't stop to fix them. Cut them off. Tell him to come quick. Big Indian camp!"

Kanipe nodded. "Yessir!"

He ran to his horse and sprang into the saddle.

Danny Kanipe didn't want to leave his men, but the general himself had given him his orders. He urged his horse into a fast trot, not willing to gamble a gallop over the unknown terrain. One gopher hole, and his important mission would be brought to an abrupt end.

He slowed the big gray as he guided the animal away from the back trail and closer to the bluffs. He wondered what Custer had seen up there on that hill that made him want that ammunition in those packs so bad. Could only be one thing—a hell of a lot of Injuns! Otherwise, he'd be tearing right into them instead of hollering for more supplies.

Mighty strange.

He saw what looked like a shallow place in the river and decided he'd make better time on the west side. As he eased his horse down the slope, he saw Reno's column firing from a skirmishing line about a half-mile away. He could see a whole bunch of Indians gathering about three or four hundred yards downstream from Reno's men.

He was going to miss a hell of a fight if he didn't find the pack train quickly and get back to his company!

"Do you have *any* idea where Benteen is?" Custer asked irritably.

"No, sir," Cooke replied.

Custer had just come down from the highest point along the line of bluffs on the east side of the valley. The peak that would later be known as Weir Point was about three-quarters of a mile north from where he'd previously viewed the scene. Up there, he'd had even a better look at the huge village extending some three miles to the north and downstream. And he had seen the vigorous activity in it. *Everything was wrong!*

"*Goddamnit!*" Custer seldom used profanity, but he knew splitting his forces was now a mistake. Reno's little battalion was still fighting as skirmishers. The sound of the firing from the edge of the village had become a steady popping like corn in a hot skillet. Never, absolutely never, had he expected this many hostiles. He had to get as much of his regiment back together as possible. "*Goddamnit!*" he snapped. "Benteen's *got* to get here!"

"Do you suppose he got into a fight?" Cooke asked.

"No, the strength is here. He could be delayed by the pack train."

"What do you want me to do?" the adjutant asked.

Custer's gaze centered on Trumpeter John Martin of H Company. "Isn't that the Italian from Benteen's own company?"

"Yes, sir."

"Send him to find Benteen, and tell that captain I said to get here *forthwith!*"

Cooke looked doubtful. "His English isn't very good, General."

"Then write an order! We can't sit here on our arses much longer!"

Cooke pulled out a pencil and quickly scribbled a message that read: "Benteen. Come on. Big Village. Be quick, Bring packs." He signed it W. W. Cooke.

Custer scowled. "And tell him to bring ammunition packs!"

Cooke added: "P.S. Bring packs." He forgot the word *ammunition*. He looked sternly at the twenty-three-year-old native of Sola Consalina, Italy.

"All right, Martini—I want you to ride back down the same trail and find Captain Benteen as fast as you can. And give him this message. Captain *Benteen*. Do you understand?"

"*Sí*, Yes, sir!" the trumpeter replied, taking the message and sticking it in his shirt pocket. He was quickly in the saddle and hurrying back upriver.

Custer unbuttoned his blue shirt another notch and thought about the little breakdowns that were occurring. When this campaign was over, he'd have to sit down and write an account of what came off well, and the little snags. Might be of value to any regimental action in the future. Cavalry officers would read it for decades, maybe centuries. He smiled to himself. It might even be regarded as a classic. . . .

Red Elk was in the vanguard of Hunkpapas, Miniconjous, and Blackfeet who gathered to meet the onrushing Long Knives as they charged down the valley. Being of little use in the close-quarters fight that was coming, his big Sharps was in its special buffalo skin scabbard attached to his saddle. In his right hand he waved the long-barreled cavalry pistol that he had used in his one-man exploit in the Powder River battle with Three Stars.

Now Three Stars was back!

Certainly the Long Knife leader had no inkling of Sitting Bull's great prophecy! His soldiers would have no chance against the mighty Lakota on this day. And the dismounted horse soldiers in front of him looked very few indeed. The smoke from their rifles began to dim the reflections the hot sun cast off the metal parts of their equipment. He looked back, seeing the war paint of some Black Kettles as they joined his brothers. He also spotted some Sans Arcs. Crazy Horse and his Oglalas, along with their allies the Cheyennes, wouldn't be far behind. The thrill of danger excited him as he swung his warhorse Lightning off to the right of the cavalrymen to get on their flank. He, of course, couldn't tell white man's time, but the first long-range shots had been fired at 3:09 P.M., and what would be known as the Battle of the Little Bighorn was quickly swelling to a fury never before seen in the land of the big sky.

☆ ☆ ☆

As the hostile warriors rode and ran on foot close to the skirmish line and around it, the din of heavy firing from the grim-faced troopers and the attackers grew louder. Shouts and Lakota war cries filled the air. The smoke and dust turned the air dark, allowing only an eerie gold from the sun to filter through. Bloody Knife tore off his white man's shirt, smeared some paint on his face, and aimed his rifle at an oncoming Hunkpapa wearing a feathered war bonnet. The shot spun the warrior partially around, dropping him in a couple of steps. Instantly, Bloody Knife sprang forward in a crouching run and ran to the fallen hostile. Ripping the bonnet from his head the scout jammed it on his own. He looked quickly around and saw a mounted Hunkpapa three yards away. Swinging his rifle up, he shot the rider in the face and jerked him from his pony.

In an instant, he was aboard the animal, galloping straight toward the village.

He had questioned the scout Frank Brouard repeatedly about Gall's family and his tipi, and now he knew what the lodge looked like as surely as if he lived in it. He also knew the usual circle layout of the village and guessed that the Hunkpapas would be on the near end.

As he galloped into the turmoil of the first tipis, women and children were still running around, shouting and calling for missing ones. A handful of warriors who had been with the pony herd were busy applying paint and hurriedly getting ready to join the fight. Dogs were still barking wildly and a few small children were crying aloud. No one noticed him as he rode around searching the tipis for telltale paintings depicting Gall's many exploits.

And there it was!

He pulled the pony up as a woman, followed by three small girls, came out the tipi flap. There was no doubt about who she could be. He aimed his revolver and shot Night Shawl between the eyes. Blue Sky screamed and he shot her in the chest, killing her instantly. A moment later, he poured two .45 rounds into the screaming Catch-a-Robe, then swung the pony around to the wide-eyed little Hurry Water. Shoving the pistol into his belt, he grabbed the five-year-old by her long hair and jerked her up into his lap. In moments, his big knife was flashing and blood was streaming out of what was left of the top of her head. Flinging her to the dusty ground like a discarded doll, Bloody Knife drew his pistol and shot her twice.

He looked around for Gall, but knew he'd have trouble finding his hated enemy, so he whirled the pony and galloped back toward the skirmish line. As he approached it, he swung into the woods on its right flank, dismounted, tore the war bonnet from his head, wiped the paint from his face, and ran to join his outnumbered comrades. He had just hurt Gall more than if he killed him, and it gave him great pleasure.

Marcus Albert Reno had seen plenty of battle during the war, and had been wounded at the Battle of Kelly's Ford. One of his brevets was for gallantry at Cedar Creek, where Crook was caught napping and Phil Sheridan saved the day. And, of course, he had been brevetted brigadier general in March of '65, in the closing days of the war, after commanding a Pennsylvania regiment. But having "seen the elephant" a number of times hadn't prepared him for this onslaught of Indian fury. It seemed that hostiles were *everywhere!* Wearing their wild war paint and ripping the air with their war cries, they were a wild visual cacophony of shooting, moving violence. He could see them on his flanks, even to his *rear!*

They were riding closer and closer to the skirmish line, continuing to grow in numbers, seemingly surreal in the murk. One, with lighter hair and white spots on his bare chest, was particularly impudent. Reno knew it would be only a matter of minutes before they would overwhelm him.

Where the hell is Custer?

Cooke had said Custer would support him. *Where the hell is he?*

He looked around in dismay. The woods by the river on his right flank would offer some cover.

He then sent a runner to his two company commanders with orders to displace their troopers into the trees to his right rear, swinging around a pivot on the end of his right flank.

He didn't know how many wounded he had, but the men would bring them.

He stood and fired his revolver at a warrior who was charging on his pony from only twenty yards away. He hit the pony, apparently in the chest; it stumbled and went down, throwing the rider. He caught his trumpeter's attention and told him to blow "Rally," then strode toward the nearby trees.

* * *

Captain Fred Benteen looked at the trail of the regiment as it reached down Reno Creek to the Little Bighorn. He gave the command to water the horses. He had led his battalion of D, H, and K Companies north through the rough country to the west of the river and had found no Indians whatsoever. Seven times during that twelve-mile trek, Lieutenant Frank Gibson with a squad of troopers had ridden to the top of ridges looking for Sioux, and each time they drew blanks. Finally it was time to go back to the regiment. Looking off to the right, he saw the pack train and its escort, B Company, coming up. He decided to wait for them and pulled out his pipe to light up.

Just then, a rider pounded up. It was Sergeant Daniel Kanipe from C Company on a courier mission. "Bring him to me," he told his first sergeant.

Kanipe saluted from the back of his sweaty horse. "Do you know where the pack train is, sir?"

Benteen jerked a thumb back down the trail. "'Bout a mile in that direction, Sergeant. Where's the rest of the regiment?"

Kanipe pointed back to the north. "Major Reno's attacking the village, and the general's on the other side of the river. I guess there's more hostiles than anyone imagined. I'm to find Captain McDougall and tell him to hurry with the packs."

Benteen nodded. "Best you get on with your mission then. He should be right back there."

Kanipe galloped off.

Captain Tom Weir strode up. "What was that all about?"

Benteen shrugged. "Apparently we've bit off a lot to chew on. That little racket we hear is probably Reno. Soon as the pack train catches up, we'll move on and get in on it."

Weir pulled out a thin silver flask and took a swig from it before passing it over to the white-haired battalion commander. Benteen took a pull on it and handed it back. At that moment, Weir said, "I'll be damned—look at that!"

Benteen turned. A handful of braying mules had broken loose from the pack train and were galloping hell-bent-for-leather toward the stream.

Shortly before reaching it, they ran into a morass, a stream bed that was still creating mud, though its flow had ceased with the dryer weather. They started to flounder. Almost immediately the struggling mules, apparently crazed by the smell of water, were stuck and needed help in getting out. The air was filled with their helpless braying.

Dan Kanipe found Captain McDougall and Lieutenant Mathey as the first runaway mules reached the mire. The sergeant jumped down from his horse, saluted quickly, delivered his message, and told him what little he knew of the situation.

McDougall turned to Mathey. "Let's get those damned mules out of that mud and hurry on. Custer must be in trouble."

"I guess I'll get on back to my company, sir," Kanipe said.

"No, too many hostiles out there. You stay with us."

Kanipe shrugged, unable to hide his disappointment. He couldn't fight a direct order.

First Sergeant James Hill, one of the oldest men in the regiment and a native Scot who had been a soldier since he enlisted in the Seventy-first Highland Infantry at the age of eighteen, spoke up, "Go see what you can do with those damned pack mules, Kanipe. I can sure use another sergeant."

Benteen decided not to wait for the pack train any longer. The fight was ahead and he was sure Custer needed him. He ordered his battalion forward and rode out to the point. Four minutes later, Private Giovanni Martini came galloping toward him from the direction of the village. As he hurriedly dismounted, the Italian was so excited he could hardly pronounce any of the English words he knew. He handed Cooke's message to his company commander, saying, "Lieutenant Cooke, he write what general say."

Benteen quickly read it and turned to Captain Weir, who was riding beside him. "Custer *is* in trouble. But I'll be damned if I can figure out what the son of a bitch wants. He says 'be quick' and then he says 'bring packs.' How in the hell can we come quick with a *pack train?*"

Weir just shrugged as he looked at the message. "You suppose Cooke meant to write 'bring *ammunition* packs?'"

Benteen shook his head. "I don't know, but send this information back to McDougall and tell him to get those goddamned mules moving as fast as he can. In the meantime, let's move smartly and see what the hell's going on."

He turned to his trumpeter. "Blow 'Trot,' Martini."

Armstrong Custer still didn't feel any imminent danger to his command. He knew he'd been hasty in splitting his forces, but that was the only way he knew to bottle up hostiles—hit 'em from more than one direction! Well, he'd have to improvise, that's all. If he attacked that big village and made that huge throng of warriors *think* he was going to smash into their women and children, *then* they'd pull away from Reno, and they'd stay put!

As he rode up to the main body after another look from the heights, his thoughts were still on how to best fight these hostiles. Mitch Boyer had guessed there might be at least two thousand fighting men in that village. But, even with his command divided, he still had the *Seventh Cavalry*. And his troopers were worth at least seven or eight warriors apiece. Most important, they had better weapons and discipline!

Indians fought like a mob.

Discipline always proved the king of the battlefield.

Now he had to find a good route.

The situation would unfold and dictate what he would do next. That was why he was such a good commander. His instinct for the best way to fight *always* manifested itself! Always.

As he trotted the last few yards to where his flags flew listlessly in the light breeze, three of his captains rode up to greet him—Keogh, Yates, and Tom. He told them what little he could add to what they already knew. Myles Keogh spoke up, "The scouts say there's a pretty good ravine ahead to the right. It leads into a bigger valley that runs down to the river a couple of miles ahead."

"Think that'll hide us?" Custer asked.

The Irishman nodded his head. "They say it's all pretty deep."

Custer made his decision instantly. "Let's take it!"

It was 3:32 P.M.

☆ ☆ ☆

At exactly the same time, Reno's beleaguered troopers had just finished swinging into their new battle line, if it could be called that, in the timber by the river. Marcus Reno was angry and flustered. Custer had *not* supported him as promised, and he was fighting an unbelievable number of hostiles—Indians who could fight like hell, and weren't afraid of anything! They were better, he'd decided, than most of the rebel soldiers he'd encountered in the war. What was this myth about a cavalryman being worth eight or more Redskins?

He had no idea how many casualties he'd taken.

Now, he'd just been told that some cavalrymen had been spotted up on the bluffs on the east side of the river. Custer? *What the hell was he doing up there?*

And ammunition would soon be gone if that damned pack train and some reinforcements didn't show up.

He looked around. How could anybody get to him? Howling Sioux were everywhere!

Captain Moylan and Captain French hurried up. French shouted, "I'm about out of ammo, Major!"

Lieutenant Don McIntosh joined them. "Me too!"

Moylan asked, "You know we're surrounded, don't you?"

Reno nodded his head. "Do the best you can, and if we don't get reinforced in another ten minutes, we'll have to break out of here."

Red Elk had been careful in the use of his ammunition. He had used his bow effectively and had unleashed a dozen good arrows at the Long Knives. He had knocked down one horse and its holder, and had hit two of the other soldiers. Most important, he had counted a first coup, and a second coup as well!

Now, with the *wasicus* having run back into the woods, he rested his pony and took stock. He didn't think any of the enemy had reached the inside of the village, but he wasn't sure. His first urge was to gallop back there and make sure Late Star was all right. But after all, wasn't he a famous *blotahunka*? He belonged in the fight.

Crazy Horse had been in the thick of it ever since he and his Oglalas had joined the fight. In fact, he'd followed the great war leader on two of his forays close to the horse soldiers. It was the way—a good warrior followed a good leader.

He was curious about something he'd seen while he was reloading his revolver. A man who looked like a Sioux had ridden out of the village and had thrown away his war bonnet. And he hadn't been able to recognize the war paint on the man's face. What was most confusing was that the man had run right into the Long Knives' line.

Suddenly he knew!

He'd heard the story about a half-Arikara, half-Hunkpapa who had nearly killed Gall. It was said that he scouted for the Long Knives. *That* was the war paint on the man's face—Arikara! It must be. Could he have done something in the camp?

Lonesome Charley Reynolds was certain that he had downed at least a half-dozen of the hostiles. There were some who thought he was the "best shot in the west," but that was certainly an exaggeration. He *was* pretty good with both a rifle and a pistol, but he never had been one to boast, or even think he was that good. Oh, he'd beaten both Captain French and Sergeant Finley in a match one night on the march out here, but that was just because they'd insisted.

Now this.

He'd warned General Custer that something strange was happening with the Sioux out here, that they had some special kind of medicine working. He'd also told him that there might be a whole lot more Indians than he expected, but the general had just grinned that funny smile of his, and had said something about there not being enough Indians in the whole West in his opinion.

He swung around to where Doctor Henry Porter was taking care of a man who'd been shot in the groin. The acting assistant surgeon had blood spattered all over his shirt and trousers, and he had a deep frown on his face as his hands flew at their work. Reynolds liked the doctor, thought he was a brave and considerate man—one who liked a joke, but had deep, serious thoughts . . . like himself. They'd shared a little whiskey together a couple of nights earlier. Around a small fire. The way a man in the West ought to spend his evenings before going to sleep.

This whole fight was getting ticklish, too many damned good warriors too damned close. Not enough shells left. He'd wanted to be a doctor once, even went to medical school for awhile. But the West called, another one of those siren songs, and Lonesome Charlie never went back home to stay.

He'd keep his eye on the doctor, keep him safe.

When Custer reached the wide ravine that would later be named Medicine Tail Coulee, he stopped and called in the two senior captains he'd named provisional battalion commanders. George Yates and Myles Keogh trotted up and tossed off salutes.

"George," Custer said, "I want you to take your company and Fresh Smith's E Company on down this coulee to where it joins the river. Go briskly, and when you get there, pour some fire into the side of the village."

Yates nodded. "Yes, sir!"

"And me?" Keogh asked.

Custer pointed up to the row of bluffs to his right front that guarded the northeast side of the ravine. "You take C, I, and L up there. When you get above where this coulee hits the river, take up positions where you can support George if he gets into trouble."

"Where're you going to be, General?"

"I'll be joining *you* for a while." Custer turned back to Yates. "If things get hot for you down by the river, I want you to break off immediately and rejoin me up on the ridge. Remember, you're just a ruse."

The Band Box commander touched his hatbrim in salute.

As the two commanders swung their horses away, Marc Kellogg, the journalist from the Bismarck *Tribune*, rode up with two familiar grinning faces—Boston Custer and Autie Reed, the Custer nephew. "Hello, big brother," Boston said.

Custer frowned. "I thought you two were with the pack train."

"We didn't want to miss anything," young Autie replied.

The general nodded. They were Custers. "By the way, where is that doggone pack train? I sent a sergeant back to tell McDougall to hurry three-quarters of an hour ago!"

"Got caught in a morass," Boston replied. "But they're coming along now, I'm sure."

Custer shook his head angrily. "You see Benteen?"

"Yes, he was with the pack train last I knew."

Custer was incredulous. *"For what?"*

Boston shrugged. "How would I know? You officers don't usually share counsel with us lowly civilians."

Custer turned away to conceal his anger. He'd deal with Benteen when this was over. The showdown had been a long time coming and this was the last straw! Insubordinate bastard! He touched Vic's flanks and rode forward to join the colors as the two columns moved out.

He had just further split his forces and had made a decision he'd never have made during the war. He wasn't leading Yates's Band Box troopers into battle! Lord knows, he wanted to. But he knew how the taste of battle would entice him. *God, how I would love it!* No, this was a wiser Armstrong Custer. He would stay above. In command. So he could support, or commit, Keogh as necessary. And he still had to get to the end of that village!

He turned back to the southwest. He could still hear firing from Reno's position.

"Doctor, we got to get out of here!" Charley Reynolds barked as he saw troopers getting on their horses in the clearing. "Major Reno said we'd be leaving shortly."

Doctor Henry Porter was still working on the trooper with the groin wound. "I don't think this man can survive a horseback ride," he said.

"Well, it's that or lose his hair," the scout replied quietly. "Here, I'll help lift him on this loose animal." He pulled a riderless horse up close.

Porter looked around and blew out a deep breath. The firing was terrible, the smoke making the woods a dark sepia in the sunlight. "I suppose you're right. You take his feet."

Together, they draped the semiconscious body over the saddle. "I'll lead him," Reynolds said, putting a foot in the stirrup on his own horse. "I—"

Charley Reynolds slumped, then slid to the ground. Porter stared at his friend a moment, then bent over him. The scout's eyes had already glazed. *"Charley!"* Porter shouted. He grabbed his wrist, but the pulse was fading. A glance told him blood was flowing from the center of his chest.

A bullet must have gotten him right in the heart. *"Charley!"* The doctor slapped his face, but it was no use.

Charley Reynolds was no longer the best shot in the West.

"By the Lord Harry," Marcus Reno sighed, "we are almost gone up."

The only man close enough to hear him in the murky din of the wooded area was the scout Bloody Knife who was busy shooting at the attacking hostiles. In fact, many of the Sioux had penetrated the woods and were closing in at that very moment! Yes, they would be gone up very shortly if he didn't do something. Reno waved at the trumpeter. "Blow 'Recall!'" he shouted.

As the rapid notes rang out, the horse holders brought the mounts into a large clearing nearby and the troopers pulled back to get in the saddle. A number of horses were dead, but so were many troopers—there were plenty of empty saddles.

Turning back to the attacking Indians, he brushed Bloody Knife. At that exact moment, a tall young Hunkpapa wearing a first-coup feather and vivid war paint ran in close and aimed an army revolver in his direction. Simultaneous with the *crack* of the pistol, Reno felt something moist strike the side of his face. He wiped it with his fingers, then stared at them in shock—they were covered with *blood and a gray mucous!*

He turned as the dying Bloody Knife slumped to the ground. The scout's head had been blasted open! He stared at the gray matter again. *Must be his brains!*

God!

Reno froze, glancing vacantly up at the tall Hunkpapa warrior leveling the revolver at him.

But nothing happened.

The warrior shook his gun and slapped it, re-aimed it. Reno shot at him and missed.

"Major!" Lieutenant Ben Hodgson shouted. *"Are we gettin' the hell out of here?"*

Reno nodded absently and told him to tell the trumpeter. He looked at his hand again. *Brains?*

Instantly the quick notes of "Charge" blasted through the trees. Reno composed himself enough to climb into the saddle and lead the command out to the east. But he couldn't stop the picture of the scout falling to the ground. He couldn't shake off the feel of the Indian's blood and . . .

It was 3:53 P.M.

Gall had been occupied with the fight with Reno, but not as a *blotahunka*. By the time he got his warhorse, the mob of howling warriors had already begun fighting the *wasicus* and he had just joined in. Now a warrior stopped him as he was ready to plunge into the Long Knives, ax swinging. It was one of his longtime scouts, Blue Horn. "Great leader," the warrior said, "Sitting Bull sends word that Long Knives have been seen high on the hills up there!" He pointed to the bluffs on the east side of the river. "The great chief thinks Three Stars may strike the village from there."

Gall's eyes narrowed as they searched the ridge. The chief was right! Three Stars would go around and come in with most of his soldiers from the side! He turned back to Blue Horn and said, "Tell Sitting Bull I will take warriors up to those bluffs and strike the Long Knives. And have him send word to Crazy Horse to attack them from the other end. Three Stars will be caught between us."

Blue Horn nodded and galloped away. Gall turned back to where the Long Knives horn was blowing and resisted the urge to fly into the fleeing horsemen in blue. At that moment he saw Red Elk and shouted at him, "Come with me! We have other Long Knives to kill!"

Red Elk turned reluctantly from the fleeing Long Knives. He must follow Gall.

The "Charge" out of the timber left several members of Reno's command behind. Lieutenant De Rudio and thirteen troopers, a couple of them wounded, and interpreter Fred Girard. While the neatly groomed De Rudio was the oldest officer in the command, Girard at forty-six was the oldest of the civilians. This group had simply been unable to mount up and join the rest of Reno's fleeing force. De Rudio pulled them back into heavier timber as the pursuing Indians triumphantly chased Reno. The Italian officer consoled the wounded as he checked their injuries. "We'll join the rest after it gets dark."

The war cries of the gleeful Indians still echoed up the valley over the sound of the rippling gunfire. Deciding it was best to remain quiet, the tiny command fearfully settled down to await its fate.

Angry Bear, the great hunter who often accompanied Gall on his raids, led his large party of Lakotas in a fast trot toward the faint sounds of gunfire. The reports of large antelope herds and possibly some buffalo to the northeast had led to the recruitment of the party from each tribe that morning. With so many men in the huge camp, the hunt had been a welcome diversion. One hundred twelve Lakotas and over a dozen Cheyennes now hurried to the scene of battle on the Greasy Grass, dabbing splashes of vivid warpaint on their faces as they rode.

Angry Bear was the same age as Gall, and had often been a *blotahunka* on minor raids. He was a tall man, and part of his hunting skill resulted from his wiry strength; more came from his absolute fearlessness. Now, he felt the excitement of a fight with the *wasicus*. It was the only reason for the distant gunfire. Perhaps it was Three Stars! He hoped so. He, too, had been sick and had missed the fight on the Rosebud; maybe now he could make up for it. . . .

There! On the ridge line ahead he spotted the blue uniforms!

Could be over a hundred Long Knives on horseback!

Was it Sitting Bull's prophecy?

Angry Bear raised his rifle and let out a war whoop as he kicked his pony into a gallop.

Up on the ridge above Medicine Tail Coulee, Custer sat on Vic beside Keogh and Tom Custer, watching George Yates approach the river with his two companies. From what Armstrong could tell, Yates and his seventy-five men should be striking the big village almost in the center. That should surely take the pressure off Reno. He raised his glasses and looked back toward the Reno fight, but all he could see was the roiling cloud of dust and smoke. He could still hear plenty of faint gunfire from that direction.

The three companies of Keogh's battalion, C, I, and L, were stretched out along the ridge. They totaled some 123 men, plus the regimental head-quarters detachment. As he had done often during the campaign, Tom

Custer was riding with his older brother as an unofficial aide-de-camp. And in his absence, Henry Harrington had assumed temporary command of C Company. Though still a second lieutenant, the twenty-seven-year-old Harrington had no qualms about leading the company.

Custer swung his glasses back to Yates, a thousand yards below, just as the sound of new gunfire reached him. The captain had brought his Band Box Troop to the point where the coulee emptied into the river and had begun firing into the village without dismounting. Fresh Smith was just behind, supporting him. The sound of the gunfire rose up sharply to the ridge.

Keogh and Tom Custer were also watching with their glasses.

Suddenly, Tom said, *"Look! There to the left!"*

Custer moved his glasses. A very large band of warriors on horseback was galloping toward Yates—could be over three hundred, maybe four! He couldn't tell for sure because of the trees along the river bank. The general turned to his trumpeter, Voss. "Blow 'Recall!'" he barked.

The trumpeter raised his bugle and complied at once. The staccato notes filled the air, mixing with the battle sounds. As the bugle call ended, Custer turned to a new noise—the drumbeat of hooves coming from behind them.

Just then Captain Jimmi Calhoun came galloping up. *"General!"* he shouted. *"Injuns, off to the east!"*

Custer turned, bringing up his glasses again. It was a pretty large party, coming hell-bent. He'd had no idea there were hostiles out there, let alone a large hunting party. He looked back down the hill to where Yates and Fresh Smith were starting up toward the ridge through a deep ravine. Sioux were piling in behind them, firing madly. He had never seen so many warriors at one time!

"Keogh!" he barked. "Mount 'em up and let's head north to where we can join up with Yates at the top of that deep coulee!"

Reno's dash from the woods began in a column of fours in a fairly orderly manner, but the enemy warriors, smelling blood, closed in to within fifty yards, firing their rifles from horseback. Many shots found their mark, as cavalry horses crashed to the rough ground. One of the last riders out of the woods was Lieutenant Donald McIntosh, commander of G Company.

His horse was killed, but he grabbed a riderless mount and swung up into the saddle. A moment later, he was killed outright by a rifle shot.

Panic struck the tiny command and the withdrawal quickly became more of a rout than a military maneuver. Myles Moylan swung around and tried to provide covering fire for the others, but it was useless. The air was continually shattered by shots and war cries. Here and there, troopers whose horses had been shot from under them managed to swing up behind the saddles of other troopers. But many of them were hit.

At just under a mile from the woods, Reno made a flash decision to make a crossing and climb the steep slope on the other side of the river. The Little Bighorn was thirty to forty feet wide at that point and didn't look very deep. He reined his horse in and jumped it into the water. The banks were a drop of about six feet, creating another problem—some horses didn't want to make the leap. Soon the river was filled with struggling cavalrymen and horses, fighting to get to the other side and climb that hill to safety! Survival was the only thought in every trooper's mind.

Lieutenant Ben Hodgson, Reno's adjutant, was shot in the thigh and unhorsed halfway across the river. Reaching for a passing trooper's stirrup, he didn't even feel the bullet that smashed into his chest, snuffing out his life.

Doctor Jim DeWolf, the former medical corpsman turned surgeon, rode dripping out of the stream, followed by his orderly. Urging their animals up a small streambed, they ran right into a small band of Cheyennes who had also crossed the river. A volley of shots killed both of them. Shouting gleefully, the Cheyenne warriors jumped off their wet ponies, knives flashing. In moments two of them held aloft the dripping scalps of the Long Knife medicos.

Major Reno, in the meantime, had urged his horse up the other bank and was directing survivors up the steep hill to the high crest above. Some were still mounted, others led their heaving horses up the abrupt slope. Lakota gunfire still raked the survivors. A few more of the warriors followed their quarry across the river, but the majority fell back, momentarily sated. At the same time, word arrived from Sitting Bull that the village might be in danger from the Long Knives on the ridges further downstream. Quickly, many of them turned their ponies back in that direction.

37

Up there where the last fight took place, where the last
stand was made, the Long Hair stood like a sheaf of corn
with all the ears fallen around him.
—SITTING BULL

Custer and Keogh's battalion hurried north toward what would later be
called Calhoun Hill, beyond where the deep coulee rose into the ridge
line. Quickly deploying Jimmi Calhoun's L Company to meet the
onrushing hunters thundering in from the east, Custer and the rest
awaited Yates and his men as they urged their horses upward out of the
coulee. But the mob of howling Lakotas that had struck Yates at the ford
was close behind. The other two companies of Keogh's command, C and I
Companies, quickly dismounted to provide covering fire for Yates.

Custer threw yet another frustrated look back to the south. *"Where is
that goddamned Benteen and our ammunition?"* he shouted at Cooke, who
could only shake his head.

Custer was angry at himself, an emotion he seldom experienced. He
knew all too well that he'd made a major mistake in having the men issued
only a hundred rounds of carbine ammunition. Unless they made nearly
every remaining round tell, they could be in deep trouble very shortly.
He'd already put out the order to be judicious in firing, but an inexperi-
enced or excited trooper could burn up a hundred rounds in a hurry. For a
fleeting second, he thought of how valuable those Gatlings might be about
now, and the other four troops of cavalry, for that matter. But that was
spilled milk. *Damn, I've never seen so many warriors!* He thought about
taking Tom and his C Company and mounting a counterattack right
straight through Yates—smash right into those hostiles charging up the
deep coulee—*smash 'em up!*

Like back in the war. Smash 'em up! as Sheridan used to say.

But then he'd be scattered all over the place, and he knew he'd never
stop until he was smack in that village! That was the Custer way!

But this wasn't *that* war, and the odds were building heavily against him. The damned enemy was like a *flood*. It was as if someone had opened a gate to a dam and a red tide was rushing toward him from different directions.

No, he'd have to keep moving north, maybe find another way into the end of that village. Draw off the enemy to protect their women and children. . . .

I've never seen so many goddamned warriors!

It was 4:03 P.M.

Sitting Bull had mounted his big black pony and had ridden to observe the fight on the south end of the village. Now, after directing Gall to meet the Long Knife threat from the east ridge, he watched as the horde of warriors followed the fighting chief up the long gully from the ford. This was a different role for him, he thought, as he watched the warriors continue to swarm into the eastern fight. He wasn't used to sitting back, not being in the forefront of the fight. But from the moment he'd heard of the Long Knives approach, something had told him that he had another responsibility, one greater than battle.

He urged his pony forward toward the north end of the camp and the Cheyenne circle. A large number of the women and children had hurried there when the fight started. Now Crazy Horse was draining off most of the warriors to follow Gall's suggestion and swing around to the north of the ridges that held the Long Knives. Many of the older people were just arriving, further jamming the area. Excitement mixed with fear showed in many of the faces, but there was no panic.

He glanced down at the sound of his wife's voice. Four Robes was standing by a small clump of bushes, one of the twin babies in her arms. Seen-by-the-Nation, his older wife, held the other baby. "Where are the other children?" he asked.

Four Robes pointed to a group of children crowded around a large rock. "They are all right," she said.

Sitting Bull nodded and rode over to where Running Antelope, Late Star's father, was trying to control the older of the young boys from racing after Crazy Horse.

Things were happening fast up on the long ridgeline. Angry Bear and his hunters crashed into Jimmi Calhoun's L Company at 4:08, outnumbering the troopers nearly three to one. The warriors rode around the kneeling troopers, firing into their defensive position from three sides.

Led horses were the first casualties, then soldiers began to fall. Calhoun had the largest company under Keogh, but it was quickly becoming the smallest. The one-eyed Second Lieutenant John Crittendon died from a bullet through his other eye two minutes after the hunters struck.

Gunfire crackled, mingling with war whoops and the screams of wounded horses.

A stream of arrows also filled the air, raining down on the grim-faced troopers.

Myles Keogh saw what was happening to Calhoun from four hundred yards away and wanted to rush back to help him. But he couldn't—Gall's warriors were pouring into the area on his west flank, firing wildly and also unleashing dozens of arrows. Another three hundred yards to the north of him, C Company, under Lieutenant Harrington, was also getting heavily engaged. And still the warriors continued to stream up from the river.

Custer now had Yates's two companies back, and he was torn between possibilities. He could send everyone back to aid Calhoun and see what developed, or he could continue north. If he gathered everyone in around L Company, he'd lose his maneuverability and any pretense of the offensive. And George Armstrong Custer didn't fight defensive engagements!

He signaled to Tom, who pulled his horse in close.

"Ride over to Yates and tell him we'll continue north and swing back down to the river the first time we find a decent coulee."

"Yes, sir!" Tom replied and galloped off.

✩ ✩ ✩

Captain Fred Benteen spotted the Reno fight at the river crossing at eleven minutes after four. Seeing blue-clad figures scrambling up the slope, he had ordered his command to proceed at the gallop, leaving the pack train to catch up on its own. He was too late to do much for Reno's retreat, so when his scouts pointed to cavalrymen on the top of a hill, he swung away from the river and hurried to the hilltop position. A quick glance at the bloodied, tired survivors told him everything.

The firing from a handful of rear-guard troopers was dying out and a good look down at the valley told Benteen that the Indians were withdrawing for some reason. In fact, they were riding pell-mell back toward the village. He could see that Major Reno was distraught.

The bulky man was dismounted and hatless, with a red handkerchief tied around his head. As he ran up to meet the newcomers, the breathless Reno exclaimed, "For God's sake, Benteen, halt your command and help me. I've lost half my men!"

Benteen coolly replied, "Of course. Don't worry about a thing. I'll set up a temporary defensive position here, while we figure out what to do. Do you know where the hell Custer is?"

Reno pointed north. "Last sight of any other troopers was up on that hill—must be an hour ago, but it seems like a century. He was supposed to back me up, but I don't know what the hell happened." He looked like he was going to cry. "Benteen," he said plaintively, "They were all *over* us!"

Benteen nodded. "From what I saw, you're lucky to be here." He looked off to the north, the source of some faint, distant firing. "That's probably him up there."

Reno shook his head, not answering as he stared at the ground. "It was terrible."

Benteen sensed that he had to take over, and Reno made it easy, saying, "I'm going back down the hill to look for Hodgson."

Lieutenant Varnum, his face streaked with grime, walked up at that moment. "And I'm going along. Benny was my best friend!"

As soon as Reno and Varnum were gone, Benteen quickly spoke with Tom Weir and Lieutenant Edward Godfrey, the commander of K company. Giving them orders to occupy the hill with the remainder of Reno's men and redistribute the ammunition, he then called the busy Doctor Henry Porter over. "How many casualties, Doc?" he asked.

The blood-spattered Porter sighed. "As far as I know, eighteen—seven seriously."

Benteen nodded. "Okay, set up your hospital over on the east side of the hill; close to where you are now. I don't know how long we'll be here, though."

Porter wiped his sweating forehead. "Do you know where Custer is?"

Benteen scowled. "*No one* knows where Custer is."

It was 4:30 P.M.

Red Elk was enjoying himself immensely. The big Sharps was heavy, and he didn't need its long range, but the battle itself was everything he'd ever dreamed about. The first fight with Three Stars had been exciting, but this was *special!* Long Knives were attacking his village, and the power of the Lakota had never been stronger. Now, riding close to Gall, he sensed that something very special was going to happen to him. The hillside was full of shouting warriors, firing up at the kneeling Long Knives, or circling, trying to get around in their rear. It seemed that nearly everyone he knew was in the fight. White Bull and One Bull, Sitting Bull's nephews, were busy, all of the young warriors who had gone on the first raid he'd led were in the thick of it. And he'd heard that Crazy Horse was leading a separate band from further downstream.

Firing and smoke were everywhere, and there were moments when the sky was nearly black with arrows.

Someone had said it was a "great day to die." He laughed. It was a great day for a lot of *Long Knives* to die! He spotted the red-and-white guidon swaying in the light breeze on top of the hill. He could barely make out a symbol on it—something like a circle, open on one side. *Now, that would be special!* Dismounting, he kneeled and brought up the heavy rifle. The Long Knife cloth was on a thin stick that was stuck into the ground. He aimed carefully, then lowered the Sharps. No, he needed a rest to steady the weapon. Reaching inside his saddle for his forked stick, he pulled it out and jammed its sharp point into the ground.

Once more he took aim, but just then a Long Knife picked up the cloth and moved it. He shrugged and grinned; that was even better. Coolly, he lined the man up in his sights and shot him.

The big bullet caught Sergeant Jeremiah Finley in the chest, knocking him backward. The acting provost sergeant and tailor to Custer fought for air as C Company's guidon slipped out of his unfeeling fingers. First Sergeant Ed Bobo saw the sergeant go down, but he was too busy to do anything about it. In the meantime, Private Iggy Stungewitz grabbed the guidon and asked Bobo where he wanted it.

"Up there, about fifty yards!" Bobo shouted. He had to move the company further west in small jumps to keep up with the general.

The Russian nodded, ran up the slope with the guidon, and rammed it into the ground near a small boulder. Just as he did so, a big caliber slug tore into his left arm, jerking him around.

Private Lucien Burnham had never faced stark fear before. He'd worried about what he'd do in the face of grave danger ever since his eleventh birthday back in Pennsylvania, when he'd been in the woods outside his grandparents' farmhouse and had encountered a nasty raccoon. The animal had screeched and attacked him. Badly frightened, he'd run howling back the way he'd come and had found the sheltering arms of his grandmother. Ever since, he'd had a fear of fear that sometimes lingered in his troubled mind.

That same fear was part of why he'd joined the army. He *had* to find out.

Now, with what looked like hundreds of wildly painted and howling Indians shooting at him and his fellow F Company troopers, he knew. All too well.

He was absolutely scared out of his wits.

He tried to fight it, to aim his carbine steadily at the Redskin horde, but his hands wouldn't cooperate. The barrel waved and his hands shook. He threw it to the ground and drew his long-barreled revolver. Maybe he could control that better.

A fierce looking Lakota in black and red face-paint rode in close, war-whooping. Burnham aimed and fired. He was shocked to see the warrior slump over his pony's neck and slowly fall off.

Burnham drew in a deep breath. He'd done it! He was all right!

A second later, a slug from a captured cavalry Springfield tore through his throat.

Custer drew a sleeve over his brow to wipe away the sweat. He had galloped at the lead of the three companies over the highest point of the ridge only to run right into the an even *larger* Indian force pouring toward him from the north. This one had to be at least five hundred strong! And it was spread out like a fast-moving curtain of yipping, howling death. He'd noticed one of the warriors in particular, a smallish bare-chested man riding in a lead position as the Indians circled around, getting ready to charge. He'd fired his Remington rifle at him, but had missed.

How many of these hostiles could there be?

He turned back to Tom, shouting, "Get Smith and E Company up out of that deep ravine! And tell the other two companies to pull in tight on the crest of that hill over there."

He shoved the Remington into its scabbard at Vic's side and pulled out his Wembley .45 Bulldog. Firing it at a nearby warrior, he turned and urged Vic up the slope toward the peak. . . .

Arrows were beginning to rain in. He didn't see his nephew Autie had just been hit in the chest by one of them. He motioned to Chief Trumpeter Voss, *"Blow 'Rally!'"*

Red Elk saw the opening between Calhoun's L Company and Keogh's I Company. Shouting to several nearby Lakotas to follow him, he urged his war pony toward the gap and galloped through to the east side of the ridge. He pulled up some seventy yards past the Long Knives. Unscathed, he wheeled his mount back toward the cavalry position. He looked around, spotting Angry Bear and his warriors fighting in close, off to his left. Away to the north he could see what was probably Crazy Horse's force, circling around some blue uniforms that were just reaching a hilltop. Even on the ridge, the smoke was getting dense, casting a brownish haze over everything.

Nearly thirty warriors, mostly Sans Arcs and Brules, had followed Red Elk and his handful of Hunkpapas. He saw some of the Long Knives turn around to face him as his presence was discovered. More warriors rode through the gap, and soon there were seventy-some firing bullets and arrows into the beleaguered troopers from just east of their position.

Red Elk smiled to himself. It was time for another of his charges, time for yet another first coup!

Myles Keogh had been hit by an arrow in his left thigh, and at least twenty of his men had been killed. Several more were wounded, and the remainder were trying to fight back from behind their wounded or dying horses. But one by one, the hammers of revolvers fell on empty chambers. Carbine shells had been expended for over five minutes.

He saw a tall young warrior no more that fifty feet away starting to urge his pony toward him. He raised his pistol, and for some reason thought of Clifden Castle back in Ireland.

Henry Harrington had taken a round in his right shoulder, but it only made him mad. He wanted to grab an extra revolver and charge right into those red bastards who were overwhelming his company. Since Tom Custer had been gone so much, he truly regarded C Company as his very own. *"Bobo!"* he shouted to the first sergeant. *"Move the company over to Keogh and join up with them!"*

He didn't hear Custer's "Recall" bugle call because a .45 caliber shell slammed into his cheek.

Iggy Stungewitz had tied his bandanna around his left arm, but blood was still seeping down to his fingertips. He rushed over to his dying lieutenant and tried to shield him, but Bobo shouted for him to stay with the remnants of C Company while he tried to get them over to I Company. But the Russian barely heard him. An arrow from a charging Blackfoot Lakota pierced his chest. As he raised his revolver, a .45 round struck him just below the sternum.

He managed to fall back over Harrington's body in a final effort to protect him.

Myles Keogh heard the *click!* as his .45 came up on an empty chamber. He dropped the revolver as an onrushing Sioux warrior rode straight at him.

He could actually see the gleam in the young Lakota's eyes as the Indian closed on him, a ribboned lance raised. He tried to reach for him, rip him from the saddle, but the lance tore into his right side, spinning him around. The pain was instant and grotesque as he stared down at the gush of blood.

Turning, he saw the tall warrior leap from his pony, knife in hand.

Keogh raised his hands. *No goddamned Injun could do this to an Irishman!*

Red Elk's knife caught him just below the belt.

And the young *blotahunka* had another first coup.

As the last of his troopers knotted together behind their felled horses, First Lieutenant Jimmi Calhoun knew he wasn't going to get out of it. For a brief second he thought of his wife, Maggie. Being in her brother's regiment was safety—the indestructible Custer. How could this be happening? Angry Bear's rifle bullet from twenty yards away caught him in the chest and killed him instantly.

Just as he led the remnants of C Company into the crumbling I Company position, First Sergeant Ed Bobo realized it was about all up. He saw Keogh's body and stared at it for a moment. Men and officers were going down all over the place, and now this handsome Irish former colonel, whom he'd always liked. *God* he thought, *Why?*

A bullet from a Springfield was his answer.

He would never have to worry about Missouri Ann again.

Custer's flags were jammed into the ground on the hilltop he'd selected. Those left from E and F Companies were clustered to his left and slightly down the hill toward the river. Fresh Smith had taken some men down the deep ravine south of the hill, but had met so many warriors that he'd tried to pull back—and was killed when he reached the command post. Wounded horses were down and screaming. Others were dying with their riders. The handsome George Yates had been shot as he tried to take on three warriors at once—scalped on the spot.

Doctor George Lord, dying from his wounds, wouldn't have to worry about shooting or doctoring when the chips were down; he'd done both well, and to no avail.

The wealthy Canadian Bill Cooke was also dying—from one rifle and two arrow wounds—wondering if some savage hostile would cut off his flamboyant beard.

Mitch Boyer had made his last scout; a Cheyenne arrow stuck out of his left shoulder and blood streamed down his arm, but he was still shooting a revolver as the hostiles closed in. He tried to hit the one with the white spots on his bare torso. He knew it was Crazy Horse.

Boston Custer was kneeling behind a dead horse, loading his last rounds into a Springfield. Beside him, Mark Kellogg, the reporter, had a long-barreled .45 revolver in each hand. One was empty, but he was still firing the other one.

Tom Custer also had a revolver in each hand. Jumping up from behind his dead horse, he threw the empty one at a nearby Oglala and jerked a Lakota arrow out of his left shoulder. A *Custer* didn't shoot back—he shot *first!* He lunged forward at a fiercely painted warrior fifteen yards away, firing the revolver in a yellow haze of anger. He'd gone only five paces when another arrow punctured his midsection. The bullet that crushed his forehead ended his charge.

Standing a few yards away by his dying Vic, George Armstrong Custer fired first the Wembley, then, with his left hand, the army revolver he'd picked up. He was aiming carefully into the maze of onrushing Indians, selecting his targets with care in the bright, brittle, and noisy sunlight. Everything was turning red on the left side of his body as blood seeped from the wound in his chest. As the Colt *clicked* on empty, he was overwhelmed by a sudden moment of silence inside him. He stared into a vacuum of swirling, mounted and running Lakota and Cheyenne warriors, most half-naked and painted, some wearing flowing headdresses, some shouting, some wild with the excitement of the kill. And if anyone knew about the kill in battle, he did. He knew its thrill. But why was it happening to *him?* All about him was death, the death of his Seventh. It couldn't be, just *couldn't!*

Not to the invincible Custer.

Not with Custer's Luck!

It was then that he knew.

God, Libbie!

A bullet struck him in the left temple, and he died with the knowledge of what he'd done.

38

Back at Reno Hill, Tom Weir took the final sip from his flask and stomped over to where Benteen was talking to Myles Moylan and Tom French. "You hear *that?*" he asked, interrupting.

"Hear what?" the white-haired captain replied.

"That goddamned firing, *that's* what. Doesn't *anyone* give a good goddamn about the rest of the command? He sent messages to *hurry,* didn't he?"

Benteen gave the other captain his owl look. "First of all, we don't know where he is, and secondly we've got wounded to worry about."

Angrily, Weir retorted, "Well, goddamnit, I'm not going to sit here on my arse if he needs me! You can do what the hell you want, Benteen, I'm going over there!"

"No, Tom, I think you'd best wait here until Reno gets back."

Weir stomped away. "I'm not waiting any longer!"

Spotting his first sergeant a few yards away, Weir barked, "Martin, get D Company in the saddle. We're moving out immediately!"

It was 4:52 P.M.

Two pack mules loaded down with ammunition from the pack train arrived on Reno Hill a few minutes after Weir galloped off to the north with his company. At the same time, Major Reno, still wearing his red bandanna, and Lieutenant Varnum came back from their search for Ben Hodgson. As the extra ammunition was being issued to all of the able-bodied fighting men on the hill, Reno slumped down on a small rock beside Benteen. He held his head in his hands for a few moments before looking up.

"Did you find him?" Benteen asked quietly.

Reno nodded toward a corpse by the edge of the ridge. "That's his body over there."

"Weir took off to find Custer," Benteen said, after a moment.

Reno looked up with a frown. "When?"

"A few minutes ago. Headed north toward that big peak. You can see his column of fours."

Reno looked off to the north, nodded. The faint sound of shooting in that direction had diminished.

"What do you want to do?" Benteen asked.

"I suppose we ought to do the same thing," the major replied. "But not until the pack train gets here. We can't leave *them* alone any longer."

Benteen nodded his head. "If you don't mind, I'm going to follow Weir with my three companies. Custer's out there *somewhere.*"

Once more Reno just nodded his head.

It was a little over a mile to the high peak where Custer had first looked down on the huge village. As Tom Weir reached the spot with Second Lieutenant Edgerly, he looked anxiously to the north with his glasses. At what he judged to be a little over three miles away on the ridgeline above the river valley, he made out what looked like a guidon moving around in the slightly smoky area. He also saw many figures, some mounted. They were moving about, apparently shooting into objects on the ground. The forms of what appeared to be many dead horses dotted the area. At a closer range, maybe less than three miles away, on the same ridgeline, he spotted another guidon, and more moving figures. *They were Indians!*

Edgerly was also looking through his glasses. "Do you suppose the general went off to join General Terry without us?"

"No," Weir replied. "He wouldn't do that."

"What do you suppose those Indians are doing?"

"Beats me."

Fred Benteen reached Weir Point fifteen minutes behind D Company. He and Lieutenant Godfrey joined Weir and Edgerly where they were still observing the smoky area in the distance. By this time, their field glasses showed that more figures had joined the others, mostly not on horseback.

In addition, it appeared that a large number of riders—definitely not soldiers—were moving toward them. Godfrey peered intently at the oncoming riders, finally saying, "Those are Lakota, and unless I miss my guess, they're riding hell-bent to finish off the job over here."

Benteen continued to watch through his glasses. "By God, I think you're right!"

The white-haired captain looked around, then walked off to his right. "This isn't a very good defensive position," he said at length.

Edgerly swung his glasses back toward Reno Hill. "The major's finally got the pack train moving this way," he announced.

Benteen looked in that direction, then back toward the oncoming Indians. "Well, he might just as well turn around. We aren't staying here."

Late Star was among the first women to reach the battle scene. She had a big knife and was just as prepared to start as everyone else. It was the Way! And particularly it was the Way for the wife of the Lakota's leading young *blotahunka*. The men did the fighting and usually the scalping. Their women did the mutilating. It was simply what women in a great warrior nation did. Time after time, they watched their beloved warriors ride off to fight or raid, and sometimes the men either didn't return or came back wounded or dead. An enemy was usually quite remote from the tribal females, but now and then the women were close enough to a victory to join in the post-battle rituals.

And part of that was mutilation.

Steal forever the enemy warrior's power.

All around on the side of this hill where the flags had stood, where Crazy Horse's Oglalas and Cheyennes had finished killing the Long Knife leaders, women were eagerly stripping bodies of the dead soldiers and taking whatever was left on the dead horses. The big animals were all around, most on their sides, eyes glazed in death. Since Late Star loved horses, she was sorry for that—but war brought many bad things, as she had known since she was very young.

Knives were flashing in the late-afternoon sunshine, and here and there a woman let out a war whoop as she ripped some part of a white body apart. And the Long Knife bodies were *very* white when one pulled off their uniforms. Late Star's knife was still bloody from gouging a hole in the stomach of a young trooper with dark hair. She had taken a locket on a small chain from around his neck. Now she watched momentarily as Little Blackbird, the champion quiller, let out a shout and pounced on a tall Long Knife with the most luxuriant facial hair she'd ever seen. The quiller laughed aloud as she straddled the long body and sliced away at the cheeks and jaw. Such black curly hair!

Late Star turned to where her best friend, Blue Feather, let out a howl of delight as she attacked the corpse of a man with vigor. "Look!" her friend shouted, "He has a bird on his chest!"

Late Star shook her head in wonder. She'd never seen such a thing—a real eagle with blue feathers trimmed in red! And he had another picture on his arm, a symbol with Long Knife writing. She had no idea what it meant, but the design was TWC. His face was badly broken, apparently from a bullet or maybe an ax. In fact, he didn't have a face anymore. She watched for a couple of moments as Blue Feather slashed off his penis and testicles, and held them in the air with an exultant shout.

Very close by was a body that another woman, Lame Bird, was just beginning to strip. The corpse was rather long, and its blue trousers had a yellow stripe, just like the one with a bird on his chest. A fancy hunting rifle and many empty shell casings lay nearby. Late Star started to turn away, when something about his face stopped her. "Wait!" she said sharply, catching Lame Bird's arm as she was about to scalp the head.

Lame Bird turned, angrily. "He's mine!" she snapped.

"No!"

"Find your own! There are plenty!"

"No, this one is mine. I'll give you a pony later."

Lame Bird stared at her a moment, then shrugged as she got to her feet. "You must be crazy."

Late Star knelt beside the body and brushed back the short golden curls. There was no doubt. A man who had once befriended her couldn't be mutilated. She thought back to a big house at Fort *Lin-cun*, and the strange but good food she had been given there. A man with a big smile had been nice to her and her father. He had a pretty wife. And he had righted the wrongs about which her father had complained.

He was Long Hair.

"How many Injuns you think are comin' at us?" Benteen asked, peering through his binoculars.

Weir shrugged. "A lot, maybe a thousand. They're everywhere!"

Benteen lowered his glasses. The hostiles were streaming up out of Medicine Tail Coulee along the main ridgeline, and from its eastern end. Some of the lead riders were no more than seven hundred yards away.

The captain looked around. "Best we get our arses back to that hill we just left. At least we'll have a steep bank behind us!"

Weir agreed. "Right, we'd better hightail it back. What about a rear guard?"

"If we don't get the hell out of here, we'll *all* be the rear guard!"

Benteen signaled for his first sergeant.

Red Elk and his nearly seventy followers were only part of the huge number of warriors galloping along behind Crazy Horse toward Reno Hill. No one knew how many fighting men were in the thundering column, but, except for a few hundred warriors who had returned to the village to celebrate and look after their families, the rest of Sitting Bull's mighty host was eager for the balance of the Long Knives' blood. Gall was among those who had returned to the village; he had just been told of the tragic death of his wife and daughters, and, stunned, had gone back to his tipi in the Hunkpapa circle.

Red Elk was full of himself! In his youthful dreams he'd often fantasized about a huge victory, but never anything that approached what had happened this day. Hundreds of dead *wasicus!* Their torn bodies dotted the slopes behind him like the white flowers in early summer. Already, he had *four* first coups on this magnificent day! And it wasn't over yet.

It was then that the Long Knives were spotted on the high peak. Red Elk immediately swung off to his right, shouting for his warriors to follow him. He'd be the first up that hill to reach them!

Farrier Vincent Charley had been urinating by a scrub some fifty yards down the north side of Weir Point when he heard the Lakota war whoops.

Spotting the band of Sioux pouring out of a shallow draw some four hundred yards away, Charley swung into the saddle and urged his horse up the hill. Reaching the peak, he saw his company saddling up and heard the bugle call. But something stopped him. Maybe it was that old thing that had been bothering him about Stungewitz, maybe it was the fact that he'd never done much of anything in his life, maybe it was that indefinable something that makes a man do something rash, something totally unpremeditated that turns into an act of courage.

He didn't know, didn't even consider such things.

He just knew that a whole bunch of Gott-damned Injuns were about to pour into the back side of his company! He quickly dismounted and pulled his horse down. Bringing his carbine up, he coolly fired at the first one he caught in his sights. The hostile pitched off his pony. All that shooting with Jeremiah Finley had made him very comfortable with the Springfield. He aimed at another warrior and saw him slump, then another. They were getting very close. He tossed the carbine away and drew his revolver. A tall, painted Lakota in front let out a war whoop as he urged his pony straight at him. The warrior's revolver blazed just as Charley fired. A flash of pain struck him in the pelvis and he crashed to the ground. The pain was terrible, but he fought off the faint and aimed the Colt at another of the warriors swarming into his position. He fired again and again, until the pistol clicked on empty.

The tall Lakota leader swung down from his pony, ignoring the bleeding wound on his bicep, and slammed his battle-ax into Vincent Charley's head—just the way Gall had taught him.

It was 6:05 P.M.

Major Marcus Reno spotted Benteen's column returning almost as soon as it had departed the tall peak area. And from the way it was moving, he guessed there was trouble behind it. He held up a hand for his column to halt. Turning to Captain Tom McDougall, he said. "Looks like someone's heading back in a mighty big hurry."

"Think it's Custer?" the B Company commander asked.

Reno studied the column through his glasses. "No, I don't see Custer's flags. Must be Benteen."

"Where do *you* think Custer is?"

Reno just shook his head. He'd quit conjecturing. "All right, let's turn around and get on back to that hill. I imagine we've still got lots of trouble."

"*It sure as hell isn't Custer!*" McDougall barked. "*Look!*"

Reno brought his glasses up again. Spilling over the hill were dozens of Sioux!

The major was exactly right. By the time the slower moving pack train, and what was left of Reno's command and its casualties, had turned around and reached Reno Hill, Benteen came pounding in at the head of his column. Jumping down from his horse, the white-haired captain strode up to Reno. "Must be a thousand goddamned hostiles behind us! We'd better get this place organized defensively at once!"

Reno shrugged. He was almost too tired to care. "Will you see to it, Benteen?"

"Yes!" Turning to Weir, Moylan, French, and the other waiting officers, Benteen barked, "Start digging in to form a perimeter around this whole hilltop. And get a watering party down to that river immediately. We're going to need all the water we can get. Also, post some sharpshooters on the north side to slow down their lead elements. Now, jump to it. Those bastards are going to be here in no time!"

There wasn't any doubt about who was in charge.

Red Elk's wound was shallow, a crease from the farrier's pistol shot. He'd tied a cloth around it, and had led his warriors forward after the battalion of fleeing horsemen. As he reached a point about five hundred yards from the hill where the Long Knives had formed a defensive position, a warrior riding beside him was shot from his horse. To his left, a pony screamed and pitched to the ground, throwing its rider. More firing was coming from the hilltop. He held up his hand as he reined in. Crazy Horse and hundreds of warriors were close behind. It would be stupid to charge up that hill into heavy fire. . . .

Sergeant Dan Kanipe listened as First Sergeant Hill gave the orders to dig in. B Company, to which he was still attached, was a big company.

And since its mission was still with the pack train, the company dug in around the corral area where the mules were still loaded down with rations and ammunition. It was also where the large number of surviving horses were gathered and huddled. Unsaddling the weary pack animals would have to wait, Hill said, until the immediate danger of the onrushing hostiles was met.

Kanipe was worried. *What had happened to the main body of troopers since I left them up on that ridge?* Rumors were rife, with everyone complaining that Custer had deserted them. He didn't think so; in fact, he was worried. His men were out there somewhere, the troopers he'd trained and knew so well. Whatever they were doing, they needed him. Captain Custer needed him, he was sure. And something was wrong. The general had been emphatic about getting the pack train up there with him, so he must have had plenty of reason. There had sure as hell been a big village down there! He'd gotten a good look at it before riding back.

Oh well, he couldn't worry about it now. He looked off to the north. That was sure one big bunch of Injuns coming toward them!

Benteen was perfectly comfortable in virtual command. Except for the brush with hostiles back on the peak, which resulted in the loss of only one man, his men were so far unscathed. And the position was a good one. Disciplined troops, well dug-in and well armed, could hold out against a huge attacking force for a sustained period of time—if properly con-trolled. And he would insure the latter. He had some good, experienced officers and NCOs, and utter confidence in himself.

As he walked up to where Tom French was using his sharpshooting rifle to annoy the closest warriors, he said, "How many do you estimate, Tom?"

"Too many to count," the captain replied, squeezing off another round and watching a Lakota fall.

Benteen gazed northward and then to the east. *Lot of warriors out there working themselves up to do something. Indians seldom charge a fixed position without big odds on their side*, he told himself. *And they sure as hell had those odds.* The breastworks from the digging were going up rapidly, augmented by hastily placed cracker boxes and packs. *Not a bad little fort*, he thought.

He hurried over to the slight depression in the center of the hill to the makeshift hospital. There, Doctor Porter and his medical corpsman were tending to the thirteen wounded men who were unable to fight. After a few words with the surgeon, he went on to his own company, where it was setting up to defend the south side.

All told, he had thirteen other officers on this hill, and 339 men, including some seasoned troopers and NCOs who were pretty damned good shots. There were fourteen others, including the teamsters and Girard, the scout.

I'll give those goddamned Redskins a fight, all right!

Crazy Horse finished riding his war pony around the three sides of the Long Knives' hill and stopped on a small knoll north of their position to study the situation. Red Elk, carrying his big rifle, rode up to him. "Great *blotahunka*, how should we go after them?" the young warrior asked.

Crazy Horse answered softly, ignoring the heavy firing that had begun, "We must keep shooting on all sides, even from down by the Greasy Grass."

Since the Lakotas and their Cheyenne friends had never had so many warriors on one battlefield before, control was a problem. Crazy Horse instinctively knew he couldn't get all of the warriors to attack in a cohesive manner because it simply wasn't the Way. They would follow their own war leaders. And, unbelievably, there just wasn't room around the hill for all of the warriors to fight! If they packed in too tightly on a line, the soldiers would hit too many of them with their rifle fire. And there were many more Long Knives in this one position than there had been spread out in the other fights.

"I'm going to go up on that ridge to shoot my Sharps," Red Elk said, pointing to his left.

Crazy Horse nodded, lost in his own thoughts.

Red Elk rode up to the point he'd indicated and tied his pony to a piece of scrub some thirty yards down the back side of the hill. Then he went back up to the highest point and found a small depression. On the edge facing the Long Knives hill, he drove his aiming fork deep into the ground. He placed the pouch of shells on the ground beside the stake, inserted the big barrel into the fork, and settled down in the sitting position. He guessed that he was about seven hundred yards from the middle of the enemy hill, putting him out of range of most of their rifles, if they spotted him. He didn't like fighting this way, but this was his chance to prove his good judgment in obtaining the big rifle, and adding to his reputation as a great warrior.

He aimed carefully, but at that distance he couldn't expect to be precise. No, the targets were too small. He could shoot horses, but what prizes would be left when the fight was over?

No, he would try to pick out soldiers, and if he couldn't, he'd just shoot into the middle of the Long Knives' position. He raised the back sight and took aim.

The first round he fired jarred his shoulder.

Five cavalrymen would die that evening on Reno Hill and six would be wounded. One of the dead and three of the wounded would be from the shells of Red Elk's Sharps.

The troopers' spirited defense held the hostiles off until darkness set in. As the last bit of light faded to black, the final shots from outside the perimeter ended the attack. The Lakotas and Cheyennes drifted away, back down into the huge village, where Sitting Bull listened to various accounts from the war leaders. Everyone was surprised to hear Late Star's story. She told it to him directly, as Red Elk and Chief Running Antelope stood behind her at the council fire. "Great Father," she said, "Not too many moons ago I went with my wise father to the huge tipi of Long Hair at Fort *Lin-cun*. There, Long Hair invited us to his house to eat while he spoke to my father of the agent who was cheating us. I watched him closely and decided I would never forget him. Today, up on that hill of the Long Knives dead, I found his body. His hair is shorter, but it is Long Hair. I stopped the women from cutting him, for he was once good to us."

Sitting Bull looked at Running Antelope, who nodded his head in agreement. "It is true, my brother," he said. "It's Long Hair."

"And what about Three Stars?"

Crazy Horse spoke up from the far edge of the firelight. "This is not his fight. Only Long Hair."

"And who are the others still fighting?"

"Not Three Stars. Three Stars has many more soldiers and uses Shoshone scouts. These scouts were Crow and Arikara."

"Can you defeat them tomorrow?" Sitting Bull asked.

"We'll fight hard," Crazy Horse replied, then he got to his feet and walked away.

As the first streaks of the peach dawn announced the twenty-sixth of June 1876, the hostiles launched their attack. They were back in heavy numbers and were determined to finish off the remaining soldiers. But what was left of the Seventh Cavalry was also determined to survive. The breastworks were better prepared, and many of the troopers had been able to get some much-needed sleep. The Indians grew brazen at times, and one warrior even ran over the fortification and counted first coup before he went down in a hail of bullets.

The biggest problem all morning had been the lack of water, particularly for the wounded. Benteen organized carrying parties, and twice led troopers down the steep bank to the river with camp kettles from the kitchens. The water-carrying volunteers, although well covered by supporting fire, still had to expose themselves to enemy fire both at the river's edge and during the arduous climb back up the hill. Fifteen of them would later be awarded the Medal of Honor. As Dan Kanipe carried a kettle up the hill, unmolested by more than a couple of rounds of enemy fire, Lieutenant De Rudio and the handful of troopers who had remained in hiding with him in the woods by the village finally made their appearance and ran to join him.

Around 10:30 A.M., Fred Benteen tired of being the punching bag and held a short meeting with Marcus Reno. A few minutes later, each led a fierce and noisy counterattack—H Company from the south side, and a force of volunteers with Reno from the north side. Each having proved a point, they fell back into the makeshift fort to rousing cheers from the rest of the command.

The survivors' morale was fully restored.

☆ ☆ ☆

Close to noon, the hostiles lost heart. They were taking casualties and making no visible gain against the entrenched and obviously aggressive Long Knives. Many of them thought their great medicine had run out, that perhaps they had used most of it up in their huge victory the day before. At 12:20 P.M., Sitting Bull, his nephews, and the grieving Gall, rode up to what would one day be called Sharpshooter's Ridge. There, they watched as Red Elk fired his last remaining round from the big buffalo gun. After a short discussion, White Bull rode down to the center of the Lakota force to tell them it was time to stop the fight and move the village.

Shortly thereafter the final shot was fired at Reno Hill.

The regiment had suffered seven more killed and forty-one wounded.

Standing beside Reno at the north barricade, Benteen quietly watched the last Lakota ride away. Through his glasses he could see the warrior was rather young, was wearing a first-coup feather, and that he carried a big rifle.

He pulled his flask from his pocket, uncorked it, and handed it to Reno. "I've been saving these final nips for an occasion of some sort. I guess this is it."

The major held the flask up before sipping. "To the Seventh Cavalry."

Benteen nodded his head. "They got their balls back today."

The ride across the ridges that Custer and his men had traversed two days earlier had been difficult. Reaching the bodies of Calhoun's I Company had been the first shock. Alabaster white and bloated, the badly torn and scalped corpses had begun to stink and were covered with flies. The dead horses, many on their backs, were stiff-legged. Those animals still alive and suffering were shot. Leaving a burial party, Benteen continued on through the carnage of Keogh's company, where his first sergeant pointed out the desecrated remains of the handsome Irishman.

Tom Weir gasped at the sight of his friend and turned away to keep from vomiting.

The huge Indian village had disappeared during the second night, and at eleven o'clock the next morning, June 27, General Terry and his staff had ridden into the Reno Hill position. It was only then that the survivors learned of the fate of Custer and the five other companies. Shock had swept over the hill, replacing the joy of being joined by the rest of Terry's command. *It simply wasn't possible!*

Now, the barely recognizable face of Myles Keogh was mute testimony of the truth. Other bodies were identified, and even the hardiest of Benteen's men had misty eyes.

Sergeant Dan Kanipe was part of Benteen's burial detail. He had volunteered for it, and now he was sorry he'd done so. Mixed in with Keogh's command were some familiar faces—C Company! He guessed they must have joined up. It didn't take him long to find the body he was looking for. Ed Bobo's corpse was stretched out on it's back, scalped, and minus its penis. He knelt, touched the cold hand, and said, "I'm sorry."

Finally, the captain reached Last Stand Hill. There, too, the identity of the bloated, mostly mutilated naked bodies was difficult to establish. Benteen, his red bandanna covering his nose, walked sadly through the closely grouped remains. One unrecognizable corpse, its head smashed beyond any identity, had an eagle tattooed on what was left of its chest. And on one arm the initials TWC grimly announced that Tom Custer had died hideously.

A few yards away, a trooper called out, "Sir, I think it's the *general!*"

Hurrying over, Benteen leaned down and looked at the swollen face of George Armstrong Custer. A bullet hole showed on his left breast and another at his left temple. It appeared that someone had cleansed the wounds. There was no sign of any other disfigurement. The body was stripped clean. Benteen stood up and heard a sob from the trooper.

"It *is* the general, ain't it?" the private whispered, tears running down his cheeks.

"Yes," Benteen replied quietly.

He turned away and fought his own emotions. He'd never cared for this glory hunter, but goddamnit, the son of a bitch was a fighter. . . .

39

Libbie heard a knock on the back door from where she was tossing restlessly in her bed. She'd gotten up at two-thirty to read, hoping that would break her sleeplessness. Now, at a little after six, she heard a deep voice tell the maid he wanted to speak Mrs. Custer. Slipping on a robe, Libbie hurried to meet her early morning visitors. There were three of them, two captains and a lieutenant, standing, hats in hand, in the parlor. One was the post surgeon, Captain J. V. D. Middleton; she didn't recognize the other two.

"I'm William McCaskey from the Twentieth Infantry, Mrs. Custer," the other captain said.

Libbie nodded, suddenly feeling a chill. No one made a casual call at this hour.

At that moment, Margaret Custer Calhoun hurried into the parlor. "What is it?" she asked, a look of anticipation on her face. "Has there been a great victory?"

A troubled look crossed Captain McCaskey's face. "Not exactly ma'am," he replied quietly. "In fact, I'm afraid I'm the bearer of bad news. General Terry has asked me to personally deliver this message to you."

Libbie stared at the captain. *Something had happened to Autie!*

McCaskey cleared his throat as he unfolded a page and read aloud, "General Custer and five companies, totaling two-hundred sixty-one officers and men, have been killed on June twenty-fifth at the Little Bighorn River in a battle with Sioux Indians and Northern Cheyenne allies."

Margaret gasped as Libbie stared, wide-eyed at the officer.

McCaskey murmured, "I'm immensely sorry, Mrs. Custer."

No! This was impossible. Bad dreams could be so real. That's right, I'll just swing my legs over the side of the bed and—

"Oh, my God!" Margaret cried out. "Who else?"

The post surgeon spoke up, "Your husband was with the general, Mrs. Calhoun." He glanced at Libbie. "And so were the rest of the Custers, including his young nephew. I'm very sorry."

Libbie's ears began to ring.

It just wasn't possible.

For an instant, the name Delilah crossed her mind, but she pushed it away. She started to speak, couldn't.

"Is there anything you want us to do?" McCaskey asked quietly.

What could anyone do?

Libbie shook off the numbness enough to say, "The other women need to be told." Yes, she was the commander's wife; she *must* hold up and help the others. She shivered. How could she be so cold in this July heat?

The *Far West*, carrying the Reno survivors of the regiment, had docked the night before at Bismarck. There, the news of the tragedy had been telegraphed to General Sheridan's headquarters in Chicago. By now, the whole country was beginning to hear the news. In the midst of its big centennial celebration, the United States was being staggered by word that its most flamboyant military leader had been killed with his famous Seventh Cavalry at an inauspicious place called the Little Bighorn by a bunch of savage Indians. Soon the entire world would be familiar with "Custer's Last Stand."

Now, looking into Annie Yates's eyes as Captain McCaskey read the news to the officers' wives, Libbie tried to appear calm. Annie, with her baby in her arms, just turned away and walked back to her quarters when the captain finished. Nettie Smith stood frozen for several moments before also turning away. "My house will be open continuously," Libbie managed to announce. "You're all welcome at any time."

Several minutes later she and the officers repeated the tragic announcement down on Laundress Row. The drab women, most with small children in their arms or in hand, listened woodenly. One screamed, and another fainted.

Missouri Ann Bobo, holding her one-year-old son in her arms, lowered her head as the Captain stated that C Company had been with Custer. The tears began slip down her cheeks. She loved two men and both were buried in some shallow grave on the side of a hill by some useless river. She shook her head and looked away. But she ran into a pair of accusing eyes. They belonged to Mary Hohmeyer, whose first sergeant husband had been killed with Fresh Smith. The German woman's look turned to hate, as she jabbed a finger at Missouri Ann and screamed, *"You did it!"*

Missouri Ann blinked as more tears filled her eyes and she stumbled away.

Libbie heard the Hohmeyer woman's words, but didn't know what they meant. She spoke up, "Ladies, we've all been struck by a terrible tragedy. If any of you need help, my door is open to you. I don't know what I can do for you, but I'll try."

As the new widows turned away, most to find solace with those women whose husbands had survived with Reno and Benteen, Libbie wondered who would relieve her anguish.

Epilogue

Ira Vandiver watched as Frederick Whittaker strode into the corner of the lobby where he had announced he would hold his press conference. All of the reporters and journalists—Vandiver could never figure out exactly what differentiated the two—attending the Reno court of inquiry were there except one from the Washington *Star*, who had been drunk since lunch. The Palmer House lobby was busy on this Sabbath afternoon, following the end of the day's proceedings.

After pausing for effect and getting all of the fourth estate's attention, the dime novelist spoke loudly in his British accent, "Gentlemen, as George Armstrong Custer's biographer, I must not let certain information pass. You all know my testimony has been refused by those prejudiced army officers sitting on the court. This, of course, proves that the whole thing is rigged, as I've been saying all along. Early in the proceedings of the court, I promised you proof—well, here it is."

Most of the newsmen were jotting down notes, while a few others like Vandiver were waiting to see what the pretender was going to spew this time. The suspense didn't last long. "All of you know of Captain Thomas Weir's illness and of his unfortunate death in December of Seventy-six. Luckily, I was able to visit him in Manhattan prior to his untimely end and get several statements from him regarding the battle."

Whittaker, the former cavalry captain who had served under Colonel Wesley Merritt, one of the members of the court, paused again, then went on. "As you know, Sheridan's bully boys on the court won't let me get this information into the record. But that won't stop me from making it known to the world. . . ."

Vandiver caught the eye of a reporter from Philadelphia and shrugged. Was there any length to which this bastard wouldn't go to get attention? Nailing Reno at the court was merely the means. And it was such an obvious ploy not only to make Custer the greatest hero in history, but to sell more copies of his book.

Whittaker continued. "Captain Weir, himself one of the heroes of the Little Bighorn, told me earnestly that both Reno and Benteen were to blame for the tragedy that happened to General Custer and his brave men. He stated that Reno's cowardice and incompetence, combined with Benteen's tarrying because of his hatred for Custer, were unequivocally the cause of the regiment's horrible disaster at the hands of the hostile Indians."

The Englishman cleared his throat. "Unfortunately, I've misplaced the captain's signed affidavit, but I assure you he was explicit in his statements. And if anyone should know, it should be that officer. You are all aware of how Captain Weir took off with his company without orders in an effort to find and help General Custer. *Alone,* gentlemen, as both the cowardly Reno and spiteful Benteen casually watched from the safety of Reno Hill."

Vandiver chuckled to himself as Whittaker continued his account of Weir's statements. The court of inquiry that had begun on January 14 had run through twenty-three witnesses, including Captain Frederick Benteen and Major Marcus Reno himself. Only one officer, Captain Edward Godfrey—who, strangely enough, was promoted to fill the vacancy created by Captain Tom Weir's death in December of 1876—was even mildly critical of Reno in his testimony. Two teamsters who had tasted the major's wrath had accused Reno of being drunk, but that charge had been refuted by other testimony. The interpreter, Girard, and the doctor, Porter, had accused the major of mishandling the retreat from the valley to the bluffs. But Girard had stayed behind in the woods with De Rudio, and the surgeon admitted that much of what he recalled was based on his limited opinion.

A strong note of support had come from a petition signed by 236 privates and NCOs of the Seventh Cavalry following the battle. It recommended that Marcus Reno be promoted to the vacant rank of regimental lieutenant colonel, and that Thomas Benteen be promoted to regimental major.

Vandiver returned to Whittaker's words. ". . . so, Gentlemen, the heroic Tom Weir speaks to us from the grave and incriminates Reno, in spite of the army's conspiracy!"

"Just a damned minute, Whittaker!"

Everyone turned as the voice of First Lieutenant Charles Braden knifed through the air. At the time of the Little Bighorn battle, Braden had been on sick leave due to wounds received in action against the Sioux in 1873, and had missed the fight. He had received a medical retirement in 1878. The former lieutenant was visiting the proceedings from New York, where he was presently teaching school. He went on, "I know the truth first-hand about Captain Weir, and what you're trying to foist on these newspapermen is simply a lie." He turned to Vandiver and his associates. "I was residing in the same apartment house with Captain Weir during his last days, and I spent many hours with him. . . ."

Braden was an 1869 graduate of West Point and was thirty-one years old. He walked with a slight limp, a reminder of the severe wound in his left thigh that had brought about his retirement.

He continued, "Captain Weir complained frequently to me about Whittaker's constant entreaties to castigate Reno and Benteen. He angrily told me that he had no intention of signing the man's statement because he disagreed with him."

Ira Vandiver looked at Whittaker, who was staring at Braden. Quickly, Vandiver asked, "What do you have to say to *that*, Mr. Whittaker?"

The Englishman shook his head and managed, "He, well, he must be mistaken."

Braden stepped in front of the novelist, looked him directly in the eye, and firmly said, "Captain Weir personally told me he did *not* believe that Reno had anything to do with General Custer's defeat."

Whittaker stood there for a moment, then pulled his eyes away from Braden and turned back to the newspapermen. "Obviously this man is part of the conspiracy. He's one of them. He has made up this story." There was a definite lack of conviction in his voice.

Vandiver spoke clearly, "I think we *all* know who has made up a story."

The small crowd of newspapermen quickly broke up.

Six miles north of the Canada–Montana border, Sitting Bull, who sat in council with his chiefs, knew nothing about the Reno court, and wouldn't have cared about it if he had. Sitting with him were Gall and the first white man he'd ever trusted, Major James M. Walsh, inspector in the red-coated North–West Mounted Police, and the senior mountie in the area where Sitting Bull's Lakota moved while chasing the elusive *pte,* the buffalo. Walsh had come to western Canada with some three hundred other redcoats in 1874 to impose the British Queen's law on its recalcitrants. Sitting Bull had come to the territory to get away from the fury of the United States Army.

The great success of the Little Bighorn battle had been short lived. Crook and Terry had come after the Lakota, literally with a vengeance. And after them came "Bear Coat" Miles, the hard-driving colonel who was every bit as self-serving as Custer had ever been. The Lakota tribes and clans had eventually splintered, to enhance their escape from the relentless Long Knives. Finally, Sitting Bull had brought his Hunkpapas to an unwelcome haven in Canada.

Canada already had its own Indians, including the Blackfeet, who had traditionally been the Lakotas' enemies. And there were just so many buffalo. This meant that when the buffalo roamed south of the border, the Sioux went after them, while the peace between the Canadian Indians and the ever arrogant Lakotas was tenuous. Sitting Bull's presence also created political problems between the two countries. The Americans had been able to get most of the rest of the Lakotas, including even the defiant Crazy Horse and his Oglalas, onto reservations. And they wanted Sitting Bull there. But the powerful chief had stated, "I never wanted to go to a gift-house, and I never will. They want my people to farm. I will never farm."

The discussion was winding down and Major Walsh had again failed to convince the great Hunkpapa to go back to a United States reservation. Red Elk, who had been asked to attend the council even though he wasn't a chief, had been permitted to speak of going back to the warpath, and he had done so eloquently. He had cited the return of many clans to Sitting Bull's lance, bringing the Lakota strength to some six hundred lodges. "We can win back our lands forever!" he barked, throwing his fist in the air in a dynamic close. "We must never let our sons forget what we did on the Greasy Grass!"

Major Walsh shook his head and replied quietly, "The American Army is too big and their people too many for you, Great Chief. Do not listen to these war cries, for it will mean the death of your people."

Sitting Bull stared into the fire, and it appeared as if the light made a patchwork of seams and canyons in his troubled face. At last he said, "I will hunt as long as there is game on the prairie, and when it's gone, I will send my children there to hunt mice."

For a short period of time just before the end of the Civil War, Ira Vandiver had served on the staff of Major General Wesley Merritt when the latter was commanding the Cavalry Corps of the Army of the Potomac. He and the general had renewed their acquaintance when the Reno court began. Now, Merritt, ever gracious, had agreed to an unofficial chat in the general's hotel room at the Palmer House. It was the night of the twelfth and the commander of the Fifth Cavalry was leaving early the next morning. The Reno court was over.

Vandiver and the general talked at random about the end of the war over a glass of the general's bourbon. After about fifteen minutes, Vandiver switched to the subject that had the country holding its breath. "Can you tell me, sir, off the record, what you think about the Little Bighorn?"

Merritt's eyes narrowed momentarily. "Absolutely off the record?"

"Absolutely."

The cavalry officer slowly blew out a deep breath. "Reno may have panicked somewhat—God knows, we heard enough testimony about Bloody Knife's death and the disorganized move from the valley timber— but I'd say, overall, that he didn't display cowardice. As far as his being able to save Custer, I don't think that's a valid point. He had barely saved the remnants of his *own* command, after facing terrible odds. And he didn't even know for sure where Custer was, or what he was doing. All right, he was the ranking officer on Reno Hill, and he could have organized the remainder of the regiment and headed north perhaps as early as four-forty-five. But I don't think he'd have gotten to Custer's position in time. I think Custer and his five companies had been finished off well before he could have ridden that four miles. No, I don't think Reno, had he been efficiently in command of everything, could have changed the outcome. In fact, by letting Benteen do such an excellent job of commanding the defense on Reno Hill until the conclusion, he may have stumbled into the best solution."

Vandiver nodded his head. "None of those survivors are going to complain about it."

"Hardly."

"Will the findings reflect what you just told me, sir?"

"Pretty much."

Vandiver paused, then smiled. "All right, General, the big question. What do you think of Custer's actions in this whole thing?"

The tall and slender Merritt shook his head as he poured some more whiskey into each glass. "I think armchair generals are going to be pondering that question for as long as there's a soldier."

He sipped some bourbon, then got up and paced for a few moments. Finally, he said, "We know some very important things that Custer didn't know. He didn't know about Sitting Bull's visions and his power to excite those Sioux and Cheyenne warriors. He didn't know that the Indians attacked Crook on the Rosebud. That was an unheard of event, Vandiver. American Indians simply *didn't* attack a major U.S. Army force in the field!"

"For Crazy Horse, or whoever it was that led the attack on Crook, to do so required an enormous amount of powerful medicine. Those damned Indians *believed* they could do anything! And when they pulled out of the Rosebud battle, essentially breaking even and of their own volition, they had, in their thinking, an enormous victory! Couple *that* medicine with all those summer roamers joining the hostiles, and there was an immensely powerful force waiting out there for Custer."

"And he had no way of knowing it."

"Precisely. Now let's take a look at Custer. As you know, he and I were contemporaries. We both went from captain to brigadier in one quick jump under Pleasanton. And some may say a strong sense of competition marked our relationship. However, he and Libbie had entertained me graciously at their house. But in this case, I must say I'd probably have done many of the same things Custer did. . . .

There was no way he could have found out about Crook's fight, and there was no way he could have known about the powerful medicine that was driving Sitting Bull's warriors. And finally, there wasn't any way for him to have expected *that* many hard-fighting Indians when he got to the Little Bighorn. I think it all boils down to numbers in the end."

"Didn't his scouts warn him?" Vandiver asked.

"Yes, but I think Custer *wanted* to find a lot of hostiles. There's been criticism about his dividing his forces, well, that was the only way he knew—from experience—to attack a hostile village. That's the way it was done. You know, he'd built this big reputation as an Indian fighter, but he actually had only one truly major battle with them, and that was the Washita. And he split his forces there. It's the only way you can bottle them up."

"What about those Gatlings and those four troops of cavalry that he turned down. Could they have swung the tide of battle?"

"I don't think those Gatlings would have been any closer than that pack train, if you get right down to it. They were too difficult to move through any kind of rough terrain. The added cavalry, nearly two hundred of them—that's a different matter. You're damned right they would have made a difference had they been with Custer's main force. A *big one.*"

"Why didn't he take them?"

The colonel shrugged. "Probably wanted to keep all the glory for the Seventh. I don't know."

Wesley Merritt pulled out his watch and glanced at it. "Well, I guess that's about it, Vandiver. It was nice to see you again, and remember—all of this is off the record."

The newspaperman got to his feet. "If you were to summarize the whole thing, General, what would you say?"

Merritt pursed his lips and nodded his head slightly. "I'd say that Custer did lots of things right—based on what he knew!"

Vandiver nodded his head. The general was right—the armchair types would be intrigued by the Little Bighorn forever.

The findings of the Reno Court of Inquiry were made public on March 11, 1879, by General Order No. 17 from the Adjutant General's Office, Headquarters of the Army, Washington, D. C.

Reno was exonerated.

The next day in Monroe, Michigan, Libbie Custer read the newspaper report for the fourth time and felt a another pang of pain. Maggie Calhoun was sitting at the dining-room table with her, sipping coffee that had cooled. At the other side of the table Annie Yates, who had arrived the day before from back East, scowled into her coffee cup. In the year following the battle, Annie's hair had turned iron gray, so now she looked far older than her thirty years.

"How can they possibly do such a thing?" Libbie asked, tossing the paper to the table.

"There must be some mistake," Maggie said. "Whittaker did such a *thorough* job of research. He could prove it was all Reno's and Benteen's fault, but they wouldn't let him testify. He told me himself that court would close ranks and cover Reno all the way!"

Libbie shook her head. "The key was Tom Weir, but they wouldn't accept what he told Whittaker. He was *there!* He knew the truth! Poor Tom. Well, we all know how sick he was before he died. He must not have been in his right mind when he told Braden those things."

"Or Braden made them up, as Whittaker said," Maggie added.

The outspoken Annie looked up from her cup. "I don't think so. Charlie Braden isn't a liar, and besides, he isn't even in the army anymore. No, much as it may displease you, my dear Libbie, I think you'd better take another look at your favorite author."

"What do you mean?" Libbie replied sharply.

"I just think he may be somewhat of an opportunist, that's all."

"I don't know how you can say that. He has preserved Autie's good name throughout all of this terrible mess."

Libbie had been doing her best to defend her husband's name. The news of "Custer's Last Stand" had washed over the American people on a hot July day in 1876, and had provided a press heyday. It was ultimately polemic, with the country immediately dividing over the Custer issue. The official commander of the Seventh, Colonel Samuel Sturgis, had lost his twenty-two-year-old lieutenant son with E Company on a ridge at the Little Bighorn, and he had strongly castigated Custer, describing him as "insanely ambitious of glory." And Sturgis hadn't stopped there, bitterly reviling him further. Others throughout the country swore he was a hero. Suddenly, belonging to the cavalry was the most popular thing for young men in America to do. It was time to join up and get even! The Democratic newspapers had practically made a martyr of Custer, while, naturally, the Republican papers took the opposite stance. "Who Slew Custer?" screamed James Gordon Bennett's New York *Herald,* and promptly blamed everyone from President Grant and his crooked Indian agents to Catholic priests. There was little middle ground, and it appeared likely it would stay that way in the public mind for a long time to come.

Quietly pushing her thoughts away from Whittaker, Libbie went back to that terrible day, the one she'd never forget if she lived to be a thousand.

She had wanted to die.

But she couldn't. It was soon after when she'd made her decision. She had to live and perpetuate him, be a hero's widow, to the end of her appointed time, in a worthy fashion.

And nothing would make her waver from doing it!

She got up from the table and went to the window, not wanting the others to see the tears trickling down her cheeks. For some reason, she remembered the poem she'd sent to Annie from New York that winter of '76:

> We smooth and fold with reverent care
> The robes they, living, used to wear;
> And painful pulses stir,
> As o'er the relics of our dead,
> With bitter rain of tears, we spread
> Pale purple lavender. . . .

Afterword

(What really happened to our characters)

DOCTOR HENRY PORTER later practiced medicine in Bismarck; became president of the Medical Society of North Dakota and vice-president of the Society of Veterans of Indian Wars. He died of a heart attack while traveling in India in 1903 at the age of fifty-four.

CAPTAIN TOM WEIR died at the age of thirty-eight in New York in December 1876 from problems related to excessive use of alcohol.

FIRST SERGEANT MICHAEL MARTIN was killed by a rifle bullet in the head at the Snake Creek fight with the Nez Perce the morning Chief Joseph surrendered to General Miles in 1877. His meanness and bigotry in the story are fictional.

LIEUTENANT CHARLES VARNUM was awarded the Medal of Honor for gallantry at White Clay Creek in 1890. He retired as a colonel and left behind many published accounts when he died at the age of eighty-six in 1936 in San Francisco.

CAPTAIN FREDERICK BENTEEN was suspended from rank of major for one year at half pay for drunk and disorderly conduct in Utah in 1884. He retired for disability in 1888. He was brevetted brigadier general in 1890 for gallantry at the Little Bighorn and later at Canyon Creek, and died at age sixty-three in 1898 in Atlanta.

MAJOR MARCUS RENO continued his starcrossed ways. He was described by one observer as "Normal when drunk and abnormal when sober." He was again court-martialed—this time for various charges, including "drunk and disorderly" by Colonel Sturgis in November 1879.

He was dismissed from the service in 1880, and died at the age of fifty-four in 1889 in Washington, D. C., following an operation for cancer. His body was finally reinterred in 1967 at the Custer National Battlefield. To this day, Marcus Reno is blamed by many staunch Custer supporters for the "massacre."

ANNIE YATES never remarried and became a dedicated Catholic. She died at the age of sixty-five in 1914 when struck by a subway train in New York City.

CAPTAIN MYLES MOYLAN was awarded the Medal of Honor for gallantry at Snake Creek in 1877. He also fought at Wounded Knee. He retired as a major in 1893 following thirty-five years of service. He died from stomach cancer at age seventy in 1909 in San Diego.

CAPTAIN TOM FRENCH was found guilty at the time of the Reno Court of Inquiry of being drunk while on duty, drinking with a laundress, and violating the terms of close arrest. He retired in 1880. His house in Bismarck was destroyed by fire, possibly by arson. He died in Leavenworth, Kansas, in 1882 at the age of thirty-nine.

LIEUTENANT EDWARD GODFREY was awarded the Medal of Honor for gallantry at Snake Creek. He later became Colonel, Ninth Cavalry, and numerous other commands, including the Mounted Service School at Fort Riley. He retired as a brigadier general in 1907, and died in 1932 at the age of eighty-eight in New Jersey.

GENERAL GEORGE CROOK pursued the Lakota following the Little Bighorn, then returned to Arizona to settle the Apache problem. He was promoted to major general, commanded the Division of the Missouri, and strongly protested broken government promises to the Chiricahuas. He died in Chicago at the age of sixty-one. He is still regarded by many as America's greatest Indian fighter.

GENERAL ALFRED TERRY was promoted to major general and commanded the Division of the Missouri until 1888. He died at the age of sixty-three in New Haven, Connecticut, in 1890.

SERGEANT DANIEL KANIPE married Missouri Ann Bobo in April 1877, and left the army in 1882 to become a U.S. Revenue Service employee in Marion, South Carolina. He served as a captain with the Nineteenth North Carolina Militia in WWI. He died at the age of seventy-three in Marion in 1926. Missouri Ann lived until 1934.

PRIVATE "OLD NUTRIMENT" JOHN BURKMAN was discharged as a private of good character in 1879 after being injured falling off a horse. He became a teamster in civilian life. This humorless man never quite got over his life as a striker for Custer. He committed suicide by gunshot at the age of eighty-six in Billings, Montana, in 1925.

CRAZY HORSE diligently pursued by Miles following the Little Bighorn, was talked into surrendering with his people at the Red Cloud Agency in May 1877. He was killed in September of that year while purportedly "trying to escape." Captain John Bourke wrote of him, "All Indians gave Crazy Horse a high reputation for courage and generosity. . . . He was one of the great soldiers of his day and generation." A huge stone monument to him is slowly nearing completion in the Black Hills.

GALL took a number of Hunkpapas with him to Canada in 1880 and finally surrendered to reservation life. He eventually converted to Christianity and also to farming, continuing in a leadership role with his people that for a time brought him into conflict with Sitting Bull. He died at the age of fifty-four in 1894.

SITTING BULL. When famine and disease wracked his followers, he brought 187 of them out of Canada and surrendered to the army in 1881. Imprisoned for two years at Fort Randall, he toured for a time with Buffalo Bill Cody's Wild West Show in 1885, but he never acquiesced to white rule. For six years he fought to preserve the 11 million acres of land guaranteed by treaty—to no avail. When the Ghost Dance mania struck the Sioux in 1890, and a major uprising was fomenting, he was shot and killed by tribal police at Grand River. Two weeks after the death of the great Sioux leader, the Battle of Wounded Knee took place.

RED ELK AND LATE STAR are fictional. Chief Running Antelope, along with his family, was treated to dinner in the Custer house, so it's possible that his daughter could have been the reason that Custer's corpse wasn't mutilated. Hostile long-range rifle fire from what became known as Sharpshooter's Ridge did cause casualties on Reno Hill.

LIBBIE CUSTER was true to her word; she never stopped fighting for the reputation of her controversial husband. Emil Justh tried to collect the money owed him, but had to settle for ten cents on the dollar. Libbie turned to writing and enjoyed wide success with her newspaper columns and her books. She was still lovely and the object of men's attentions well into her sixties. She died on April 4, 1931, just four days short of her ninety-first birthday.

Strangely, the big losers of the Battle of the Little Bighorn were the Indians. It was the greatest victory by Native Americans over the army in U. S. history, but it also brought about the eventual end of freedom for the western plains tribes, and the demise of the Sioux as the rulers of that world.

And, yes, the armchair generals are still trying to sort the whole thing out.

Robert Elwayne Skimin

A Note on the Type

The text was set in 11 point Adobe Caslon with a leading of 15 points space. William Caslon released his first typefaces in 1722. Caslon's types were based on seventeenth-century Dutch old style designs, which were then used extensively in England. Because of their incredible practicality Caslon's designs met with instant success. Caslon's types became popular throughout Europe and the American colonies; printer Benjamin Franklin hardly used any other typeface. The first printings of the American Declaration of Independence and the Constitution were set in Caslon. For her Adobe Caslon, designer Carol Twombly studied specimen pages printed by William Caslon between 1734 and 1770.

≈

The text display font is Caslon Open Face, issued by the Barnhart Brothers & Spindler foundry in 1915. It was originally called College Oldstyle and was initially a reproduction of Le Moreau de Jeune, a type from France's G. Peignot foundry; BB&S admitted to taking a liberty when they put it in the Caslon category. Caslon Open Face is nonetheless a useful display face that leaves an impression of elegance when used sparingly in display work.

≈

The jacket and title page display font is Willow, an Adobe Originals typeface designed in 1990 by Joy Redick for the Adobe Wood Type series. Willow is a condensed typeface modeled on nineteenth-century wood types known as Clarendons (wood type Clarendons do not resemble the English metal types of that name). Clarendon condensed faces were originally so well-designed that words or a line of display type have an even color that is remarkable for wood types. Willow is taken from proofs of type in the Rob Roy Kelly Collection housed at the University of Texas at Austin.

Composed by Jean Carbain
New York, New York

Printed and bound in the U.S.A.

About the Author

Robert Elwayne Skimin was born and raised in Medina County, Ohio. He enlisted in the Army at age eighteen and was soon its fourth youngest officer. He saw combat as a paratrooper, an artillery officer, and Army aviator. He was the first Army pilot to wear the famed Green Beret, and was decorated several times. Skimin is the author of nineteen books including *The Booze Game; Soldier for Hire*, a four-volume male adventure series; *Chikara!*, which won the prestigious Ohioana Book Award; *Gray Victory*, an alternative history in which the South has won the Civil War; *Renegade Lightning* (with Ferdie Pacheco), a WWII air-war novel; and *Apache Autumn*, an historical novel of the Apaches that was nominated for a Pulitzer Prize. He went on to publish *Ulysses*, a biographical novel of U. S. Grant, later titled *Ulysses S. Grant, A Novel* in paperback; *Custer's Luck*, a "what if" in which Custer wins; and *Footprints of Heroes, From the American Revolution to the War in Iraq*. His sweeping novel of twentieth-century Russia, *Derzhava*, is in progress. Skimin is also the creator of an illustrated history series for children *Danny Drumm's Heroes*, launched in 2006. Skimin has lectured extensively on a variety of subjects and has conducted several seminars on the business of publishing. He lives in El Paso, Texas.